MW00581021

Just Trying to Have School

Just Trying to Have
SCHOOL

The Struggle for Desegregation in Mississippi

Natalie G. Adams and James H. Adams

University Press of Mississippi / Jackson

The University Press of Mississippi is the scholarly publishing agency of
the Mississippi Institutions of Higher Learning: Alcorn State University,
Delta State University, Jackson State University, Mississippi State University,
Mississippi University for Women, Mississippi Valley State University,
University of Mississippi, and University of Southern Mississippi.

www.upress.state.ms.us

The University Press of Mississippi is a
member of the Association of University Presses.

First printing 2018

∞

Library of Congress Cataloging-in-Publication Data

Names: Adams, Natalie G., author. | Adams, James Harold, 1955– author.
Title: Just trying to have school: the struggle for desegregation in
Mississippi / Natalie G. Adams and James H. Adams.
Description: Jackson: University Press of Mississippi, [2018] | Includes
bibliographical references and index. |
Identifiers: LCCN 2018021897 (print) | LCCN 2018025248 (ebook) | ISBN
9781496819550 (epub single) | ISBN 9781496819567 (epub institutional) |
ISBN 9781496819574 (pdf single) | ISBN 9781496819581 (pdf institutional)
| ISBN 9781496819536 (cloth) | ISBN 9781496819543 (pbk.)
Subjects: LCSH: School integration—Mississippi—History. | Educational
equalization—Mississippi—History. | Discrimination in
education—Mississippi—History. | School integration—Massive resistance
movement—Mississippi—History. | African
Americans—Education—Mississippi—History.
Classification: LCC LC214.22.M7 (ebook) | LCC LC214.22.M7 A43 2018 (print) |
DDC 379.2/6309762—dc23
LC record available at https://lccn.loc.gov/2018021897

British Library Cataloging-in-Publication Data available

To the many educators who have influenced our lives,
but most importantly to our parents,
Harold and Ruth Adams and John and Bonnie Guice

Contents

ix   Preface

xiii   Acknowledgments

3   **Introduction**
The Daily Work of Doing *Brown*

11   **Chapter I**
With No Deliberate Speed: The Road from *Brown* to *Alexander*

34   **Chapter 2**
"A Cruel and Intolerable Burden": Black Mississippians and Freedom of Choice

51   **Chapter 3**
Big Bulls in the Local Herd: Superintendents Enforcing the Law of the Land

76   **Chapter 4**
Weathering the Storm: Principals and Local Implementation

100   **Chapter 5**
Love, Hope, and Fear: Teachers Guiding Desegregation

124   **Chapter 6**
"We All Came Together on the Football Field," But . . .: The Role of Sports in Desegregation

146   **Chapter 7**
"We Never Had a Prom": Social Integration and the Extracurricular

167   **Chapter 8**
"Hell No, We Won't Go": Protest and Resistance to School Desegregation

188   **Chapter 9**
Resistance through Exodus: Private Schools as a Countermovement

213   **Chapter 10**
Unfinished Business: Lessons Learned through School Desegregation

237   Notes

269   Bibliography

291   Index

Preface

"You realize you are digging up some old bones." These were the haunting words Leon Johnson uttered as Jim and he ended their phone conversation, one initiated in hopes that Leon would talk to us about his experiences as one of the first black students to attend DeKalb High School (Kemper County) under "freedom of choice" in 1969. Leon's reference to "digging up bones" is an apt one to describe the researching and writing of this book. We knew revisiting the story of school desegregation in the Deep South would be an emotionally charged one. We ourselves experienced desegregation forty-five years ago. Jim was a ninth grader at DeKalb High School during the first year of school desegregation in Kemper County, and Natalie was in third grade in 1970 when her elementary school in rural north Louisiana (Franklin Parish) was desegregated. We are both children of educators who were part of desegregation; our mothers were teachers, and Jim's father was a school administrator. Both of us are children of white parents who agonized over the decision to leave their children in public schools when many of their friends were fleeing to newly opened private academies. When we began this research in 2010, we knew we could not write the story of school desegregation in Mississippi as emotionally detached, "objective" scholars. We were not outsiders sweeping in to write about "the South" and then retreating to a distant enclave far removed from our topic of study. We live here; we reared our children here; we work here; we play here; we go to church here. We are products of the South—the good, the bad, and the ugly.

Like an archeologist who stumbles unexpectedly upon a bone from the Pleistocene era, we, too, stumbled upon thrilling finds in unexpected places: a sermon from a Methodist minister delivered in the pulpit days after a local white coach woke to a burning cross in his front yard simply because he allowed a black boy to try out for the basketball team; FBI field reports explicating the daily activities of the Citizens' Council in Mississippi in the mid-1950s; a copy of a letter written by one of the fifty-three black petitioners in Yazoo City in 1955 to the executive secretary of the NAACP; an athletic facility in Columbia named after a black coach who was passed over repeatedly for the head coaching position at the newly integrated high school; and letter after letter from Senator James Eastland to his white constituents back home assuring them that he would fight desegregation with every fiber in his being. These historical finds (along with many others) provided the backdrop and colored the contours for telling the stories of local Mississippians who were in the schools during the years between *Brown v. Board of Education* (1954) and *Alexander v. Holmes County Board of Education* (1969).

But we did not want to rely solely on archival research, historical documents, and published primary and secondary sources to weave a narrative about school desegregation. We wanted the stories of people in the trenches during school desegregation to be front and center. We had to dig deep and long and hard to find the diversity of people needed to tell the multiple stories of how school desegregation was and was not accomplished in Mississippi. We began by sending letters to current superintendents and to local newspapers asking for participants willing to talk to us; the response was disappointing. This changed in 2011 when Sid Salter featured our research in one of his editorials appearing in numerous Mississippi newspapers. We received a swell of responses from people—primarily white teachers, principals, and students—eager to tell their stories. Finding superintendents and school board members who were major decision makers during this time period proved much more challenging. Quite sadly, most of them were no longer alive. We were fortunate indeed to find Clyde Muse, Tom Dulin, Julian Prince, Virgil Belue, and Harold "Hardwood" Kelly, who had been superintendents and gave graciously of their time to talk about those events of fifty years ago. Unfortunately, Harold Kelly died shortly after we interviewed him.

But painful bones were also excavated. Incredibly racist remarks were made nonchalantly by some of our white interviewees who assumed we shared their beliefs because of our shared skin color. We were often confronted by people, typically white, who made it very clear that we had no business digging up old bones. "Why are you still talking about race—bringing all that mess up?" one elderly white woman asked Jim as he waited in a restaurant in the Delta to interview a black former teacher. In Carrollton, we experienced firsthand outright hostility manifested in a white high school girl working in the local ice cream shop, who refused us use of the bathroom. This occurred after she found out we were interviewing the local superintendent, a white man known for his vocal criticism of Carroll Academy, the private school she attended. During our research, we were also met with skepticism from potential black interviewees, and we had to dig much harder to find blacks willing to talk to us. Their silences and hesitancies during interviews reminded us that we cannot escape the history of our region where whites are/were not to be trusted no matter what gifts (i.e., "the opportunity to tell your story") we purport to bear.

As we spent hours talking to teachers, coaches, and principals, we were reminded of a Sunday School song from our youth based on Ezekiel and the Valley of the Dry Bones—"The knee bone's connected to the thigh bone; the thigh bone's connected to the hip bone—" Our shared rootedness in the South allowed us many opportunities to reach across race and share commonalities around a love of family, church, sports, music, and food. We swapped stories about our personal lives growing up in the South, playing sports, teaching lovable but often unruly children, coaching football, serving as the dance team sponsor, and socializing with our co-workers outside of school. Coach Charles Boston and Coach Harry Breeland shared our interminably hopeful belief in the transcendence of sports. Cyndie Harrison, whose stories about her first year as a white teacher in an all-black school staying up all night to prepare lessons so that she would be worthy of the label "teacher" reminded us why we became teachers in the first place: it was a calling. Fenton Peters, who sadly passed away midway through the study, whose insightful quips about the power dynamics always present (yet rarely articulated) during court-ordered desegregation (a term he insisted on using instead of integration), forced us to constantly check our own privilege as white academicians writing a book on desegregation.

One of the most exciting discoveries during the initial phases of this work was that little scholarship had been published about this important period of civil rights history. For researchers, this is a gem—"a gap in the literature." Many moments of the civil rights movement in Mississippi (e.g., voter registration, James Meredith and the integration of the University of Mississippi, the Freedom Riders, Freedom Summer) have been extensively covered in film and literature. The heroes and villains are well preserved in the historical transcripts of this time period. Yet, the story of public school desegregation in the state has been largely ignored. We owe a debt of gratitude to Luther Munford, whose 1971 senior thesis entitled "Black Gravity: Desegregation in 30 Mississippi School Districts" is a brilliant analysis of the immediate effects of desegregation in Mississippi, and to Charles Bolton, whose book *The Hardest Deal of All: The Battle over School Integration in Mississippi, 1879–1980* is the definitive historical account of this time period. We are also incredibly grateful to James Loewen, author of *Lies My Teacher Told Me* and *Sundown Towns*, who began a book on this topic when he was teaching at Tougaloo College back in the 1970s but never finished it. He generously gave us a copy of his unpublished manuscript complete with penciled-in notations. While several teachers and students have written personal *memoirs* about their experiences in a particular locale during this time period, no book had been written combining the voices of educators, parents, and students statewide.

Dr. Lamar Weems, a retired neurologist in Jackson and son of Mack Weems (superintendent in Scott County at the time of the *Brown* ruling) insightfully remarked that the civil rights movement in Mississippi was as much about evolution as it was about revolution.[1] By this he meant ordinary people changed as they participated in the process of actualizing *Brown* and in doing so altered the cultural landscape of race in the South. Admittedly, this is a progressive and disputable interpretation of the history of race in the South. His point was that ordinary people, with their prejudices, character flaws, and resilient human spirits, were as important to the civil rights movement as were those that have been lionized in statues, historical markers, literature, and film.

In closing, we return to Leon Johnson. Leon and Jim both attended DeKalb High during the first year of desegregation; they have little recollection of each other. Jim moved away after one year, and Leon continued to attend DeKalb High. However, for the short time in which they occupied the same school, Jim and Leon experienced DeKalb High and school desegregation very differently. After their initial telephone conversation, Leon never returned Jim's repeated calls to schedule a time for them to discuss his experience at DeKalb High during school desegregation.[2] That is and was the reality of living race in the Deep South.

Acknowledgments

We come from a long line of public school teachers who instilled in us an unwavering commitment to public schools. This book is an extension of their dedication. We are grateful for their influence and hope the book is a tribute to each of their legacies. The heart of this book is the oral histories of more than one hundred educators, parents, and students who shared their individual stories with us. It is impossible to include all of their names, but each of them helped shape this book. Thank you for allowing us into your lives. A special thanks to our colleague Ed Davis, who first planted the seed for writing this book and helped us secure initial funding. Thanks also to Sid Salter for mentioning our book in his weekly column back in 2011, which helped tremendously in identifying people to interview. We thank our universities—Mississippi State University and The University of Alabama—for granting us sabbaticals to research and then complete the writing of the book. We give special thanks to our colleagues in the Department of Instructional Systems and Workforce Development, New College, and the Social and Cultural Studies in Education program who helped cover the minutia of our daily lives, so we could devote time to writing the book. Thanks to Eric Torres of Hosteeva Vacation Rentals for giving us the "family discount" so we could get away for writing retreats at the beach. We are especially grateful for Marty Wiseman and the Stennis Institute at Mississippi State University for their support. Last, but not least, we are thankful for each other's patience, sense of humor, and willingness to take risks. When we met each other in 1985 in New Iberia (LA), we were a middle-school English teacher and a coach who fell in love, married, and had children—all very quickly. In 1992 we almost divorced over wallpapering our bathroom. Who would have thought that twenty-five years later, we would write a book together and have a whole lot of fun doing so?

Just Trying to Have School

The Daily Work of Doing *Brown*

Wars and elections are both too big and too small to matter
in the long run. The daily work—that goes on, it adds up.[1]

On Monday, May 17, 1954, at 12:52 P.M., Judge Earl Warren began reading his first major opinion as the chief justice of the US Supreme Court. It was the "school desegregation" case that had been making its way through the courts since 1951.[2] "These cases come to us through the State of Kansas, South Carolina, Virginia, and Delaware. They are premised on different facts and different local conditions, but a common legal question justifies their consideration together in this consolidated opinion." The common factor among the five cases was that all plaintiffs had been "denied admission to schools attended by white children under laws requiring or permitting segregation according to race."[3] Midway through his brief opinion, Chief Justice Warren underscored the essential role of public schools for a strong democracy and for the self-actualization of every child:

> Today, education is perhaps the most important function of state and local governments. Compulsory school attendance laws and the great expenditures for education both demonstrate our recognition of the importance of education to our democratic society . . . In these days, it is doubtful that any child may reasonably be expected to succeed in life if he is denied the opportunity to an education. Such an opportunity, where the state has undertaken to provide it, is a right which must be made available to all on equal terms.[4]

He then posed the central question of the case: "Does segregation of children in public schools solely on the basis of race, even though the physical facilities and other 'tangible' factors may be equal, deprive the children of the minority group of equal education opportunities? We believe that it does."[5] Finally, the highest court in the land unanimously (9–0) and unequivocally declared that

3

segregated schools had no place in public education. With the *Brown v. Board of Education* (1954) ruling, segregated schools were deemed unconstitutional, and desegregated schools were now the law of the land. However, the Court did not offer specific guidelines for implementation or a timeline for enforcement. Instead, Warren announced at the end of the ruling that the Court needed more time and input to determine the specifics of implementation: "The formulation of decrees in these cases presents problems of considerable complexity . . . In order that we may have the full assistance of the parties in formulating decrees, the cases will be restored to the docket."[6]

The NAACP immediately began preparing its arguments for the upcoming hearing on implementation orders. Some leaders (e.g., Kenneth Clark and Spottswood Robinson) called for immediate desegregation within one calendar year, while others expressed uncertainty about the best path forward. Thurgood Marshall told a group of NAACP insiders in September 1954, "It will, of course, not do us any good to take the exact same position as we took last year . . . On the other hand, I am not certain as to what position we should take this year."[7] Chief Justice Warren appointed his own advisory group to make implementation recommendations. The issue of timing was a vexing one for them as well. One member opposed any form of gradualism, while the other five argued that "immediate desegregation was 'impractical' and was likely to be ignored by almost all elements in the South as clearly arbitrary and unreasonable."[8] Even those recommending a more measured approach did not agree on what would be considered a practical and realistic timeline. One wanted twelve years to complete the entire desegregation process, while another favored leaving the issue of timelines to district courts to decide based on local "conditions and sentiment."[9]

While the NAACP and the Supreme Court prepared for the second round of the desegregation case, black leaders in the states affected by *Brown* organized their own grass-roots responses to how desegregation should be accomplished. In the summer of 1954, one hundred black educators met in Hot Springs, Arkansas. At the end of their meeting, they issued a formal statement calling for blacks to be fully included in all future decisions about school desegregation:

> Good statesmanship in a democracy requires that all segments of the population participate in the implementation of the court's decision, which is of common concern. The idea is still too prevalent that the issues involved can be resolved without Negro participation. Some public officials speak as if only white Americans are involved. We are all, Negro and white, deeply and equally involved . . .

We as Negro citizens stand ready to cooperate whole-heartedly in the progressive fulfillment of these democratic objectives.[10]

On May 31, 1955, more than a year after the *Brown* decision, the Supreme Court ruled again on school desegregation in what came to be known as *Brown v. Board II*.[11] Once again reading the opinion was Chief Justice Warren. He reiterated that the "transition to a system of public education freed of racial discrimination" required attention to the complexities and diversity of problems at the local level and that his Court did not want to usurp the authority and expertise of local school authorities who "have the primary responsibility for elucidating, assessing, and solving these problems." The Court decreed that matters of school desegregation would be settled in the district courts where federal judges would decide whether or not the actions of school authorities, charged with enforcing desegregation, would constitute "good faith implementation of the governing constitutional principles." Warren ended with the following: "The judgments below, except that in the Delaware case, are accordingly reversed and the cases are remanded to the District Courts to take such proceedings and enter such orders and decrees consistent with this opinion as are necessary and proper to admit to public schools on a racially nondiscriminatory basis with all deliberate speed the parties to these cases." The Court's vague language on the timetable for school desegregation gave white southerners the ammunition needed to wage a long, drawn-out battle to circumvent *Brown*. "All deliberate speed" quickly translated into "never," or, at least, "not in my lifetime."

No state fought more fiercely to preserve segregated public schools than Mississippi. A month before the *Brown* ruling, Attorney General J. P. Coleman told Governor Hugh White and the Legal Education Advisory Committee (LEAC), established in 1954 by the Mississippi legislature to preserve segregated schools: "We're not in any danger of getting our schools mixed up. We should quit running around like a mother partridge trying to divert attention from her nest and get the psychology abroad that we are the ones who are holding the ball." Governor White similarly declared, "We will continue to have segregation in our schools, the supreme court notwithstanding."[12] Meanwhile, Mississippi circuit judge Tom Brady lambasted the ruling while addressing the Greenwood Sons of the American Revolution. He referred to Monday, May 17, 1954, as "Black Monday." Brady expanded his speech to a ninety-page booklet entitled *Black Monday,* in which he called for every southern state to create a new resistance organization. Seeking to distinguish these new organizations from the Ku Klux Klan, Brady said they would be "law abiding" and their membership and meetings open to all. Their main goal was to inform citizens of the dangers of amalgamation or "race mixing." Brady suggested a name for these resistance organizations in Mississippi: "Sons of the White Magnolia."

Inspired by Brady's book, Robert Patterson formed the first such organization in his hometown of Indianola. Called the Citizens' Council, this group flourished in the 1950s and was one of the most powerful forces in the state in fighting school desegregation. Its members wielded great political influence in local and state politics and publicly harangued any white politicians or business leaders who did not toe the segregation line. While they boasted of being different from the "white ruffians" who comprised the KKK, members of the Citizens' Council regularly used economic retaliation, intimidation, and harassment to prevent or deter black Mississippians from filing school desegregation petitions and lawsuits.[13]

So successful were resistance efforts in Mississippi that ten years after the *Brown* ruling, every school district in Mississippi still operated a dual system of segregated schools with no students attending schools with someone from a different race. In 1966–67, two years after the passage of the Civil Rights Act, only 2.1 percent of black students in Mississippi attended schools with white students, and as late as 1968–69, that percentage had only increased to 7.1 percent, the lowest in the South.[14] For fifteen years, Mississippi quite successfully used every legal and legislative tactic available to delay the implementation of *Brown*. This delay came to a crashing halt on October 29, 1969, when the Supreme Court ruled in *Alexander v. Holmes Board of Education* that "all deliberate speed" was no longer constitutionally permissible: "Under explicit holdings of this Court the obligation of every school district is to terminate dual school systems at once and to operate now and hereafter only unitary schools."[15] Thirty of the thirty-three Mississippi districts named in the case were ordered to open as desegregated schools after the Christmas break. On the eve of massive school desegregation in January 1970, Mississippi governor John Bell Williams despondently told his radio audience:

> I speak to you in a fateful hour in the life of our state . . . The moment that we
> have resisted for 15 years, that we have fought, hopefully to avoid, or at least, to
> delay, is finally at hand. We have reached the millennium. The children of Mis-
> sissippi, white and black, have been denied the right to attend the school of their
> choice by an arbitrary edict of the United States Supreme Court . . . Through a
> series of decisions, the high court has taken away from the people the right and
> the responsibility to run their own schools and to safeguard the best interests
> of their own children . . . So, let us accept the inevitable fact that we are going to

suffer one way or the other, both white and black, as a result of the court's decrees. With God's help, let us make the best of a bad situation.[16]

Left to deal with the hundreds of decisions that had to be made to reopen as fully operational desegregated schools were the principals, teachers, superintendents, secretaries, custodians, coaches, cafeteria workers, and other school personnel employed by their local public schools. With little guidance from state officials, often working in a hostile local context, and with no formal training and experience in effective school desegregation processes, these ordinary people were thrown into extraordinary circumstances. How did they work through school desegregation once the judges, politicians, attorneys, and policy makers stepped out? That question was the genesis of this book.

Over the last seven years, we have interviewed more than one hundred parents, teachers, students, principals, superintendents, community leaders, and school board members who were the "boots on the ground" in one of the most significant social and educational changes in the twentieth century. We have pored over historical documents and read the fine print of dozens of small-town newspapers to understand how school desegregation was being talked about, debated, and understood at the time that it was occurring. In the chapters that follow, we share the findings of our research by focusing on the arduous task left to local Mississippians in implementing school desegregation in their local communities. Because every school district had to create its own desegregation plan, the particularities of school desegregation varied greatly. Thus, no singular narrative can adequately capture the complexities of school desegregation, and no one explanation (e.g., the black/white ratio in a community) can account for its success or failure. By focusing on the various ways in which local communities implemented school desegregation, our intent is to complicate the tendency to present desegregation as a monolithic narrative emphasizing macroforces while minimizing micropolitics and micropractices. We hope to show that the daily minutia mattered.

The focus of the book is primarily on the years 1968 through 1971 as courts began vigorously enforcing school desegregation. However, we begin in chapter 1 with a more detailed analysis of what transpired in Mississippi between the *Brown v. Board of Education* decision in 1954, the passage of the Civil Rights Act in 1964, and the *Alexander v. Holmes County Board of Education* ruling in 1969, as local blacks fought to hold their school districts accountable to the principles of *Brown,* and whites devised a host of ever-changing ways to delay or impede desegregation efforts.

In chapters 2 through 5, we introduce the four key players in the school desegregation process: black parents and students, superintendents, principals, and teachers. In chapter 2, we examine how school districts employed "free-dom-of-choice" (FOC) plans after the 1964 Civil Rights Act to comply ostensibly with school desegregation orders. We relay the stories of several black parents and students in Mississippi who were the first to test their school district's desegregation plans. Some of them were closely associated with their local NAACP chapters; others had no prior history or experience in challenging segregation, and they acted without help from local or national civil rights organizations. All were tenacious in waging the fight in their local communities to desegregate their schools. In chapter 3, we examine the role of superintendents in local school desegregation efforts, focusing particularly on the stories of Julian Prince, Clyde Muse, Tom Dulin, and Harold Kelly, who between them led seven school districts through school desegregation. Their stories demonstrate the many challenges school leaders faced in trying to mitigate the daily operations of school desegregation. In chapter 4, we focus on the school-level administrators responsible for translating school desegregation plans into a workable model for their particular students, teachers, and staff. We examine how principals approached such issues as discipline, curriculum, extracurricular activities, and classroom assignments. We also demonstrate how race was a determining factor in the principal selection process. School desegregation provided unprecedented opportunities for many white, male teachers and coaches to advance into administration early in their careers. At the same time, a disproportionate number of experienced black principals lost their administrative positions either through dismissals, demotions to assistant principal, or reassignment to bogus positions at the central office. In chapter 5, we turn our attention to teachers. Faculty integration was often the first step a school district took in trying to meet school desegregation orders. A young, recently graduated white teacher would be hired to teach in an all-black school, or a more experienced black teacher would be transferred to an all-white school. When the courts ruled this method of compliance unacceptable, student desegregation then took place. Teachers had to figure out how they and their students could live and learn together in classrooms, cafeterias, halls, bathrooms, locker rooms, and teacher's lounges, where the public and private spheres of people's lives often intersect.

In chapters 6 and 7, we shift the focus from the formal structures of school to the informal spaces where students have some autonomy, power, and control. In chapter 6, we dissect the role of sports in the transition to desegregated schools. "We all came together on the football field" was an oft-repeated comment in the oral histories of both our black and white participants. We explore the many ways in which sports helped ease a transition to desegregated schools by uniting black and white fans around the common goal of beating their opponents on the field. However, we also examine how sports was not the panacea many had hoped, and discrimination of black players and coaches persisted both on and off the field long after the initial desegregation dust settled. In chapter 7, we delve into the world of proms, cheerleading, band, pep rallies, homecoming court, and student government, where the racial politics of the day had a direct impact on the lives of students. We analyze how the micropolitics embedded in extracurricular activities both helped and impeded the loftier goal of reducing prejudice through social integration.

In chapters 8 and 9, we examine the role of resistance, broadly conceptualized, in school desegregation efforts. In chapter 8, we look at more conventional forms of resistance, such as protests, demonstrations, marches, boycotts, and violence. We link the resistance efforts of students and parents during school desegregation to the larger freedom movement. While the focus of the chapter is primarily on the resistance efforts of blacks, we end the chapter by describing how whites employed the strategies of the civil rights movement and the antiwar movement to protest court-enforced school desegregation. In chapter 9, we propose that the establishment of private segregationist academies throughout the state was the ultimate form of white resistance to school desegregation. In some school districts, the entire white, school-age population left the public schools in the first few years of desegregation, never to return. But the varied responses to private schools also demonstrates that the white community was not unified or homogeneous in its beliefs about race, the role of public schools for a strong community, or the personal choices parents should make on behalf of their children's education.

In the closing chapter, we summarize the lessons learned from studying the stories of school desegregation in Mississippi. We return to some of the towns and school districts discussed in earlier chapters to look at how public schools are faring today. We probe how the contemporary state of public education and recent school reforms (e.g., charter schools, vouchers, and school choice) are related to the history of school desegregation in the 1960s and 70s. We argue that one of the rallying cries for those who fought for school desegregation was that public schools were imperative for a strong economy and a strong community. We ponder what seems to be a diminishing commitment to public schools in the twenty-first century and end with an appeal to the importance of local leadership, community organizing, and individual commitment to strong public schools as foundational and still relevant principles of a democratic nation.

Writing in the *Commercial Appeal* (Memphis, TN) in January 1970 just as massive school desegregation was occurring, William Street predicted that "the time will come years from now, when the story of Mississippi school integration can be set down clearly and simply, but, for now, that is impossible. There is too much emotions, too many fears, too few concrete statistics."[17] In the chapters that follow, we tell the story of school desegregation in Mississippi, but fifty years later, that story is still complicated and still fraught with emotions. Our intent is not to tell that story "clearly and simply" (for such a story cannot be told), but to capture instead the nuances of "just trying to have school" during this tumultuous time of social upheaval and possibility.

Chapter 1

With No Deliberate Speed

The Road from *Brown* to *Alexander*

"We'll go on as always." "It won't affect us." "Let them enforce it." "Just a lot of confusion." "Bound to cause changes." The speakers of these words were Herbert Nix, Travis Strickland, Rufus Huddleston, L. I. Myers, and J. T. Schultz, all superintendents in Mississippi in 1954. They were responding to the Supreme Court, who had, days before, on May 17, 1954, declared segregated schools unconstitutional.[1] In *Brown v. Board of Education Topeka, Kansas,* the Supreme Court overturned the separate-but-equal doctrine established fifty years earlier in *Plessy v. Ferguson* (1896).[2] In their ruling, the Court specifically addressed the damage that segregated schools inflicted on black children: "To separate them from others of similar age and qualifications solely because of their race generates a feeling of inferiority as to their status in the community that may affect their hearts and minds in a way unlikely ever to be undone ... Separate is inherently unequal."[3] At the time of the ruling, seventeen states and the District of Columbia mandated segregated schools by state constitution or statute.[4] Mississippi was one of those states. "It shall be unlawful for any member of the white or Caucasian race to attend any school of the high school level or below wholly or partially supported by funds of the State of Mississippi which is also attended by a member or members of the colored or Negro race."[5] With the ruling, desegregated schools were now the "law of the land." It was clear from the beginning that the white power structure in the Deep South had no intention of obeying. On May 27, 1954, Mississippi's Senator James Eastland stood on the Senate floor and delivered a vehement attack on the Supreme Court ruling, declaring, "Let me make this very clear. The South will retain segregation."[6]

The immediate response of white southerners to *Brown* varied. Some resigned themselves to the inevitability of school desegregation; others promised fierce defiance, and many simply clung to the belief that it would never be enforced. Many of the border southern states complied quickly to the ruling. The District of Columbia announced that it would reopen in fall 1954 as a desegregated school system. Maryland and Delaware followed suit with little incident. The southern states of North Carolina, Arkansas, Alabama, Kentucky, Oklahoma, Tennessee, Texas, and Virginia adopted the strategy of "let's wait and see." By 1956 Kentucky, Oklahoma, and Texas had voluntarily complied with *Brown*. Mississippi, Georgia, Louisiana, and South Carolina (with Alabama quickly joining their ranks) vowed to wage an all-out fight to preserve segregation.[7]

In June 1954, a month after the *Brown* decision, Mississippi governor Hugh White convened a meeting with a group of eight black leaders in the state to ensure their support of segregated schooling. Attending the meeting were Percy Greene, editor of the *Jackson Advocate*; H. H. Humes, a Baptist minister; J. H. White, Jacob Reddix, and J. R. Otis, college presidents; and J. D. Boyd, N. R. Burger, and E. S. Bishop, former presidents of the Mississippi Teachers' Association.[8] Governor White interpreted his meeting with this small contingency as affirmation that blacks would cooperate with him in defying *Brown*. On July 30, 1954, he followed up with another meeting in Jackson with a larger group of black leaders who presented a "Statement Issued by Negro Leaders from Every Area of the State of Mississippi," which began:

> The spotlight of our nation and of the world of free democratic peoples is upon the state of Mississippi today. They are looking to see what we are going to do. Even the Kremlin enemies of democracy are watching for an opportunity to catch us in a moment of weakness and to ridicule our institutions. Facing such a challenge we pray God that we may not fail in our duty toward our state, toward democracy and toward our people. In this our destiny and for the sake of our posterity we cannot do otherwise than take our stand for the ideals of our America and the whole free world—for justice, human brotherhood and equality of opportunity for all.[9]

This was not the response the governor expected as reflected in his address to the Mississippi House of Representatives on September 7, 1954:

> We have explored every possible solution. We have expended considerable time and effort to learn the true attitude of the Negro leadership in the State, in the hope that they would appreciate the sacrifices that have been made to equalize their opportunities without integrating the races. In this effort, as you know, we were most positively and unexpectantly disappointed. These leaders not only repudiated what had been told us in private conference but demanded things that even the Supreme Court decision had not pretended to try to give them. It

remains only for me to say that no hope for solution can now be predicated upon the cooperation of these men. We can go forward, however, with the clear conscience of knowing that we gave them the opportunity to cooperate for the best interest of all, including themselves, and they spurned the offer. Upon them, not us, rest full responsibility for rejection.[10]

Earlier in the 1954 regular session the Mississippi legislature established the Legal Education Advisory Council (LEAC); its stated purpose was to "preserve the best interests of both races and the public welfare" by "maintain[ing] separate educational facilities for white and colored races." The LEAC consisted of twenty-five white men, including Governor White, J. P. Coleman, the attorney general, and John C. Satterfield, who would later be the lead attorney for the state in the *Alexander v. Holmes* case.[11] After his failed meeting with the black leadership in the state, Governor White, with the support of the LEAC, called a special session in September 1954 to consider a constitutional amendment to abolish public schools if necessary. The legislature approved the resolution, and on December 21, 1954, the citizens of Mississippi approved this amendment by a margin of 2 to 1.

In 1956 the Mississippi State Sovereignty Commission was created, with a state appropriation of $250,000. Ostensibly, it was to "perform any and all acts and things deemed necessary and proper to protect the sovereignty of the State of Mississippi, and her sister states, from the encroachment thereon by the Federal Government."[12] In practice, it became the segregation watchdog agency. Governor Coleman likened the commission to the FBI "during times of war seeking out intelligence information about the enemy and what the enemy proposed to do."[13] In a candid account of his tenure as the commission's director of public relations under Governor Ross Barnett (1960–1964), Erle Johnston explained the Commission's purpose: "The agency . . . had authority to use state money and statepaid manpower to oppose federal encroachment on the states. 'Federal encroachment' was a sophisticated version of 'integration.'"[14]

Prior to the Court's ruling in *Brown*, southern states realized they needed to demonstrate some pretense toward equalizing black and white schools. The Mississippi Citizens Council on Education (MCCE), a biracial committee formed in 1950, presented the state legislature a school equalization program with a price tag of approximately $180 million.[15] In 1952, Senator James Eastland helped Biloxi public schools secure funding from the federal government for almost $100,000 to build new elementary and junior high schools for black children and for additions to another segregated black school.[16] In 1953, the Mississippi legislature passed its first serious equalization program that included paying black and white teachers the same salaries. It designated 65 percent of construction bonds to building and updating black schools.[17] The proposal remained largely unfunded as legislators argued the wisdom of passing sweeping and costly reforms when the verdict on the *Brown* case was still out. However, after the ruling, the state legislature did begin allocating more money to black schools in an attempt to garner black support for maintaining segregated schools. From 1952 through 1957, the state increased funding for black libraries by 563 percent compared to only 54 percent for whites. During the same time period, the salaries of black teachers increased by 83.4 percent compared to 24.3 for whites.[18] New facilities for black students were built in many school districts: three new schools were built in west Tallahatchie after 1946; Black Hawk Elementary was built in Carroll County in 1956; Kemper County erected a new high school in DeKalb in 1957; and Natchez built four new schools between 1953 and 1964.[19]

George Owens, chairman of the Senate Education Committee, knew that if the state was going to resist school desegregation, state politicians had to convince black Mississippians to stand in solidarity with whites in opposing desegregation regardless of how the Court ruled. Writing in March 1953, Owens stated that "the only possibility of maintaining a segregated school system in Mississippi is by persuading the Negro to attend of his own volition schools provided for him."[20] They naturally reached out to black educators who were beholden to their white superintendents and school boards for their jobs. In 1956, at its annual convention in Jackson, the Mississippi Negro Teachers Association publicly supported the state's equalization program.[21] However, many blacks, particularly local activists, did not share the views of the black teachers. In 1958, Medgar Evers, the state NAACP field secretary, expressed the frustration of many about the seemingly all-too-cozy alliance between black middle-class teachers and the white power structure: "As much good as the NAACP has done to make the opportunities greater for teachers who once made $20 a month and are making up to $5,000 [a year] now, we don't get their cooperation. The professionals are the same way. Only in isolated cases do they go all out to help us. Some ministers are almost in the same category . . . [They] won't give 50 cents for fear of losing face with the white man."[22]

Knowing that Mississippi would wage an all-out battle to prevent the implementation of *Brown*, the national NAACP sent Ruby Hurley and Gloster Current to the state to help start new branches of the NAACP, to reinvigorate dormant ones, and to galvanize local blacks to assume the everyday operations of these chapters. One of their main priorities was to help their local branches develop strategies for forcing local school boards to comply with the *Brown* decision.[23]

Filing the First Petitions

In August 1954, the Walthall County NAACP branch attempted to file the state's first desegregation petition. The petitioners were immediately shut down by their local school board and, after being subpoenaed on false charges, dropped the petition.[24] On July 18, 1955, 140 black parents in Vicksburg signed the first school petition in the state after the *Brown II* ruling demanding their school system comply with desegregation orders immediately. Days later, 42 parents in Jackson, led by Medgar Evers, and 19 parents in Hinds County filed a similar petition. The Jackson petitioners asked that the public schools be immediately reorganized with no reference to race as proscribed by the *Brown* ruling. The petitioners noted that "the time for delay, evasion, and also procrastination is past. As we interpret the decision, you (the board) are duty bound to take immediate concrete steps leading to early elimination of segregation in public schools."[25] On August 11, a similar petition was filed in Clarksdale.[26]

In Natchez, the local NAACP was also organizing. It held a meeting on July 18, 1955, to discuss the school petition. Fifty attendees signed the petition. Dr. A. Maurice Mackel, a local dentist and the secretary of the Natchez NAACP chapter, was ecstatic about the turnout, writing to Roy Wilkins, executive secretary of the NAACP: "The enthusiasm was high throughout. Many who are not parents begged to sign."[27] One week later, he followed up with Mr. Wilkins, still optimistic their efforts would produce results: "This is quite an experience. It is delightful. Many parents have sought me in an effort to sign."[28] On July 25, 1955, Dr. Mackel and David Bacon, the president of the Natchez branch of the NAACP, sent a letter on behalf of the petitioners to Brent Forman, president of the Natchez School Board of Education. It read:

> The subscribers, whose names are written on the attached petition respectfully petition you and the Natchez School Board of Education for equality of educational opportunities for all of the people in light of the Supreme Court decision on education. In the past, school plans have been made for us rather than with us. This in itself is detrimental to the growth and development of individuals. Kindly be advised that we are willing to cooperate with you in making the transition in our educational system. We are certain that the majority of the citizens believe in and respect the law of the land and with the proper approach in this matter we will put democracy in action, the most effective answer to communistic propaganda, and strengthen our position among nations. It is incumbered upon those in the know from a national and international point of view to implement legal and progressive movements toward the end that America will eventually be in a position to utilize its manpower in war and peace to the maximum degree. It can

only do this by having a well trained citizenry, a satisfied citizenry, and a happy citizenry. With due respect, we the parents and friends of parents, most urgently request that the Natchez Public School Board of Education take immediate steps toward compliance with the laws of our great country.[29]

As blacks throughout the state presented petitions to their respective school districts, Mississippi attorney general J. P. Coleman was reassuring the LEAC that he would personally handle any petitions or lawsuits brought by black parents: "I am going to take 90 days to try the first case. It will take that long. There's no use anyone worrying about them (Negroes) running any cases through Mississippi during the next six months. I'll see to that." Coleman dismissed the Vicksburg petition, stating that it "could not be used as a basis for initiating federal court action." He noted that because the petition failed to include the names of the children requesting admission to the white school, the petition did not "amount to a hill of beans." The Vicksburg school board dismissed the case, saying it "did not meet requirements [and] would be given no further consideration."[30] A similar fate fell on the Natchez and Jackson petitions—dismissal on the part of the white power structure.

By the time fifty-three black parents signed a petition in Yazoo City on August 6, 1955, demanding that the schools abide by the *Brown* decision, the Citizens' Council was well mobilized and ready to exert their power. The local Citizens' Council chapter took out a full-page advertisement in the *Yazoo City Herald* listing the names and addresses of every person who signed the petition. The ad was also prominently displayed in many local white restaurants and other business establishments. The ad ended with "this list is published as a public service by the Citizens Council of Yazoo City, Mississippi."[31] Retaliation was swift. Many of the black petitioners lost their jobs, their credit, and their businesses as detailed in a report to the NAACP:

> One man here, _____, whose name was on the petition draws a Disability check from the War department. He received his check last week and tried to cash it. And not a store or bank in Yazoo City would cash it. The Delta National Bank here in Yazoo City also is applying pressure. The president of the Delta National Bank—Herbert Holmes has phoned to every Negro that signed that school petition and told them to come down and get their money out, that the bank did not want to do business with them any longer.[32]

Eventually all but three of the petitioners removed their names from the petition, and many moved out of Yazoo City.

J. H. Wright, a local plumber, was one of those petitioners. He reported in a November 8, 1955, letter to the national NAACP that 99 percent of his business was with whites. After the ad in the paper, he lost all of his work, such that he could not afford food, clothes, or materials. The NAACP advised him to move to Detroit and contact Congressman Charles Diggs, which he did. Clearly frustrated that neither Mr. Diggs nor the Detroit NAACP had reached out to help him, Wright wrote to Roy Wilkins that "the white people told me that I wouldn't get any help from the N.A.A.C.P. [and] so far I have found that to be true."[33] Wilkins promptly responded with assurance that he had personally contacted the executive secretary of the Detroit branch with the specifics of Mr. Wright's situation and that someone would be contacting him immediately.[34]

So successful were the tactics of the Citizens' Council in shutting down blacks' attempts to force their school districts to comply with *Brown* that the Yazoo City petition would be the last one submitted by black parents during the 1950s. According to William Simmons, the organizer of the Citizens' Council in Jackson, the successful efforts to prevent school desegregation in the summer of 1955 were "a turning point in public opinion in the South, a turning from a feeling that 'integration is inevitable' to a determination that 'we aint' going to do it.'"[35] With these resounding defeats, the national NAACP abandoned its efforts to force school districts to comply with *Brown* through appeals to legislative logic and judicial action. As Dittmer notes, the traditional strategies of the NAACP failed miserably in Mississippi because "the national office made several miscalculations, underestimating the ferocity of white resistance and overestimating the federal government's commitment to law enforcement."[36]

Despite the success of the Citizens' Council in stopping blacks from filing petitions with their local school boards, many blacks in the South continued in those early years after *Brown* to hold onto at least a modicum of optimism that the law of the land would ultimately prevail. W. A. Bender, director of public relations at Tougaloo College and editor of the *Journal of Negro Education*, recognized the depths to which Mississippi would go to prevent *Brown*, writing in his 1956 editorial: "The naked truth is that Mississippi does not want to do so and has no intention of making a move to that end now or in the years of the future."[37] However, he ended that editorial with the following passionate declamation: "Desegregated schools are coming and all the children will take them in stride just as people elsewhere are taking them. The forces of justice are on the march. The momentum is too great for any one to get in the way and try to stop them. It cannot be done; it will not be done. The new day is not far away. Mark you this!"[38]

In the years following the *Brown* ruling, violence against blacks escalated. Local civil rights activists were often the target. On May 7, 1955, Reverend George W. Lee, Belzoni native and local business owner, was killed in what was called an "odd" car accident shortly after a voter registration rally. No one was ever charged with the murder. In November 1955, Gus Courts, also a Belzoni resident, was shot in his store. He had recently contacted an attorney about filing a lawsuit against the Belzoni Citizens' Council. Courts survived the attack but, knowing his life was in danger, relocated to Chicago with help from the NAACP. That same year another local civil rights activist, Lamar Smith, was murdered on the courthouse lawn in Brookhaven. Again, no one was charged with the murder. However, the murder that captured the attention of the national news media was that of Emmett "Bobo" Till. On August 28, 1955, Till, a fourteen-year-old boy from Chicago who was visiting his aunt in Money (MS), was brutally murdered—his body found three days later in the Tallahatchie River. He was tied to a cotton gin fan. There was overwhelming evidence to convict J. W. Millan and Roy Bryant, the husband of the woman with whom Till allegedly flirted. The two were arrested, tried, and found "not guilty."[39] In the trial, the defense argued that the body recovered was not that of Emmett Till. In his closing arguments, defense counsel John Whitten warned: "There are people in the United States who want to destroy the customs of southern people . . . They would not be above putting a rotting, stinking body in the river in the hope he would be identified as Emmett Till."[40] The murder of Emmett Till and the subsequent trial were well covered by national and international presses. *Jet* magazine published the photograph of Till's horribly bloated, disfigured body. Four years after Till's murder, in April 1959, in Poplarville, a brutal mob of white men abducted Mack Parker from the local jail, beat him, shot him twice, and then deposited his body in the Pearl River. Parker had been arrested two months earlier for raping a white woman, an accusation he vehemently denied to his death.[41]

As the 1950s dragged to an end, the hope of desegregated schools promised in *Brown* seemed a distant dream for blacks living in Mississippi. William Robinson captured the frustration of many when he wrote in 1959: "When the Court handed down its decision, not even the most optimistic among us felt that integration was at hand or just around the corner, but even the most pessimistic little dreamed that is was so far off."[42] By the end of the decade, the "new day" did indeed seem "so far off." No school district in the state had made any movement toward integrating its schools, and by all indications staunch segregationists seemed to be prevailing in the fight over school desegregation.

Citizens' Council Vows Never

In 1953, Robert Patterson, a farmer, paratrooper, and former football captain at Mississippi State University, attended a meeting at his daughter's elementary school in the Delta town of Indianola. Patterson and the rest of the parents gathered there were told that it was quite possible that the Supreme Court would rule in favor of school desegregation, and they should prepare themselves and their children accordingly. Patterson left that meeting irate and resolute in his belief that whites must fight the high court's ruling. He wrote in a letter: "[W]e cannot and must not accept this scourge as inevitable. The people of America must call all their resources and stand together forever firm against communism and mongrelization."[43] Two months after the passage of *Brown*, in July 1954, Patterson and five other Sunflower County businessmen began strategizing about how they were going to fight this "scourge" of integration. That meeting led to the official formation of the White Citizens' Council in October 1954. By December they had established headquarters in the small town of Winona, and Patterson assumed a full-time position with the organization as their executive director. By November 1955, they claimed more than sixty-five thousand members in Mississippi and began publishing a monthly newspaper called the *Citizen*.[44] Their purpose was clearly articulated in the first issue:

> To preserve separation of the races against assaults from the National Association for Colored People. In alliance with the federal government. At the same time, they are dedicated to protect the rank and file of Negroes from the wrath of ruffian white people who may resort to violence. "Economic pressure," a method of combating Negro pressure from the North, is not organized by the Councils. Individuals who belong to councils may have persuaded Negroes to remove their names from school integration petitions by various means short of violence. These means include firing employees, or refusing to renew leases for sharecroppers who have followed the NAACP line.[45]

The Citizens' Council was well organized, with local chapters throughout the state. They launched an intense statewide membership drive in 1955, mailing letters to their local chapters encouraging them to recruit as many members as they could: "The cotton harvesting is at a close and money is beginning to flow. Every Mississippian should be proud to spend the little amount it takes to be a part of this great cause, the outcome of which will mean the very survival of the white race in this Nation."[46] Comprised, in part, of well-known business leaders and politicians, neither their meetings nor their membership was secretive.

Using economic intimidation of blacks who tried to push their local school boards to desegregate their schools coupled with a well-orchestrated and financed propaganda campaign and a close connection to state politicians who introduced and often passed laws to prevent school desegregation, the Citizens' Council was highly effective throughout the South, but particularly in Mississippi, in preventing the implementation of *Brown*. Steeped in an ideology of white supremacy, the Citizens' Council distributed nationwide a plethora of printed materials warning whites that integration was a Communist plot to take over the United States through the mongrelization of the races. They published pamphlets on how to circumvent *Brown*, and they created booklets to be used in schools to indoctrinate white students into a belief in the inherent inferiority of blacks.[47] For example, elementary students were taught eleven essential differences between whites and blacks, including "the Negro's arm is about two inches longer than the White man's," and "the skulls are different."[48] In 1958–59, they sponsored an essay contest for high school students (awarding two five-hundred-dollar scholarships) in which students were asked to write on one of the following topics:

1) Why I believe in social separation of the races of mankind
2) Subversion in racial unrest
3) Why the preservation of States Rights is important to every American
4) Why separate schools should be maintained for the White and Negro races.

Pictures of the winners and copies of their essays were featured in the *Citizen*.[49]

The Citizens' Council exhorted its white members to fight integration, including "token integration," with every means possible. In a 1959 pamphlet entitled "How to Save Our Public Schools," it blames white moderates in the state for their acceptance of the "inevitability" of integration and their too willing cooperation with the federal government under the auspices of preserving public schools. It warns its white readers that there is no middle ground when it comes to integration:

The latest fraud the integraters are trying to perpetrate on a partially-unsuspecting public is "Your choice now is accept token integration or close your public schools"... Mention is carefully avoided, of course, of the fact that there is no such thing as token integration. Those unfortunate "moderates" in certain areas of North Carolina and Virginia know by now that you can't do business with the

NAACP. You are either for segregation, or you are for integration, without prefix, suffix, or affix.[50]

The pamphlet continues by stating the onus of responsibility for implementing *Brown* falls on black parents who must file individual lawsuits; such suits are "difficult, time-consuming, and expensive." Although no lawsuits were successful up to this time, the council proposed certain "conditions" favorable for blacks to win their lawsuits, including a weak school board, moderate whites, and law enforcement controlled by moderates. To deter any blacks from filing such a lawsuit, it proposed the following strategies:

> Every community needs a strong pro-segregation school board, composed of fearless men who will defy the mixers; municipal, county and state officials equally fearless, determined and capable of providing the necessary leadership; an honest local press; speakers for civic clubs to keep community leadership informed as to their vital financial stakes in this struggle; and last, but most important, alert, capable, strong organization which will guarantee the existence of the other conditions, which will solidify the will to victory, and translate into constructive action.[51]

Ominously, it declares that the Citizens' Council would shut down public education if the state complied with *Brown*. If this were to happen, it would not hesitate to create an alternative private school system for white students. Five years later the threat became a reality when in 1964 the council began calling for the mass exodus of whites from public schools.

Petitions, Lawsuits, and More Resistance

By the beginning of a new decade, not much had changed in the public schools in Mississippi. A dual system of public segregated schooling continued to operate with no movement toward complying with *Brown*. As late as January 1964, not one desegregated public school existed in the state. Blacks benefited modestly from the delaying tactics and the concomitant equalization efforts with a few new black schools built, some facilities upgraded, the addition of new science equipment, library books, and athletic gear, and an equalization of teachers' salaries. But by and large, black schools were still dreadfully underresourced, underfunded, and far from equal as Dr. Gilbert and Natalie Mason discovered when their son, Gilbert Jr., began kindergarten in 1959 in the segregated black school system in Biloxi. The Masons were active in the PTA, and Dr. Mason served as the team physician for Nichols High, the black high school. Despite having some excellent teachers and some modest upgrades to facilities and course offerings, the black schools in Biloxi were nowhere near the level of the white schools. Nichols High offered no college preparatory courses, no advanced math and science courses, and no foreign language courses, all of which were offered at Biloxi High. The curriculum at Nichols High focused on manual training, yet even typewriters were scarce at the school. The Masons realized just how unequal the two systems of schooling were when Gilbert Jr. brought home a report card with a grade of "C" in music, art, and physical education. These courses were not offered at his elementary school. When the Masons began investigating, they learned that the entire system used the same preprinted report cards. The central office had instructed the teachers at the black schools to assign a grade of "C" on the report card in the subjects not offered.[52]

By the early 1960s, the Masons and many other blacks in the South were clearly discouraged and frustrated. They were also worried about the effect the obvious delaying tactics were having on their children. Since 1954, they had been preparing their children for the realities of attending desegregated schools; yet, black children continued to languish in segregated schools—the very schools that the Supreme Court had declared in 1954 to have harmful and possibly irreversible effects on their social and psychological well-being. As William Robinson noted, black parents were forced to do what they had always done to protect the psyches of their children:

> An integral part of the process of growing up in the South, the Negro child develops a tolerance toward the traditional disadvantages to which he is heir as a member of [a] depressed racial minority group. This tolerance has kept the growing Negro youth from being beaten down spiritually while riding in the back of the busses and street cars, while being excluded from movie houses and restaurants, and while being denied recreational and employment opportunities because of his race . . . Now parents and teachers must help black children develop defenses against knowing legally they are supposed to be attending desegregated schools but are still not there. Teachers have to begin immediately to indoctrinate their pupils with attitudes of tolerance to the frustration of integration's delay.[53]

In October 1960, Medgar Evers, the NAACP field secretary in Mississippi, contacted Robert Carter, an attorney with the NAACP, asking for guidance in a desegregation lawsuit brewing in Biloxi. At the helm of the Biloxi movement was Dr. Mason, who earlier that year had led 125 blacks in a "wade-in" protesting segregated beaches on the Gulf Coast. The peaceful protest turned bloody as white bystanders attacked the protesters while the police sat idly by and watched. Five white men jumped on Mason, pummeling him with a pool stick. Mason was arrested for disturbing the peace, and the white attackers walked away.[54] Concurrently with the planning and execution of the segregated beach protests, the Masons petitioned the Biloxi School Board for their son to attend one of the white elementary schools. They were refused. One year later in 1961 the Biloxi NAACP, of which Mason was president, followed up with another petition demanding the Biloxi School Board desegregate its schools. Again, the school board refused their request. For two years, the Masons and others persisted in filing petitions, to no avail. Getting nowhere with that tactic, they decided to file a lawsuit against their school board.

In October 1962, the NAACP's legal counsel contacted Mason, suggesting that the federal government file the lawsuit against the Biloxi Municipal School District, rather than individual black citizens. A few days earlier, violence had erupted at the University of Mississippi when James Meredith attempted to enroll at the school. The NAACP feared that Mason and the other black Biloxians initiating the lawsuit would be easy targets for more violence. Given the timing and the racial tension permeating the state, Mason agreed. On January 18, 1963, on behalf of the children of military personnel stationed at the Keesler Air Force Base and the Veterans Administration (VA) Hospital in Biloxi, the Department of Justice (DOJ) filed the first school desegregation lawsuit in Mississippi. On March 18, 1963, Mason and twenty-one other parents once again petitioned the Biloxi School Board to desegregate their schools beginning September 1963. Once again, the school board refused their petition.[55]

Federal judge Sidney Mize dismissed the Biloxi lawsuit because "the federal government has no standing as plaintiff in this court and does not have the requisite interest in the subject matter to maintain the action . . . [O]nly natural persons are entitled to privileges and immunities of the Fourteenth Amendment."[56] Mason was not surprised by the ruling, and he stood ready to pursue the case further. On June 5, 1963, Gilbert and Natalie Mason along with twelve other families filed a lawsuit against the Biloxi Municipal Separate School District as "natural persons" with an obvious interest in the case. Within days, Joe Patterson, attorney general for Mississippi, filed a motion to dismiss the case on the grounds that the black families had failed to exhaust all the "administrative remedies" available to them. Judge Mize ruled in favor of the attorney general and dismissed the case. However, the Fifth Circuit Court of Appeals disagreed with the lower court's ruling and agreed to hear the case. It combined it with two other school desegregation lawsuits filed in the state—one by Medgar Evers and other black parents in Jackson and the other by Winson Hudson and Dovie Hudson in Leake County.[57] On February 14, 1964, the Fifth Circuit reversed the lower court's ruling, stating, "If Selma, Alabama can commence with desegregation of four grades for 1965–1966, Jackson, Mississippi can at least catch up. And indeed, in all but the most exceptional cases, all school districts commencing desegregation in fall 1965 should be expected to do as well."[58] The case was remanded back to Judge Mize and the district court for a speedy hearing.

During the trial in May 1964, the black parents heard a plethora of "scientific" explanations justifying segregation, including "conclusive [evidence] to the effect that cranial capacity and brain size of the average Negro is approximately 10 per cent less than that of the average white person of similar age and size, and that brain size is correlated with intelligence."[59] Reluctantly, however, Judge Mize ruled in favor of the plaintiffs although he cited the testimony about the correlation between brain size and intelligence as indisputable scientific fact. Nevertheless, he said he was obligated to "enter the order although it is contrary to the facts and the law applicable thereto" because of previous rulings by the higher courts.[60] He ordered the three school districts to submit desegregation plans immediately. The Biloxi, Jackson, and Leake School Districts all submitted similar plans calling for the desegregation of first grade in September 1964 with one grade desegregating every year thereafter.

In fall 1964, ten years after the *Brown* decision, sixteen black students in Biloxi and thirty-nine black students in Jackson became the first students in Mississippi to attend school with white children.[61] In Leake County, it took weeks for local black leaders to find parents willing to send their children to an all-white school. Finally, A. J. and Minnie Lewis agreed to send their daughter Debra to Carthage Elementary.[62] The local newspaper reported Debra's first day of school:

> Debra took it all calmly. She was delivered to school in a dusty 1954 automobile by her parents shortly before the first bell rang at 8:15 am. Dressed in a starched plaid dress, she walked 20 feet toward the one story brick building, was met by two teachers and a man who came out, then climbed a dozen steps and walked inside. "I'm a little bit excited," her father, A. J. Lewis, said later at the family's tin-roof, four-room house. He said the FBI had been watching his home, but he had received no threat as other Negro parents claimed prior to the start of the new term.[63]

In a separate case, the Delta town of Clarksdale was also court-ordered to desegregate in 1964; however, no blacks were willing to send their children to a white school. It was reported that one white student in Clarksdale tried to enroll at one of the black schools but was turned away by the principal because he did not have a birth certificate with him.[64]

As with the earlier cases when parents filed petitions against their school boards, those filing the first lawsuit faced immediate reprisals. A. J. Lewis expressed optimism the first day he dropped his little girl off at Carthage Elementary, but soon thereafter he was fired from his job, and his house was torched. A white man poured scalding hot coffee down Gilbert Mason's back in the newly desegregated hospital cafeteria in Biloxi. When Mason grabbed a chair and struck the man in retaliation, Mason was arrested for fighting in a public place. And Medgar Evers was murdered in his driveway on June 12, 1963—a year before his children integrated the Jackson public schools.[65]

One Step Forward, Two Steps Back:
The Civil Rights Act, Freedom of Choice, and Continued Delays

In July 1964, Congress passed Public Law 88–352, the Civil Rights Act of 1964. An important component of the new law was Title VI, which prohibited discrimination on the basis of race, color, and national origin in programs and activities receiving federal financial assistance. The Civil Rights Act provided both a carrot and a stick to force recalcitrant southern school boards to comply with *Brown*. School districts failing to desegregate could have their federal funding terminated. For those who complied, not only would they continue receiving federal monies, but Title VI also provided a program of federal technical and financial assistance to help school districts during the desegregation process comply with the *Brown* ruling. In 1964 Mississippi received approximately $38 million in federal funding for public schools. The Civil Rights Act also authorized the DOJ to file suits against local school districts on behalf of black parents and students being denied a desegregated public education.[66] Finally a crack in the school segregation wall seemed to emerge, triggered by the unusual alignment of the judicial, executive, and legislative branches around the enforcement of *Brown* in the South.[67]

One year later on April 7, 1965, Congress gave teeth to Title VI by passing the Elementary and Secondary Education Act (ESEA), which allocated $1.3 billion to aid in the education of low-income students. As the poorest state in the country with the most underresourced schools, Mississippi could ill afford to refuse federal funding, but this financial boost was predicated on school districts' complying with school desegregation mandates. As William Peart, writer for the *Clarion-Ledger*, noted in a 1965 story: "For Mississippians, that was a bitter alternative to consider. They were confronted with a distasteful

choice: either comply with the government's desegregation directive or lose
the federal aid they had come to depend upon."[68] Twelve school districts in
Mississippi forfeited the Title I federal funding for which they were eligible
because they refused to desegregate their schools.[69] The West Tallahatchie
school district was one of the districts that lost the bulk of its federal funding over a two-year period, from almost $217,619.84 in 1965–66 to $36,758 in
1967–68. Frustrated with the abrupt termination of federal monies, Superintendent Robert Taylor wrote Senator Eastland in December 1967: "[T]here
is no possible way for a school administrator to plan a program under the
present method of allowing cut-off funds for alleged non-compliance in the
middle of the school years."[70] Superintendents, like Robert Taylor, suddenly
found themselves in the ironic position of decrying, on one hand, the federal
government's intrusion into state affairs by enforcing desegregation while, on
the other hand, asking the federal government to fund its schools at a greater
percentage than any other state in the country.[71]

Undeniably, the threat of termination of federal funding finally forced
school desegregation throughout the South. By 1969, 115 school districts in
Mississippi were receiving Title I funds from the ESEA. In some districts,
federal funding accounted for 30 percent of the school district's budget.[72]
However, throughout the mid-1960s, many Mississippi school districts mis-
used ESEA funds as a last-ditch attempt to maintain a dual system of segregated schools. They bought band uniforms for their black schools, hired black
teachers for the segregated schools to reach a teacher-student ratio mirroring
the white schools, and diverted monies to newly opened private academies.
So rampant was the abuse of ESEA funding that the Department of Health,
Education and Welfare (HEW) inspectors accused the state of misspend-
ing $3 million between the passage of the ESEA in 1965 and the *Alexander v.
Holmes* ruling in 1969. In the early 1970s, many school districts were ordered
to repay the federal government for misappropriated ESEA funding.[73]

Local school districts were given little directives or guidance from their
state Department of Education or their state politicians on how to respond
to these new congressional mandates. Jack Tubbs, the state superintendent of
education, declared he had no authority to instruct school districts to comply or not with desegregation orders. Governor Paul Johnson never called a
special session to discuss how the state should approach school desegregation
under the new orders.[74] In December 1964, the HEW published a three-page
manual entitled "Instructions to School Districts Regarding Compliance with
Title VI" to help school districts navigate Title VI mandates. To prove compliance with the law, school districts had to submit a voluntary desegregation plan or a final court order. The HEW's "how-to" manual suggested two

primary ways to achieve desegregation: "geographical zoning" or "freedom of choice." Whatever the method selected, schools needed to demonstrate a "good faith effort" to desegregate their schools by the 1965–66 school year.[75] In March 1966, the US Office of Education issued a *Revised Statement of Policies for School Desegregation Plans under Title VI of the Civil Rights Act of 1964* to help provide more specifics about what would be considered appropriate compliance according to the HEW. These guidelines made clear that school boards bore the affirmative duty to desegregate their schools. The HEW set fall 1967 as the date for the extension of desegregation to all grades as a qualification for federal financial assistance. All desegregation plans had to be submitted to the US Office of Education for approval. The new guidelines were very specific on how freedom of choice (FOC), the most prevalent method of compliance, was to be implemented:

> Under the Freedom of Choice plan, students are given the opportunity once a year to choose the school they wish to attend. Each year, several months before the beginning of the new school term, the Board of Education must send students and their parents a letter explaining the particular plan under which the district's schools are being desegregated. The letter must inform the students and their parents that they may choose the school they wish to attend. It must list the schools in the district, their location, and the grades covered. The parents and students should return the name of the school they select to the office of the school superintendent within 30 days after receipt of the letter. Students who are 15 years old or who will enter Grades 9 through 12 in the following school year may make their own choice of a school to attend under the Freedom of Choice Plan unless the parents wish the student to make a different choice . . . The local school board has the further responsibility of notifying the community each year that the Freedom of Choice Plan is available to all students, of developing community support for it, and taking the steps necessary to protect all persons exercising their rights under the plan.[76]

The new guidelines acknowledged that the FOC plan would continue to place the burden of desegregation on black parents and students since it would be highly unlikely that a white parent or student would choose to attend an all-black school. According to the guidelines, the effectiveness of FOC plans would be evaluated on the *results* of such plans: "The single most substantial indication as to whether a free choice plan is actually working to eliminate the dual school structure is the extent to which Negro or other minority group students have in fact transferred from segregated schools."[77] "Freedom of choice" ostensibly provided a mechanism for black parents to exercise their right to send their children to desegregated schools. In reality, it proved in many school districts to be yet another way to delay school desegregation.

Challenging Freedom of Choice

Several school districts, particularly in the northeastern part of the state where the black population was sparse, voluntarily moved to a unitary system of schooling. In 1965 in the southern part of the state, the Long Beach Separate Municipal School District voluntarily desegregated its school system.[78] However, the majority of school districts between 1965 and 1969 continued, in practice, to operate a dual system of schooling in which the majority of whites attended a primarily all-white school, the majority of black students attended segregated black schools, and a smattering of black students attended white schools. Often these black students were handpicked by the superintendent or school board to attend the white schools, or black parents, typically those involved in their local civil rights movement, would send their children to "integrate" the white school.

Black parents who availed themselves of this option were often treated much the same way as the first school petitioners in 1955 with threats of economic retaliation and harassment. In 1967, when one hundred black parents in Noxubee County filed FOC plans on behalf of their children, they faced immediate reprisals. Eighty of them eventually withdrew their forms after they were fired, lost their credit, or were physically harassed. The DOJ charged thirteen local white residents with "interfering with court-enforced desegregation by threatening and intimidating parents of Negro children."[79] Among the thirteen named in the suit for harassment and intimidation were the mayor and several law enforcement officers. Other prominent community members, including the sheriff, the superintendent, a principal, several Board of Trustees members, and the administrator of the local hospital, were also charged with harassment and contempt of court for refusal to comply with previous desegregation court orders.

As school districts continued to stall in desegregating their schools, black parents and students began challenging "freedom of choice" in court. The first major victory came in December 1966 in a ruling consolidating two cases originating in Alabama and Louisiana. The Fifth Circuit Court of Appeals ruled in *United States v. Jefferson County Board of Education* that states had an affirmative duty to "integrate students, faculties, facilities, and activities . . . to effectuate a transition to a racially nondiscriminatory school system."[80] Acknowledging that FOC had failed to produce desegregated schools, Judge

Wisdom declared "the only school desegregation plan that meets constitutional standards is one that works." The ruling also made clear that the courts would give "great weight" to the HEW guidelines in determining judicially whether or not school districts had adequately desegregated their schools. The Court also emphatically made clear that school desegregation was not an option. Regardless of whether a school system chose to accept federal funding or not, they were legally bound to create a unitary school system. Two years later in 1968, the Supreme Court dealt another blow to FOC. In *Greene v. County School Board of New Kent County* (1968), the Court ruled that "freedom of choice is not a sacred talisman; it is only a means to a constitutionally required end—the abolition of the system of segregation and its effects. If the means prove effective, it is acceptable, but if it fails to undo segregation, other means must be used to achieve this end. The school officials have the continuing duty to take whatever action may be necessary to create a 'unitary, nonracial system.'"[81]

All Deliberate Speed Means Now: The *Alexander v. Holmes* Ruling

The court ruling that finally forced school districts in Mississippi to end their dual system of segregated schooling began, as all the previous cases did, with black parents upset with their school's district obvious delaying tactics in enforcing school desegregation. In 1968, Mrs. Beatrice Alexander of Holmes County joined with eight other petitioners involved in similar lawsuits against thirteen other Mississippi school districts and filed suit in the District Court for the Southern District of Mississippi against the Board of Education of Holmes County.[82] The district court refused to hear the suit; thus, the 1968–69 school year began as usual with an FOC plan on paper but little desegregation in practice. The petitioners applied to the Fifth Circuit Court of Appeals for summary reversal of the lower court's refusal to hear the case. The Fifth Circuit ordered the district court to give these cases "highest priority." The district court consolidated the nine cases under *United States v. Hinds County Board of Education* and began hearings in October 1968.

On May 13, 1969, the district court ruled in favor of the school districts, approved all their FOC plans, and even praised them for their efforts in desegregating their schools. The court noted no instance of a black child being denied admission to any school through FOC. Rather, according to the Court, segregated schools were the result of the will of the people—both black and white:

It simply cannot be said under such circumstances that FOC plan has not worked in such a case! The vast majority of colored children simply do not wish to attend a school which is predominantly white, and white children simply do not wish to attend a school which is predominantly Negro, and that ingrained and inbred influence and characteristics of the races will not be changed by any pseudo teachers, or sociologists in judicial robes.[83]

As evidence of how well FOC was working, the court noted that black teachers had testified as such in court:

> Well trained colored teachers in active service in formerly colored schools and in formerly white schools in this district have appeared before this court and convincingly testified under oath as a matter of fact that freedom of choice was actually working in their schools; that perfect harmony and understanding existed in the school and that no danger in the school system lurked in the implementation of the Freedom of choice plan, but that any kind of forced mixing of the races against the wishes of the involved parents (colored and white) would result in an absolute and complete destruction of the school and it system."[84]

The plaintiffs appealed to the Fifth Circuit for summary reversal and the motion was granted on June 25, 1969 with a July 2, 1969 court date set. On July 3, 1969, the Fifth Circuit Court of Appeals ruled in favor of the government and the plaintiffs. In sharp contrast to the lower district court, the Appeals Court ruled that FOC had failed to achieve desegregation. They instructed the thirty-three school districts named in the suit to work with the HEW to prepare desegregation plans that would eliminate dual systems of education. They further instructed that such plans should include "student and faculty assignments, school bus routes if transportation is provided, all facilities, all athletic and other school activities, and all school location and construction activities."[85] They set August 11, 1969, as the deadline for all thirty-three districts to submit desegregation plans to the district court and August 27, 1969 as the implementation date. On July 25, 1969, the Fifth Circuit changed the implementation date to September 1, 1969. As ordered, on August 11, 1969, the Office of Education submitted desegregation plans on behalf of the thirty-three school districts. Thirty of the thirty-three were mandated to start school immediately as desegregated districts. Hinds County, Holmes County, and Meridian were given until fall 1970 to implement their desegregation plans.

In an intriguing turn of events, having to do primarily with the 1968 election of Richard Nixon and his subsequent retreat from an aggressive federal enforcement of school desegregation in the South,[86] HEW Secretary Robert

Finch sent a letter on August 19, 1969 to Judge William Harold Cox, chief judge of District Court for the Southern District of Mississippi, requesting that the desegregation plans submitted earlier be withdrawn and the HEW be given to December 1, 1969 to submit new plans with an implementation date of an "unspecified future time." On August 21, 1969, the US Attorney General filed a motion in the court of appeals to modify the July 3rd Fifth Circuit order to a submission date of December 1, 1969. Unsurprisingly, on August 26, 1969, the district court recommended the delay be granted. On August 28, 1969, the Fifth Circuit withdrew its September 1 implementation date and set December 1969 as the new date for submission of desegregation plans. Suddenly the HEW, long-considered by most school districts an adversary, seemed to now support the same argument southern school districts had been making for the last five years: we need more time.[87] The United States Commission on Civil Rights called this new delaying ploy a "major retreat in the struggle to achieve meaningful school desegregation."[88]

Not to be deterred, on August 30, 1969, Mrs. Alexander and the other plaintiffs applied to Justice Hugo Black, Circuit Justice for the Supreme Court, for a stay on the Fifth Circuit August 28, 1969 order and a reinstatement of the July 3 order. On September 5, 1969, Justice Black reluctantly denied their application stating it was "deplorable" that he had to uphold the August 28 ruling because he could not rule with certainty that the full Supreme Court would agree with the request for relief. Mrs. Alexander and her fellow plaintiffs filed writ for certiorari on September 23, 1969, which was granted by the Supreme Court on October 9. Once again, the highest court in the land would rule on school desegregation.[89]

On October 29, 1969, the Supreme Court handed down its landmark *Alexander v. Holmes* decision saying "all deliberate speed" meant now:

> The Court of Appeals' order of August 28, 1969, is vacated, and the case is remanded to the court to issue its decree and order, effective immediately, declaring that each of the school districts here involved may no longer operate a dual school system based on race or color, and directing that they begin immediately to operate as unitary school systems within which no person is to be effectively excluded from any school because of race or color.[90]

The Court remanded it back to the Fifth Circuit Court of Appeals to set an implementation date. The Fifth Circuit met in New Orleans several days later and set December 30, 1969, as the deadline for school districts to have a plan in place for the immediate opening of desegregated schools after the Christmas break.

Responding to the *Alexander* Ruling

On Monday, January 5, 1970, a bitterly cold day, twelve school districts in Mississippi began operating as unitary school systems.[91] However, the specifics of how these school districts responded to the Court order varied significantly across the state. In Kemper County, the school board and superintendent responded by segregating black and white students into different parts of the building at DeKalb High with neither group having any contact with the other during any part of the day. In Amite County, white parents gathered immediately after the ruling to discuss the formation of a private school. It was an emotional meeting with one county official proclaiming, "If the federal courts want to operate the schools, then let them operate them . . . We're going to turn them over to the blacks." Other parents declared they would never send their children to school with black children. Dr. Ray Lee, a physician in Liberty, who led the meeting noted: "Right now we have two things to worry about. We have to find some place for white children to go to school and also we have been worrying about somebody blowing up the public schools we've got." In Kemper County and Amite County, the exodus of white students to private academies was almost total by January 1970.[92]

Other school districts responded by adopting policies and practices designed to maintain some modicum of segregation within "integrated" schools or school districts. Carroll County, Coffeeville, and Amite County instituted sex-segregated schools.[93] The desegregation plans in Sunflower and Bolivar Counties proposed assigning students to schools based on scores on achievement tests.[94] Many school districts adopted an approach called "ability grouping" in which students were assigned to classrooms within desegregated schools based on their scores on achievement tests (e.g., California Achievement Test or the Iowa Basic Skills Test) or some other form of academic evaluation. The classes were often referred to as "high, middle, and low" or some variation thereof. In some school systems, four or five "ability group" classes were set up per grade. For example, in Okolona, one sixth grade was reported to have five different tracks:

A—composed of all white students
B—comprised of 17 white and 5 black students
C—reflected almost equal representation of black and white students
D—comprised of 7 white students and 25 black
E—comprised of 29 black students and no whites.[95]

In Yazoo City, black and white students were in the same buildings, but their classroom composition was exactly as it was the previous semester—white children taught by their white teachers with their same white classmates and black students and teachers similarly segregated.

The road from the *Brown* decision in May 1954 to the *Alexander v. Holmes* ruling in October 1969 is indeed an intriguing story of political maneuverings and unlikely alliances, court rulings and resistance, and a well-documented rhetorical battle about state versus federal rights. After fifteen years of fighting desegregation with every political and legislative means available, massive school desegregation finally came to Mississippi in January 1970. Six months later, forty-four school districts had voluntarily complied with desegregation. Seventy-eight districts were under court orders to desegregate, and twenty-six were still in litigation.[96] In August 1970, Charles Johnson, executive secretary of the Mississippi Education Association, optimistically declared that when schools opened in fall 1970 as fully desegregated there would be no violence. "The private schools," he stated, "seem to have provided a safety valve." His prediction proved true. Massive school desegregation occurred in Mississippi in 1970 with little of the violence associated with earlier fights for civil rights, but the road to get there was far from smooth.

Chapter 2

"A Cruel and Intolerable Burden"
Black Mississippians and Freedom of Choice

On a hot August day in 1964, Alean Adams left her home in Fannin headed for a meeting in Philadelphia, Mississippi, located in Neshoba County. The plan was that she and the other passengers in her car would follow Jay Lehay, a white civil rights organizer from California who was also carrying a group of people to the meeting. It was a dangerous trip for a group of civil rights leaders to make in the summer of 1964. Days earlier, the murdered bodies of civil rights workers Michael Schwerner, Andrew Goodman, and James Chaney were found buried in a dam on the outskirts of Neshoba County. As Alean neared Philadelphia, she lost sight of Jay's vehicle, and her car began sputtering. She explains what happened next:

> I kept circling and circling. And each time I would circle, there was a service station, and some whites started coming out with ax handles and shovels and whatever else they had. I couldn't find my way, but I saw a black guy. He was fixing a tire. But he was afraid to stand up and talk to me to try to tell me where I was trying to get to. So he just kept fixing his tire, and out the corner of my eyes, I could see those white men advancing on us to the car where we were. And he said to me, "Get in the car and go—now!" That's how he said it, "Now!" But he kept on working on his tire and acting like he didn't see us. So when he said that, it was cold steel. He didn't have to shout. I knew what he said and what he meant. That it's getting dangerous and he didn't want anything to happen to us, so he was trying to help us. So, I got back in my car and started again. By that time, Jay had missed us, and he came back to try to pick us up, and then we followed him on out and went across the railroad track and went to the meeting. And to this day I don't know what they did at that meeting. It was such a horrible kind of whatever. But we were glad to be alive, because we really thought we were going to get buried in that dam that day also.[1]

Alean and her husband, John, would go on to lead the fight for school desegregation in Rankin County several years later. Their four children would be
some of the first black students to attend an all-white school there under FOC,
and the desegregation lawsuit brought against Rankin County in 1973 bears
their son Kenneth's name.[2] Pioneers yet quite ordinary individuals, Alean and
John Adams were but two of hundreds of black parents and students who, at
great personal cost, led the fight in their own backyards to force their school
districts to comply with desegregation through a plan called "freedom of
choice." For Alean, it was a choice that began years earlier when she faced her
deepest fears on that road to Philadelphia. "Everybody has their Philadelphia.
It's a moment when you face your greatest fear knowing that you may not survive. But you do survive, and when you come out the other side you find that
your Philadelphia has stripped away your fear. You know for certain that you
can survive fear, and that you are stronger than you ever knew you could be."[3]

As reflected in the stories told in this chapter, being the first in their communities to send their children to formerly all-white schools or being the
first black student to attend such a school was a fearful experience. Certainly,
many suffered greatly for their "freedom of choice." Their commitment to
persevere in the face of their own "Philadelphia" is testimony to their courage,
strength, and fortitude.

"Getting a Piece of the Pie": Being the First under Freedom of Choice

Mae Bertha and Matthew Carter were poor sharecroppers who farmed
twenty-five acres of land in Sunflower County on the Pemble Plantation.
Sunflower County was the home of Senator James Eastland, a staunch and
vocal opponent to school desegregation, and civil rights activist Fannie Lou
Hamer.[4] It was also the birthplace of the White Citizens' Council, formed in
1954 in Indianola for the purpose of preserving segregated schools. Mae Bertha and Matthew were as active as poor blacks living in the Delta could be in
the growing civil rights movement. They joined the NAACP in the late 1950s
and attended, when they could, the weekly meetings at the New Kingdom
Baptist Church in Cleveland, Mississippi.[5]

In summer 1965, the Drew Municipal Separate School District mailed FOC
forms to the black and white parents in their district. They were confident
that no black parent or student would actually complete and return them.
As Mae Bertha notes, they made a serious miscalculation: "[T]hey were sure
that they had fixed everything around Drew so no blacks would be coming

around their schools. They were so sure of that. But they didn't know about us out there on the farm."[6] On August 12, 1965, Mae Bertha and Matthew Carter drove the nine miles to Drew to drop off the FOC forms. They did not talk much on the ride there; both knew the enormity of what they were about to do. They handed their forms to the Drew High School principal, C. M. Reid, who took them and said not a word. Mae Bertha and Matthew turned around and left.

The next morning Mr. Thornton, the foreman of the Pemble plantation, paid the Carters a visit at their home, in which he told them it would "be best" if they withdrew their FOC forms. He chided, "Your children will get a better education at the black school. Your children won't have any friends at the white school. The other blacks aren't going to have anything to do with you." As Thornton hummed through a list of reasons why the Carters should reconsider their decision, Mae Bertha walked into her house, retrieved a record player and an LP record and returned to her porch. She began blaring the January 11, 1963, speech President Kennedy had delivered about the importance of the Civil Rights Act. Thornton told Matthew he would slip away to the barn while he talked some sense into Mae Bertha. Mae Bertha promptly told her husband: "[Y]ou go out there to the barn and you tell Mr. Thornton that I am a grown woman. I birthed those children and bore the pain. He cannot tell me what to do about my children, like withdrawing my children out. And I'd be a fool to try and tell him where to send his kids."[7] Matthew informed Thornton that they had decided to keep their children in the white school. Several nights later their sharecropper's cabin was peppered with gunshot; fortunately, no one was hurt. Later, their family garden and animal pens were destroyed—their cows and pigs lost—and their credit was discontinued at the commissary. But the Carters refused to back down.[8]

When September 3, 1965, arrived, Ruth, Larry, Gloria, Stanley, Pearl, Beverly, and Deborah Carter were on the school bus ready to be the first black children to attend Drew High School and A. W. James Elementary School. Accompanying the bus were four local deputies charged with getting the children safely inside the school. They did not, however, protect them from the angry whites lining the streets shouting, "Go back to your own schools, nigger." They also did not protect them from the daily abuses suffered on the bus, in the school classrooms and hallways. For four years, the Carter children were the lone black students attending formerly all-white schools in Drew. Mae Bertha recounts that she and Matthew did a lot of praying and counseling their children. Every afternoon when they stepped off the bus, safely back at home, Mae Bertha greeted them and then listened as her children vented, cried, and ranted about their day. Deborah explains one of the primary messages her mother tried to convey to them: "If Mama heard me say 'I hate white people, I just can't stand them,' she always answered, 'Don't you ever say that. Don't you ever say that you hate white people or anyone—it's not right' . . . The other thing she wouldn't let us say was that we wished we had never been born."[9]

Although Mae Bertha and Matthew Carter were tangentially involved in local civil rights activities, they received little support from other blacks in their community when they decided to desegregate the schools through FOC, and no other black parents in Drew signed the FOC forms. They acted alone, albeit with significant help from outside civil rights organizations, such as the American Friends Service Committee, Operation Freedom, and the NAACP Legal Defense Fund. However, in many communities, local civil rights leaders worked together to strategically choose several students, usually their own, to desegregate the schools as a group so no one student or family would have to bear the burden alone. Such was the case with Alean and John Adams.

John was the president of the first chapter of the Rankin County NAACP. Both he and Alean were actively involved in voter registration efforts in Rankin County in the early 1960s. They housed white northerners involved in early civil rights efforts in Jackson and the surrounding area, and they participated in the 1964 march in Selma. In 1965, John was fired from his job with the Rankin County school district because he participated in a boycott of local white merchants. The Adams helped start the first Head Start in Rankin County, and Alean was one of its first teachers. Alean, along with four of her five children, participated in a twenty-mile, two-day protest march from the Beat community to the Brandon courthouse in May 1965.[10] In the early years of their activism, John attended community-organizing meetings in the small town of Pisgah. At first, Alean stayed at home with the children while John was on the front lines, but, as Alean explains, she, too, wanted to be actively involved in the movement:

> Usually it was the men that were going to the meetings at first, but every time they would go to the meeting, somebody would get a ticket. Either your headlights or your taillight or for whatever reason, you would be stopped. And I would be sitting at home with five kids, and I thought I needed to be with them at home. But finally we decided. We loaded them in the car and took them with us. So the kids were sitting in the back of the truck doing their homework. And we'd be in front of the church carrying on other business and what have you. And that way I didn't have to sit at home and worry if John got a ticket. Plus I was longing for freedom too. I always knew there was something wrong, that there was something better that the Lord had in store for us other than going through the kinds

of things that we were having to go through. It wasn't that we were brave, but there comes a time when there's nothing to fear except fear itself. So you make up your mind: "I guess this is what we have to do."

As leaders of the local movement, the Adamses, along with four other families, agreed to test the FOC option in Rankin County. It was an emotional decision for the parents who knew their children would, more than likely, be subjected to harassment, humiliation, and perhaps violence. "It was a terrible decision to have to make," Alean said. "And I truly think in some cases we put them through a lot in order to get to where we had to go. But somebody had to do it. It was painful, but once you bit it off, you got to chew it, every day." Once the decision was made, John and Alean spent most of their time worrying about their children. They prayed a lot and hoped for the goodness of white teachers, bus drivers, students, and principals to treat their children fairly. It did not always go well, such as the time when their daughter Linda was kicked off the school bus in the middle of nowhere. Alean explains what happened:

We had a bus driver once, and he wasn't a real bad person, but he assigned certain seats for the children. You get in the seat, and you couldn't move. Well, for some reason Linda moved or did something. And to this day I'm not really sure what happened, but he put her off on that road on the other side of 471 because she got up or something. And there probably was a rule that she shouldn't get up, but he had no business to put her off the bus and leave her standing beside the road. So when he came by the next day, I was ready for him. He got off the bus and talked to me, and somehow he figured that to make her understand the rule, he had to do that. But my argument was that I wanted her to obey the rules on the bus, but I don't want you putting her off by herself, leaving her. And she was still pretty young at that time, and she would not be able to protect herself. So he apologized, but anyhow I was very angry, so you had to watch out with the schools.

It was a fine line for black parents who made the decision to send their children to school environments that they knew would be potentially dangerous. Do you let them fend for themselves and fight their own battles, or do you step in to fight for them? Alean and John did both. One day while checking her youngest son's schoolwork, she came across a paper on which he had written, "I hate Mrs. King. I hate Mrs. King." Alean knew Tony was a good-natured child, so she could not understand why he would write such strong words about his teacher. Alean decided to pay Mrs. King a visit:

I was always of the opinion you listen to the teacher, you listen to the child, and you try to come up with "What is the problem?" So I went to see Mrs. King, and I didn't ever say anything else to him anymore about hating Mrs. King. You had to be kind of a mediator between hate and love and the things . . . we had been taught all our lives. You don't hate her, but she was just old, and it was time for her to go home. She didn't want to accept black children coming to the schools. She didn't want to teach them. I didn't tell her what he wrote—that he hated her—but she chilled my bones.

Their son Kenneth, who attended Brandon High, had a particularly tough time, recounts Alean: "Kenneth caught the devil going to Brandon High School." He was spit on, excluded, and treated unfairly by many white teachers and students. Alean explains why Kenneth's experiences were much worse than her other children: "It's always been worse for black boys than it is for black girls. They let the girls go through pretty well, but boys—they always have a tendency to say, 'they're big, they're black,' and they have a fear of them. Even when you teach them not to be outspoken and do whatever in order to get along, it seems like they're always seen as a problem." Alean readily admits that her children were often resentful of their parents' activities and sometimes felt they were the sacrificial lambs in their parents' fight for civil rights. But John and Alean were relentless: "This was a battle—a battle for the future, a battle for our rights."[11]

The Adamses were part of a collective movement in their communities to test the legitimacy of FOC, and while they and their children suffered financially, socially, and emotionally for their decision, they were not the lone wolves in the fight for desegregation. However, many black parents throughout the state carried that torch alone.

Ola and Isom Crockett lived in Laurel in Jones County. They had been closely following the unfolding drama surrounding school desegregation in the mid-1960s. It was through the newspaper and the nightly news they first discovered the FOC option, and as a couple, they decided they were going to use it to send their children to the white school. Ola had already broken the color barrier by being one of only two black students enrolled in a nursing program at Jones County Community College, but challenging the segregated school system of their hometown was even riskier for the Crocketts because Isom was a teacher in the school district. In Mississippi, a black teacher being affiliated with the NAACP or any other form of "subversive" civil rights activities often led to being fired without cause. Ola recounted an incident that occurred earlier when they lived in Canton and were pulled over by the police: "We lived in Canton briefly and was questioned by the police if we belonged to any of those organizations like the—he couldn't say it plain—like the N-double. My husband finished it out for him, 'the NAACP'? Well, it really wasn't any of his business, but that's what we ran into."[12] Despite the risks, the Crocketts were determined that their children were going to attend the white school.

Ola first visited the principal of one of the white schools to discuss her intentions to file FOC papers on behalf of her children. The principal informed Ola: "I can't be responsible for your children." News about Ola's visit spread quickly in their small hometown. They were targeted as troublemakers and soon became the victims of violence. Ola explained:

> With me entering the nursing program and taking the children over there, somebody along the way did not like it. We went to a basketball game one night, and when we returned there were no lights at my house. We came in. My husband says, "Somebody has fire bombed our house." Why? Why would you do that? As the year progressed, we had night riders that decided they were going to shoot us off the hill. Then our insurance was canceled. They thought we were too much of a risk.

Despite threats and violence, Ola and Isom were not dissuaded. Their children would attend the white school under FOC. Ola arranged another meeting to discuss their plans, this time with the superintendent. This meeting went much better than the first. The superintendent knew he had no legal rationale for preventing the Crocketts from filing FOC forms, but he tried to negotiate for more time. Ola describes their meeting: "So I took all five of my children and went down to the superintendent's office. I told them, 'Sit on this bench and don't move.' And I went in. And I was yakking back and forth, and I told him, 'My children are going to school out there.' He says, 'Well, don't take them back until a certain time.' 'Ok, but I'll take them back, and when I do there better be some books there for them.'" Ola tried to prepare her children for the ill treatment she knew they would face in the white school. She told them, "[I]t's 900 kids over at Northeast. It's 3 of you. That means 300 to each 1 of you. And they're going to get you." For one year the Crockett children were the only black children attending white schools in Jones County.

Ola also had to determine when she needed to assert herself into her children's education and when she needed to back off and let them resolve their own issues. One day a white parent handed out birthday invitations to all the children in her son's elementary school class. When Ola called the parent to ask for directions to her house, the mother told her, "Well, I was hoping you weren't going to bring your child." Ola responded that her son had received an invitation and they were most certainly planning on attending. The mother replied, "Well, your son is not really welcomed." The next school day Ola marched into the school office and demanded a meeting with the principal, where she told him, "[D]on't permit parents to come in and invite a class to something when you know there are black children in there and they aren't welcome." Ola's children were able to negotiate their all-white schools and find some success. Their oldest son, Dale, was the first black drum major at his high school and was relatively well accepted by his peers. However, the Crocketts always kept a close eye on their children to ensure they were safe and treated fairly. When Dale rode the band bus to out-of-town events, Ola and Isom were right behind the bus, trailing them in their own car.

Ola is quick to say that she did not send her children to the white school because she thought white teachers were superior to black teachers in segregated schools. Rather, she sent them to the white schools because the black schools were underresourced, and opportunities, such as traveling to band competitions, were not available to black students in segregated schools. Like most black parents making difficult decisions during school desegregation, the Crocketts simply wanted their children to have access to the same resources as white students, so they, too, could develop their talents and fulfill their dreams. Ola explains:

> Those [white] teachers weren't any better than the black teachers in my estimation. They just had all the materials and everything that they needed for the children in that school. We wanted a piece of the pie and we were determined to get a piece of the pie. So I've always said being in a white school does not give you any more mental capacity. Doesn't make you smarter. Because over here at Mount Olive [a segregated black school] that little school where they had to buy a microscope with money from cotton picking, they produced teachers, orthopedic surgeons and writers. So, like I always contend, going to a white school does not give you more sense, it just gives you more equipment to work with. It gives you access to more. And we took advantage of it.

Ola and Isom Crockett were not civil rights activists in the traditional sense, yet they represent an important group of black parents who were part of the school desegregation story by acting individually, with no outside support, to wage their own personal battle for the rights of their children to have the best education possible. As Ola notes, "One year all seven of us were in school. And we were all fighting different demons." As a family, they decided what did not "kill them would make them stronger":

While I was in nursing school, after all the insurances were canceled, my instruc-
tor called me, and she says, "Why don't you just give up?" I told her, "No, I'm not
giving up anything." And this was midyear. I put those many months in; I'm not
going to give up the rest of it. But you see how they paint this: "If somebody does
this to you, then RUN." I'm not going to run, and they [her husband and chil-
dren] didn't either. And it did not affect my grades. It did not affect my husband's
grades. It did not affect my children's grades.

Like the Crocketts, the Adamses, and the Carters, Gilbert and Natalie
Mason fought a long, drawn-out battle with their school system in Biloxi to
obtain the right for their son to attend a white school that had all the resources
they knew he deserved. In hindsight, Gilbert believes the fight was well worth
every bruise and personal affront he endured because Gilbert Jr. attained an
education that opened doors that would have otherwise been closed. Gilbert
wrote:

> In spite of the vicissitudes of those early years, I think that we as parents con-
> cluded that desegregation was worth the sacrifice made. I know that Gilbert,
> Jr., for example, got access to the best science labs and the best advanced math
> courses available in the Biloxi schools. He excelled and went on to become a
> medical doctor himself . . . We proved that desegregation could be made to work
> peacefully. Our children did not have to give up their black identity to do this.
> Gilbert Jr. stayed very involved with his church, the NAACP Youth branch, and
> with his neighborhood Boy Scout troop. Because our child got the best high
> school education available, and because he learned to cultivate friendships among
> every race of people, I considered school desegregation a success."[13]

Other parents and students were not as profuse as Dr. Mason in extolling
the benefits of school desegregation; however most agreed that the long-term
benefits outweighed the costs. But for the students living "freedom of choice"
in those early years, there were certainly costs.

A Lonely Existence: Attending Schools under Freedom of Choice

Gloria Carter Dickerson was one of the seven Carter children who desegregated the Drew City school system under FOC in 1965. When the FOC papers
arrived in the mailbox at their home, Gloria and her siblings ripped open
the letters and excitedly called their mother, who was in St. Louis vising her
mother: "Mama, we got some letter in the mail today, and when you get home

we want you to sign these papers so we can go over to the white school."[14] When Mrs. Carter returned home, she asked her seven school-age children, "are you sure you want to do this? It's not going to be easy, and they are not going to want you there." All seven responded, "We want to go, Mama."

They began their venture into desegregated schools as innocent children excited about riding "shiny busses," going to school year-round, and learning from brand new textbooks—all facts their mother had relayed to them about the benefits of attending a white school. On the first day of school, they woke up early, donned their best clothing, and waited eagerly for the bus to arrive. They were the first to be picked up, and all seven children sat in the front three rows of the bus. However, as the white children began boarding the bus, the abuse and harassment they would endure for years quickly began. The white children jumped to the side as they passed their row, exaggerating their attempts to avoid physically touching them. By the second or third day, the abuse got physical and nastier. Gloria recalls:

> On the bus the kids were just out of control. They started throwing all kinds of stuff, paper, chalk. And they called us all these names and talked about how much we stinked and said things like, "Don't get close to that nigger." We were terrified and uncomfortable, and all we wanted to do was get off this bus because we did not fight back. We did not do any fighting because we were in the non-violence of Dr. King. We didn't say anything back to anyone.

Every afternoon they related to their mother their treatment on the bus. "You can't blame the children," Mae Bertha told them. "That is what they are being taught and they do not know any better." A few days later, the bus driver told the children, "Y'all need to go to the back of the bus where you belong." The Carter children dutifully obeyed, but when they told their mother what had transpired on the bus, Mae Bertha was not so sanguine. She promptly made a few calls and resolved the situation. The children no longer were sent to the back of the bus.

Once off the bus and in the classroom, the Carter children's experiences varied, depending largely on the white teacher in charge of the class. Pearl, Gloria's younger sister, who was in elementary school, had a particularly horrible experience with her teacher. None of the children wanted to sit by Pearl, so the teacher devised a plan in which the children rotated sitting in the desks next to her. The teacher told the students, "It's your turn to sit by the nigger today." When the students objected, she directed them, "Push your chair as far back as you can to get away from her." Gloria's experiences were a bit better. Most of her teachers made sure that she was not visibly harassed, but it was a very lonely existence. No white students tried to befriend her or go out of their way to make her existence any easier. Gloria responded by losing herself in her books. She explained: "I did a lot of studying and a lot of listening to the teacher. When we had library period, I would put my head in a book and not look up and just study and study and study. I would block everything out and just focus, and I sure learned to focus and always try to block them out."

The children painfully learned how to navigate school being as invisible as they could. They determined what places to avoid—the cafeteria being the primary one. On most days—hot, cold, or rainy—they met on the front steps during lunchtime. They tried to maneuver through the halls during class periods, making as little contact with whites as possible, and unstructured school activities, like pep rallies, were just torturous. Unfortunately, their school lives did not get any better during the four years they were the sole blacks attending the white schools. The 1969–70 school year was probably the worst. By then *Alexander v. Holmes* was making its way through the courts, and the whites in the Carters' hometown knew that soon a critical mass of other black children would inevitably be attending white schools. According to Gloria, that year was dreadful:

> In 1969 the whites heard that they were going to integrate the school, and the kids were so ugly to us. They were like, "My daddy is really upset; he's so mad because them niggers are going to come over to our school. This is going to be so hard on our parents because our parents don't have enough money for tuition to the private schools 'cause we have to get out of here before them niggers get here." I am listening to every word they are saying 'cause they are saying it so I could hear it, and things like you know how lazy and stinky and dumb and stinky and "We don't want to be around no niggers."

In 1970, when the rest of the black students joined Gloria at Drew High School, she was relieved more than anything else. After four years of enduring isolation and exclusion and hearing daily how inferior blacks were and how integration would ruin the schools, Gloria had grown weary of being the only black in her classes. She spent her senior year at Drew High School back in a largely segregated black school because the majority of whites left to attend the newly opened Sunflower Academy.

When she integrated the schools as a twelve-year-old, Gloria did not realize that she and her sisters and brothers were on the vanguard of the school desegregation movement. She also did not realize how dangerous the situation was and how fervently her parents prayed for their safety every time they left for school. What she did know—and it was the reason why with grit and determination they continued—was they were getting the education their parents knew was imperative for them to move ahead in life. Her mother often reminded them:

> You go to that school, and you listen to every word that teacher has to say 'cause she is teaching their kids, and they want their kids to learn, so you learn while they are learning, so no one can say you are not educated 'cause you are getting the same education as those white kids. No one can ever tell you that you are not qualified because of your education. If someone tells you that you are not quali- fied, you tell them, "I went to school with you, so what do you mean I am not qualified?"

Gloria graduated from Drew High School in 1971. She attended the University of Mississippi, where she graduated with a degree in accounting and later earned her CPA license. She worked in Jackson for Job Corps and then with the Kellogg Foundation, first in Michigan and then in Mississippi. When she retired from Kellogg, she returned to Drew and started her own nonprofit organization called We2Gether Creating Change.[15]

Clarence Hall, who lived in Glen Allan in Issaquena County, joined the army in 1941 and fought in Europe for three years. Like many civil rights activists, Clarence's life-long commitment to equality began in the military where he fought for his country, discovered that blacks in other parts of the country had far more rights than he, and then returned to the United States no longer willing to accept his second-class citizenship. He explains: "I don't regret the time I spent in the service because the time I spent in the service really enlightened me that people should be treated like a human being. And I knew that didn't happen in Mississippi. I returned from WWII a changed man. God was preparing me to come back to help change Mississippi." Before becoming active in school desegregation efforts in his hometown, Hall was a leader in the voter registration movement. He vividly recalls going to the courthouse to pay his $2 poll tax and being accosted by several whites who demanded, "Ain't you doing alright?" City leaders made promises to him to try to deter him from registering. They said they would replace the dirt road leading to his house with a gravel road. But he stood firm, saying that he sacri- ficed his life for this country and he deserved the same rights as any citizen in any state. When he tried to register to vote, he was given a literacy test. He was asked to define "eminent domain." He knew the answer but the clerk inter- preting his answers said he did not pass the test. He was denied the right to vote. In fact, he did not get the right to vote until 1965 when the Voting Rights Act was passed. According to Hall, whites were afraid of the enfranchisement of blacks because they numerically outnumbered whites in Issaquena County and they "didn't want the blacks to be in power in positions of supervisor or sheriff." In one night alone, 27 crosses were burned in his community, one at his front door.

His daughter, Ann, recalls waking up and seeing the fiery cross blazing on her lawn. She was only a first-grader and, at first, she was terrified. However, her fears subsided when she conjured up the image of her father: "He was a giant to me. I had no fear of the Ku Klux Klan or what racist people were trying to do because I felt that my dad can conquer all." Indeed, when it came to protecting Ann and his family, Clarence advocated a different approach than that of Dr. King: "I'm not non-violent. I prepared for five years in the service. If you touch her [Ann], you will hear from me. If you do anything to her, I will protect her." In 1965 Clarence led the efforts in Issaquena County to desegregate the schools using FOC. Clarence enrolled Ann at Riverside Elementary, an all-white school.[16]

Ann remembers well the solitude of first grade being one of only a few blacks in her grade: "I suffered in silence. I don't think my parents really knew some of the things that I went through."[17] The day after the cross was burned in her yard, she was sitting in her classroom when the principal's voice boomed over the intercom: "Ann Hall, please come to my office." Ann was petrified. She did not even know where the principal's office was located. Her teacher pointed her in the direction, and off she set.

> Me, going down the hall. I had to go past the other classroom, the second-grade classroom, third, fourth, fifth, sixth, in order to get to the office. The white children—because there were no black children except for the second grade—they were looking at me as I'm walking down the hall. I remember the old teacher chairs sitting by the window at the entrance of the office. So, when I walked into the office, the secretary told me to have a seat in the chair. And I can remember being cold in the office, temperature wise. I had to wait until the principal called me into the office, and when he called me into the office, he asked me, "Did anything happen at your house last night?" I told him, "Yes." He said, "What happened at your house last night?" I told him the Ku Klux Klan burned the cross in the front yard. He asked me, "Were you scared?" I said, "No, I wasn't scared, and I'm still coming to school here." Then he dismissed me and told me to go back to my classroom. I went back to my classroom, but thinking back on that for years and years: why and who would subject a little child to an interrogation like that?

The few black children in her first-grade classroom were segregated in one row on one side of the room. They were prohibited from interacting with the white children. At recess, the children were segregated on the playground. One week, the white children played on the side with the merry-go-round, and the black children congregated in the area with the swing sets; the next week, they switched areas. One morning, a little white girl called Ann over to her desk to show her something. Ann was excited about the invitation. When the teacher spied her at the white student's desk, she grabbed her ruler, spanked her on the leg, and ordered her back to her own desk. Ann was humiliated. She had always been a good student, a good girl, and someone who respected her teachers. She had no understanding why she would be physically punished simply because she crossed the color barrier established in the room to prevent black and white students from talking or playing with each other. As Ann notes, "We were clearly segregated within the integration."

In second grade, Ann returned to Glen Allan, which was an all-black school that year because all the white students, under FOC, enrolled at Riverside Elementary. Ann describes her new school situation: "It was like a totally different world. It was a culture shock because I had not been in an all-black setting, and it was different. I existed, but it was just different." During her third-, fourth-, and fifth-grade years, Ann attended Riverside Elementary under FOC, where she was the only black student in her classroom. Most of the time, she was by herself. Occasionally, a few white girls made overtures to her and asked her to play dolls with them. But these white girls were soon targeted as "nigger lovers," and they quit playing with Ann. In 1970, when Ann was in fifth grade, wholesale desegregation took place in the Western Line School District. After being the minority for most of her school career, suddenly she was thrust into a largely segregated setting with black students. According to Ann, her years of being isolated from her black peers rendered her an outsider within her new school setting:

I went back to Glen Allan because it was the neighborhood school. Most of the white children from that area decided to go to private schools. So, I was in a majority black situation. I got a chance to see from the flipside because we had one or two white students that were there. We would go to the bathroom, and the black girls in the bathroom would treat the white girls real bad. They would pull their hair, throw tissue at them, and the girls, they were afraid to say anything. When they got back to the classroom, they'd be afraid to tell the teacher because they don't know what's going to happen to them. I didn't like it, but there's nothing that I could do about it. Every time I would speak up about it, the black girls would turn on me, and they started calling me names and say, "You think you're a little white girl?" They even started pulling my hair because I had really long hair, and they would pull my hair, and they would treat me mean. I was isolated again.

I was isolated within my own race. "Oh, she thinks she's more than anybody else. She thinks she's white. She talks white." I heard that throughout my fifth grade to the twelfth grade.

For seven years, until she graduated, Ann endured a different type of racial intimidation; this time from girls of her own race.

Ann eventually became a teacher, then a principal, and always an "advocate for children." Ann believes the long-term benefits of school desegregation outweigh the costs, even if she herself endured a rather lonely existence throughout her school years. Her own views about race, education, and the possibilities of change took root in these formative years. According to Ann, attitudinal changes are imperative for societal change, and such changes are initiated first through exposure to people of other races:

> If you have not been taught better, then that's all you know. I've had a lot of white friends, associates, that have had certain prejudices that are embedded in them, and while talking to them and getting them to understand both sides, then you could see the wheels turn, and they've changed their point of view. There are some people, I believe, in the society, that no matter what type of education they get or exposure they received, they'll always be the same. But then, there are others who begin to get a deeper understanding, and they let go of all of the hatred for no reason. Why would I hate you, someone who I don't really know, just because of the color of your skin? Once you learn the character of the person and get to understand that person, you connect to that person on that level. You got to have bad sometimes in order to get to the good, because if all of those things had not happened back in the past, we wouldn't be where we are today. I'm not saying that the world is perfect today, and I realized that the world will never be perfect. But, as years go by, it gets better, and you see the progression.

One of the provisions of the FOC plan was that ninth- through twelfth-grade students could complete their own FOC form (as long as their parent approved their choice). However, sometimes students were not fully aware of the repercussions of completing these forms. Such was the case with Robert Jackson, now a state senator representing the Eleventh Congressional District of Mississippi. Robert was born in 1955. His parents were sharecroppers on a plantation, and he attended segregated schools in Quitman County for most of his life. In ninth grade, he and his fellow students were given what he thought was a "survey," asking them, if required, if they would be willing to attend the white school. Jackson wrote on the survey, "Yes," for the simple reason: "I did what people told me to do. I can't say no to an adult."[18] He was soon sent to Marks High School. He recalls that meeting:

The next day, I was snatched from my school and taken across the track to the white high school. And I just remember going with my parents over there—such a shock. Sitting in the principal's office there—the principal was R. T. Warden—who later became superintendent of Quitman County Schools. Mr. Warden was kind of tall and kind of a big protruding kind of belly. And he had thick glasses, and you could see his eyeballs through his glasses. It was the scariest thing for me—sitting in his office. And then talking to my parents, telling them that I had been brought over here to attend classes. So that was kind of disruptive for me to go from one community, one culture, to another.

Several other black students were sent to the white school as part of Quitman County's limited efforts at desegregation. Robert notes that his white peers had no idea that the black students were "forced to go as opposed to being our choice to go."

Being one of a few black students at the white high school was a challenge for Robert; in fact, today he recalls little of that first day: "I really tried to block it out. Everything was a challenge." Robert concedes it was not a welcoming environment; however, he notes that it prepared him to function in predominantly white institutions, like the University of Southern Mississippi, where he attended college, and the Mississippi Senate, where he has served since 2004. Like many blacks interviewed for this study, Senator Jackson is ambivalent about school desegregation, recognizing its importance in breaking the segregationist hold on the South but saddened about the loss of black community around their school. He laments: "I remember so many aspects of growing up black that we lost when we went through integration. Looking at some old albums, you see Hi-Y, Tri Hi-Y and those groups that were formed at black high schools at the time but are no longer in existence."

"We Thought They Meant It": The Fallacy of Freedom of Choice

When Mae Bertha and Matthew Carter drove to Drew High School in August 1965 to deliver their FOC forms to the school officials, they believed the school board was acting in good faith to abide by the Civil Rights Act. As Matthew noted, "we thought they meant it."[19] The Carters believed they had the law and the courts on their side to protect them. They, along with many black parents, soon discovered the fallacies inherent in "freedom of choice." In 1967, Mae Bertha Carter filed a lawsuit against the Drew School District on behalf of her children. The lawsuit detailed the many ways that the school system, despite receiving federal funds, continued to maintain a "racially segregated and discriminatory system that placed a 'cruel and intolerable' burden on black persons and pupils."[20]

Chapter 3

Big Bulls in the Local Herd
Superintendents Enforcing the Law of the Land

When *Brown v. Board of Education* was ruled in 1954, every superintendent in Mississippi was white, male, and firmly entrenched in the white power structure of the day. As the final arbiter of most educational matters in their school district, they wielded great political influence and enjoyed a high-status position in their community. In return, they were expected to reflect the values of their southern, white culture and make decisions accordingly. Dr. Julian Prince, who began his career teaching physics in McComb in 1949 and went on to serve as a superintendent of three different school districts in Mississippi, describes the superintendents in the 1950s as "big bulls in the local herd":

> This type Mississippi school superintendent (always white, always male) was an icon. He represented his culture. Tall, short, fat, or slim his demeanor would be one at ease with his surroundings. But underneath he saw himself as the big bull in the local herd. He expected to be treated with deference. His characteristics in general were these: he rose to his position in maturity; he expected a long tenure in his position; he had the respect of his white community; and he ruled his school district with an iron hand. This superintendent was a product of, and a part of, his culture. If he was a hard-core racist (and not all were) and that racism was expressed in the manner he treated his Negro charges, there was no one to check his behavior. [1]

With few blacks registered to vote in Mississippi when the *Brown* decision was rendered in 1954, superintendents did not have to bow to any political pressure from their black parents, teachers, principals, and students. Charged with overseeing both the black and white schools, they could choose how they would administer their black schools. Many superintendents left their black schools alone and allowed the black principal to lead his school how he saw fit. Others ruled with benign neglect and did little to improve the conditions of the black schools or the education of their black students. Others were much more involved in the operations of the black schools; they frequently visited and knew the black teachers, students, and parents well. Some were certainly sympathetic to the complaints of their black patrons about the blatant inequalities existing between white and black schools and earnestly tried to help, given the conditions of the time, to improve the education of blacks in their schools. While there were few repercussions from the black community if the superintendent governed unjustly or heavy-handedly, appearing too sympathetic to the plight of their black patrons could have significant repercussions from the white community, as was the case with Mack Weems, who served as county superintendent of Scott County from 1940 to 1955. Under his leadership, significant improvements were made to the black schools, as described by Mrs. Lilla D. Ware, one of the guest speakers at a 1955 retirement dinner for Weems sponsored by the black teachers, students, and employees of Scott County:

> Mr. Weems I wish to thank you for all you have done for Scott County. YOU have brought us from creek cisterns and open well water to fountains on the campus. You have brought us from pine knot fires to gas heaters. You have brought us from carrying lunches in tin buckets, paper bags and boxes to nice lunchrooms with well prepared nutritious food. Yes, I am proud to look out and see 23 nice warm school buses transporting children who used to walk 2 1/2 to 3 miles daily, until Mr. Weems put them riding.[2]

In the post-*Brown* election, Superintendent Weems was defeated. The primary reasons being his unfaltering commitment to supporting and improving the black schools and the discovery that his youngest daughter, a student at Millsaps College, attended a lecture at Tougaloo College, a historically black college near Jackson.[3]

Despite the good intentions of some white superintendents to work toward equalizing black and white schools in their districts, no superintendents in Mississippi were leading the charge to desegregate their schools in the aftermath of *Brown*. As part of the power structure of their community, most stood steadfast in their resistance to school desegregation even after the passage of the 1964 Civil Rights Act as explained by Prince, who was part of the statewide superintendent meetings in 1964:

> The prevailing attitude with long-term administrators across the state in 1964 was to battle racial change. Many of my peers thought efforts at cooperation were

those of a wimp, or worse. Participants in school administrative meetings that fall were obsessed with finding ways to foil desegregation actions . . . I kept my mouth shut about what I knew to be coming down the pike for school desegregation. There was a logical reason for my reticence. In 1964 unless I was dealing with one of several dozen other administrators who thought like I did, I could never know the hidden background of another, or what a person's motives would be. There was an atmosphere of intimidation in the state. People not expressing the stand-pat, resist to the bitter end, party line might find themselves in very uncomfortable positions.[4]

After ten years of delay, blacks were rightfully suspicious of the white power structure in their communities as reflected in this 1965 article in the *Journal of Negro Education*:

> The leadership of the schools, the superintendent and the school boards, are the surrogates of the power order. Their chief responsibility is to protect the equities of the status group. By and large, their behaviors in these years since "Brown" have been those of artifice, obfuscation, and fancy footwork in their effort to keep faith with the power structure to which they are beholden as the schools have been challenged by the minority groups.[5]

However, the Civil Rights Act thrust superintendents into school desegregation whether they wanted to be there or not. As chief educational administrators, they were responsible, along with their school boards and school board attorneys, to submit desegregation plans that would please both the HEW and their constituents and keep them out of court.

In 1965–66, the HEW published guidelines to aid school districts in formulating their specific desegregation plans. Districts were instructed to demonstrate a "good faith" effort immediately in desegregating their schools, with 1967 as the targeted deadline for achieving school desegregation.[6] The specifics of how to assign teachers, faculty, administrators, staff, school buildings, bus routes, and a host of other particulars were left to the individual school districts. In some towns, desegregation plans were readily adopted and implemented. For example, Greenville and Tupelo adopted a voluntary desegregation plan in 1964. However, the majority of school districts in Mississippi spent 1965 through 1969 creating desegregation plans based on FOC, which often resulted in little more than token desegregation. The implementation of desegregation throughout every school district in the state varied greatly as did the relationship between the local superintendent and school board and the federal government. Certainly, the leadership of the superintendent was paramount in how a school district complied with desegregation orders, but other variables also determined actual implementation efforts: board and community opposition to desegregation, civil rights activism in the community, the black/white ratio in their town, and the logistical ease of implementation—just to name a few.[7] Even after the *Alexander v. Holmes* ruling in October 1969, which called for an immediate end to segregated schooling, many superintendents with their school boards continued to wage a fierce battle with the HEW over their desegregation plans. Some superintendents retired early in the fight; others resigned in the midst of their district's desegregation process, and a few abdicated their responsibilities and let chaos and violence rule the day. One superintendent reportedly committed suicide during the desegregation of his school. Still others took a very different approach and tried, sometimes quite unbeknownst to most in their community, to work willingly with the federal government. Regardless of how they went about desegregating their schools, the superintendent as the educational leader of his school district was expected to direct and lead his school through the turmoil of school desegregation.

Superintendents as Obstructionists: The Case of Okolona

In January 1969, Henry C. Hull, superintendent of the Okolona Municipal Separate School District, received the following letter:

> Title VI of the Civil Rights Act of 1964 and the Regulation promulgated thereunder provide for a periodic review by the Department of Health, Education, and Welfare of school districts receiving Federal financial assistance. Where evidence is found that a school district is not in compliance with the requirements under the Act, efforts are to be made by this Office to secure compliance by voluntary means. If these efforts are not successful, the law requires that we initiate appropriate enforcement proceedings. Based on a careful analysis of all available information, it is my conclusion that your desegregation plan is not adequate and is not working effectively to accomplish the elimination of the dual school system ... Accordingly, I am referring this matter to the Office of General Counsel of this Department with a request that administrative enforcement proceedings be initiated. In addition, this letter is to notify your district that final approval of any application filed with this Department for Federal funds for new programs and activities is hereby ordered deferred ... Sincerely yours, (Mrs.) Ruby G. Martin, Director, Office for Civil Rights.[8]

This was "the letter" that superintendents dreaded receiving. Their district was not in compliance with Title VI; administrative proceedings would be initiated against them to enforce desegregation, and their district would not receive any federal financial assistance. Superintendent Hull immediately wrote Senator James Eastland, a staunch supporter of segregated schools, explaining the "unusual circumstances" of his district: "We have more Negro than white pupils enrolled in the school. Since we have only two schools, pairing the schools will cause us to have more Negro than white pupils in every grade in schools. You can readily see that the community would have difficulty in accepting such a plan, and many white pupils would withdraw."[9] He ended by asking Eastland's help in removing them from the district's deferred status designation, so they could have their federal money restored. Senator Eastland promptly responded stating he would "do everything humanly possible to be of assistance." He further advised that a hearing was a positive step in that it offered the school district a reprieve from immediate implementation of a desegregation plan. With President Nixon now in office, Eastland was hopeful that the federal government would back off a bit in the enforcement of Title VI. He replied to Hull, "[W]e are hopeful here that the President will maintain his campaign promise not to withhold funds in order to coerce integration of schools."[10] Superintendent Hull seeking the intervention of Senator Eastland was not unusual. The Southern Regional Council reported that throughout the South "local officials appealed to their congressmen, who gained special dispensation for their districts from the White House."[11]

In response to the January 3, 1969, HEW letter, the Okalona Municipal School District adopted a desegregation plan on February 21, 1969, in which it proposed a gradual adoption of full-scale desegregation. In fall 1969, it would use FOC to desegregate first grade only. Grades 1–4 would be desegregated in 1970–71; grades 1–8 in 1971–72, and all grades desegregated in 1972–73. It concluded its submission to the HEW with the following:

Finally, may we respectfully point out to you as you review this plan that we are aware of your impatience with what you consider slow progress in meeting requirements of the Civil Rights Act. However, isn't it just possible that we may be proceeding so rapidly that traumatic consequences in the southern community to both Negro and white citizens outweigh the dubious gains for society as a whole? Perhaps ten, fifteen, twenty or even fifty years may be a short time to achieve the ambitious goals you have set for us. There are numerous people in communities such as Okolona, Mississippi and Chickasaw County who are so conditioned that they cannot change. Only the great institution of death will remove this opposition . . . We do feel that you in H.E.W. are exercising your tremendous power without regard to the rights of others or for the quality of the educational programs that results. What you are doing may be "legal" but certainly not ethical nor reasonable for our point of view . . . We still have some small hope that H.E.W. will be sufficiently sensitive to the nationwide disillusionment with its unrealistic guidelines, that it will cease its drastic demands. After all, what could be more in harmony with our great democratic traditions and heritage than "Freedom of Choice"?[12]

The HEW refused the voluntary desegregation plan, and Superintendent Hull was ordered to appear on March 19, 1969, in Washington DC for an administrative proceeding under Title VI of the Civil Rights Act of 1964. Hull was obviously frustrated that the HEW was not willing to accept the four-year desegregation plan as reflected in a February 28, 1969, letter to Senator Eastland: "I'm sure that you will notice that we have violated all of the principles that have to do with the 'power of persuasion.' That is because we feel that it is futile to try to reason with them. These power-mad bureaucrats are beyond reason and beyond persuasion."[13]

Superintendent Hull is not an anomaly, and the many ways in which superintendents directed efforts to delay desegregation, to support private schools, and to put the needs and concerns of white parents and students over black patrons is well documented throughout this book. However, to paint all superintendents with a single swath or to simplify superintendents' decisions and actions to a singular motive (i.e., preserve segregated schools at all costs) fails to capture the complicated economic, educational, and cultural contexts under which each superintendent was working; it also dismisses the complexity of school reform at the level of local implementation. A more nuanced picture of the superintendent's role in desegregation reveals some similarities, but, as the following cases illustrate, the particulars of how desegregation was achieved in school district after school district is as varied as the school districts and towns themselves.

Leading a School District through Desegregation: The Tales of Four Superintendents

Julian Prince, Clyde Muse, Tom Dulin, and Harold "Hardwood" Kelly were all "native sons of Mississippi." Born in the 1920s and 30s and attending schools in the 1940s and early 1950s, they grew up in a state in which Jim Crow laws were a way of life, and white supremacy pervaded every facet of social, political, economic, and cultural life. Given the power and influence of the Citizens' Council and the deeply rooted racism of southern culture in the midtwentieth century, it is fair to assert that none of them began his career as an ardent desegregationist. But school desegregation hurled them into a very different position of leadership, that of chief mediator among the HEW, the DOJ, the district courts, their school board, and their local communities— including not only parents, teachers, staff, and students but also civil rights organizations in the black community and the Ku Klux Klan and the Citizens' Council in the white community. The four helped lead seven different school districts (Corinth, McComb, Hinds County, Meridian, Carrollton, Winona, and Yazoo City) through the desegregation process from 1965 through 1972.

The Expert: Dr. Julian Prince

In 1962, the small town of Corinth, Mississippi, captured the attention of the federal government when its city council passed a resolution condemning the actions of Governor Ross Barnett when James Meredith attempted to enroll at the University of Mississippi. The White House invited several community leaders in Corinth to fly to Washington to help the federal government develop more effective ways of working with a beleaguered state embroiled in racial tension and violence. Julian Prince, as superintendent of the Corinth public schools, attended that meeting and returned to Washington DC several times in the next few years.[14] On a trip in 1964, Prince met a young lawyer from Harvard named David Seeley who had just been appointed the assistant commissioner for equal educational opportunities for the US Office of Education. Seeley's job was to monitor the newly enacted Title VI of the Civil Rights Act. He asked Prince to be part of a small group of people charged with hammering out the implementation details of Title VI. Prince agreed and returned to DC to be part of what would be called the "Arlie Conference." (It was held at the Arlie House in northern Virginia.)[15] He was one of the only superintendents sitting around the table debating such questions as "What would HEW consider voluntary compliance?" and "At what point would the DOJ step in to enforce compliance?" Prince was well aware that his fraternizing with DC officials put him at odds with the majority of whites in his home state: "There I was with what many Mississippians considered a den of iniquity with top Federal people who were going to force desegregation on the south. Worse I was involved in making the decisions how the job would be done!"[16] Devising implementation guidelines with such a diverse group was not an easy task. The representatives of various civil rights organizations wanted nothing less than immediate desegregation of all schools. The superintendents called for a more gradual approach, so they could prepare their communities. The DOJ representatives sought clarification on how much time was realistically needed and at what point they should initiate legal proceedings against districts refusing to comply. The HEW representatives pushed for more specificity on what constituted minimal, but acceptable, compliance with Title VI.

Prince returned to Corinth after this meeting and informed his school board that compliance with school desegregation was inevitable, and the best way to achieve that was through the FOC plan. The board held a series of community meetings to discuss desegregation efforts and ultimately decided to voluntarily desegregate its schools. Prince and the board attorney returned to DC to work out an FOC plan acceptable to the HEW.[17] The relative ease of Corinth's transition to desegregated schools contrasted greatly with that of other school districts with much higher percentages of black students. One such place was McComb, which came courting Prince in 1965.

Racially, McComb and its surrounding areas was a far cry from Corinth.[18] It was a dangerous place for black residents. The Ku Klux Klan in Pike, Walthall, and Amite Counties was notorious for its brutal attacks against blacks, often with the full cooperation and participation of local law enforcement officials.[19] But the KKK did not have the sole claim on racism and violence. Like all southern towns in the 1960s, racism filtered through all facets of community life, including the church. One church in McComb appointed some of its members to serve on the "nigger committee." Their job was to stand at the front door to intercept any blacks who attempted to enter the sanctuary.[20]

This area was also the home of some of the strongest NAACP chapters in the state. It was a logical place for the newly formed Student Nonviolent Coordinating Committee (SNCC) to move in 1961 to help local activists launch a vigorous voter registration campaign. The showdown between local black activists, the so-called "outside agitators" from the SNCC, and the KKK soon turned violent. In September 1961, E. H. Hurst, a member of the Mississippi state legislature, shot and killed Herbert Lee, a black farmer and a member of the NAACP involved in the voter registration movement. Hurst was never charged for the murder nor spent a day in jail.[21] "A wave of terror swept over the area," wrote J. Oliver Emmerich, editor of the *McComb Enterprise-Journal*.[22] Black churches, homes, and meeting places were routinely bombed or burned. So violent was the area that the *Washington Post* dubbed McComb the "bombing belt" of the country.[23]

In 1963, Charles Nash was the student body president of Burglund High, the black segregated high school in McComb. He remembers well the dangerous atmosphere for black residents as reflected on the worst argument his parents ever had. It concerned what he should do if stopped by the police:

> Mother's position was to stop; don't say anything; keep your mouth shut; don't sass; don't disagree with them. If they give you a ticket, just get your ticket and come on home. Daddy's position was get home; don't let them stop you; get home; if you get home, we'll take care of you. And they couldn't agree on that. Mother was right because Big John Smith was terrible. He was a police officer in the McComb Police Department; he beat many black persons for nothing.[24]

In 1964, in an attempt to restore some peace and order in the community, 650 white residents signed a declaration calling for a halt to the violence and police brutality against blacks. The "Statement of Principles" was published in the local paper. The black community immediately responded with its own statement signed by twelve black organizations in town. According to Emmerich, "the citizenry has finally evinced responsible concern."[25] A biracial committee was appointed to help formulate a plan for easing the racial strife in McComb. At its first meeting, one of the black members, an elderly minister, asked everyone to stand, hold hands, and sing "Amazing Grace" together.[26]

This was the context in which the McComb School Board members found themselves in 1964 as they debated how to comply with school desegregation orders. They were fearful that fights over school desegregation would erupt into another round of violence. They needed someone with experience and expertise in desegregating schools. Julian Prince instantly came up. Prince was a frequent visitor in Washington DC and was on a first-name basis with David Seeley and many federal officials charged with enforcing school desegregation in the South. He had already led one school district through desegregation, and he had close ties to McComb. He began his teaching career there and was appointed director of instruction in 1959. His primary responsibility was to compare the instructional quality between the black and white schools in McComb. But when Frank Watkins, chair of the McComb school board, called Prince about the superintendent position in McComb, Prince quickly and emphatically responded: "Frank, there ain't no way I am going to McComb. Let's face it; life is too short."

Eventually, Frank's skills of persuasion won out, and in July 1965 Julian Prince assumed the superintendent's position of the McComb schools. Knowledgeable about the intricate details of Title VI and what the federal government considered acceptable desegregation under these guidelines, Prince's approach to desegregation was two-tiered. First, to appease the federal government, he needed to demonstrate "good faith" efforts with evidence of short-term progress and a plan for moving to wholesale desegregation. He did this by implementing an FOC plan, which called for desegregating grades 1, 10, 11, and 12 immediately. In fall 1965, twenty-one black students enrolled in formerly all-white schools under the "choice" option.[27] Second, he needed to convince his black and white constituents that academics would be enhanced, not hurt, by desegregation. His mantra, often repeated, was "quality education for all." He emphasized that school desegregation afforded opportunities and funding to enhance the curriculum offerings for McComb students. He knew his white patrons were concerned about the quality of education in desegregated schools and had another option. They could withdraw their children from the public schools and enroll them in one of the new private academies. He also knew that the McComb black community, galvanized by an active civil rights ethos, would not tolerate any digression in the fight for equal rights. Prince began searching for new and innovative educational practices that would position McComb as a leader in cutting-edge curriculum, pedagogy, and technology in the state and nation.

In April 1967, Prince was awarded a grant from the Office of Education to implement computer-assisted technology (CAT) in mathematics. A group of black and white teachers traveled to Stanford (CA) during the summer of 1967 to learn how to use the ASR 33 Teletype machine to teach mathematics skills beginning fall 1967.[28] Charles Nash, one of the black educators traveling to Stanford, explained how CAT was used as a way to transition into desegregated schools:

> That was "desegregated" only in the sense that they bussed white children to West Brook Elementary where I was the principal, and some of our children went to Otken School, and children from all white Otken came to ours. They bussed them over; they came down the hall; they went into the room where the teletype machines were. They worked on the teletype machines for an hour or so. They got off the machines, walked back down the hall, got on the bus. I wouldn't call that desegregated. They were in the same building with us; our children were in the same building with them. But it was the first attempt to bring black children into the white community where the schools were and white children in to the community where the black schools were.

Prince attributes much of his success in his early years as superintendent to the guidance he received from the black leaders in town—one of whom was Robert "Bob" Moses, who alerted him to a march planned by a group of black students in 1965. Prince's first reaction was to call the police. Instead, he decided to meet with the students. Prince explained what transpired at that meeting:

They came, and it was a hundred degrees day in July, and I went out from the central office to see the group. There were about a hundred children grade 1 to grade 12, and they were so hot they were melting. They had marched in the heat for about four miles from over in the black community. So I told Robert to bring them on inside, and we sat them all over the building and gave everybody a coke. And I said, "Who wants to talk?" They got the children who wanted to talk to me, and they demanded that we desegregate voluntarily. They didn't know we had a desegregation plan. So, I said, "Ok, here are the grades that we are desegregating this fall. If you are in any of those grades, you are welcome to come to a desegregated school. That is how the plan is going to work."

After his meeting with the black students, word got out in the white community that Superintendent Prince was too "moderate" on the issue of school desegregation and a "black sympathizer." These rumors soon reached an FBI agent who contacted Prince:

Agent Reese Timmons said to me, "You have put your foot in it. You got a problem. I'm going to show you how to look under the hood of your car every morning before you crank your car. You will not go to any meeting in this area at night. You will not go to any meeting in this community until you check with me first. Here are the people in this community that you can trust. You don't trust anybody I don't name."

It was not long after that Prince came face to face with the white hostility in his school district. Returning from a meeting in Bude, about thirty miles northwest of McComb, he noticed he was running low on gas. He stopped at a gas station to refuel. The attendant filled his gas tank, Prince paid him, and then the attendant asked him, "Ain't you the new superintendent down in McComb?" Prince was pleased that the man seemed to know who he was. "Yes, I am," he replied. "Well you nigger loving son of a bitch, don't you ever come back in here again." After that encounter, Prince heeded the advice of the FBI agent and did not go anywhere before first checking under the hood of his car.

Prince's expertise in school desegregation made him a sought-after consultant and guest speaker throughout the state. In October 1969, Prince addressed an advisory committee to the Pascagoula School Board, appointed by the Pascagoula Moss Point Area Chamber of Commerce. Prince was touted in the local paper as an educational leader who brought his school district from being one of the lowest in the state to being in the top ten in only three years. By then, Prince was also serving as the director of manpower resources for the Mississippi Research and Development Center. He told the crowd that he had used "unorthodox methods" to move his district to desegregation, but his primary emphasis was and would continue to be "quality education."[29]

Despite Prince's status as an expert in school desegregation with deep ties to Washington, he eventually ended up at odds with the federal government. His voluntary five-year desegregation plan came under fire after the 1969 *Alexander* ruling for not moving quickly enough to a unitary school system. In February 1971, the Office of Civil Rights informed Prince that the district's federal funds would be terminated for failure to comply with desegregation. Although its desegregation plan was court approved in April 1971, the Office of Civil Rights demanded that the McComb School District repay the federal money it received in 1970–71 during noncompliance. On April 23, 1971, Prince wrote to Senator James Eastland apprising him of his concern that the HEW was intentionally delaying the school district's request for compliance confirmation:

> On Tuesday, April 20, I had a conversation with Dr. Lloyd Henderson of Mr. Pottinger's office. Dr. Henderson said that he did not like our plan and that he would fight it with every tool at his disposal. At the moment I placed no substance on that comment—i.e., that he could. Reflection since that time has caused me to worry that Dr. Henderson and Mr. Pottinger may be delaying our return to compliance in order to keep us from being eligible for an Experimental Schools Grant. Would you be kind enough to discreetly check into this and determine if Dr. Henderson is delaying our compliance approval? Speed is of the essence."[30]

In November 1971, Prince and board attorney Joe Pigott flew to DC to argue their case during an administrative hearing. Prince describes the results of that meeting: "They had no case . . . We left town well satisfied. The Atlanta OCR [Office of Civil Rights] had shot themselves in the foot. And that was about it with the OCR. They dropped out of sight in our rear view mirror. We went on about our business having school."[31] In 1975, the residents of McComb rejected a millage increase for public schools, and Prince left McComb in 1976 to become the superintendent of the Tupelo City School system.

The Negotiator: Dr. Tom Dulin

Tom Dulin began his career in education as a math and physics teacher in 1952 in Vaiden in Carroll County. In 1962, he was appointed Attendance Center superintendent at J. Z. George High School—a segregated 1–12 white school in Carroll County. During his third year in that position, Carroll County was ordered to desegregate, first by FOC and then total integration the next year. Dulin traveled the back roads of his rural community as the megaphone for explaining the district's school desegregation plan. That role did not endear him to many of the white parents he was addressing in community meetings. During a particularly heated meeting with an all-white audience of several hundred, a man stood up and pointed a pistol directly at Dulin uttering these chilling words: "If you do not take care of my child—if anything happens to my child, I will kill you." Crosses were burned in Dulin's front yard; he received death threats and was under FBI surveillance for three months. Dulin explains the atmosphere: "It was just a difficult time, and that's just part of it because it was such a historical change, and it came so suddenly, and we might not have done as good a job as we should have there preparing the community for what was taking place. But I learned something there that I was able to use when I went to Winona."[32]

In 1966, Dulin became superintendent of the Winona School District in nearby Montgomery County, which was still a totally segregated school system. In his first year as superintendent, Dulin, his school board, and the board attorney began working on a voluntary desegregation plan using FOC. Unknown to the community, they were furtively negotiating with officials from the HEW on this plan. Dulin describes a particularly intense meeting that ended successfully but not without concerns for their personal safety:

> We had an eight-hour telephone conversation—a conference call—and what we were doing was, we were pleading with them [the DOJ and the HEW] to let us integrate the school system partially and then do it wholly at the beginning of the school year, so we would have time to prepare our people, and we spent a great deal of time telling them that we think we can get some black people to come. We will work at it, and we will try to swap teachers. White teachers go to the black schools, and black teachers come to the white schools. Just give us a little time to get our community ready. Just don't throw it on them all at once because they would leave. We were afraid they would leave, and I believe they would have. It was an interesting eight hours. I had those tapes, and I hid them because during the process of negotiating with them we were actually begging them to let us integrate the school system, which was a strange tune for Mississippi at that time. We were going against the grain, probably the only school in the state of Mississippi that actually begged the government to let us integrate.

Their negotiations resulted in the decision they wanted, and they were allowed to adopt a more gradual approach to school desegregation. Dulin

immediately began contacting some black families to convince them to send
their children to the white school under FOC. They were reluctant, but he
assured them that he would personally make sure they were welcome and safe
in their new school. Several finally agreed.

Dulin thought he had prepared his teachers and staff for the first day. He
had planned every detail, even to the speech teachers were to give to their
white students in introducing the black students to the class. Dulin thought
he had covered all his bases and everyone was prepared for this first step
toward desegregation. According to Dulin, he had forgotten one detail:

> All of our school staff—we had them well versed on what was going to hap-
> pen—but we had one custodian that was sick during that period of time, and
> I did not know he was coming back the very morning the little black children
> came to school. We had asked the black children to come at fifteen minutes after
> eight. We had a little morning devotion planned, and after that we would take
> them and put them in the proper classes and try to get them as comfortable as
> they could be. Well, this black custodian called me at about 7:30 and said, "Come
> over here quick." I said, "What's going on?" He said, "You are not going to believe
> it, but there is a whole gob of black children over here wanting to go to school."
> And I thought, my Lord, we worked so hard to get them over there, and they had
> worked hard. They did not want to come, and they had worked with us to work
> out everything, and there he was. I said, "What are you doing with the children?"
> He said, "I am running them off. I got a broom." I said, "Lord, you just wait and sit
> down, and I will be right over there." I thought, well you can work your gizzard
> out, and one thing come up and disturb the whole deal.

Meanwhile, Dulin and his school board began holding numerous meetings
in the black and white community preparing for school desegregation. They
publicized the FOC option on the radio and in the newspaper, and they
hired Dr. Roscoe Boyer from the University of Mississippi and Dr. Douglas
McDonald from Delta State University to conduct workshops with their
teachers.

One of Dulin's main concerns was that white parents would leave the Winona public schools to enroll in one of the recently formed private academies
in the area. To curtail a possible exodus, Dulin implemented an unusual policy. He mandated that all teachers, administrators, and school board members
in his district send their own children to the public schools. If they enrolled
them in a private academy, they lost their jobs or their seats on the board.
Dulin explains this unusual policy:

If you taught in the Winona public school system—whether you were white or black—or if you were on the school board in the Winona public school system, your children went to the public school. If you were a teacher and decided you did not want your children to go to the public school, you left the school system. If the school system was not good enough for your children, it ain't good enough for you, and we stood by that. A school board member, if they decided they didn't want their children to go to public school, you had to resign. That is the only way I would stay in Winona when we integrated the school system, and it worked. Might not have been legal, but it worked.

For three years, the Winona City School system continued to use FOC to desegregate its schools. In 1969, several black parents filed a complaint against the school district for failing to implement a wholesale desegregation plan. The district court ruling in the Winona case in August 1969 offers an interesting case of the variance in how federal judges decided school desegregation cases during this time period. After hearing testimony from Dulin, the black plaintiffs, and several witnesses, district court judge Orma Smith ruled that he would not interfere with Winona's 1969–70 school year, and Dulin and his board were to proceed as planned. He encouraged the district to use this year to "pave the way" for total desegregation through implementing faculty integration first. Yet, he told the district he would not hold them in contempt of court if they failed to do so immediately. Instead, he said, "I urge you to do all in your power to comply." He ordered them to submit a plan for abolishing their dual system of schooling by December 1, 1969, but again he was quite lenient in the specifics. He declined setting a firm deadline for implementation but iterated he would not favorably respond to a plan that called for more than two years to implement. He reminded Dulin and the board that it was their affirmative duty to disestablish a dual system of schooling and that their desegregation plan could not place the responsibility for successful desegregation on black parents. He praised Dulin and the school board for "being diligent in following its agreed upon freedom of choice plan" even though the plan had produced very little desegregation. Judge Smith lauded Dulin and his board for their good faith efforts, persistence in meeting with community groups, and communication with black parents in encouraging them to utilize the FOC option.[33]

Dulin was summoned to federal district court multiple times as part of the lawsuit against his district. After one particularly grueling occasion where he had been on the witness stand for several hours, Dulin issued a request to the judge:

"Will you let me ask him something?" He said, "It's rather unusual, but I am going to let you ask him." So I asked him, "Do your children go to the public schools?" and he was from Chicago or somewhere, and he didn't want to answer, and the judge said, "Yes, you are going to answer. He's been answering your questions, so now you answer his." And his children did not even go to the public schools. He had his children in a private school, and he was down here doing what he was doing, but he was not even living by his own principles, and you would have thought by listening to him that he was deep into desegregation, and he was not even a part of an integrated system where he lived. We had a good bit of that kind of stuff. People making us do things, but they weren't doing it themselves.

Dulin acknowledges that the South would have never desegregated had there not been judicial intervention. "If it was left up to society as a whole, a hundred years from now we would probably still be segregated, so someone had to take care of it. It just so happened it was the courts that took it, and I think it was the right thing." However, like many white southerners of the era, he was distrustful of "outsiders," like the attorney he queried in the courtroom, whom he viewed as a hypocrite for failing to live out in his personal life that which he was advocating professionally. Yet he himself was concerned that his local community would perceive negotiations with the federal government in a secretive meeting as evidence of a position outside the norms of conventional thinking about race and integration. "We knew if we could get this worked out amongst ourselves, it would be to our advantage," said Dulin. Nevertheless, they hid the tapes of that meeting for many years from their peers. Years later, when Dulin tried to retrieve the tapes, they had mysteriously disappeared. Dulin remained the superintendent of Winona public schools until he retired in 1990.

The Enforcer: Dr. Clyde Muse

When Clyde Muse began his first job as superintendent in July 1969, in Hinds County, the second largest school district in the state, he was not a seasoned superintendent with extensive experience leading a district through desegregation. As principal of Starkville High and then assistant superintendent of the Starkville city schools, Muse's experience with desegregation, thus far, had been limited to a few black students attending white schools in Starkville under FOC. However, he had a solid reputation as a "good school man." As a relative outsider to the Jackson area with no political ties or local community affiliations, Muse was brought to Hinds

County to enforce school desegregation in a district with 17 different schools, 132 bus routes, and 13,000 students. His education happened fast, for Hinds County was one of the school districts named in the *Alexander v. Holmes* case. On the second day on the job, he accompanied Bob Cannada, one of the attorneys defending the school systems, to New Orleans for the Fifth Circuit Court of Appeals ruling. Muse describes this experience:

> There were thirty-two school districts that were going to be affected by this order. Stacked in front of the court was pleadings and stuff this high from all over the different school districts represented there. But I never shall forget. They came in with the black robes and all of the Pledge of Allegiance and other pomp and circumstance of the Fifth Circuit going into session. And the chief judge called order, and he said, "Let's get on with this damn school case. I'm tired of it." That woke this "li'l' ole country boy" up. Finally, I said to Bob, "Can I speak to the court?" And he asked the judge would he allow me to speak, and he said he would. And I just began to say as a school person, please give me at least the second semester so that students, teachers, parents, and everybody can make decisions. And anyway, it's just not educationally sound to do that. Well, he said, "Well, Dr. Muse, we think you can do it with school people like yourself. It can be done." So I sat down.[34]

The Fifth Circuit ordered the school districts to submit desegregation plans immediately with an implementation date of August 27, 1969. Muse left that court hearing thinking it would be impossible to transform his school system in a matter of weeks from a dual to a unitary school system. He contemplated defying the court order. "What would be the repercussions if we don't comply?" he asked his attorney. "Ten-thousand-dollar-a-day fine for every day it's not implemented on time, and you have to pay the fine personally." To that, Muse replied, "Bob, I couldn't stand two hours of that, so I guess I better get it done."

Muse and the other thirty-two school districts named in the *Alexander* case received a reprieve of sorts. At the last hour, Robert Finch, secretary of the HEW, asked that the date for submitting desegregation plans be changed to December 1969 with no specified start date. From July to November 1969, no school leader was sure of what was going to happen the next day—so fast were the rulings and orders coming down. Finally, on October 29, 1969, that delay was no longer possible when the Supreme Court ruled in *Alexander v. Holmes* that "continued operation of racially segregated schools under the standard of all deliberate speed is no longer constitutionally permissible." Schools were ordered to open in January 1970 as desegregated schools. Muse spent November and December, including most of the Christmas break, planning and preparing. This entailed visiting all the local black and white communities in Hinds County. He noted, "[I]t was the toughest time of my entire school career." His "no-nonsense" approach to enforcing school desegregation and his message to every community group were the same. He addressed the crowd, explained the court order, described his plan for how that order would be accomplished in Hinds County, and then fielded questions. According to Muse, he tried to relate the same message to every audience he addressed: "We're going to treat every student fairly. We're not going to let any person be harassed in any way because of their race. We are going to have good discipline, and we will require students to come to school properly dressed, and we will require them to get up their lessons, and if one of them is mistreated, I don't care what color he is, by one of my faculty members or my people, they will be dismissed that day." This steady refrain communicated a powerful message to the people in his district. Muse stated, "By and large, they realized that I meant business."

The decisions he made were always with one eye on appeasing the HEW and the courts, who "were looking right down my throat," and the other eye on calming the concerns of his faculty, students, and parents. He was able to keep all the schools open, which went a long way in placating whites and blacks who did not want to lose their schools. Muse prided himself on being fair and not playing favorites or having any particularly political agenda during the implementation phase. His decision on how to assign teachers, which he thought was fair to all, was not well received by many white teachers as he explained:

> But then I did a system, I guess you might call it a lottery system, to change teachers. Each one was given a number, and we just spun a wheel so to speak. We'd turn out a number, and if Ms. Smith might be teaching now at Clinton, she may be transferred to the same grade down at Pearmont in Terry. And I lost a good many of my really good teachers, and so we had to make some adjustments during that second semester. But we made them, but I had a fruit basket turnover for sure.

Muse was anxious the first day of school and spent his time circulating from school to school. The press as far away as England had descended into Jackson to report on the first day of massive desegregation in the state's most populous city. Muse's goal was to have school as normal, which meant keeping the press out of his school buildings. He promised he would give a press conference at the end of the day. With thirty-five microphones in front of him, he succinctly told the waiting reporters, "It went real well. We had a good day at school." That night he received a phone call from a man who had seen him on TV. The caller questioned Muse's pedigree as a native son, believing that his report about a "good day" could not have been delivered by a Mississippian. Muse describes that conversation:

> He told me who he was and that he was a retired military person. Then he said,
>   "I want to ask you a question."
> I said, "Alright."
> He said, "Are you a Mississippian?" I said, "Yes sir. I was born and raised in
>   Mississippi."
> "How about your daddy?"
> I said, "Yes, sir. He was born and raised in Mississippi."
> "How about your granddaddy?"
> I said, "Yes, sir."
> He said, "Well, I want to tell you something. You sure as hell don't sound like one."
>   Because he wanted me to get on there and say how bad it was, and how ter-
>   rible it was, but I just stated the facts the way there were.

Many whites left the Hinds County school system for private schools, and shortly after Muse began his tenure as superintendent, the town of Clinton split from Hinds County, taking with it a sizable portion of white students. In 1971, the Meridian school system hired Muse to enforce desegregation in its school district. This time, however, he had a much more supportive white power structure behind him that was committed to preserving the public school system. However, his message and approach in Meridian was the same: "If you could provide the leadership, and the people can trust you, whatever you say, that's what you're going to do whether they like it or not. You're going to be successful, and they're going to support you."

Muse's decisions were not always popular. When he expelled a black student in Meridian for hitting a white student, a group of black parents and community members staged a protest in front of his office. They marched for several days. He finally met with them, listened to their complaints, explained his position, and then told them he was not going to rescind the expulsion. Muse describes the outcome of that meeting:

> Finally, it wound up me with two of the ringleaders as the only ones left in the
> room. I just sat there not saying a word. [One] finally turned around and said,
> "Oh hell, let's go. He's not going to do anything." But they took the pickets down.
> But that's the way I was. And they had to see that, and they had to know it, and I
> would discipline a white child just as fast as I would a black child. And I was the

same way when I was here in Hinds County. So [if] there's anything that helped get me through that, besides the good Lord, [it] was just the simple fact that I'm going to be fair to everybody.

Muse served as the superintendent in Meridian for seven years. In 1978, he became the president of Hinds Junior College. Once again, he was thrust into the role of enforcing a desegregation court decision, the *Ayers v. Allain* case, which began in 1975, when the plaintiffs brought a class-action suit against the state for maintaining a racially dual system of black and white public colleges and universities. The case was not settled until 2002.[35] In 1978, the federal court ordered Hinds Junior College and nearby Utica Junior College, a black institution, to merge. That merger was complete in 1982, and Dr. Muse became the president of the Hinds Junior College District.[36] Muse notes, "So I get to go through all this again at the college level. And I told somebody, 'You know, maybe that's what I was intended to do as an administrator.'" At the age of eighty-six, Dr. Muse still serves as the president of Hinds Community College.

The Rogue: Harold "Hardwood" Kelly

Harold "Hardwood" Kelly earned his nickname because of his skills on the basketball court. He played for the University of Mississippi from 1945 to 1948. In 1949 he began coaching and teaching in Yazoo City and for the next fifteen years rose through the educational channels in his school district. In 1966, he was appointed superintendent of the Yazoo City Municipal Separate School District. At that time Yazoo City was still operating a dual system of segregated schools. Kelly was part of a close-knit network of superintendents who spoke frequently and shared their mutual desegregation woes. Kelly, Tom Dulin, and Clyde Muse were part of a group of schoolmen who met once or twice a year at a fellow superintendent's deer camp. Kelly describes the camaraderie that developed among superintendents facing desegregation travails:

> We used to get together—maybe a couple of times in a year on an informal basis where we really talked about things that were happening at our school. And, in fact, we used to go out to Joe Tally's camp out in Forrest. Joe was the superintendent in Smith County and he had a camp down in Forrest. A deer camp—a really nice place. There used to be 30–40 school superintendents all up in the Delta. And we would go down in the morning and cook and have meetings at night. Get

up the next day at 5 o'clock and be back at work at 8 or at least by mid-morning. It was nothing but school business, talking school business. You'd pick up the going-on's from all over the state and some good ideas. We got a lot of good ideas from swapping stories. Clyde Muse was one of the big deals to come to that. All the Delta boys—Greenwood, Western Line, Cleveland, Bolivar County—they were there too.[37]

Yazoo City was one of the thirty-three districts named in the *Alexander* case. Kelly traveled to New Orleans with his board attorney in November 1969 to hear the Fifth Circuit Court of Appeals implementation date. According to Kelly, the attorney convinced him to attend a movie instead:

It was real funny in that all these school districts had to go to New Orleans and appear before a three-judge panel, and a lot of the superintendents went. At the time, we had a young lawyer that just got out of school at Ole Miss named Tom. We were supposed to go down to have a precourt hearing, and Tom says, "Coach, do you know what a precourt hearing is?" I said, "No. How would I know?" And he said, "They're gonna call you down there and tell the school districts what they have to do." So we went down to New Orleans. We were down there, and all the lawyers, about fifteen or twenty of them, were all worked up. They were going to go before this three-judge panel in the morning. Tommy looked at me and says, "Coach, let's go to the show." I says, "Tommy, no." He said, "Why do we want to go to that? Let's go to the show." So we went to the show. We got back, and they were still working, but when we got to the court hearing that next morning, and John Satterfield, who was the prime counsel for the thirty-three school districts, he got up and says, "Your Honor," and he stands up, and he wants to make his case. So, the judge let him make about three or four sentences, and he said, "Mr. Satterfield, would you please sit down?" And he sat down. About the third time, he said. "If you do this one more time, Mr. Satterfield I will have to get you for contempt of court." And that ended. Then they read out what they wanted these school districts to do, which was come home and pair all the grades. That's the way we got it done.

The threat of being charged with "contempt of court" did not prevent Kelly from implementing a school desegregation plan that defied court orders and HEW mandates. For the spring 1970 semester, the Yazoo City school system practiced segregation within supposedly desegregated schools. This meant that in the elementary schools black and white students were physically together on school campuses, but they were segregated in the same classroom with the same students being taught by the same teachers as they were in the previous semester. The high schools had a similar arrangement with students being integrated only in their elective courses (e.g., band, chorus, and physical education). This arrangement did not please the courts. Kelly insisted it was the only viable, educationally sound approach to dealing with such a change in the middle of the year. He explained:

> What if you were in the fourth and fifth grade or any grade for that matter, and this teacher had been teaching you the whole year. She had given you a grade for the first semester. You had made a B. And she knew what you needed to study for the next semester in order to a make an A. And she told you that. Then that person was in a position to grade that child for the rest of the year. Whereas, if you switched the teacher, the teacher would have to have this information on the child, and she'd have to learn that before she'd have an opportunity to take the child where they are and teach them, you see. Now I don't know whether that makes sense or not, but that was the reason why I did it that way. And it seemed to work. They could give a yearly grade and actually continue to know the children that they were teaching.

Kelly firmly believed that as superintendent he was the one most qualified to make educational decisions on behalf of student learning. He explained, "Hell, I'm the one that's trained to do this." He thought the HEW plan of total desegregation by pairing schools was educationally unsound given the timing. Under Kelly's plan, the school district would then open in fall 1970 as totally desegregated schools—classrooms and all.

Kelly met with all the faculty in his school district and explained how they were going to respond to the court's mandate to open as a desegregated school system in January. At that meeting, he said to his faculty, "If you don't think you can do what I'm telling you, please have a letter on my desk on Monday morning. I don't care about your reason why, but I need the letter by Monday morning." He went home that Friday afternoon and told his wife, "Come Monday, I don't know if I'll have a staff or not." On Monday he had two letters of resignation.

On January 26, 1970, Melvyn Leventhal, primary counsel for the NAACP Legal Defense Fund, filed a contempt of court motion against Yazoo City for violation of the November 7, 1969, court order. The federal court ordered an investigation. Kelly explained: "So it did not suit the courts completely. So I got a contempt of court order, which says you haven't done it right. In fact, the courts came in here and sent their representative to live with me to see what is going on. So he stayed with me about two or three months, and I still had the contempt of court order against me because this was my decision to do it this way. He got to be a coffee-drinking friend of mine." Kelly's decision also put him at odds with many in his own community, including the board attorney who did not know of his proposal until he unveiled it at a meeting. "I had to appear before HEW, the Justice Department, and the local NAACP, all the groups, and half of those agreed with me, and half didn't, but my lawyer said 'Kelly, you have messed up. That's not the way we should have done it.' And I said, 'Well if it's not anything left for the people in education to do, then I will find out.'" Kelly's school board, by and large, stood behind him, and for the first semester, the majority of white students remained in the public schools, probably due, in part, to Kelly's plan and a concerted community "Friends of Public Schools" campaign.

As one of the first districts to open under court orders in January 1970, Yazoo City was teeming with reporters from all over the world. CBS, NBC, and ABC were on site, as was Willie Morris, the editor of *Harper's Magazine*, who had grown up in Yazoo City and played basketball for Coach Kelly. Kelly kept members of the press at bay for opening day with the promise that he would escort them through the schools and answer their questions on the third day. According to Kelly, who had a great fondness for his former student, Willie tried to persuade him to bend the rules: "Willie wanted to get into school the first day. He says, 'Coach, I'll dress like one of the students. They won't even know who I am.' I said, 'No, Willie, you're not going to do that. Others can't get in; you can't get in either.' So he sat in my office for two days, and he'd say, 'Coach, can I go?' I said, 'No, but on the third day, Willie, we're going to give you an escort. You can go anywhere you want to go.'" [38]

Yazoo City's move to a unitary school system in January 1970 was heralded throughout the nation as a shining example of a successful school desegregation effort. Unlike other school districts with large black populations, Yazoo City had managed to retain most of the white students in its public schools. Yet, the feeling of optimism was tinged with an underlying concern about the future of the Yazoo City public schools. Would the white students remain once classroom segregation was eliminated in the fall? "All's Well in Yazoo City, but What about Tomorrow?" was the headline of the *Commercial Appeal* after opening day. It captured the sentiments of many, including Harold Kelly, who cautiously offered the following at the end of the first day, "So far, everything has gone smoothly. There have been no incidents." Even more circumspect, one local businessman told a reporter, "All I'm prepared to say is that at 2:30 this afternoon it was working." [39]

Kelly's "coffee-drinking friend" reported back to the court in July 1970 that the district had, indeed, assigned students to classes on a "racially discriminatory basis." However, Judge Dan Russell did not hold the school board or

Harold Kelly in contempt of court.[40] The Yazoo City school system opened with wholesale desegregation in fall 1970 with significantly different enrollment figures than in January 1970. Whites were now only 25 percent of the student population as compared to 50 percent in the previous semester. As feared by Kelly and others, many whites left the public school for Manchester Academy, a private school opened in 1969. Kelly never left Yazoo City. He retired as their superintendent in 1988. He was once approached by the private school to be its principal. He declined: "I said no way. I finished in the public schools, and public schools meant a lot to me. And I always think that any community has got to have a good public school if they're going to progress economically and every other way."

The Toughest Job in the State

In August 1970, Dr. John S. Martin, the superintendent of the Jackson Municipal School District, abruptly resigned his post. The *Clarion-Ledger* attributed his sudden departure to the emotional toil desegregation was playing on school leaders:

> "It's the toughest job in the state." That was a leading educator's description
> Thursday of the superintendency of a public school system in Mississippi under
> the stresses of mass integration—and integration in a state with the highest per-
> centage of black pupils in the nation. Several administrators have gone into early
> retirement, several have suffered heart attacks, two or three fatal, and there has
> been one suicide, the official said.[41]

It was a tough job indeed, and every superintendent faced with school desegregation did so under extreme pressure, often with little positive guidance from his board and surrounded by a cacophony of conflicting voices demanding their needs be met first. Dr. L. O. Todd, who preceded Muse as superintendent in Meridian, described the context under which superintendents were working in 1969 as "the most revolutionary and abrupt thing that has ever happened to education."[42] As the educational leader of their district, the superintendent was charged with completing the difficult task of determining the nuts and bolts of school desegregation: How do we ensure there will be no violence and all the children will be safe? How will teachers be assigned? What schools will be closed? How will students be assigned to classes? How will bus routes be determined? Do we have enough textbooks and desks? Many made decisions that put them either at odds with the HEW and the courts or in conflict with their local constituents. Others were doomed from the beginning because of recalcitrant school boards and powerful white constituents stalwart in their commitment to segregated schools. Certainly, many deserve the blame for openly defying court orders and HEW mandates and caring foremost, and often only, for appeasing their white patrons either by devising ways to keep them in the public schools or diverting precious resources to the newly opened private schools. However, some superintendents soared to the challenge and led their school districts through this social and educational crisis much more successfully than many expected.

Chapter 4

Weathering the Storm
Principals and Local Implementation

On August 17, 1969, Hurricane Camille, a category 5 storm, decimated the Mississippi Gulf Coast, leaving homes, businesses, and schools flattened. In Louisiana and Mississippi, 172 people were killed, and another 150 perished in Virginia (primarily Nelson County) in flash floods. One of the strongest hurricanes in recorded history, Camille caused $1.42 billion in damages.[1] On the day that it hit, Lamar Beaty, recently appointed new principal of Pass Christian Junior High, was in Starkville waiting to take his final exams to complete his master's degree from Mississippi State University. Beaty, like most folks living on the coastal South, had been carefully monitoring this hurricane. It first made landfall in Cuba on August 15 as a category 2 hurricane and then returned to the Gulf. As it strengthened in intensity as it stormed across the warm gulf waters, it appeared to be veering toward northern Florida. However, around noon on August 17, it took a turn and began heading straight toward the Mississippi coast. Beaty's wife was in Mobile with their daughter, who was hospitalized, and their son was staying with grandparents in nearby Houston (MS). Waiting anxiously in Starkville, Beaty decided to go to the highway patrol station to receive the most up-to-date reports on the storm. It was there he received the devastating news from a radio update from Civil Defense. Their team was sitting in an amphibious vehicle in 30 feet of water in the parking lot of North Street Elementary in Pass Christian. One of the highway patrolmen looked at Beatty and said, "Do you know where North Street Elementary is?"[2] "Yes," Beaty replied, "it's one block from my house and on a little bit higher ground." Beaty knew he, his family, and his community were in trouble. He sat up all night at the highway patrol station, and early Monday morning made a quick visit to his advisor, who offered him a "B" in the class and an exemption from the final exam. Lamar shook his hand and said, "You got a deal." When Beaty finally arrived back in Pass Christian, there was nothing left of his home. Schools were canceled until October 1, 1969.

At a principal's meeting days before school was to open, the superintendent unexpectedly announced to him: "Beaty, you're going to be principal of the junior high and the high school." Beaty's first reaction was "Sir, I'm not sure I'm ready for this." To which the superintendent replied, "Then turn in your resignation, and I'll get someone who is." Beaty quickly retorted, "I'm ready."

When Beaty began his first principalship in October 1969, not only was he dealing with the move to a unitary desegregated school situation, but he was also trying to lead a school through the chaos left in the aftermath of Hurricane Camille. Surprisingly, the opening of schools almost two months later than usual and the transition to a desegregated school occurred fairly smoothly. Looking back on the events of 1969, Beaty wondered how these two significant events impacted his school district that year: "If the hurricane hadn't hit, what would have happened? Would the blacks have resented having to leave their school and go to another school? I think there was probably some resentment, but that school [J. W. Randolph] was pretty much totally destroyed. Would the whites have resented having to go to what had been an all-black school? You know, we don't know because of Hurricane Camille."

Most principals in Mississippi did not face a literal storm, as did Beaty, when they first opened their doors in 1969 and 1970 as desegregated schools, but every principal who worked through this time of desegregation weathered his own storm—perhaps a teacher ill-prepared to teach in a diverse heterogeneous classroom, students upset about the canceling of prom, parents dissatisfied with their child's classroom placement, overcrowded facilities, inadequate resources, vocal criticism of recently adopted discipline policies, an appearance before a district judge to defend an action taken, or a student walkout in protest of school policies. Certainly, some principals endured the storm much better than others. Many white principals resigned or retired. Some did so bitterly, but others recognized it was time to turn the reins over to a new cadre of school administrators ready to take on the challenges of school desegregation. William Lewis, a high school coach in 1969, vividly recalls the meeting in which the long-term principal of Harrison Central High decided to retire:

Mr. Barnett was a great big fellow. Had this big rough voice, and he really commanded the school and ran it his way, the way the old school guys used to run the school house. He really didn't take kindly to any interference from anybody, and the students were respectful of him. And he called us together the spring of 1969 and said he had made the decision to retire. And I can remember this big strong gruff fellow and tears running down his cheek. And he made this statement that has always stuck with me. And I think it was really prophetic: "Ladies and

Gentlemen. The time has come for my kind of education to come to an end." And I think he was exactly right.[3]

Waiting in the wings were a number of white men, who were given an unprecedented opportunity to hone their skills as administrators at a very young age. Unfortunately, their opportunity often came on the backs of older, more experienced black principals who did not weather the desegregation storm so well. Many of them were demoted or lost their jobs entirely.

It would be at the school level that the "rubber met the road" in determining the implementation of desegregation in the daily work of doing school. Some principals had significant input into major decisions affecting their schools; others had little or no involvement in creating the districtwide desegregation plan but were expected to explain it and enforce it. A primary challenge for many principals working through school desegregation was that they were expected to be the internal change agents responsible for enacting court orders and HEW desegregation plans, yet their own authority to enact substantive change was often curtailed by the bureaucratic and hierarchical structure of educational decision making.[4]

The Christmas Break: Preparing for Integration in a Hurry

Charles Boone was a principal at Quitman High School in Clark County, Mississippi. Like many of his fellow principals in 1969, he had received no formal training on how to lead a school through desegregation. He was jolted into reality a few weeks after the *Alexander v. Holmes* (1969) ruling when two men from the HEW walked into his office, handed him a book that was as "thick as a Sears Roebuck Catalog," and said to him, "When you open up your school after the Christmas holidays, the ninth grade through the twelfth grade will be in this building. And it's all in the book."[5] They turned around and walked out. He quickly picked up his phone and called his superintendent who said, "Yeah, I just got the same book." With little guidance from the superintendent or his school board and the "book" being basically useless, Boone realized he needed to get busy and get busy soon. He called the principal at the black school and asked if he could address his student body. The principal agreed. Boone's strategy going in was that he would build rapport with the black students by demonstrating how similar his own background was to theirs. He shared with them how he had grown up poor and had to struggle to get an education. He thought he was giving an inspirational speech about how one can work hard and overcome life's obstacles to become successful. He intentionally used "we" throughout his address to emphasize that they would all need to work together to make integration successful. He gave what he thought was a "good citizen talk." It was an abysmal failure. When he finally stopped for a breath, a hundred hands went into the air, and he began addressing their concerns:

> Will we change the school mascot?
> What will be our school colors?
> Is it true that you are going to make us cut our hair?
> Will I be able to take Algebra?
> Will we get to play on the basketball team come January?
> Who will be our teachers?

Boone tried to answer their questions as best he could, quell their fears, and dispel the rumors behind many of the questions. But he returned to his school with the realization that it would be the seemingly mundane decisions he must make that would determine whether or not desegregation would be successful at Quitman High. Boone explained what he did during the month he had to prepare: "During the Christmas holidays, many a night, I'd work all night and all day. I'd come home and shave, take a bath, and put my clothes back on and go work straight without sleep at all or maybe just an hour, trying to get ready during the Christmas holidays to open up January 7."

Boone and his assistant principal, Arthur Nelson, who was black, spent the Christmas break studying the students' current schedules, examining their cumulative folders and determining the semester schedule for each student. Boone created a master chart to provide a visual image of the racial breakdown of each class. When he placed a white student in the class, he used a red pen; when he placed a black student in the class, he used a black pen. Boone realized that several of the black seniors transferring to his school in January were going to be a half-unit short of meeting state requirements for graduation. Boone sought guidance on what he needed to do: "I called the State Department. I want it in writing what I'm supposed to do. They didn't know. I told them, 'I'm going to fudge on the evidence so these kids can graduate.' They said, 'Mr. Boone, we're not going to question anything you do this year.'" By the end of December, Boone felt confident that he was ready for school to open: "Now, I've got it all set up. A new handbook. I've got everybody's schedules, and I've got the teachers being in this room or that room. I've got it mathematically all worked out during that two weeks over Christmas holidays. Met with my teachers a day early and gave them their assignments. And I'm ready to start. I'm not bragging, I'm praising the Lord. He got me through it."

Boone cites his deep religious faith and daily prayer life as the reason for his success that first semester. "Everything was through prayer and what I thought was right for the kids." He specifically believes his prayers were answered in the assignment of his assistant principal, whom he did not know before the Christmas break. He described their first encounter:

> That was my first night with Mr. Nelson. And I said to him, "Well, I've got this problem, and here's what I think we ought to do." And he would say, "That sounds fine, Mr. Boone." Then I would say, "That is what I think we ought to do here." And he would say, "That's fine." I thought to myself, "Oh my goodness, I got an Uncle Tom. I don't want somebody that agrees with me on everything. I want somebody that tells me if they disagree with me." So I said, "I'll outsmart this fellow." So the next problem I had, I said, "Now, how do you think we ought to handle this?" And he would think, and I would agree with him on his answer. I said, "That's weird." And I'd give him another problem. He said, "Well, I think we ought to do this." I couldn't believe it. Two individuals, one in the black system and one of the white system, and under an integrated coming event, we had the same goals and were trying to solve them the same way. I said, "Something's wrong." So at 2 o'clock in the morning, I walked outside. And I looked up and saw his car tag, and on his car tag it said, "Christ is the Answer." Now, I can take you to this graveyard right up here and show you a big tombstone—me and my wife—and across the bottom to this day it's got "Christ is the Answer."

Tragically, Mr. Nelson and his daughter were killed the following year in a car accident.

Like Charles Boone, John Allen Flynt was a somewhat seasoned principal when desegregation occurred in his school district. In 1960, he began teaching in New Hebron (Lawrence County), a small rural school housing grades 1–12. In 1966, he was appointed principal and coach. When the *Alexander* ruling came down in October 1969, Flynt began visiting the black schools to gather information about their teachers and their students. He knew he would have some input concerning what black teachers would be assigned to his school, so he wanted to be armed with information about their teaching. However, with Christmas break right around the corner and the superintendent providing no logistical details about the desegregation of their schools, Flynt was anxious. How was he supposed to open his school doors in January as an integrated school when he did not even know who would be teaching at New Hebron or what new students would be enrolling? Finally, right before schools were to open in January, the superintendent called a meeting with all the principals. He asked them to go around the room and state their main priority in terms of teacher need. After the last person made his declaration, the superintendent stood up, told them to "work it out," and then left the room. The principals began vying for teachers. Flynt and another principal both wanted Coach Swancy Brown at their school. Flynt wanted him to teach math; the other principal wanted him to coach. At the end of the day, after much discussion and negotiation, Coach Brown was assigned to New Hebron along with eight other black teachers.[6]

Unlike Charles Boone and John Allen Flynt, Jim Brewer was a brand-new principal when he took over the leadership of Jefferson Middle School in Columbia, which was to open on January 7, 1970, as a desegregated school. Similar to many black high schools during desegregation, Jefferson High School, the formerly all-black school, was converted to Jefferson Middle. Jefferson High was the pride of the black community, but it had been woefully underresourced. When Jim and his superintendent took a tour of the school before Christmas break, Jim was appalled at the condition of the facilities—broken desks, unusable electrical outlets, peeling paint, and a general disrepair.[7] The neglect of black schools and the sudden need to improve them in preparation of white students was a challenge many school districts faced as they hastily prepared for desegregation. A 1970 NEA report about the status of desegregation in Mississippi and Louisiana observed: "A fortunate result, regarded by black students with some cynicism, has been the renovation and remodeling of the black schools to make them fit for white students. As noted by the earlier task force, great emphasis is placed on repainting of restrooms and locker rooms, replacing commodes, and on obliterating all emblems of school and racial identity."[8] Brewer's first order of business as the new principal was to spruce up his school building. He asked twenty black and white high school boys to help over Christmas break. He thought it would also be a good opportunity for them to get acquainted before they began school together in January. These student volunteers helped repair the school and moved books, furniture, supplies, and equipment to the "new" Jefferson Middle School.

Jim Brewer knew that many of the whites held lingering doubts about sending their children to a school located in an all-black neighborhood, and black parents were concerned about how their children would be treated in an integrated setting with a new, white principal. To help alleviate their concerns, Brewer held an open house the Sunday before the opening day of school. To his surprise, 735 students and adults attended. As black and white parents greeted each other walking down the halls, Jim felt confident and prepared for the next day as he explained: "I was fairly young, and I looked at it as a real challenge. To be very frank I was excited the Sunday afternoon went down so well. The teachers were prepared; the classrooms were prepared, and I was pretty wrapped up. I didn't expect any trouble, and we didn't have any."

Starkville city school superintendent B. Hall Buchannan had spent some time trying to prepare his school personnel for desegregation. He met regularly with the principals, apprised them of upcoming changes, and on occasion solicited input from them. Fenton Peters, who was principal of the all-black Henderson High, described those meetings of which he was a part:

> It was a joint effort, preparing for what was going to happen. I was part of the process, but it was not left entirely up to me. The rules and what not came down from on high. [Superintendent Buchannan] and his assistants, the central office staff and the school board, devised and contrived a major plan and process about what was going to happen and what way we were going to do it. Now we had an administrative council. It was all the administrators there surrounding the superintendent, and we came up with some things that we felt, as professionals, would probably go best or work better as opposed to that way. Of course, as I said, everyone had their input. I don't know if everybody got heard. Some people got heard a little more than what others did.[9]

Starkville's desegregation plan was based on grade centers using all existing school buildings. There was a first-and second-grade school, a third-grade school, and so forth.[10] Starkville High was the only school in the district for grades 10–12. This grade-center approach to achieving desegregation alleviated competing schools in which the black/white ratio had to be carefully monitored since citywide all students in one grade attended one school. The plan was effective in meeting the requirements to implement a unitary school system, but it was not without its critics. Many members of the black community were upset about losing Henderson High, a school with a rich history and a centerpiece of the black community. Also, Fenton Peters would not continue as the high school principal when the Starkville schools desegregated; he was demoted to principal of the middle school.

Making It through the First Day

Was today a success? This was the question looming over every principal's head at the end of opening day in January, February, August, or September 1970. The decisions, the all-nighters over Christmas and summer break, and the constant worry all culminated in having a successful first day. The measures for judging that success varied from school to school. For many principals, a successful first day meant no violence and few disruptions inside or outside the building. For others, the main criterion for claiming success at the end of the day was that white students showed up. For yet others, it was that teachers were prepared, students were in the classrooms, and learning took place. High on every principal's list for a successful first day was making sure that his school opened in an orderly manner and the day was as "normal" as possible.

Jim Brewer sought the help of parents and community members to ensure no disruptions occurred on opening day at Jefferson Middle School. He asked key members of the community to serve as hall monitors. Their job was simply to check for any disturbance or commotion and to praise the students for good behavior as they changed classes or walked to and from bathrooms and the cafeteria. At the end of the day, Brewer was proud of their accomplishments: "We had class on the first day. The students went to their classrooms; they knew where to go, and the teachers were teaching that first day, and we were extremely proud of that."

Fenton Peters did not know what to expect the first day of school desegregation at Armstrong Middle School in Starkville. Perhaps he was a bit preoccupied with other matters since his wife was in the hospital giving birth to their second son. He described opening day: "While my son was being delivered by cesarean, the superintendent and I were walking around my school making sure that nothing happened. The superintendent was touring schools to make sure, as much as he could, that nothing out of the way happened, that nothing went wrong, and nothing did. To be honest, compared to other places, it was smooth as a dollar. I did not think it would go that smooth, but it did. It fooled me and a lot of other folks." On opening day at Beaumont High School (Perry County), a concerned white father waited outside while his daughter entered her newly desegregated school. He admitted to the local paper that perhaps desegregation may work better than he thought; however, he added, "if anything happens to my girl. If she's insulted by a nigra, I'll come over there and knock hell out of Adcox." Bill Adcox, the principal of the high school, considered the man's comment indicative of a first good day and a sign of progress in the community: "Last year the same man said he would shoot me if we desegregated the school."[11]

The local, state, and national press was out in full force in January 1970 eager to capture for the rest of the country the drama unfolding as the state that had fought *Brown* the longest was forced to comply finally with school desegregation. Many principals had to expend considerable time and energy on the first day keeping the press at bay and out of their schools. Like most principals, Jim Brewer had no formal training on how to deal with the media, deliver a press conference, or write a press release. But Brewer quickly received a crash course in school-media relations. On the morning Jefferson Middle School opened its doors as a desegregated school, Principal Brewer was dealing with two immediate concerns: determining the veracity of a rumor circulating that a band of one hundred white parents was marching toward the school to protest integration and disrupt the school day and preventing the press from entering his school building. The rumor about the marchers proved false, but he did have to confront the media. Brewer explained how he dealt with the press: "I had to tell them they couldn't come in and take pictures inside while we were having classes. 'No way are you going to disrupt our school.' But they took pictures of the outside, and that was about it. That lasted only about twenty minutes, and they went somewhere else to take pictures."

When the reporters from the national networks, including Dan Rather, showed up at Neshoba Central High School in Philadelphia (home of the horrific murder of civil rights workers in 1964), Principal Leo Salter solicited the help of the police to keep members of the media off his campus. A few tried to force their way into the building. The police escorted them out as they and Salter exchanged shouts with the press calling for "first amendment rights" and Salter replying, "You don't have any right to be here while we are having school." It took about two weeks for all the press to leave Neshoba County. The experience left Salter with a rather low opinion of journalists. His son, Sid, would go on to become one. Sid commented, "I think my dad would have been happier had I told him I wanted to be a horse thief than I wanted to be journalist because he didn't have any use for them."[12]

Larry Van Dyke did not have the luxury of a Christmas break to prepare for the first day of desegregation. He was appointed principal of Holly Springs Elementary the day before school was to open in January 1970. Larry knew he was specifically chosen for the job because he was a "Yankee outsider . . . someone you can hate more easily."[13] Larry was from Memphis, and he and his wife, a physician, had recently returned from Africa, where they served as missionaries for six months. According to Van Dyke, they approached their new jobs in Holly Springs with a religious zeal: "We were both being missionaries in our fields. And we thought it was important because we could talk and socialize with the movers and shakers in the town of Holly Springs, so we felt that was more than just a ministry to the poor and needy. So that was where we were coming from." He met his teachers and students for the first time the morning that school opened. By then, almost all the white students and most of the white teachers had fled to the private school. However, a group of whites tried to intimidate black parents and students. Van Dyke explained:

The day we opened there was a narrow road to the main entrance to the primary building. The cars were lined up and down. The school bus [with black students] could hardly get through. Of course, there was the yelling and shouting and all that, but they stopped at the front door. They were hoping that they [the black students] wouldn't come to school if they saw all those white people there defending their school. I called the superintendent. He said, "I know. We've got it the same way at the junior high." And the bus driver was black, which I thought was pretty brave of him to drive in. The superintendent had notified the police and sheriff in case they needed help. Once the kids got into the school, the cars that were parked along the sides drove away. This continued for a few days.

While Larry Van Dyke was trying to contend with whites parked beside his school, he was also dealing with the media determined to "get some real good candid pictures of what the classrooms were going to be like." He refused them entrance and tried his best to limit their contact with students or teachers. This meant that he had to make the decision on that first day of school to cancel recess. He noted that the first few days were simply about surviving.

Spare the Rod, Spoil the Child: Rethinking Discipline

After the first few days, the press left and initial uncertainties were abated, principals were faced with the real challenge of having school. Weighing heavily on both black and white patrons was the issue of discipline. They expected their principal to be first and foremost a strong disciplinarian who would establish and maintain a safe environment conducive to teaching and learning. He was also expected to allay the fears of white parents as reported in an article in the *Meridian Star* on January 11, 1970:

> A major concern among white parents is discipline. Parents were assured in meetings at Yazoo City that any trouble would be stopped immediately. Robert Barrett, the no-nonsense principal of Natchez desegregated high school complex, told an audience of 200 black and 200 white juniors that any fight, racial or otherwise, would result in a two-week suspension. "Your conduct must be above reproach," Barrett said. "The administration has worked 18 to 20 hours a day for weeks to get ready for this semester. We don't have time for petty problems.[14]

Despite their concerns rarely being expressed in the local papers, black parents were equally concerned about discipline, and with good reason, given the ill treatment of many black students attending schools under FOC and the elimination of black leadership in newly integrated schools. Black parents worried that their children under massive desegregation would face a hostile learning environment that threatened their children's safety, academic achievement, and emotional and physical well-being.

During the early years of school desegregation, concerns about discipline were often veiled in the language of "cultural differences"; that is, blacks and whites in the South lived in such different "cultures" that conflicts over appropriate school behavior would inevitably occur. School districts often held workshops for their teachers and staff to prepare them for cross-cultural differences between black and white students. Principals were expected to be the mediators when conflicts occurred, as illustrated in the following 1955 article appearing in *Educational Leadership*:

> The principal, of course, has the responsibility for maintaining order and discipline in his school . . . It must be remembered that in many areas of the South we have had in effect what amounts to almost two separate cultures developing and proceeding parallel to each other. In some instances, these cultures have not had many points of contact which can serve as a basis for integrating the youth of the two different groups into one harmonious student body. When the two cultures begin to come into contact at this common point, the public school, frictions may occur.[15]

Many principals were surprised to discover during the desegregation process that black and white students in their segregated schools were, in fact, held to remarkably similar expectations about student conduct. When comparing the discipline policies of Quitman High to the black high school, Charles Boone found the biggest difference between the two was the severity of punishment: "Where our policy would say, 'You'll get a day out of school [suspension] for doing so-and-so,' theirs said, 'You'll get two weeks off.' Their rules were much, much, much more strenuous than mine."

Most school districts in the throes of school desegregation devised new discipline policies in hopes that community fears and anxieties about student integration would be alleviated. Stringent and often quite detailed, these policies were widely disseminated and published in the local paper. The following excerpt from the Starkville City school system, published on September 9, 1970 in the *Starkville Daily News*, is representative:

> The following list provides specific examples of misconduct requiring immediate suspensions and-or expulsions. It is not intended to be a complete listing of all possible actions of breach of contract.

1. Skipping school or class and-or leaving a campus without permission
2. Fighting or provoking a fight or disturbance
3. Possession or use of weapons of any nature, or objects that could be classified as a weapon, such as knives, sharp pointed or blunt instruments
4. The theft of objects belonging to individuals or any item or items of school property
5. The possession or use of drugs
6. Possession or use of fireworks in any form
7. Possession or use of alcohol
8. The use of vulgarity, profanity, or obscenity whether spoken, written, or through action or implication[16]

The discipline policy of the Vicksburg Public Schools, published in the local paper on September 3, 1970, went into great detail defining the many different ways in which students could violate appropriate and expected norms of behavior. For example, number 17 of their violations specifically addressed "intimate associations of students":

17. Intimate association of students must be kept on an honorable and reasonable level at all times during the school day and at school functions and at school sponsored activities. Gestures and acts beyond holding hands and arms will be considered interruptive to the learning atmosphere of the school. The first offense will call for a firm warning to students involved and a letter to parents. The second offense will bring about a one (1) day suspension from school. The second offense will result in a three (3) day suspension from school. The third offense will call for a five (5) day suspension from school.[17]

Recognizing his community's concerns about discipline, one of Charles Boone's first orders of business was to create a new student handbook. He sought the help of his students:

It was one of the smartest things I did in this whole integration. I met with the black girls. You think about it. Girls of the same color will ask different questions [than] they would if white girls were there. They'll ask different questions [than] they would if boys were there. They asked some pretty good questions, and a lot of my answers were "What do I need to do?" I took good notes. I did it with the black boys. I did it with the white boys. Then I would put the black and white boys together and see if they had a question, and the white girls and the black girls together. So I hashed the rules out, and we cut them crossways anyway. But they taught me a lot of things that I had to solve that I didn't know were going to be problems to work out at the time.

As part of his new discipline plan, Boone required all students to wear a photo name badge at all times. If a student misbehaved, then the teacher took his/her name badge and then contacted the office. He explained, "Here was the system. The teachers stood at the doors and dismissed the students when the bell rang. They watched the hall. If a young lady walked up to you, and said, 'That boy just pinched me on the behind,' then the teacher walked over to that young man and said, 'May I have your ID card?' They were then called in later so not to disturb the class."

Like most principals, Lamar Beaty, principal at Pass Christian Junior/Senior High, took his job as head disciplinarian very seriously. He was constantly worried that mayhem would suddenly erupt, and he would be unable to control the situation. Beaty was particularly on edge when students congregated in places with little teacher surveillance. The pep rally was one of those angst-inducing places: "I had a tendency to put a lot of pressure on myself worrying about things that might happen that never did. You think, What's the worst that could happen? You have a race riot? Man I dreaded pep rallies because you get a large crowd together. You know something is more likely to happen then than any other time, and I used to dread those—hated them with a passion, but nothing ever happened. I don't think the kids—they weren't thinking the same way I was." What Beaty is speaking to in the above quote is the conflicting beliefs about how to manage student behavior during desegregation. On the one hand, some subscribed to the belief that if adults would just leave students alone and allow them opportunities to get to know each other, they would resolve potential conflicts on their own. Strict, militaristic discipline codes would be counterproductive if the aim was to encourage black and white students to get to know each other as individuals and discover they shared many more similarities than they did differences. Potential behavior problems would be lessened because of students' own self-regulation and monitoring. On the other hand, the prevailing belief of the time was that the best way to control student behavior and actions (at school or at home) was by firm, heavy-handed adult intervention. The old adage "spare the rod, spoil the child" dictated discipline in most homes and schools (both black and white) in the South during this time period. Thus, corporal punishment was an expected component of any school discipline policy.

Mississippi did not have an official state policy about the use of corporal punishment in school; local school districts were free to make their own rules about whether or not it would be used and under what circumstances.[18] Thus, paramount on everyone's mind going into school desegregation was not whether corporal punishment would be used but rather how it would be used and who would administer it. This concern was further complicated by the South's history of whites using force and physical violence to punish and discipline blacks. Understandably, when discipline policies were adopted in newly desegregated schools, many black parents recoiled at the thought of a white principal inflicting physical punishment on their children. Conversely, many white parents objected to the reversal of power relations and stood firm against black teachers inflicting physical punishment on their children.

One common way of dealing with discipline during the transition to desegregated schools was to assign the administration of corporal punishment based on race. John Allen Flynt, principal at New Hebron, explained the district's policy: "We had rules in the county office on paddling. I would paddle the white kids, and Swancy Brown and Smith Lucas, two of the black teachers, one of them would take care of the black kids. I had a couple of black boys in my office one time, and I told them I was going to give them a paddling, so let's go get Coach Brown. And they said, "Why don't you do it?" I didn't whip as hard as the black teachers did." A similar arrangement existed at Magnolia Junior High where George Dale as the principal disciplined the white students, and the assistant principal, Inez Green, took care of the black students as Dale describes:

> Mrs. Green would walk around with a long ruler. A lot of the black ninth-grade students had been held back for whatever reason and were older than the ninth-grade white kids. And the white parents were concerned that there were older black boys in the junior high. If one of them misbehaved, they were sent to the office to Mrs. Green. She would either make them lean over the desk, and she would pop them with that long ruler. It wouldn't hurt, but I'm sure it would embarrass them to death that Mrs. Green made them grab their ankles and lean over her desk.[19]

However, sometimes central administration or principals adopted a race-neutral approach to administering discipline. When Charles George was appointed assistant principal at West Tallahatchie, his principal, Larry Garvin, put George, who is black, in charge of all the discipline. George explained why:

> I took care of the discipline—both white and black. The reason why I was chosen by the principal to do the discipline was because everybody knew me. The whites and blacks knew me. And they felt that it would be done without any difference. In other words, what was good for one was good for the other. So I paddled whites. I paddled blacks. And those that didn't want to get paddled, I gave them the opportunity. I said, "Now, you take this paddling or you go home for three days." If they went home, I told them, "Now your parents have to bring you back."

So I had some of the white parents brought their children back same way as the blacks. So when they came back, those white parents told me, "Now if my child does wrong, I want you to tear them up."[20]

Lamar Beaty felt that the divvying up of discipline based on race ran counter to the intentions of desegregation. Beaty had two assistant principals—one white and one black—working with him at Pass Christian Junior/Senior High. He explained how he intentionally implemented a different approach to discipline at his school: "The first thing I told them was that there will be no you're white, you discipline the white kids. You're black, you discipline the black. No, Mr. Kirk [white AP] is to discipline grades 7 and 8, and Mr. Swanier [black AP], you've got 9 to 12. And I basically gave him all the discipline to transportation and few other minor things, and this freed me up to deal with primarily faculty and staff and everything."

The pervasive belief of the time was that principals should lead their schools with a heavy hand, albeit a "fair "hand. "No tolerance" policies, particularly toward fighting, were often adopted. John Allen Flynt met with his students at the still-segregated New Hebron right before Christmas break and clearly laid out the discipline policy: "If you get in a fight with a black student, then the two of you will be going home [meaning suspended]." Early on, his policy was tested. A white boy broke in front of a black student in the cafeteria line, and the black boy hit him. Flynt suspended both of them. The white boy never returned. Lamar Beaty faced a similar situation; however, he responded differently when a white boy, known as a troublemaker, decided on the first day of school to start a fight with a black student:

He picked the meanest, biggest black he could find and was going to whip him on the front campus one afternoon, and he got beat into the ground by this black kid. And I suspended the white kid, and I did not discipline the black, and oh Lord, the "you know what" hit the fan, but everybody said that John started it, and John admitted that he started it, so he got the punishment for it. And I had problems with that family the entire year.

Making judicious decisions about discipline often put white principals at odds with their white constituents who presumed they shared their racist beliefs. Flynt explains what happened when one of his white students refused to address his black teacher with a professional title: "Some were going to hold out. I had one boy that a teacher sent to my office, a white boy. He was not going to say Miss or Mr. to any black teacher. And I told him, 'Well go to your locker and get your books.' He said, 'What for?' I said, 'Well, you are going home. You can't go to school here if you're not going to show your teacher respect.' He said, 'Give me another chance.' So he went back to class." When Flynt opened the doors of his new school in January, a white parent offered to buy small Dixie drinking cups so black and white students would not have to drink out of the same water fountain. Flynt declined his offer, telling the father: "No need for that. We'll make it." When Larry Box was principal of Sudduth Elementary in Starkville, a white parent was furious that black children were touching his daughter's carrot-colored hair. Box felt the children were simply demonstrating natural, childlike curiosity. However, the father believed differently. He called Box one night and threatened him: "If you don't stop that, I'm going to be in the bushes outside your building with a gun, and I'm going to stop it."[21]

Two areas of discipline were of particular concern to black parents who felt their children were being unfairly targeted. The first was the classification of "weapons." Concerns about safety on school campuses meant that most discipline policies of the time contained a clause that students could be suspended for "possessing any object that could be classified as a weapon." This translated in many high schools to prohibitions against students bringing an Afro or pic comb to school. Fenton Peters, a principal in Starkville, explains: "A big Afro was the style at that time, and a pic comb was made of metal, so it was considered a weapon. So black kids could not bring a pic comb to school." This ban on one type of grooming tool while others were allowed (e.g., a hairbrush) appeared discriminatory toward black students. The second concern was the ban on facial hair. This was particularly problematic since many of the segregated black high schools in the late 1960s allowed students to wear beards, mustaches, and goatees, while white schools typically required male students to be "clean shaven." This conflict about personal taste and appearance led to a showdown between the white principal and forty-one black students at Riverside High School (Western Line School District) when the schools desegregated in 1970. The black students transferred to Riverside from O'Bannon and Glen Allan, where facial hair was permitted. However, the principal at Riverside implemented a "no facial hair" policy. He justified his decision as a way "to prevent students who deviate from 'normal' appearance from becoming 'distractions' from classroom work." In defiance of the Riverside policy and citing that mustaches were a symbol of black identity and pride, the black students refused to shave. The principal suspended all of them. Three students filed a lawsuit, and one week after their suspension, federal Judge William Keady ordered the reinstatement of the students and a "relaxing" of the enforcement of such dress codes, citing no evidence that facial hair was an academic disruption. In nearby Greenville High School, a similar incident occurred in which a former Coleman High student was suspended for refusing to shave.[22]

Defiance of school dress codes was not unique to southern school districts undergoing desegregation in the late 1960s and 1970s. This was the height of the student protest movement, and students from California to Chicago to New York fought for the right to wear longer hair, black armbands to protest the Vietnam War, and for girls to wear shorter dresses and pants. Judges throughout the country adjudicated dozens of dress code and "hair cases," often with conflicting rulings.[23] But the regulations against facial hair and the classification of Afro combs as weapons were not merely fights about adolescents' rights to freedom of expression; in newly desegregated schools in the South, these were racially charged conflicts spawned by deeply ingrained beliefs and fears about black masculinity and black power, which played out in the disciplinary policies adopted in many schools.

Disintegration: The Loss of Black Principals

In the segregated South, black educators held an esteemed position within their communities as middle-class professionals with status and some semblance of financial security. Black principals were particularly revered, as they held one of the few positions of power and leadership available to blacks during Jim Crow and often served as liaisons between the black and white communities as described by Frederick Rodgers:

> The principal was the man who ran the school and, in many cases, the Black community. His influence in community affairs was almost without exception great. He was, therefore, central in community life and was indeed more knowledgeable about what was going on than anyone else. Also, as head of the Black high school, he had a role in the white power structure as well. This usually put him in the position of knowing more about the larger community than any other Black in the Black community. He was often the only Black with whom influential members of the white community had anything approaching professional contact.[24]

However, with school desegregation in Mississippi, the black principal was almost entirely eliminated, which would be one of the most detrimental consequences of school desegregation.[25]

In 1970 the National Education Association (NEA) commissioned a task force to study the effects of school desegregation in seventy school districts in Mississippi and Louisiana. What they discovered was, indeed, bleak: "[W]hat is happening in Louisiana and Mississippi schools is not *integration*; rather, it is *disintegration*—the near total disintegration of black authority in every area of the system of public education."[26] The task force described four ways in which black principals had lost their status and authority:

Outright demotion
"Phasing Down" of the Black Principals' Schools (i.e., closing Black schools)
Retention of Title with Diminution of Authority
Paper promotion[27]

The loss of black principals was not only devastating to individuals who lost their jobs, their livelihoods, and their authority, but it was equally demoralizing to the black community as further indication that the school desegregation for which many had fought so valiantly would extol a grave price on black individuals and the black community.

According to 1970 NEA testimony before a Senate Committee, 5,000 principals and teachers in southern states either lost their jobs or were demoted as a result of desegregation.[28] According to James Haney, between 1967 and 1970, "the number of black principals in North Carolina dropped from 620 to 170, in Alabama from 250 to 40, and Mississippi lost almost all of its 250 black principals."[29] While exact figures are difficult to confirm, plenty of anecdotal data exists to confirm Adam Fairclough's poignant assertion that the "main casualties of integration were the black schools and the men who had run them."[30] In Rankin County, a black principal was demoted to administrative assistant to the white principal at the school where the black principal was formerly in charge. In Hinds County, a black principal with more than twenty years of experience was demoted to a classroom teacher, and in Winston County, the black principals demoted to assistant principals were "in name only with no authority."[31] In Houston (Chickasaw County), Warren Cousin was demoted from principal to assistant principal in 1970–71, despite having ten years of experience as a principal. In 1975 his assistant principal position was eliminated, and the school district failed to assign him to a principal position.[32] In his 1971 senior thesis analyzing the immediate effects of the *Alexander* ruling, Luther Munford offered additional examples. In Covington County, a black principal with a degree from Cornell was demoted to "administrative assistant" in the new high school when his school become a junior high; a black high school principal in Leake County was made co-principal but assigned to oversee the "black side" of the building; and a black high school principal in Franklin County became an elementary principal.[33] The underlying reason why black principals lost their jobs during school desegregation was succinctly explained in a 1969 article in the *Chicago Tribune* about the attempted demotion of the black high school principal in Humphreys County (MS) to assistant principal at his own school: "It's traditional in Mississippi that no Negro has authority over any white." [34]

Fenton Peters was in his second year as the principal of Henderson High School, the only black high school in Starkville, when the Starkville city schools were court-ordered to desegregate in 1970. He was quick to correct the usage of the term "desegregation" to explain the events: "The term is *court-ordered* desegregation. Had it not been court ordered it probably would not have happened till this very day . . . the powers that be at that time had to have a scapegoat to lean on and say 'they made me do it,' and that's how it got done." Peters was not chosen to be the principal of Starkville High. He was, however, appointed principal at Armstrong Middle School. A newspaper reporter at the time interviewed him because, according to the reporter, he was one of only a handful of black principals leading integrated schools in Mississippi during the first year of desegregation.

As the principal of Henderson High School, Fenton Peters had status and power in the black community. Well-respected by the superintendent, Peters was part of the administrative council comprised of all the principals who met regularly with the superintendent during initial discussions about how to implement desegregation. Nevertheless, when the superintendent and his close allies were working out the desegregation plan for Starkville city schools, which included the closing of Henderson High, where Peters was principal, he had little clout. He noted, "None of our recommendations—when I say 'us' I mean black people at that time—they took very few recommendations from us. Most of them came from the white community." His main charge during the planning phase was to disseminate information about the desegregation process to the black community, many of whom were incensed about the proposed closing of their beloved high school. Eventually, the superintendent decided to convert Henderson High to a junior high, rather than close it. Peters found himself in the middle of this tension—being a spokesperson for the black community but having to take orders from the white power structure. In 1976 Peters was appointed principal at Starkville High, the first black principal at the high school and one of the few black men leading desegregated high schools at the time. Despite his reputation in the community as a strong educational leader, many whites were not pleased with his appointment, and he soon became the target of their wrath. Peters explained:

> About two, three months into my tenure that first year, the house rumbled, shook. I went to the back and looked—smoke everywhere. My mailbox has been blown

up. Of course, I called the sheriff, and they came out and didn't see anybody. A couple of days later, I put a new mailbox, and it rumbled again, shook the house. This time, it was found down near the intersection. The sheriff and I were personal friends. A mailbox is federal property. The sheriff called the FBI. I told the sheriff that that sounds like dynamite, but he said, "Fenton, that is nothing but a cherry bomb." I said, "No, a cherry bomb doesn't shake the house." I asked the FBI agent, "What do you think caused this?" and he said, "Probably a blasting cap and a third stick of dynamite."

Charles Nash was one of the few black men appointed lead principal during the first year of massive desegregation. Nash was twenty years old when he began teaching science in the segregated school system of his hometown of McComb. During his second year of teaching, he was appointed assistant principal of Burglund High School, the segregated black high school in McComb; two years later, in 1968, he was appointed principal of West Brook Elementary School. Nash was part of a team of teachers who traveled to Stanford (CA) the summer of 1967 as part of an innovative program to bring distance learning to the children of McComb. The supervisor of the Stanford program recommended Nash to be the director of the program back in McComb. However, Superintendent Julian Prince did not offer him the job. According to Nash, Prince did not think McComb would accept a black man in a districtwide leadership position: "The time wasn't right for them to choose me to direct this system-wide activity, so instead of giving me that job as coordinator, [Prince] offered me the job as principal of West Brook Elementary School, so that's how I got to be a principal."[35]

When full-scale desegregation took place in McComb in 1971, Nash was appointed principal of Hughes Elementary School, the school for all first-graders in McComb. It was a significantly symbolic appointment in a town with a violent racial past.[36] Every first grader in McComb would have as their first exposure to a principal—a young, black man. He describes his first year as a positive experience for him, his students, and their parents: "It was the best year I have ever had since I've been in the academic area. Most often I would be at the entry to welcome the children to school in the mornings. They didn't see me as the black principal, and the parents, apparently it didn't bother them. The black children would come up and hug the principal, and the little white children would come up and hug the principal." Nash was principal for one year before deciding to make a major change in his professional career. Two factors contributed to that decision. One, in devising the hierarchy of leadership in the newly desegregated McComb schools, the superintendent created the position of "supervising principal," to which all the elementary school principals reported. This position lessened the power and authority of the school building principals, which Nash said rubbed him the wrong way. According to the 1970 NEA Task Force report, these types of new positions were created in many districts in Louisiana and Mississippi: "In a number of districts visited, . . . various new positions, held by whites, have been created since desegregation. These positions held such titles as 'area principal,' 'supervising principal' and 'curriculum coordinator.' It is widely believed by blacks that these newly titled whites constitute the real authority behind the black principals, who have been reduced to a more figure head status."[37] Nash also felt he was not getting paid enough for the job he was doing. He asked Superintendent Prince for a raise: "We had a very nice conversation. We always had a great relationship, and he said, "Charles, I understand. I hear what you are saying, but I'm already paying you as much as I'm paying the most experienced principal in the school district, and he named the person who was that." He returned from his meeting and called Dr. Leonard McCullough at Mississippi State. McCullough had contacted him earlier about enrolling in a doctoral program and working for the Mississippi Educational Services Center, whose purpose was to help schools through the desegregation transition. Nash told McCullough that he was ready for the new challenge, and two weeks later, he packed his car and headed to Starkville.

When Nash was appointed principal at Hughes Elementary, he already held a master's degree, which served him well during the transition to desegregated schools because academic credentials were often used as justification in the throes of hastily devised desegregation plans for promoting young, white assistant principals to principals. When Lamar Beaty was appointed principal at Pass Christian, his superintendent told him, "Don't come back to Pass Christian in August without your master's, because if you do, we won't have a job for you." Beaty traveled to Mississippi State to complete his master's degree. Later, he learned the reason behind the superintendent's order: "I didn't know it at the time, but there was a gentleman at the black school who had been there longer than I had in the system, but he did not have a master's degree, but I think they felt like if I didn't have a master's degree, they would have to offer it to him." The demotion to assistant principal was a bitter pill for many black principals to swallow, often serving under a principal with far less experience and sometimes at the same schools where a year earlier they had served as principal. Certainly, many white principals and black assistant principals were able to forge professional relationships and work collaboratively and cooperatively through the desegregation process. Indeed, in many communities, the white superintendents and principals desperately needed their black assistant principals to help smooth the transition into desegregated schools. They were expected to serve as the bridge between the black students and the white principals as well as between the white superintendents and school boards and the black community. Charles George was one of many black principals in Mississippi who served as an assistant principal during school desegregation, and in that role was vital to the smooth transition to school desegregation in his community.

George graduated from Tougaloo College in 1957. Shortly thereafter he received a call from the superintendent of West Tallahatchie offering him not only a job teaching but also the position of principal of the elementary school, so right out of college he became both a teacher and principal. Three years later the superintendent appointed him assistant principal at Tutwiler High School, the black high school. In 1969 with court-enforced desegregation looming, the superintendent met with George and his principal to solicit their help in implementing a peaceful transition to desegregated schools in their district. According to George, they devised a strategy to help get their community on board:

> My principal and I came to the conclusion that the best thing for us to do is sit down, select some influential people in the black community and some influential whites, and let's have a dialogue. We selected a black person from every community where we had a school. We had five school districts and we pulled five blacks from those districts. So we sat down and had dialogue and he explained to them that integration was here. It wasn't a thing that had been spoken of and what hadn't been done, but it's here. So we went back to our different schools and began talking to our teachers and students.

George met with his teachers, telling them, "if you think you aren't going to be able to work in an integrated situation, we want you to say 'yes' now and then you may go seek employment someplace else." No black teachers left. However, when principals were appointed to the newly desegregated schools, no black principals in West Tallahatchie remained as the head of a school. George explains, "The superintendent decided that it would be more successful as far as integration was concerned if that head person were white." He was appointed the assistant principal. Charles George was not promoted to principal until 1980.

George Dale, who was principal of Magnolia Junior High in Moss Point, gives much credit to his assistant principal, Inez Green, for the success they had the first year despite the tension citywide surrounding school desegregation. When a riot broke out at the high school, it was Mrs. Green that ensured no violence spilled over to the junior high. Dale explains:

The best thing that happened to me was that in my new job as principal of Magnolia Junior High, he gave me an assistant—a black lady by the name of Inez Green. Mrs. Green had been a guidance counselor at the black high school. A delightful lady who pretty much ran the black Methodist church. She knew everybody in the black community. The day of the riot at the high school—since we were in the black community—the black kids were leaving the campus in droves, and white parents were getting up there to pick up their kids. Mrs. Green, my assistant, walked in front of the campus, and as the black high school kids were coming down the street to the black neighborhood where our school was located, she said to them, "Get on down the road! Don't the first one of you get on this campus. Get on down the road, and go to your house." And we had nobody come on our campus.

Charles George, Dr. Charles Nash, and Dr. Fenton Peters went on to have very successful careers in education. Charles George and Dr. Fenton Peters both served as superintendents later in their careers. In 1997, Dr. Peters received the Education Hall of Fame award presented by the Greater Starkville Development Partnership. After Charles George retired, he served on the West Tallahatchie School Board. Today the school district's office is housed in the Charles M. George Facility for Educational Services. Dr. Charles Nash now serves as the vice chancellor for academic and student affairs at the University of Alabama system. In 2008, he was inducted into the McComb High Hall of Fame. However, their inclusion here should not be read as the norm or as a story that with a little time, all turns out well. For every George, Peters, and Nash, there were dozens of black principals who never regained their position or status in the community. As well documented, school boards across the South closed black high schools or converted them into junior high or elementary schools. Schools that had been named for black teachers or historical figures were given new names (e.g., Rosa A. Temple in Vicksburg was changed to Vicksburg Junior High). Black principals were demoted or given meaningless titles. As Dr. Peters poignantly noted as he described the many losses brought about by school desegregation, "They gave us desegregation, but they gave it to us on their terms, so it didn't turn out like we thought it was going to be."

The "Average Joe" Doing What Had to Be Done

Many principals, like Charles Boone, found the changes brought about through school desegregation professionally stimulating. As Boone declared,

"I like a challenge. So I was excited just as though it was my first football game of the year. I knew it had to be done, and I knew God was on my side. And I didn't see how I could lose." For ambitious black men, like Charles George, they had to wait years before they were appointed principal. Many others were never given the chance to prove themselves as administrators in charge of their own school. A number of principals simply quit, retired, or sought employment in other fields. For many who stayed, it took a tremendous emotional and physical toil. Leo Salter, the principal at Neshoba Central High School, suffered a stroke at a Rotary Club meeting while discussing upcoming desegregation efforts. He was hospitalized for several weeks. When released, he went straight back to work, telling everyone, "We are going to have school." Salter's health continued to deteriorate, and over a period of five years, he had four strokes. Unable to endure the physical stresses of the job, he retired in 1973. As his son, Sid Salter, notes, "integration physically took all the starch out of him." Sid is proud of how his father handled school desegregation and argues that principals and teachers, like his own parents, have been sorely overlooked for their role in moving the ideal of equal educational opportunity into the reality of integrated schools.

My dad got the bronze star, but if you asked me what I was proudest of about my father's life; it's not D-Day. It's January 1970 because he was able to go into the cauldron and have school. Did he do it perfectly? No. Did he make mistakes? Yes. Was some of it luck? Absolutely. He'd tell you the same. There was nothing exceptional about my parents. They were just average Joe schoolteachers, and there were hundreds of people just like that who should get the credit for that whole exercise working. Not the politicians but the black and white small-town Educators (capital E educators) who decided to have school.

Chapter 5

Love, Hope, and Fear
Teachers Guiding Desegregation

In the fall of 1967, Harriet DeCell Kuykendall and JoAnne Prichard Morris, both white teachers in the segregated Yazoo City School system, began team-teaching a high school humanities/social science course. The idea for the class began as a lark of two teachers who were bored in a workshop they did not want to attend. Harriet explained:

> I didn't want to take the class. It was just a waste of time. I didn't need it, and I went to the superintendent, and I said, "I've already had it in my course of study," and he said, "We can't let you off because we are not going to let any black teacher off, so you have to do it." So JoAnne and I were sitting on the back row, and we were almost being rude to the nice man who was teaching the class and leading us into writing the course of study. At one point, he came back to see what we were doing on the very back row, and because we didn't want to be rude to him, we began to make things up, and we said we were writing the perfect class, and it's a mixture of English and history because she [JoAnne] taught English, and I was teaching history at the time. He said, "That's a good idea, just keep on writing."[1]

Their concocted class morphed into an experiment; they would teach the course in the morning to all white students at Yazoo City High School and then repeat the course in the afternoon to the black students at N. D. Taylor High.

JoAnne and Harriet's experiment was met with skepticism and resistance from some of the black teachers at N. D. Taylor. Harriet was a veteran teacher with close to twenty years of experience. JoAnne was a fairly new teacher, but both were part of the established white power structure of Yazoo City. Harriet was the wife of newly elected state senator Herman DeCell, and JoAnne's husband, a Harvard graduate, worked as the assistant to the president of the Mississippi Chemical Corporation. When they arrived at N. D. Taylor on the first day of class, a teacher pulled them into the principal's office and prof-fered this frank warning: "You women need to know right now that we're not going to tell you the truth. Black people are not going to tell you the truth."[2] JoAnne understood his message. Black teachers might greet them with polite triviality ("We're so glad to have you here"), but a veneer of distrust simmered beneath that civil façade. Their mere presence as "volunteer" teachers teach-ing a class they created reflected the long-standing inequities and power rela-tions between black and white teachers in the school system. It was a privilege no black teacher would ever have—to create a new course with little or no input from anyone, team-taught with a friend and colleague, and be trusted with the freedom to travel from school to school.

While the class originated accidentally, JoAnne and Harriet were dedi-cated to it and to the students at both schools. It was also an adventure to them, a foray into uncharted territory that held an element of excitement. In April 1968, when word got out that the black students were planning a march in response to the assassination of Dr. Martin Luther King Jr., one of JoAnne's black students called her and warned her not to come to the school that day. The principal at Yazoo City High was also fearful for them and sent Harriet a note: "Do not leave campus today." Harriet and JoAnne ignored his warning, as Harriet explained: "So we hid in the ladies' room, so we couldn't be found, and we usually waited until one o'clock to go, but this time, we left at twelve and had lunch elsewhere, and then we went to that class." Their volunteering to "integrate" the black school with this two-hour class also served an instru-mental purpose for the superintendent and school board. It gave them evi-dence to present to the HEW that their district was cooperating with school desegregation mandates. JoAnne recalls, "I don't know how many times Mr. Kelly [the superintendent] said, 'Y'all saved my neck.'" He then left them alone to teach the class as they wanted with the caveat, "As long as I don't hear about you at the post office, do what you want to do."

Like many white teachers thrust into school desegregation, their experi-ence at N. D. Taylor High transformed Harriet and JoAnne's attitudes about segregation. Harriet explained:

> I went over there thinking that separate but equal could work and that what you had to do was to make certain that the black school was as well run and was challenging to students as well as the white school because we had a good school in Yazoo City. Once I got into the school over there teaching, I realized it was impossible—that there was not any way that you were going to turn that school around without having white students in it because the presence of white people was going to be very important.

Teaching in both schools, they saw firsthand the inequities between the two. Beyond the noticeable discrepancies in textbooks, resources, and equipment, other less obvious differences surfaced. For example, at Yazoo City High, students could take chorus as an elective course that met every day. Such an elective was not available for the students at N. D. Taylor, where they had an outstanding choir. Instead, the choir teacher pulled students from their core classes to prepare for shows and competitions. According to Harriet, "Promptly, we went to the superintendent and said, 'She needs a class period,' and the next year, she got it." During court-enforced desegregation a few years later, Harriet and JoAnne became part of the Friends of Public School movement in Yazoo City, a campaign launched by white business leaders to support public schools in their community.

However, the role of white teachers in desegregating schools is not a monolithic narrative, nor does it always end in the transformation of teachers' heads and hearts. Indeed, many white teachers left the public schools at the first sign of desegregation. According to one report, one thousand of the twenty-three thousand public school teachers in Mississippi quit in the spring of 1970, many of them to teach in the new private academies.[3] The exodus of white teachers was greatest in the school districts where white students also left the public schools en mass, most notably in the Delta. In Indianola (Sunflower County), thirty-nine teachers resigned in spring 1970, leaving only two white teachers in the entire system. In the small town of Pickens (Holmes County), the entire faculty of seven white teachers resigned. In Coahoma County, one-third of the white teaching force left in February 1970 when school desegregation was enforced there.[4] In Tunica, nineteen white teachers resigned in January 1970 to teach at the newly formed Tunica Church School, a private academy that did not charge any tuition the first semester. These former public school teachers received their full semester pay from the Tunica County School Board.[5] As discussed in chapter 2, some of the white teachers who stayed treated their black students intolerably, addressing them with derogatory names, isolating them from the rest of the class, and encouraging white students to harass them. Others looked the other way as their black students suffered innumerable abuses, like a white teacher in Rankin County who sat silently by while in his classroom the white students poured syrup over a black student's head.[6]

Unlike many white teachers who had other teaching options, black teachers were completely dependent upon their local public schools for employment. However, they, too, approached school desegregation in various ways. Many celebrated it as the culmination of a long-awaited victory begun in 1954. Others were more wary, worried about their own job security and the education of their students in a potentially unwelcome, if not outright hostile, learning environment. They worried that the white teachers replacing them at the segregated black schools would not be as committed, compassionate, or concerned as they. Many black teachers outright balked at leaving their segregated schools, and others were anxious that the gross inequities inherent in segregated school systems would put them and their students at a disadvantage in a desegregated school system with, in many cases, higher academic standards and expectations.

However, the majority of teachers, both black and white, stayed. Undoubtedly, many did so because in small-town Mississippi jobs were scarce. They needed a job and were not willing or able to compromise their and their family's financial livelihoods. But many remained because they viewed teaching as their calling and were determined to work through school desegregation despite the many obstacles. Superintendents and schools board members hashed out desegregation plans with judges and the federal government, and principals took those orders and implemented them in their local schools. However, it would fall on the shoulders of teachers, more than any other adults, to determine how they and their students would live and learn together in the intimate space of the integrated classroom. As Dalton McAlpin, a young white teacher assigned in 1970 to a formerly all-black school in Jackson, reflected, "We had school, and learning occurred. It was tense for a while for sure, but we just kind of kept going, just trying to have school."[7]

Coercion and the Luck of the Draw: Teacher Assignment during Desegregation

Lillie V. Davis was born and reared in Quitman County in the Mississippi Delta. A child of sharecroppers, Lillie graduated in 1947 as the valedictorian of the first high school graduating class from Marks Industrial High School. In 1957, she graduated from Rust College in Holly Springs and began teaching in the segregated schools in her hometown. By 1969, she was a seasoned teacher with a reputation of being a good, but firm, teacher. Lillie had heard rumblings about some black teachers being sent to Marks High (the white school) as part of the school desegregation plan. Lillie did not want to be one of those sent to the white school under the auspices of integrating the schools. So, Lillie spent the summer of 1969 deliberately avoiding the superintendent. However, one day his secretary managed to out-maneuver her. When she was at the courthouse for an unrelated matter, the superintendent's secretary cornered her.

"The superintendent wants to see you," she told Lillie.

"About what?" Lillie asked.

The secretary replied, "You know what."

Once inside his office, the superintendent informed Lillie that if she wanted to continue being employed in Quitman County, she would be teaching second grade at Marks High (which housed grades 1–12) in the fall. Not one to back down, Lillie told the superintendent, "I'll go because I don't want my children to go, and I know I don't have any choice. You white people are vicious. You believe in killing black folks. That's why I don't want to go."[8]

Lillie was concerned about the black students she would be leaving behind, whose educational and psychological needs were clearly not driving decisions about how to implement desegregation. Such decisions were made first and foremost for the benefit of white students. Who was looking out for the interests and needs of black students? This was a paramount question for Lillie as she was forced to leave her children to the care of teachers, most likely white and inexperienced, who she thought would not love, teach, or understand her black students as she had. She explains:

> I liked where I was. I enjoyed teaching where I was. I was satisfied where I was. I would teach any children, but I would rather have been over there because nobody understands how to teach black children but black people. And I knew that I would be able to help my black children, and I knew they needed a lot of help. White teachers don't really understand our black children and how to teach them. They think that black children can't learn, their knowledge is limited; they have a poor home environment, their parents are ignorant; they are uneducated.

When the schools opened in August 1969, Lillie Davis was one of four black teachers teaching in predominantly white classrooms at Marks High.

Maye Dee Martin found herself in a similar situation in Cleveland (MS) in 1968. Maye Dee was not a native of Mississippi. She moved to Cleveland from Texas in 1954 and began teaching in 1957 in a segregated school in which black students had a split session built around the cotton-picking season. In 1968, Maye Dee and four other black teachers were chosen to teach in the predominantly white schools as part of the district's desegregation plan. Two of the teachers were assigned to teach only handwriting and spelling; one taught home economics at Cleveland High; another was a librarian who rotated among three schools. Maye Dee explained why they were given these teaching assignments: "They didn't think blacks knew too much about teaching or being a teacher." However, Maye Dee was assigned to teach reading. She is not sure why: "perhaps because I came here with a master's degree." According to Maye Dee, there was another reason why these five teachers were chosen to be the first to integrate the white schools: "We had fair skin and nice hair and had been in the school system for several years. Dr. Morris [the superintendent] knew us all. I guess you could refuse if you wanted to, but they chose who they wanted. Nobody too black."

Black teachers, like Lillie and Maye Dee, were pawns in their school system's efforts to implement court-enforced desegregation plans, which often began with faculty integration. Indeed, as late as 1969, many school districts were still clinging to the hope that school desegregation could be accommodated with some carefully selected black teachers at white schools (and vice versa) and the continuation of FOC to desegregate white schools with a few black students. Their superintendents specifically handpicked Lillie and Maye Dee to integrate the white schools because they were good teachers. As Lillie noted, "They wanted the best teachers to teach *their* children." They had little say about their transfer; neither felt that refusing was an option. Cyndie Harrison, on the other hand, was not coerced or even strongly persuaded to be one of the only white teachers teaching at Central High, a black school in the Oxford City School system. Fresh out of college with an English degree and no other job prospects, Cyndie eagerly accepted the only job offer she received in fall 1969.[9]

Like Lillie Davis, Cyndie Harrison was born and reared in the Mississippi Delta. But their worlds were vastly different. Cyndie, who graduated from Ruleville High in 1964, could attend the college of her choice. When she chose Millsaps College, her grandmother was mortified. She believed, according to Cyndie, that there was "a communist behind every bush at Millsaps." She graduated in 1968 with a degree in English. Cyndie did not immediately find a teaching job, so she worked for one year as a receptionist. In 1969, she moved to Oxford so that her then-husband could attend graduate school at the University of Mississippi. Her father-in-law, through a Rotary Club connection, arranged for her to meet with the superintendent of the Oxford city schools. Much to her disappointment, he told her that he had no openings for an English teacher. Cyndie was relentless, "I really, really wanted to teach"—to which he said, "Well, I need a ninth-grade English teacher over at the colored school." Cyndie jumped at the opportunity.

Immediately after securing the job at Central High, Cyndie drove to the school to meet the principal, who informed her of a meeting the following day for all the teachers. He quickly added that she was not required to attend, which troubled Cyndie. She wanted to fit in, and she did not want to be treated differently because she was white. So the next day she walked into the Central High auditorium where she received her first glimpse into the inequalities of black schools—rows with no seats in them and seats with no backs or bottoms. She eyed a group of teachers congregated in the front row. She wanted to join them, but all the usable seats were taken, so she sat a few rows over, segregated from the black teachers. She soon discovered the rest of the school was in equally bad repair: worn, musty-smelling furniture; no air conditioning, no ceiling fans; torn blinds, wooden floors that bounced; a teacher's lounge with one couch and no chairs. She wandered into the library and was horrified to find that many of the shelves were totally empty. The holdings were scant, and in a high school library, she found elementary-aged books such as *Brim's Boat* and Maurice Sendak's picture book *A Is for Alligator.*

Because very few employed white teachers volunteered to transfer to black schools, superintendents had to rely on new hires, like Cyndie Harrison, to fill racial faculty quotas at black schools. The assignment of Cyndie to a black school and Lillie and Maye Dee to white schools during the early implementation phases of massive school desegregation illustrates three significant findings of the 1970 National Education Association (NEA) Task Force, created to study the progress of school desegregation in Mississippi and Louisiana:

1. Consistently, school officials transfer the most highly qualified blacks to formerly all-white schools, while replacing them in the formerly all-black schools with the least qualified whites in training and experience.
2. Black teachers are assigned to such subjects as Physical Education, Social Studies, Home Economics, and Shop, while white teachers are assigned Language Arts, Math, and Science . . . Apparently, the subject assignment of black teachers is based less upon their qualifications than upon the particular racial taboo of each white community.
3. In some districts, it was reported, white teachers are asked to transfer and are given the option to refuse, whereas black teachers are told; their alternative is dismissal.[10]

Superintendents were the final arbiters in hiring and assigning teachers. In many school districts, they assumed a very hands-on approach to doing so. In other districts, superintendents delegated the responsibilities of teacher assignment to their white principals. However, in some school districts forced to devise desegregation plans immediately, a rather unconventional method was adopted: the use of a lottery. In December 1969, Dr. John Martin, superintendent of the Jackson Municipal Separate District, announced a two-pronged approach to achieve faculty integration in his district. They would first ask for voluntary transfers. After that, "names of teachers would be drawn in a lottery to decide teachers transferred." Exempt were teachers within eighteen months of being sixty-five, the age of compulsory retirement.[11] Martin further declared a four-day holiday for students to "shuffle the teachers." The new semester would begin on February 2, 1970, with the new assignments of teachers. Martin declared the lottery a success in that only twelve to fifteen white teachers resigned rather than transfer to schools in black neighborhoods. However, he concluded, "The teacher reassignment plan, based on a lottery was the most difficult, most unpleasant and the most distasteful job I have ever done in my life."[12] Six months later Martin resigned his post as superintendent.

Dalton McAlpin was a second-year teacher at Callaway Junior/Senior High in Jackson when he read Martin's announcement in the paper. He and several of his fellow teachers attended the lottery held on the stage at Provine High School. Dalton describes the strangeness of the method for those of them standing around watching: "It was like picking ping pong balls out of this thing, like a lottery. I stayed for probably an hour because you really couldn't tell what was what. They weren't calling out names; they were just picking balls with numbers on them. So we couldn't figure it out, so we left." Two days later Dalton received a letter with his new assignment: Jim Hill High School, one of the formerly all-black schools.

In many ways teacher assignment by lottery was a game of chance, not clearly understood but with the odds (i.e., not being transferred) heavily skewed in favor of veteran teachers. When the Starkville City School system used a lottery system to determine teacher assignments in January 1970, they devised an intricate procedure for how many "chances" one would have in the lottery. For example, teachers with three years or less teaching experience had three "chances" in the lottery, while teachers with more than seven years of experience had only one chance. Teachers within eighteen months of retirement were exempt from the lottery as were principals, special education teachers, coaches, teachers who were already teaching in a school where they were the minority, and individuals with key assignments that could not be transferred because the assignment did not exist in another school.[13] To ensure that all lottery procedures were followed, and that all was fair and upfront on the day of the lottery, the Starkville School Board appointed a monitoring committee. Larry Box, a principal in Starkville, describes the logistics of the lottery:

> They borrowed a bingo machine from the local country club, and they took all the white second-grade teachers at Overstreet, for example, and assigned them a bingo—B1, B2, whatever. They developed a rubric of experience and degrees. And

you got assigned a number of bingo balls based on that. The net result being the more degrees you had and the more experience you had, you might not have but one ball in the machine. If you were a beginning teacher with a BS and no experience, you might have four balls. The more experience you had, the less chance you were going to be picked. And they would turn the machine on, and whatever ball came out of the bingo machine, they would look and say, "Well, that's so-and so."[14]

Hinds County also used a lottery system to assign teachers in the first semester after the *Alexander* ruling, but teacher assignment based on a lottery system was short-lived. As school systems, like Jackson and Starkville, scurried to comply with student desegregation in the fall of 1970, they developed alternative ways of hiring, placing, and transferring teachers, which led, in many districts, to the dismissal, demotion, or displacement of many black teachers.

"Martyrs in the Crusade": Black Teachers and School Desegregation

Writing long before the *Alexander* ruling, Willard Gandy opined in a 1962 article in the *Journal of Negro Education* that "the Negro teachers might very well be martyrs in the crusade to desegregate the schools."[15] His ominous words would come to fruition in Mississippi and elsewhere in the South. According to a report published in 1970 by the American Friends Service Committee, 462 black teachers were fired or did not have their contracts renewed in the 127 southern school districts visited for their study.[16] Willie Morris was one of the first to document the loss of black teachers in Mississippi in the aftermath of the *Alexander* ruling: "Fifteen per cent of the black teachers in the state who were teaching in 1969 did not have jobs in 1970 . . . In 26 school districts in Mississippi, 800 new teachers were hired in 1970. Of these, only 158, or 19.7 per cent, were black."[17] In a study of the effects of desegregation on teachers in Mississippi from 1970 through 1973, Bobby Jean Cooper reported an increase of almost 9 percent in the number of white teachers as compared to an almost 12 percent decrease in the number of black teachers.[18]

According to the 1970 NEA Task Force, black teachers were displaced using three primary methods: (1) dismissals and nonrenewals, (2) discriminatory assignments and transfer practices, and (3) the use of newly devised "qualification standards."[19] Identifying the "displacement of black educators" as one of the major problems of desegregation, the task force provided a terse explanation for the dismissal of so many black teachers: "white racism."[20] Gandy ends his 1962 article with a similar insight: "[T]he area of greatest difficulty is in the attitudes and mores of the Southern people . . . Attitudes, intense in nature and reinforced by the culture, will prove very difficult to alter."[21] The "attitude" to which Gandy refers was the prevalent belief among whites that black teachers were not academically strong enough to teach white children. This belief was articulated in two ways. The first was explicitly racist and steeped in the ideology of white supremacy; that is, black teachers were believed to be innately less intelligent than white teachers. The second reason (and the one most likely to be expressed publicly) was that black teachers were *not* innately less intelligent than white teachers; however, because of the vestiges of Jim Crow and years of denied opportunities in segregated schools, blacks were viewed as culturally and educationally disadvantaged. As a result of their "cultural and educational deprivation," they not only lacked the academic credentials and specialized training needed to teach white students, but they were also less "worldly" in terms of exposure to art, music, language, and other forms of high capital markers.[22] Newspapers of the time were rife with references to the concerns of white parents about the teaching capabilities of black teachers. For example, the *Leland Press* reported the following in a 1969 article: "[Whites] believe, rightly or wrongly, that black students are basically inferior to white students in aptitudes and educational achievement levels. More than that, they consider black teachers as being far below the abilities of white teachers of equivalent training."[23]

Dr. Charles Nash, who began his educational career as a teacher and then a principal in the McComb city schools in the 1960s, is quick to offer a rebuttal to claims about the educational and cultural deficiencies of black teachers. He notes that precisely because black teachers were barred at the time from pursuing advanced degrees from the University of Mississippi, Mississippi State, and the University of Southern Mississippi, they sought opportunities out of state for educational advancement, often in large cities and in universities with much better reputations than those locally. Nash recounts:

> The best teachers in McComb during this time were black teachers. I'm going to make this claim. The black teachers, the Ratcliff's, the Tobias's, the Clay's—these people had degrees from Indiana and New York University and places like this. Back then black schools in the South did not have graduate degrees, so black teachers were given a stipend, by law, so they could study out of state to get their master's degrees. So they would go during the summer, and after two or three summers, they'd earn their master's degrees, and they'd come back. I had a bunch of those folk. Now I'm not saying that Ole Miss didn't do good, quality teaching preparation at the master's level, but it was probably not as good in those days as was Indiana or New York University. Those people were very sophisticated; they

were very well learned; they brought us not just mathematics, English, and history; they brought a lot more than that to the community.[24]

Fenton Peters, a black principal in the Starkville city schools, recalls an incident when such assumptions about black teachers were challenged by the results of a teacher training workshop offered at both the black and white high schools in Starkville:

> A couple of instructors from Mississippi State came over and taught an extension course on the Henderson [black school] campus. Some of their counterparts went to Starkville High School and taught the same course. Turned out that some of our people at Henderson scored as well or better than some of them [the white teachers] did and, of course, they got themselves in a little bit of hot water by saying that some of them over there [the black teachers] are as good as y'all are. That did not set well with some of the powers that were at that time. They were not supposed to say that. That was *not* supposed to happen.[25]

In addressing a predominantly black readership, Emma Bragg in a 1963 article in the *Journal of Negro Education* challenged the prevailing attitudes about the superiority of white teachers while also acknowledging that black teachers had been denied professional development opportunities readily available to white teachers. She argued that, in the course of school desegregation, the lack of such opportunities might disadvantage black teachers forced to compete with white teachers for jobs. Bragg wrote:

> We as teachers may be equal and in some instances superior in the *extent* of academic training as compared with our non-Negro counterparts, but do we have the quality of experience which does not appear on the academic transcript and which has been the privilege of the non-Negro teacher? Have we had the opportunity for world travel? . . . Have we had the opportunity for workshops, seminars, conferences under sponsorship of the influential and rich foundations?"[26]

Bragg noted that these "qualitative differences in professional preparation" were the reason for the differences in the comparative scores between black and white teachers on the National Teachers Examination (NTE) in which whites on average earned higher scores. By the end of the 1960s, school systems throughout the South increasingly began requiring teachers to take the Graduate Record Exam (GRE) or NTE as part of the hiring or retention process. They then used the scores on these standardized tests as justification for the dismissal or non-hiring of black teachers.

In April 1968, the Starkville City School system adopted Policy 13–69, which required all teachers, including those already working for the school system, to achieve a certain score on the GRE or to have a master's degree in hand. According to Fenton Peters, the intent of this policy was clear and extremely effective in getting rid of black teachers:

> It was a tool for elimination because it was felt—this is a racial thing—the inferiority of black people compared to white. We had to resign and reapply for our jobs, meeting the new criteria that had been set forth by the school board and superintendent and it was to make a certain score on the GRE. It turned out that the lawyers who helped to handle our case found out that only about (I believe I am right) 5 percent of blacks scored that score, so it became very evident what that was for from the start. Well, we went ahead. You had to take the test or else you had to enroll in a graduate school and get a master's degree in a certain length of time, and, of course, couple all of those things together and weeding out about 50 percent of the black teachers . . . There was a time when I was going into the central office file to look at probable teachers and could not find a black one in there, and if I found one, it had been marked "could not meet the criteria." That left no doubt in our minds what was going on. That was a tool that was used to purge us and that specter still hangs over Starkville schools right now.

In May 1970, thirty black teachers in Starkville were dismissed based on the new criteria for job retention. Their dismissal sparked a series of protest marches and the arrest of more than one hundred black protesters.[27] When the school district had to hire thirty-two new teachers for the upcoming school year, no black teacher was hired even though at least six black teachers who applied for the openings had the requisite GRE score. By 1970–71, the number of white teachers in Starkville had increased by 13 percent, while the number of black teachers decreased by 46 percent.[28]

Similarly, the Okolona Municipal Separate School System and the Columbus Municipal Separate School system used scores on the NTE for hiring and retention purposes. After such a policy was enacted in Columbus in 1970–71, the number of black teachers dropped 22 percent from 133 to 103; the number of white teachers dropped 3 percent from 243 to 234. The day before schools were to open in August 1970, Superintendent James E. Goolsby announced there were 36 teaching vacancies. When asked if he would hire black teachers to help fill these vacancies, the superintendent replied, "I hope to fill with the best, qualified teachers I can find, regardless of color."[29] Nine black teachers who met the NTE requisite score applied for the vacant positions. None was hired.[30]

With the help of the NAACP Legal Defense Fund and the NEA, black teachers in Starkville and Columbus filed lawsuits against their school districts for unlawful dismissal. In 1971 the U.S. District Court for the Northern District of Mississippi ruled that the use of NTE and GRE scores for selection and retention of teachers was unconstitutional. Both school districts were ordered to reinstate their dismissed black teachers. In their ruling, the federal court reprimanded the school district for using the GRE and NTE examinations for purposes for which they were not designed. The intended effect of this misuse clearly was, as the Court stated, "to bar proportionately more black teachers than white teachers for reemployment and hiring." [31]

Throughout the 1970s, black teachers continued to file lawsuits against their school districts for unlawful displacement using the "Singleton factors" set forth by the Fifth Circuit Court of Appeals in *Singleton v. Jackson Municipal Separate School District* (1969). In the *Singleton* case, the court set forth guidelines for how school districts were to handle faculty reductions (i.e., dismissals, demotions, and nonrenewals) due to the exigencies of school desegregation. First, the school system must implement and communicate clear, objective, nondiscriminatory standards for handling dismissals and demotions. Second, any reduction could not alter the ratio of black and white teachers in the system. Last, no vacancy, after the reduction, could be filled by hiring a teacher of a race different from the teacher dismissed.

The rulings in the multiple teacher dismissal cases in the 1970s varied greatly. For example, in *McCormick v. Attala* (1976), the federal district court ruled that Mrs. Earlean McCormick, a black teacher in the Attala School District who was not rehired for the 1973–74 school year due to a decline in the district's average daily attendance (ADA), was *not* entitled to reinstatement under the "Singleton factors" because Attala County had achieved unitary status before she was not rehired. The "Singleton factors" were only applicable to school systems that had not achieved unitary status. In this case, the courts ruled that the Attala School District had achieved unitary status because "during the three years following the 1970 desegregation order, public school integration was well accepted by the black and white communities throughout Attala County and by school students, patrons, teachers, and administrators . . . The transition . . . was accomplished without undue impediment or confusion." [32] On the other hand, In *Keglar v. East Tallahatchie School District*, the court ruled that Elbert S. Burten, who was dismissed in 1972 because of a decrease in student enrollment, *was entitled* to reinstatement for unlawful dismissal. The East Tallahatchie School District argued that *Singleton* did not apply since the district implemented its desegregation plan in 1970. The court disagreed and ruled that the school district had failed to achieve unitary status because the two years since 1970 were "marked by hectic school and community upheaval and delayed faculty reduction"; thus, teachers in East Tallahatchie fell under "the umbrella of *Singleton's* protection."[33] The school district was ordered to rehire Burten.

The displacement of black teachers during massive desegregation led Victor Solomon, associate director of the Congress of Racial Equality (CORE), to assert in December 1969 that school desegregation was a failure because it had "sapped black schools of talented teachers and Negro scholars." Solomon pleaded for a return to black neighborhood schools run by black school boards with black teachers given the resources equal to that of white schools. Solomon stated, "It is an insulting assertion to say that a black school cannot be a good school because of its blackness."[34] In Mississippi, most black teachers in 1969 were not ready to abandon school desegregation efforts yet. Rather, they organized. In January 1970, the Negro Mississippi Teachers Association formed the Educational Resources Center to act as an umbrella organization for the various individuals and entities filing complaints and lawsuits against their school systems. The coalition was particularly vocal about whites "setting up private schools for themselves but fighting to retain control over black people in public schools." They vowed to take appropriate action to stop "new ways of discrimination."[35]

Teaching in the Unknown

On the first day of school in her new teaching assignment at Marks High, Lillie V. Davis did not know what to expect. "I was scared as a rabbit from a dog. My husband told me, 'Now I don't know how things will go for you, but if things don't go well, I'll be driving up and down the street, just run out now and I'll pick you up in the truck.'" Lillie gives credit to the principal who made the decision that the two sections of second grade would both be taught by black teachers. This prevented white parents from requesting that their child be placed in the white teacher's classroom. Of the twenty-seven students in her second-grade class, only three were black. Lillie explains how the first day was a trial for all of them, but day by day, classroom interactions improved:

That first morning I went in, and I stood before the children and I tried to have a devotion, and they just looked at me. They just stared at me; they didn't open their mouths. I tried to sing a little song that children used to sing, but they didn't say anything. I said a little scripture. I said a little prayer; then I introduced myself to them, told them that I would be their teacher, and they were still quiet. And then I tried to get them to loosen up. I like to teach reading as my first subject, and I wanted to start it with a little playful game where you clap your hands, and I finally got them to do that. And the next morning we were back in school, and the children did better and better. You see children will do well if the parents will not talk about them and try not to make them dislike people. Children will just naturally love you anyway. So later on, the children just started—they would line up to hug me before they leave in the evening.

Cyndie Harrison was also nervous about her new teaching assignment at Central High in Oxford. Unlike Lillie, she did not have any teaching experience to help prepare for the first day of class. What she did have was a passion for teaching with a good dose of youthful idealism. She recalls her excitement when she received from the principal a list of the names of her students: "It's like being pregnant. You love your baby before you see it, and I loved those students before I ever saw them. I thought some of the names were strange, and I wondered how I was going to pronounce some of them, but I thought, 'well, we can get through this together.'" On the night before the first day of class, Cyndie could hardly sleep:

> The night before I was to meet my students, I had the weirdest thought. I wanted to be the best teacher that these kids had ever had. And I just sort up woke up in the middle of the night, and I thought, "What if somebody asks me to explain what a nominative absolute is." So, the very next morning I got up early and flipped through my old notebooks, and I went over some very difficult grammar constructions because I wanted to be ready.

As they prepared for their first days of teaching in a new setting, Lillie and Cyndie relied on their professional training and their academic backgrounds to plan what they would do in the classroom. But being an effective teacher requires more than just content knowledge and a toolkit of instructional strategies. Teachers complete dozens of ordinary tasks and routines every day based on "taken for granted" knowledge. But when school desegregation occurred, nothing could be taken for granted. Suddenly the mundane, such as faculty meetings, Christmas parties, hall duty, parent conferences, and cafeteria small talk, took on significant import, and teachers, caught in the desegregation crosshairs regardless of their own political beliefs and actions, had to negotiate both the mundane and the larger cultural changes occurring around them as they tried to fulfill their duties as a classroom teacher.

School desegregation often put black and whites together for the first time; yet, years of segregation had bred distrust, fear, and ignorance of each

other. Thus, many teachers were ill-equipped to negotiate the social integration brought about by school desegregation. The teachers' lounge could be
a particularly tense place since it was one of the few spaces on campus for
teachers to socialize and interact on a more informal basis. For Lillie V. Davis,
her outsider status as one of the only black teachers in the school was most
pronounced when she entered the teacher's lounge. Far from being a solace
from the students and the constant challenges of teaching, the lounge was an
inhospitable place as Lillie describes: "I would walk into the teachers' lounge
and everybody would get quiet. I'd go in there and do what I needed to do,
take care of my needs, and come on out." Maye Dee Martin spent a year at
an elementary school in Cleveland as the only black teacher and one of only
three blacks in the entire school (the other two being the cook and janitor).
Maye Dee describes the importance of the lounge for her in demonstrating
that, yes, she wanted to be an integral part of the faculty, but she would not
allow anyone to intimidate her:

> I am not a coffee drinker, but I would go to the lounge and get some coffee and
> have sugar and cream because I am going to sit in there. You see I grew up in
> Texas. I didn't grow up in Mississippi. I didn't grow up in the cotton fields. We
> owned over two thousand acres down at the old home place, and I didn't have
> to go and work for anybody, but I went to the lounge, and they all respected me.
> I never had a problem. I knew how to mix. But one of the black teachers at the
> other school would take her lunch and go in the lounge, and she would cry 'cause
> she didn't want to be over there.

For James George, a black teacher at Carrollton High School in 1970, the
strain between his white principal and him began the first day they met.
George was a native of Carroll County. When he graduated from Alcorn
Agricultural and Mechanical College in 1967, he began teaching agricultural
education at Vaiden High School, an all-black school in Carroll County. At the
time a few black students attended the white schools under FOC, but in 1969,
the schools in Carrollton were still largely segregated. In fall 1970, Carroll
County was court-ordered to desegregate its schools. When school opened
in fall 1970, George was still teaching "shop" at Vaiden High, although it had
been converted to an elementary school. In late September, he was informed
that he would be transferred immediately to JZ George High School, the formerly all-white school. [36] When George casually called the white principal at
JZ George High School by his first name in a conversation between the two,
the principal quickly reprimanded him, "That's Mr. to you." When the STAR
student (an award given to the top student in the school), who was white,

chose Mr. George as the teacher that most influenced him, the principal failed to tell George of the day and time of the awards banquet held in Jackson. Fortunately, the secretary of the school gave him the information. Problems between the two began to escalate when George discovered tools taken illicitly from his shop strewn about the school campus. The principal blamed him for failing to properly store school property. The discord reached a climax when George discovered that his principal had ventured into his shop while he was not there and cut the locks off three of his tool cabinets. Seething, he confronted the principal. He explains what happened next:

> I told him off. He said, "Let's just ride to the superintendent's office." And I said, "No, you get in your car, and I'll get in mine cos I'm not riding with you." We headed to the office. The superintendent asked him, "Did you do that?" And he said, "Yeah, I needed some tools." The superintendent said, "Are those from James's classroom?" He said, "Yeah, but those are tools everybody uses." The superintendent said, "No, I am going to buy him nine new locks, and he can put locks on all the cabinets, and don't you cut another one." The principal said, "Well, I'll just fire him." The superintendent said, "If you don't do what I ask you to, I will fire a principal." Then he went storming out of there.

After two years, the principal left, but for the time he was there, he and George had little to say to each other. "It was tough, very tough. The thing is you did your job, but you didn't feel free doing it. I was on pins and needles all the time," he recalls. When asked if he ever thought of leaving, George summarized the thoughts of many black teachers who felt unwelcome in their new desegregated school environment: "Where you going? There was trouble everywhere. It takes a whole lot more than that to run me away from my home."

Like James George, Lillie V. Davis was determined that she would be not be intimidated in her new teaching environment, but surviving that first year was definitely a challenge. She received harassing phone calls rife with vulgarities and profanities. On several occasions, she was refused service in the local grocery store. But it was the social isolation and the feeling that she simply was not wanted that most tested her resolve. Her position as an outsider was made abundantly clear to her in December when she was not only excluded from planning the annual Christmas party in her own classroom but also shunned during the festivities. Lillie describes that lonely event:

> So coming up for the Christmas party, the parents came and met. And they decided how they were going to give the party and what they were going to do

for the party, and I was not included. So on the afternoon of the party I was just somebody sitting there. I wasn't asked anything. I was just a nobody over there. I just sat there. Sometimes they're things in life we have to accept them. We can't do nothing but accept them because I know that things are going to get better. I knew that.

One of the changes that occurred in many elementary schools as part of school desegregation was the departmentalization of elementary schools. Instead of a first or second grader staying in the same classroom all day with the same teacher responsible for teaching all subjects, the students rotated between two or more teachers. In upper elementary, it was not uncommon for students to have four to five different teachers: one for language arts, one for mathematics, one for science, one for social studies, and one for physical education. Maye Dee Martin describes how departmentalization was utilized at her elementary school in Cleveland to ensure that white students had limited contact with black teachers: "As a 5th grade teacher, they never would let me teach them the entire six weeks. I would teach three weeks reading, and I was paired with a white lady, and then she would swoop in and teach my students English for three weeks. It was to satisfy the parents so they were not taught everything by one black teacher." The sudden adoption of such practices as team teaching or departmentalization did not just coincidentally occur concomitantly with school desegregation. According to the 1970 NEA report of seventy desegregated school districts in Louisiana and Mississippi, departmentalization at the elementary school was used "excessively." The report notes that both black and white teachers said this "irrational scheduling" of classes was not educationally sound for young children. One task force member declared, "Some children have four to six teachers in a single day. White teachers, as well as black, are disturbed about this."[37] The NEA report notes that the new ways of organizing the day and assigning students to multiple teachers in the elementary school was explicitly designed to limit the contact white students had with black teachers.

When Cyndie Harrison began teaching in the segregated black high school in Oxford, she was not prepared for the abject poverty of most of her students. Of the 125 students she taught, only one wore glasses. Most suffered terribly from toothaches because visiting a dentist was a luxury they could ill afford. A ballpoint pen was practically unheard of, and most of her students came to school with no pencils or paper. After a few days of noticing that many of her students stepped off the buses in the morning clutching lemons, Cyndie asked her principal for an explanation. "To kill hunger pangs. They suck on a hole in the lemon," he replied.

Despite her noble intentions and a solid educational background at a strong liberal arts college, Cyndie felt she failed miserably those first few weeks. "I tried to explain these things, but I could see they were confused, or they'd put their heads on the desk. I was losing them. I was constantly reminded of what the years of discrimination had done to them. I cried every night for the first few weeks. I really didn't know what I could do with them. How could I ever give them grades? How could I ever work miracles, and make everything better for them?" Cyndie persevered. She introduced diagramming sentences; she created her own worksheets with humorous grammatical errors for them to detect (e.g., I found a purple lady's coat"), and she introduced poetry reading and writing in which some of her students found success as they penned poignant expressions of their life experiences, such as the following:

> On a farm
> Your work is never done.
> And you work from morning,
> Noon,
> And night.
> On a farm
> Your work is never done.
> Oh, how I like to be in the city,
> And I am here on a farm.
> And my work is never done.

At the annual Christmas party, Cyndie's students surprised her with a gift they bought from money they had pooled together: two placemats and three napkins. The gift brought her to tears. As she was thanking her students for all they had taught her that semester, Francis, one of the poorest girls in the class, who had spent most of her recesses in Cyndie's class because she did not have a coat, presented her with her own Christmas gift: a blue ballpoint pen. "I really could not say anything. I tried. I think I said, 'Thank you Francis.' But that was about all I could say. But I looked up at her, and she had gone back to her chair. And she sat down, and she was just hugging herself and trying to smile and cover her mouth at the same time. She was so proud of what she had done."

At the end of the semester, the principal announced that when school resumed after Christmas break, their school would be a junior high, housing grades 7–9, and all the white students from Oxford Middle School would be joining them. Central High would no longer exist. After this announcement at a school assembly, many of the students and teachers broke out in tears. They stood to sing their alma mater for the last time. Then they joined together to sing a song Cyndie had never heard:

> Lift ev'ry voice and sing, till earth and Heaven ring.
> Ring with the harmony of liberty.

Every student in the auditorium was singing the Black National Anthem.

Cyndie concedes that she did not begin her job teaching in a segregated school with a "political bone in her body," but she received a crash course in the politics of race and schooling. Not only did she experience firsthand the inequalities between black and white schools in terms of facilities, resources, and funding, but when the Oxford city schools opened in January 1970 as fully desegregated schools, she discovered that her students' second-class status would continue in the new schools. The method would be called "ability grouping" or "tracking," and most of Cyndie's students were placed in the lowest track, thus continuing to learn in largely segregated all-black classrooms.

Dalton McAlpin also was thrust into the racial politics of the day with little preparation on how to handle the ramifications of those politics in his school or classroom. Recently graduated from Louisiana State University, Dalton began teaching in 1968 because he was not quite sure what he wanted to do with the rest of his life. During the second semester of his second year, he was assigned to Jim Hill High School, a formerly all-black high school. On the first day at this new school, Mr. Emit Hayes, the black principal, corralled the ten or fifteen new white teachers into a classroom. He introduced the assistant principal, gave his spiel about how this was going to be a trying year, and asked them to please work together as a team with the black teachers to make the school year a success. When he finished, one of the white teachers asked, "Mr. Hayes, do you have any advice to give us? Some of us haven't been working in a desegregated situation at all. What would be a good piece of advice for us?" Mr. Hayes bluntly responded, "Well, the first thing that I would suggest to you is that you do not use the word 'nigger' in this school." Such were the realities, Dalton discovered, of teaching in the midst of the controversy of school desegregation.

At their first faculty meeting, the tension between the black and white teachers was palpable. Dalton explains,

> It became painfully obvious to us that many of them were not happy that they had us. It was more body language than anything. Nobody said anything, but it was just real stand-offish. It took about a month for the ice to break. But that initial first week or so was real tense among faculty because they—looking at it from

their standpoint—they didn't know who they were getting as their colleagues and what our attitudes were going to be. And we didn't know what their attitudes were going to be. I mean it was kind of a Mexican standoff.

After about a month, the "ice broke . . . they realized we were not monsters and vice versa." Dalton attributes the mostly positive interactions between the black and white teachers to Mr. Hayes, "a shining example of what a principal should be like in that kind of situation because he had the ability to spread oil on troubled waters." One of those potentially troubling times was when Mr. Hayes found out that the white teachers were meeting together socially on the weekends. Dalton describes those meetings and Mr. Hayes's response:

> And during the spring we got together two or three times at various people's apartments to kind of commiserate with each other about our lot in life being in the middle of all this. And somebody dubbed those get-togethers as white survival parties. And, of course, word immediately got back to the black teachers and administrators that the whites were having these parties. And Mr. Hayes asked me specifically by the end of the year, "Let's not do this anymore. It's a problem and y'all have certainly survived, and we have survived you. So is it OK? Can you not do that next year?"

Dalton and most of the white teachers stopped meeting for "white survival parties"; however, sometimes the tension between black and white teachers or principals was not so easily resolved. Dalton concedes that at Jim Hill High there were a few black and white teachers who "never did warm up. They came; they did their job, and they went home."

On May 15, 1970, on his usual morning route to school, Dalton encountered what seemed to be a riot of some kind:

> When I turned the corner, the street was full of kids—all black. And it was clear that there was some kind of disturbance. I hadn't had the radio on or anything, so I slowly drove through them, and people are pounding on my car and pounding on my windshield, and I got through that group and went around the corner to get to the staff parking lot. And I went inside and I said, "What the hell is going on?" Mr. Hayes said, "You haven't heard the news?" And I said, "No." And he says, "Well, the highway patrol shot up Jackson State last night, and a couple of people were killed. This is a very dangerous day for all of us because it's really incited everybody."[38]

For the rest of the day everyone was on edge. Many of the black students were absent, and not much instruction occurred. Mr. Hayes vigilantly walked the halls making sure no disturbances or incidents of violence occurred in his school. At the end of the day, they found out that one of those killed was a student in Dalton's class: James Earl Green. For the next few days, Dalton and the other social studies teachers suspended their planned teaching activities. Instead, as Dalton explains, "We got together—the black and white social studies teachers—and we thought, 'maybe the thing to do is just discuss civilly in our classes and let people vent about it, without getting out of control.'" On the day of Green's funeral, classes were dismissed. Dalton and the white teachers that attended the funeral rode in the car with the black football coach, who was concerned for the safety of his colleagues, given the racially charged atmosphere of the day.

With a Hope and a Prayer

Hollywood loves to make movies about heroic white teachers (e.g., *Dangerous Minds, Freedom Writers*) who sweep into horrific schools marked by violence, neglect, and incompetent teachers to "save" their black and Latino students from the predetermined fates that await them because they are black/Latino, poor, and victims of structural and institutional racism. That is not the story told in this chapter. Neither heroes nor villains, the black and white teachers featured in this book were, in many ways, simply trying to make it through the day, week, and month implementing a top-down educational reform that was still being challenged and debated in the courts, at their local school board meetings, at the Department of Justice and HEW offices in Washington DC, and in their state capital. Mandates, policies, and directions changed constantly. Yet, they and their students were directed to have school as usual. Working through school desegregation required teachers to attend to the technical professional requirements needed to be a good teacher while also trying to make sense of their own racialized personal and collective histories as the social, cultural, and educational landscapes they knew so well were rapidly changing.

In his book *There Goes My Everything: White Southerners in the Age of Civil Rights,* Jason Sokol notes that "most white southerners identified neither with the civil rights movement nor its violent resisters."[39] This is an apt description of many white teachers, like Cyndie Harrison and Dalton McAlpin, who fell into the throes of teaching through desegregation by timing more than anything else. Cyndie admits that back in 1969 "I didn't have a political agenda. I wasn't trying to right any wrongs. I needed a paycheck, and they needed a teacher." But the experience was life changing for Dalton and Cyndi and countless other white teachers. Teaching during this time of social and racial upheaval created a critical dissonance between their own comfortable and often sheltered upbringing in the South and the lived realities of their black students and colleagues, who heretofore had been largely invisible to them. They were forced to question the racial politics, etiquette, and mores of their white upbringing, and in doing so, unlearn and relearn much of what they had been taught growing up white in the Deep South. Certainly, it is easy to portray Cyndie Harrison's enthusiasm and prodigious declarations of love for her black students at Central High as a form of naiveté possible only because of the privileged life she had lived as a white southerner. But such an interpretation fails to capture the sense of *hope* that drove many white teachers, like Cyndie Harrison, Dalton McAlpin, Harriet Kuykendall, and JoAnne Prichard Morris, to approach their teaching through school desegregation as if their decisions made a difference. This hope is what David Haplin calls "absolute hope": "Absolute hope entails a basic, even naïve, kind of faith in the future involving a taken-for-granted belief that it is always better to seek ways of improving things that are not working out rather than to leave them as they are."[40] Absolute hope is what kept Cyndie Harrison from falling into despair over her teaching conditions, her classroom, her own lack of preparation, and the impoverished lives of her students. Absolute hope is what drove Dalton and his co-workers to abandon their lesson plans for several days so that students could talk through their grief over the death of their classmate and work through their anxieties about racism and violence. And it was hope undergirding the many decisions white teachers made to create classrooms where their students (both black and white) would be protected from the disorder and negativity occurring outside the school walls.

Haplin refers also to a different form of hope, called "ultimate hope" which unlike absolute hope is "an aimed hope . . . [which] has an object or, more accurately, a better specific state of affairs in mind."[41] This is the type of hope that kept Lillie V. Davis, Maye Dee Martin, James George, and other black teachers persevering through the trials and tribulations of school desegregation. They withstood the obvious affronts based solely on their race, the routinely displayed lack of respect for them and their black students, and the institutional tactics aimed at keeping blacks oppressed because, as Lille Davis explains, they kept their eyes squarely focused on the prize: "We wanted educational equality for our children. That's all we wanted, and we wanted them to have the same chance, and the same opportunity that other children have." Black teachers knew that goal would not come quickly nor would it be easy, and far too many suffered professionally. What kept them getting up and going to school every day was an "ultimate hope [that] holds up . . . the

prospect of a better way of life—for oneself, for others and for society generally—while recognizing there are likely to be obstacles on the way that will
need to be challenged and overcome."[42] As Lillie Davis sat alone in the corner of the room while her white students and parents celebrated the annual
Christmas party, she did not fall into despair. She kept the faith, and she kept
coming back—day in and day out. "I know that things are going to get better.
I knew that." For twenty years, Lillie continued to teach in the public schools
in Marks, facing multiple obstacles, including the return to segregated schools
for black children when the entire white population fled to the private school.
After retiring, Lillie decided to run for school board in 2006 because she was
concerned that the school system was still failing to provide "the prospect of
a better way of life" for the hundreds of black students in her school district.
She was elected and worked tirelessly for another ten years as a school board
member in Quitman County.

Chapter 6

"We All Came Together on the Football Field" But . . .

The Role of Sports in Desegregation

Avid high school sports fans in southern Mississippi knew about Coach Charles Boston and the talent he cultivated on his Jefferson High football team in Columbia. Eddie Payton had played for Coach Boston, and his little brother, Walter, was considered as good, if not better, than his older brother.[1] So when school desegregation occurred in Columbia in January 1970, there was some excitement about Coach Boston, Walter, and several other outstanding football players joining the Columbia High football team. Tommy Davis was the young new head coach who had just moved to Columbia in the summer of 1970. He remembers well the talent on that first team and the excitement of fans elated over a winning team:

> We had a very good team, the best team Columbia had had in years. We lost two ballgames: one to McGee and one to Monticello. And that was the only two games that we lost. Walter [Payton] was a senior. He was in the backfield with Archie Johnson and Sugarman Moses. And we had some excellent players, excellent linemen, excellent backs. We just did real well that year. And they worked together, played together well.[2]

Davis was proud of the accomplishments of his team both on and off the field, and he credits Coach Boston for much of their success during that first year: "He was the kind of man that wanted everybody to succeed. And all the players loved Coach Boston." What is missing in Davis's account of the role Coach Boston played during the desegregation process is that Coach Boston had applied for the head coaching position at Columbia High. Rather than hire a local seasoned black coach with a long track record of winning and producing collegiate athletes, the school system hired Tommy Davis, a young new white coach. Coach Boston was demoted to assistant coach.

We place great faith in the unifying potential of sports, and every Friday and Saturday night in high school and college football stadiums throughout the United States, we are provided tangible evidence that sports can transcend barriers of race and economic disparities. Black boys can be chosen "all-Conference" while white boys sit the bench. Cam Newton is just as likely to win the Heisman as is Tim Tebow. Sports speaks to a human hope that in some ways race and social class really do not matter. It is no surprise, then, that many of those involved in the early years of school desegregation, including Coach Boston and Tommy Davis, laud the role sports played in this historical social transition and locate the football field or the basketball court as the place blacks and whites, sitting by each other and cheering together for a common cause, worked through the initial tensions of school desegregation. However, as the story about Coach Boston's demotion illustrates, "we all came together on the football field" is only one side of a very complicated story about the role of sports during desegregation.

Sports in the Preintegration Era

In small towns throughout the South in the pre-*Brown* era, it was not unusual for a group of black and white boys to find a vacant lot or grassy field and play a pickup game of football or basketball after school or on weekends. Such was the case in Laurel as remembered fondly by Coach Charles Boston: "This was a sawmill town. And it was understood—well I knew I had to stay on my side of the tracks, so to speak. But we played with, against white boys. Not organized, but on Sundays we'd go over down at the train station. We never had any problems until some busybody would drive by and see us out there and tell the cops. And they'd come break us up."[3] One of his playmates was Bobby Collins, who later became the head football coach at the University of Southern Mississippi. Boston describes the camaraderie between the two: "We delivered newspapers together. His uncle had the paper franchise. He went to Mississippi State and I went to Alcorn. While we were waiting around for our newspapers, we'd go down in the alley down there and punt. And we could have played together. He was a quarterback and I was a receiver. He could have passed the ball to me, but it was just that we were separate." Hamilton Stevens, a school board member in Forrest during desegregation, has similar fond memories of his youth in the 1940s:

> We had a pretty good grassy area down there. And the black kids and the white
> boys would gather up down there, and we'd play football. And sometimes we'd

have a mixed-up crew. Some blacks and whites on each side. And then somebody would decide, "Let's just put all the black boys on one side, and the whites on the other." And then we would play the same bunch. We all went fishing together, hunting together, and of course a lot of their mothers worked in different white homes.[4]

Hugh McCarthy, who was on the school board with Hamilton, shares a similar memory: "Most of us were integrated back then. Didn't really know that—what the word was because the black younguns and the white ones played football together on a—just a pickup game-type thing. And the high school players were called White Bearcats and the colored school, they were the Black Bearcats. And the black boys came to our football game free of charge. And we went to theirs free of charge."[5]

An easy togetherness may have existed between black and white children playing sports outside of school; but in school settings such integrated competition was prohibited through an informal, yet strictly enforced, policy, by which most colleges and universities abided. For example, in 1956 the University of Mississippi withdrew from playing in the All-American Basketball Tournament because their opponent, Iona College of New York, had a black player. In 1957 Jackson State College had to forfeit their game in the NCAA small college tournament because there was a possibility that they may play a mixed-race team.[6] Mississippi State University won the SEC title in basketball in 1959 and 1961; both times they declined the invitation to play in the NCAA Tournament because of the possibility of competing against black players. However, in 1955 the Jones Junior College football team challenged the unwritten policy and accepted an invitation to play in the "Junior Rose Bowl" in Pasadena (CA). The opposing team was Compton College in California; five of its starting players were black. Despite threats from some state politicians to eliminate Jones Junior College if they played and the Citizens' Council's warning that playing an integrated team would usher in school desegregation, Jones Junior College played the game, with its marching band and school officials in tow. They lost 22–13, but they became the first team in Mississippi to defy the unwritten policy prohibiting sports teams from playing integrated teams.[7] The next to do so would be Mississippi State University—eight years later.

In 1963, one year after the infamous riots at the University of Mississippi when James Meredith became the first black to enroll there, the Mississippi State University basketball team was relishing yet another Southeastern Conference basketball championship. Tired of his team being denied the opportunity to showcase their talents in a national spotlight, Coach "Babe" McCarthy appealed to his student and alumni fan base to put pressure on MSU president Dr. D. W. Colvard to allow the team to play in the NCAA conference tournament. The students, fans, and alumni rallied around Coach McCarthy and the team. They staged a sit-in on the president's lawn, wrote letters and circulated petitions, and contacted state politicians and members of the College Board, demanding that the team be allowed to play.[8] President Colvard finally relented and issued the following statement minutes before MSU was set to play its last game of the season against Ole Miss: "As president of Mississippi State University I have decided that unless hindered by competent authority I shall send our basketball team to the NCAA competition."[9] Still reeling from the Ole Miss riot, Governor Ross Barnett was unusually quiet. He made one public statement that reaffirmed his commitment to segregation but acknowledged that under the Mississippi Constitution he had no power to reverse the decision of President Colvard or the College Board. In an 8–3 decision, the board voted to allow Mississippi State to play in the tournament. After various forms of subterfuge (including using the freshmen team as decoys to trick the sheriff charged with serving an injunction to keep the team from flying out of state to the tournament), MSU played in the NCAA tournament against Loyola University (Chicago) who had four black players.[10] MSU lost, but the coaches, the players, and the fans' response was significant, for it demonstrated that the segregationists' hold on Mississippi was waning. Henderson noted: "Though racial southerners employed athletics as a weapon for the social and political cause of segregation, the values and ideals of sport (especially the enthusiasm for winners, egalitarianism, and reward for achievement) both justified White support of MSU's basketball team and allowed previously silenced moderates to espouse disapproval of their 'closed society.'"[11]

In a region obsessed with high school and college sports, perhaps it is no surprise that sports became a vehicle to challenge segregation in athletic competitions. But the significance of sports during the period of school integration was not simply about competing on the field. As we heard repeatedly throughout our interviews, "coming together on the football field" created a symbolic space for blacks and whites to forge new interracial identities, discover shared interests and passions, and unify around a common cause. This went a long way in helping ease the transition to desegregated schools. In fact, according to a survey of superintendents involved in the desegregation process, athletics was the "one protruding factor contributing to the peaceful transition in Mississippi's schools."[12]

Friday Nights and New Identities

Sitting side by side, sharing the same bathrooms, concession stands, and water fountains, Friday night football became a visible symbol of changing times, and it offered hope to many that perhaps this school desegregation just might work. Such was the case in the fall of 1970, when, for the first time, black and white fans crowded into the Starkville High stadium to cheer on the mighty Yellow Jackets. Fenton Peters, who was the only black principal of a school in Starkville in 1970, remembers well those Friday nights:

> The football teams kind of pulled things together and made them gel for Starkville schools. The teams melded. They got together, and the 1970 team coming up that fall were the conference champs as a result of that. They did spring training together. They coalesced during spring training. The football and the athletic programs went well. Sports did help. That is a pretty well-established fact here. There are some people who believe so strongly that it was the oil on the water and if that had not happened we would have had a lot more problems than we had.[13]

George Dale, who was principal of Moss Point High in southern Mississippi during the first years of desegregation, notes that when Moss Point High became a powerhouse in the Big 8 Conference after school desegregation, both black and white fans rallied around the team, and getting a seat on Friday nights was almost impossible. Dale notes, "My analogy is the athletic field did more for desegregation in Mississippi than anything else, and it probably took the place of the church."[14] Mike Johnson, a white coach in Rosedale and Leland, during this time period, succinctly summarized the power of sports during school desegregation: "Sports saved the school. And I hate to say that, but I think that's what happened. People could rally around a successful team."[15]

In a region in which sports is second only to religion, perhaps it is no surprise that sports provided a place for blacks and whites to come together. When winning was the primary goal, many white coaches and fans suddenly discovered they could disregard the skin color of a powerful running back or a high-scoring point guard. William Lewis, a young high school coach during the early years of desegregation, recounts how the Harrison Central High community rallied around a black athlete, Larry Hawthorne, whose nickname was Sugar Bear.

> And Sugar Bear could really score with the basketball. He could run up and down the floor, and he could really score. And Sugar Bear was one of the first two black players to ever play in the Mississippi High School All-Star Game—summer of

1970. And Larry was a great player. Obviously, they were trying to key on him. We ended up having a big ball game. Defeated them rather easily. Sugar Bear scored thirty-three points that night, and at the end of the ballgame, when they announced the All-Tournament team, Larry was announced as the Most Outstanding Player in the tournament. And led by the people from Hancock High [the opposing team], they actually led the standing ovation for him. I can well remember sitting there and saying to myself, "You know? Things are starting to change." It was kind of a great moment. Something that's kind of hidden in the history of our state and the integration of our schools. But just the fact that the people had the appreciation to stand up for that physical basketball talent and support somebody of a different race. That before that year they had not even seen him play on a basketball floor.[16]

Desegregation also introduced to white fans a new style of high school basketball. The "fast break" and dunking made basketball a fast-paced, much more exciting game to watch. Coach Lewis recalls how electrifying their pregame warm-ups were:

I can remember our kids—our boys' team—coming out to warm up, and our white fans had never seen somebody dunk a basketball back then. And all of a sudden now, I've got half of my kids that could dunk a basketball. Even one or two of the white kids learned to dunk. There was no prohibition back then about in warmups about dunking. And our kids would start dunking the ball, and the crowd would just get into a frenzy because they had not seen that. And you've got to keep in mind that most cases, this was a year ahead of other schools along the Coast, that they hadn't experienced that yet. So it was something new for them. But it was kind of novel and exciting. And then we were good.

Dalton McAlpin, a second-year teacher in Jackson at Jim Hill High School, recalls the packed gymnasium in his previously all-black school: "Jim Hill was a football powerhouse in those days, as well as basketball. And so we all went to the football games and the basketball games. That's where I learned what the term 'fast break' basketball was because those boys played faster than any basketball players I had ever seen—just storming up and down the court."[17] Thomas James Evans, one of the first black students to attend Madison-Ridgeland High during FOC, remembers well the 1971 basketball season when black players joined the Madison Ridgeland team: "I don't know what was more entertaining—the fast-paced, shoot-out-style play or the look on the faces of the white people in the stands. The whites had never seen basketball like that before nor had they witnessed fan support like that."[18]

As black and white players played together, white and black coaches coached together, and black and white fans cheered together for the same team, the football field and the basketball court provided a space for the partial dismantling of historical racial boundaries. The hope of many was that this camaraderie would transfer off the field and into the classroom.

Practicing Integration

The box office hit *Remember the Titans* is based on the true story of what happened the first year of court-enforced desegregation in Alexandria, Virginia. As the town prepares for school integration, everyone is anxious. No one knows what the upcoming school year will bring. The black and white football players are forced together two weeks earlier than everyone else as they hit, tackle, and punch their way through a two-week, grueling summer training camp. They return to school and become the unifying symbol for the rest of the community. In a true climatic (and made for Hollywood) ending, they have a perfect season and win the state championship. A Hollywood film that took some liberties with the actual truth, *Remember the Titans* illustrates the symbolic role of spring and summer football practice immediately prior to desegregation. Football or basketball practice was not just about honing one's skill as an athlete and a team member; it was a test to see whether or not this experiment called integration could actually work. The stakes were high. If athletes could get along on the football field, then adults and other students might just follow suit.

Students received very little preparation for desegregation. Thus, football practice became a miniexperiment in how black and white students would respond to each other once they were forced to go to school together. According to Richard Dent, a senior at Waynesboro High School (Wayne County) in the fall of 1970, school desegregation "just happened."[19] No one sat the students down and said "Be prepared for this" or "Look, this is how we're going to do this." The uncertainty and fear of the unknown made for a tense opening day of school. He recalls that the sheriff, several deputy sheriffs, the highway patrol, and a few marshals lined the road to ensure that the busses carrying the black students could peacefully get to the school. But as a white football player, he had already met several black students during summer practice, and he did not share the same apprehensions of many adults. He attributed that to summer football practice:

> We had already started practicing two weeks before, and the black students fell in, fell right in. And went to the same dressing room. We didn't think anything about

it. I mean we were just students. We didn't have anything as far as prejudging whatsoever. We just knew that they were coming to us, and when they came, we just moved on. I think sports extends that bridge when you have those gaps out there. And they did. The timing was good. It was the beginning of the school year. School hadn't really begun. Even though we had practices for a couple of weeks, school hadn't really begun. And they came in, and they made that transition. And it went well. I don't think it would have been successful in that, again, athletics helps transcend a lot of things.

William Lewis explained how the informal nature of football practice helped diffuse some of the uneasiness felt the first few weeks of school:

One of the things that helped us was that we had summer football practices. And they [black football players] came and participated in summer practices with us in a less structured, less formal situation than the normal school day. So when school started, they already knew us, and we already knew them. They might not know the rest of the student body, and the student body may not have known them, but at least from the athletic standpoint, we already knew them. That may have taken the edge off.

Archie Johnson, who was a junior in Columbia in 1970, was worried about spring football practice. He had never been around any of the white boys going out for practice; he did not know their skill level, and most importantly, he was concerned about whether he would retain his position as quarterback. According to Archie, spring practice helped him and his teammates sort out a number of contentious issues:

We started spring practice. There was a concern about who would keep their position. Me, as quarterback, I was concerned about that because I didn't know if it would be talent or something else. I was concerned about my position and didn't know what to expect. But spring practice rolled around, and spring practice does a lot of running, a lot of seeing who's who and position-wise. I pretty much held my own, had a slightly different system, but picked it up quickly. The football battling, sweated and bled, and once things were sorted out, everyone accepted it, position wise—who was who. And I think we both realized that the team as a whole that athletic ability has no color.[20]

The close proximity to each other, the trust built when players eat, shower, bleed, and sweat together, and the bonding inherent in team sports creates a certain athletic intimacy. This intimacy often extends beyond the field and locker room and, during desegregation, helped create a space for athletes to learn about their teammates' lives in ways that reduced the social distance between them. Players could form relationships with each other based on commonalities shared as teenage boys. Exchanging details about their lives, they began relating to each other as individuals. Sid Salter, who played football for Philadelphia High School in the 1970s, describes this special bonding between players and how it helped pave paths for common understandings:

> I remember being in the huddle on the field, third or fourth quarter, tired, and the manager had come out there, and at some point in the game I realized we're all drinking out of the same bottle. We're all wiping with the same towel. I also noticed how many kids, black and white, were hanging around each other after school. After football practice, a black kid would ask for a ride. It was more like giving your teammate a ride than it was giving a black kid you didn't know a ride. You learned where each other lived, their families, and their girlfriends.[21]

Sports allowed students to play a vital role in desegregation efforts. Often, athletes were the role models for others, including adults, to emulate. Working as a team but getting to know each other as individuals represented a cultural shift in interracial relationships. On the football field, the basketball court, and the locker room, students in newly desegregated schools worked out differences and discovered commonalities. They were not merely practicing for an athletic competition; they were practicing and leading others for the realities of living and learning together in a new educational environment.

Coaches as Enforcers, Mediators, and Peacekeepers

The role of white coaches in the South during desegregation sometimes takes on a mythic quality as illustrated in the oft-cited story of how one of the South's most revered college football coaches, Coach Bear Bryant of The University of Alabama, helped ease that university into desegregation seven years after Governor George Wallace's infamous stand at the school house door where he tried to prohibit James Hood and Vivian Malone from enrolling there. The story goes that in 1970 when the all-white University of Alabama football team suffered a resounding loss (42–12) in their opening game to an integrated Southern Cal team, Coach Bryant walked to the Southern Cal locker room after the game and asked black running back Sam "The Bam" Cunningham to come with him to the Tide's locker room. It is there that Bryant supposedly told his players (pointing to Cunningham), "This is what a football player looks like."[22] One of Bryant's assistant coaches reportedly said of this incident:

"Sam Cunningham did more for integration in the South in sixty minutes than Martin Luther King had in twenty years."[23] According to popular legend, this single event ushered in the integration of the University of Alabama's football team the next year with the full support of administrators, students, alumni, and fans.

Interestingly, there is no written documentation that this locker-room incident ever took place.[24] However, the persistence of this story in football folklore forty-five years later speaks to the revered status of coaches in southern communities and their potential to bring about social change. As discussed in chapter 5, in school districts that used the lottery to assign teachers during the first semester or year of desegregation, coaches were often excluded. Their positions were deemed too important to be held to random chance. Many white coaches used their influence and power in the community to assure white parents and students that desegregation was not as detrimental as they imagined or had been told it would be. As Pamela Grundy notes in her account of the integration of sports in North Carolina, white coaches played a significant role in "bravely facing the powder keg of segregationist sentiment."[25]

During the tumultuous events of school desegregation, coaches were often called upon to be the disciplinarians whose very presence was meant to convey peace and order. At Riverside High School in the Delta, no one was prepared for school desegregation. "It was complete pandemonium," recall Grey and Alice Spencer, teachers at Riverside during this time. It was the coaches, both black and white, who walked around and tried to keep some semblance of calm and order.[26] Coach Owen Makamson was one of the coaches at Riverside. He describes how they spent January 1970 patrolling the school hallways.

> It was helter skelter, and it was really the coaches. We didn't even do any teaching. We just ran, walked the halls with paddles and tried to keep order. Oh no, it was not organized. We didn't have fights and stabbings and all that. It was just uncertainty, and we, as coaches—of course coaches have always been respected—and that was our job. We just walked the halls and tried to keep peace and quiet and especially when the bells would change.[27]

In January 1970, Billy Brown was the only white coach left in the Kemper County public schools. Ordinarily it would have been the middle of basketball season, but all games had been suspended via an edict from the Kemper County School Board. It was a strategy, according to Coach Brown, to convince the few remaining white students to leave the public schools. Numerous white athletes transferred to nearby school districts to play sports.

Transferring rules suddenly disappeared, and Coach Brown watched several of his white players from the semester before playing in nearby Noxubee and Lauderdale Counties when schools reopened in January. Despite the exodus of many of his white players, Coach Brown had decided that he was not leaving the Kemper County public schools, and he held spring practice, not knowing whether or not he would even be allowed to field a team in the fall. In those first few weeks of January 1970, a group of white men congregated every afternoon at a gas station near DeKalb High School. Their presence was meant to intimidate blacks and the few whites left in the public school. Coach Billy Brown, who was born and reared in Kemper County, described his confrontation with these men:

> On the first day of school, a few whites came, and there were some men out there—six or seven of them. When school was out, they would cross the street like they were taking someone's names. So I don't know whether or not they thought they were the Ku Klux Klan or whatever, but that night, I called them up. I knew most of them, and I knew it was a bad joker or two, but anyway, I call one [of] those bad jokers up and I told him. I talked to him plain, and they know me. I grew up here, and I said, "You're not scaring anyone. If y'all want to kluck, by God, I'll put you to klucking." You know back in those days most everybody kept shotguns or rifles. I had an old .22 I kept in my truck.[28]

In fall 1969, two black students, Lindy and Leon Johnson, enrolled at DeKalb High under FOC. Coach Brown assumed the responsibility of ensuring that Lindy and Leon were not mistreated, at least under his watch. He recalled Lindy's first day in his history class: "Lindy Lou sat down up at the front, and I guess she was probably scared to death. She's sitting in front of my desk, and these two prim little girls jump up and ran back. I made them come up there, and I sat one of them on one side of her and the other on the other side. I wouldn't let them pick at her or nothing else." A few weeks later while walking in the halls he noticed several white boys had Leon penned next to the lockers. "They were really harassing the student. And I mean I ate them damn alive. I told them 'If I ever see this again, and I'm not always going to be around all the time, but if I do . . .' I mean I ate them alive. I put a stop to that because they knew I'd eat them alive." During desegregation coaches were called upon to enforce order and contain chaos. But their role in many schools extended beyond simply being the disciplinarian. They were often the bridge between blacks and whites, intervening when necessary, stepping back when restraint was needed, and diverting pent-up energy by a command of "Give me five laps." Such was the case of Coach Harry Breland.

Coach Harry Breeland was the coach at John Jefferson High, a segregated black high school in Purvis. John Jefferson High was an athletic powerhouse in the black conference, and, like Coach Charles Boston, Breeland had a reputation for grooming excellent college athletes. One of his players, Willie Heidelburg, was the first black to play football at the University of Southern Mississippi. When desegregation occurred in fall 1970, John Jefferson closed, and the black students dispersed across several schools. Coach Breeland described the sentiment of his colleagues and him during this period of uncertainty: "You didn't know what to expect. You knew how you taught kids in the black schools, for you had been teaching for four, five six, seven, eight years. And what was expected there. But you were willing to try it because that was the state that I was in and most of the people were in, and they said, 'We'll go in and give it all we got and see what happens.'"[29] Breeland was sent to Oak Grove where there were thirty-two black students in the entire school (grades 1–12). He was the only black teacher. Breeland described his first year as "lonely, very lonely—I guess you could say I felt kind of like Lone Ranger without Tonto because even though I can't recall anything bad for me, it was just different being the only black there."

Breeland knew what desegregation typically meant for black coaches, and he did not expect to be asked to coach. He explained, "Nobody told me that, but I just felt like they were going to use that for a year or two. Kind of get integration started within the school." Six weeks into the semester, he was asked to coach basketball, so he became the assistant coach. He attributed this move to coaching as helping him feel more connected to the school and the students. Oak Grove was not known for its athletics, and the baseball team had not been competitive for years, so Breeland was surprised when a group of white students asked him during that first year to coach the baseball team.

I guess I would say that the thing they saw in me was I wanted to win, and I was willing to work and put in the time. So the kids, along with the principal, decided that I would be the baseball coach. So when they asked me, I said, "You know, I've never coached baseball." And I told them, "Most of the black schools down on this end don't have baseball with the exception of the Big 8 teams." And I remember the words they said, "Coach, we'll learn together." I thought I had really, really reached a real special relationship with them. To be that young and to say that. That's expressing to me that they wanted me to be a part of what they wanted.

Coach Breeland agreed to be the baseball coach. In 1976, Oak Grove won their first state baseball championship "We won it all. It was huge for our school. It brought our students together. You know, because we had—we didn't have problems that much with integration. We had problems with the new and the old line." Oak Grove went on to win eight more state titles under Breeland's leadership. It was an anomaly for sure—a black coach coaching a "white" sport comprised predominantly of white students.

Coach Breeland knew he had made progress toward building the kinds of relationships he enjoyed with his athletes at John Jefferson High when the Oak Grove students started referring to him as "Coach." Breeland explains:

> I saw a lot of good things happen with relationship building during that time. I received a lot of respect from the parents, and I give a lot of credit to the kids. I know the kids were going back and telling their parents how hard we worked, how sincere I was, and how much they enjoyed playing for me. I would be standing in the hall getting ready for class, and they'd call me "Coach." And prior to that time, they would call me Mr. Breeland. Then they made the other kids call me "Coach." I guess I need to explain it this way, and I don't want you to think this is special. But some kids look at that a little different when they can call you "Coach." It was a tremendous help to me in the classroom because they would relate things to how I made them work.

Black coaches served a particularly important role for black students transferred (sometimes in the middle of the year) to formerly all-white schools where they were often considered the outsiders and expected to assimilate into the already-established culture of the school. For these students, black coaches became their guiding light, their cheerleader, and a voice of reason. Coach Boston stayed at Columbia High School, despite being demoted to assistant coach, because he wanted to be there for his black players and students during this time of change and uncertainty. Boston explains, "I just decided to stay. I felt like I could help. It helped them by me being there." When Coach Boston did not get the job of head coach, some of the former Jefferson High players talked about staging a walkout to protest the hiring decision. Archie Johnson, one of Boston's players, explains how they looked to Coach Boston in dealing with the insults and lack of respect paid to black students and teachers when forced to give up their leadership roles, their traditions, and their history in the new school:

> We had some problems in terms of who the head coach would be. Coach Boston was the only coach we ever had. But at some point, we accepted the decision and were not surprised by it, and I think looking back, Coach Boston made it easy for us in terms of looking at compromise. The next year we were looking at who would be assigned what numbers. At Jefferson I was number 10. When we got to

Columbia High, we discovered that the number had been retired from a former player. I had an issue with that. I said, 'Aren't we starting all over again? You know, from the beginning?" Anyway, we compromised. So it's retired. We accepted that. It's a compromise. Our colors at Jefferson were green and gold and Columbia High was blue and gold. Again, we said, "We got some gold in the deal." And again, we looked for ways to compromise and finding that room for compromise. Coach Boston was kinda like that too. He would encourage us, "We're getting something and look at the good side of it."

Seeing Inequalities through the Prism of Sports

In the segregated world of the South, whites could ignore, choose to be ignorant of, or dismiss the racism, prejudice, and discrimination faced by blacks every day. Likewise, blacks could try to shelter their children (with differing levels of success) from overt discrimination and racism by keeping them closely guarded in the segregated spaces of church, home, and school. When Archie Johnson played football at the all-black Jefferson High School, they never ate meals on the road. Finding a restaurant that would welcome a busload of black boys traveling to an away football game was not only difficult but potentially dangerous in Mississippi during the 1960s. Johnson explains what they did instead: "When we were at the black school, the tradition was that the hosting school would provide the pregame meal and the postgame meal, and that was a tradition that I always loved. All together we would mix and mingle and chit chat before we went to battle. We just drove straight there and back. I don't ever remember stopping." This was not the custom for white players who freely traveled on busses to away games, stopping for a meal at any number of restaurants or cafes along the way. But playing sports together on an integrated team forced many white students and coaches to witness the blatant racism and discrimination that heretofore they could ignore. As the team traveled on busses to away games, white coaches and players witnessed their black athletes not being served at restaurants or being denied bathrooms or entrance to certain venues. At games, they heard white fans from the opposing team sling racial slurs at their black players. Sometimes white players stood up for their black teammates; sometimes they responded with silence. Coaches and administrators, in coordinating the logistical details of arranging sports competitions, were suddenly forced to deal with the implications of racism on the lives of their black players.

In January 1970, John Allen Flynt was the principal and head football coach in New Hebron. It was the middle of basketball season and two black boys had joined the team. New Hebron was scheduled for an away game the very first week of desegregation. Flynt explains what happened on that first bus trip as an integrated team: "We had a basketball game one week and we had two black boys playing. It was an away game. One of the boys did not come, and the other boy rode the bus by himself. And I know he was nervous, and they stopped to eat on the way back to get a hamburger. He stayed on the bus and told them that he wasn't hungry. One of the white parents got a hamburger and carried it out to him."[30]

Later in the season, the basketball team played in Florence. Once again, they stopped at a restaurant to eat a pregame meal. This time the black players did go inside. Flynt describes the scene that occurred:

> We were playing in a south Mississippi basketball tournament in Florence, so I told the coach to run by and get them a sandwich or hamburger. We went to a place in Florence, and we lined up and went through the line to place your order. About halfway through the line a guy came up, and they said, "We don't serve blacks." About half the team had already eaten, so we got the other boys to order, so the black boys would have something to eat. From then on if we were going to Timbukto, and if we were going to get them a hamburger, I would call and make sure they served blacks there.

During segregation, black students were well-aware of the inequalities between their school and the white school. They saw the football stadium and the well-kept school lawns at the white schools. They knew their textbooks were often the ones discarded from the white school. But many did not realize just how "separate and unequal" the two schools were until they saw the differences in athletic facilities. John West was a junior at the segregated Thompson High in Natchez. When he walked onto the Natchez High campus for the first time, he was astounded. "I saw fiberglass [basketball] backboards I had never seen before. I saw a white guy pole-vaulting; I had never see that before. A track field that looked like a track field, and a parquet [gymnasium] floor."[31] Waffling a bit about whether to transfer to Natchez High under FOC, his decision was sealed when he saw the athletic facilities at the white school. His senior year, he joined the Natchez High basketball team. He was the sole black player.

Integrated sports brought with it a heightened level of competition for starting positions, and for the first time, whites could not assume the superiority they generally took for granted in every other aspect of their lives. Sometimes white players accustomed to being the star athlete suddenly lost their starting positions to a more skilled black player. Coach William Lewis recalls a phone call from an irate white parent indignant that his son had been replaced by a black player on the Harrison Central basketball team:

> And so I went back there and took the call and some very harsh language. All I had to say was "Hello," and I got an earful pretty quickly. And it was all about why had I taken his son out and replaced him with this black player. And he was using some pretty strong language. And we finally just decided to disagree on the way that the team was to be handled. But the young man [the white player] performed a lot better the rest of the season.

But competition in sports on integrated teams also provided tangible evidence to black students a message their parents, teachers, and principals had been preaching for years: whites were not inherently or innately superior, either on the field or in the classroom. Charles George, a black assistant principal at West Tallahatchie, explains this valuable lesson of sports:

> Integration made the blacks realize that whites were no better off than they were—intelligence and everything else. You see, they—the blacks—thought, for the most part, that whites were better than blacks. But when they came together in the classroom or in an athletic competition they saw that some whites were good, some blacks were good. You see? And some weren't. Some blacks weren't and some whites weren't. So, in other words, they got to know each one as a participant—what he could and couldn't do.[32]

"We all came together on the football field" is a story with a happy ending. It is an appealing story, and we can all find individual and specific examples of how sports provided an impetus for positive attitudinal changes. It is a progressive story of well-intentioned, rational people working through differences toward a common goal and in doing so creating positive social change. But, as in most stories, there is always another side. We all came together on the football field but . . .

No Black Coaches Need Apply

Today Coach Charles Boston is an icon in Columbia, Mississippi. He is a vibrant, wiry eighty-three-year-old who seldom misses a football practice and attends just about every sports event held at Columbia High. The newly built athletic field house is named in his honor. Coach Boston began his coaching career at Bassfield in a small all-black school about eighteen miles from

Columbia. He still gets excited when talking about the time his little team in Bassfield beat Jefferson High:

> We were working all week leading up to the game, and I kept pumping them, "We can do it." And the day of the game, Jefferson came up and they got off the bus. And normally you see a football team, and they jog on the field. These guys were so cocky, they walked. They'd been scoring seventy points. They just walked out, and I told my guys, "Look, they're disrespectful; they don't even count you." So we kicked off. Anyway, the game is going along, and they scored first, missed the extra point, leading us six nothing. Somehow, we battled around. I had seen them play a couple of times and I noticed they played man defense. And so I designed a play. I called it "the banana." I had the two ends come in and then go out and pull it out. And I had a little boy that weighed 124 pounds—a halfback. I sent him in the middle, and he button-hooked right in the middle there. A little ole guy. We were on our 35. And boy when he caught it, he decided he wanted to score. Our quarterback got down field and he threw a block. He missed the guy, but the guy had to adjust to it. This little guy shot past him and touchdown! We kicked the extra point. We're leading 7–6 in the second half. It's tight. And I had a little kid—and most of my kids were small—but this little boy was playing in the line. A little short guy. He was short, but all his weight was here. He was real chesty. He caught Jefferson's quarterback in his own end zone for a safety. So we beat them 9–6.[33]

In 1963, Coach Boston took a job at Jefferson High School where he was the head coach, the one and only coach, the athletic director, and the assistant principal. He knew how to win ballgames, and his players were highly recruited by Mississippi Valley State, Alcorn State and Jackson State. When Columbia desegregated their schools in the spring of 1970, Coach Boston and his Jefferson High students transferred to Columbia High where there was a vacancy in the head coaching position. He applied for the position fairly confident that with his track record and reputation he would have a good chance of being hired. He was not selected head coach at Columbia High. This was a pattern repeated throughout the South. Black coaches at the segregated black schools, regardless of their knowledge, skills, and rapport with their players, were not hired in chief positions of leadership in integrated schools.

At his new school as an assistant coach and the only black coach, Boston was involved in the football program. A seasoned coach accustomed to calling all the shots, Coach Boston had to adjust to being in a secondary position where he was not allowed to call plays. It was a change for his players as well. He was their coach; he was Coach Boston—the head man. Finally, one day the head coach turned to Coach Boston and asked him about a play. According to Boston, it was a turning point in their relationship:

> One day this coach that was head coach. He and I worked through it together. I'll give him credit. He would ask me things, and he'd let me have input, but he'd never ask me about any plays. So, finally, one day, we're sitting up in a meeting, and he asked me did I have any plays that I like. I said, "Yeah, there's a lot of them that I like." It kind of struck me as odd that I would always have to demonstrate my plays. So I had to go to the board and show him what I was going to do. So, I'd start. I'd run that play. Run it, and the next time I'd fake it to this guy and give it to this one. And Walter [Payton] and Sugarman loved that play. When I walked out in practice, he said, "Well, I want you to put it in today." I guess he thought it would work. So I went out and when I demonstrated it, their eyes lit up. They were glad to see the play. So we put it in. So after that one worked well, he asked me about some more.

Coach Boston became much more involved in play calling, much to his delight and that of his players. Eventually, Coach Boston was even able to convince the head coach to run a reverse, a play the head coach disdained: "But I thought that was the idea of the T-formation—to trick you. Start one way and come back. Hide the ball or whatever the case is. But anyway, we had a big tight end—a black kid—that loved to run that. So we put that in. Worked well. Everything I did just turned to gold for me. I guess the Lord blessed me with it." After the first year, Coach Davis resigned from the head coaching position to take a job at a community college. Once again Coach Boston applied for the position, but this time he had a master's in hand since this was the reason given for why he was not selected head coach the year before. Once again, he was not selected.

Superintendents offered a number of reasons why black coaches were demoted during the first years of school desegregation. They were not equipped to deal with the administrative side of coaching; they did not want head coaching positions in newly desegregated schools; they lacked the proper academic credentials; they lacked training in coaching pedagogy. But Coach Boston offers a more pointed reason for why he was not chosen despite earning an advanced degree and years of successful coaching: "It had to be my race. What else could it be?" Coach Boston resigned from his coaching position after being passed over for the head coaching position a second time. He went on to have a productive career as an assistant principal at Columbia High, but even today one can detect in his voice the disappointment and sense of loss over not being able to do what he loved the most—coaching: "I sometimes wish things had been different. It might not of worked, but I would have liked to have the chance to see what I could do. You know what I mean?"

In Greenville, superintendent W. B. Thompson in 1970, much to the ire of his black patrons and some white constituents, appointed William Morgan, who was white, to be the head football coach at Greenville High School. Passed over for the position was Davis Weathersby, coach at the formerly all-black Coleman High. Weathersby's record over a fourteen-year period was 112 games won and 26 lost. Morgan's record from the last two years he coached was 7 games won and 12 games lost. Weathersby was demoted to line coach and the head coach of track although he was offered a salary increase in line with the other coaches' salaries. In justifying his hiring decision, Thompson admitted that he was concerned that selecting a black coach would scare off white parents and white players, and coaches might resist taking orders from a black head coach. "My concern is to provide the best quality education program possible and keep as many black and white students in the system," Thompson told a meeting of the Greenville Community Relations Committee, a biracial committee. One of the white supporters of Weathersby told the crowd that choosing Morgan over Weathersby would be similar to merging Ole Miss and Mississippi State and choosing MSU coach Wade Walker over Ole Miss's nationally recognized head coach Johnny Vaught.[34] Weathersby declined the job offer as head track coach and went to work at Mississippi Valley State University, where he served as athletic director and later won a lifetime achievement award from the Southwestern Atlantic Conference.[35]

While Coach Boston was eventually allowed to call plays, many black former head coaches found themselves in assistant coaching positions with little authority and no significant coaching responsibilities, often taking orders from white coaches far less experienced than they. William Lewis was only twenty-one years old when he was hired to be the head basketball coach at Harrison Central High in 1969. As part of the district's desegregation plan, North Gulfport High, the black school, was closed, and all its students transferred to Harrison Central. Coach Johnny Anderson was one of the coaches at North Gulfport High, and, like Coach Boston and Coach Weathersby, he was demoted during the desegregation process and stripped of any real decision making. At basketball games he helped with the scoreboard and kept the scorebook. In football he was an on-field assistant. His primary job was to help keep the black players in line. Lewis recalls how Coach Anderson handled his demotion: "Those students from North Gulfport looked up to him. He could have easily had a chip on his shoulder and not been cooperative— not helped us. But if Johnny harbored any problems—personal ill will—about not being named one of the head coaches back then, he never showed it." The reality is that Coach Anderson, like most black coaches, had little recourse to being demoted. Employment opportunities for black coaches were limited; a few were asked to join college coaching staffs, but this typically meant uprooting one's family and moving to another town. Looking elsewhere for a head coaching position was pointless because no school districts in the state were recruiting black head coaches. Thus, most stayed on as an assistant coach with the hope they would eventually be promoted.

In January 1970, while attending the American Football Coaches Association (AFCA) convention in Washington DC, fourteen black college football coaches from predominantly white colleges in the Midwest and West held a separate meeting to address the racial problems they saw brewing at their schools. All attending were assistant coaches. Among issues discussed were "boycotts, facial hair, and black identity." The bulk of their three-hour meeting was devoted to the role of the black coach in the lives of their black players: the need to build relationships with them, earn their trust, and help them navigate the muddy waters of playing on an integrated team. "Black coaches are hired as a buffer and a coach, in that order," they iterated. While no high school coaches attended, and none of the coaches represented there were from the South, the group expressed the sentiments of many black assistant high school coaches who lost their jobs at head coaches but remained for one primary reason—their black athletes.[36]

"No Mixing Off the Field": The Black Athlete Paradox

Like many whites in Mississippi, Beverly Moon grew up poor. When schools were desegregated in her hometown of Jackson, she could not afford to go to any of the new council schools or private academies that most of her white friends attended. So, she was one of about forty white students attending Blackburn Junior High, the public school to which she was assigned. Cheerleaders at her school were chosen based on their grades. Because she was a straight-A student, Beverly was selected cheerleader, the only white cheerleader on the squad. Her father was supportive of her being a cheerleader, but, much to her disappointment, he would not allow her to ride the bus to any out-of-town games. Beverly explains why:

> As much as he was OK with me being there—dropping off, picking up—he said he was going to protect me against black boys. And so, when I said that the cheerleaders were going to ride the bus over to a junior high football game in Vicksburg one afternoon, and he wouldn't let me go. And I just couldn't understand

it. "Why can't I go? I'm a cheerleader. I have to go." And he's like, "No, you're not going." And he finally said to me, "No, because you have no idea what those boys are going to try to do to you on that bus. And I won't let you be on that bus with them. I'm not going to let you." And he was just determined. I always tried to appeal to my stepmother, and she said, "No. There's no way we're going to let you on a bus with a bunch of black boys." [37]

Beverly's account of her family's reaction to riding on a bus with black football players reveals the insidious side of the sentimentalized story about sports as the great healer of racism. The adoration lauded upon black players for their athletic talents and contributions to winning games did little to challenge or change long-standing and pervasive racial stereotypes, power relations, and racial dynamics off the field. White fans may have been comfortable with black and white boys touching, tackling, and hitting in the context of an athletic competition, but white fans celebrating black athletes on the field did not translate to embracing them off the field. As discussed in the next chapter, social integration in the form of interracial relationships, dancing, dating, and socializing outside the parameters of sports and a few other school activities were not only frowned upon, but prevented with the codification of certain school practices, such as eliminating the prom and other school-sponsored dances.

Unpacking the Blissful Clarity of the Redemptive Power of Sports

As we write this chapter, Super Bowl XLIX is right around the corner. As always, a media frenzy surrounds this annual cultural phenomenon. We are inundated with cooking tips for the big day, teasers about the upcoming ads, titillating stories about the seamy side of football (this year it is the Patriots deflated ball debacle), and human-interest stories illuminating the positive cultural role football plays in the United States. The Friday before the game, *Today* featured a tear-jerking reunion between two former high school football rivals in Gary, Indiana—one black and one white—and how a handshake after the game was a transformational moment for both. In 1944, Carl Biesecker's white football team competed for the first time against Horace Mann High, a black high school, where George Taliaferro played. Horace Mann won. After the game, Biesecker offered Taliaferro his hand, saying, "It was a pleasure playing against you with all that we have heard about what kind of a football player you are." Taliaferro went on to play for the Chicago Bears as one of the first blacks in the National Football League. The two did not see each other for sixty years until Carl's daughters arranged for the reunion. Taliaferro speaks of that handshake and conversation as a life-changing moment for him: "That is the moment that I became a human being with worth and dignity because he showed me in one single gesture by a shake of hands that, 'you are all right with me.' And I took the symbol of friendship and ran with it. And everything that I have attempted in my life, every opportunity that I have ever had stems back to him and a handshake."[38]

This is a touching story that reaffirms a powerful narrative in our country's storied racial past: in the midst of racial strife, violence, and unrest, sports provides a bridge for blacks and whites to reach across huge racial divides, recognize the humanity in each other, and come together around common goals and interests. Indeed, the redemptive role of sports has achieved a myth-like status not only in the United States but throughout the world. However, as Roland Barthes warns, the danger of myth is that it "establishes a blissful clarity" and "abolishes the complexity of human acts."[39]

Unquestionably, initial attempts at desegregation were made smoother in many schools because of the intense male bonding of black and white boys who came together on the football field for a common goal of beating their opponents and making their school proud. In many cases, sports provided a mechanism for an integrated group of spectators to sit together, cheer together, and share their love of the game. However, juxtaposed against this positive reading of sports as the great unifier is an equally true story of loss, disappointment, the perpetuation of racism, and the failure of sports to be the panacea some had hoped. "Coming together on the football field" did not suddenly transform the historical relations between blacks and whites or eradicate institutional and structural racism. Racial disparities in sports persisted as black coaches were demoted or dismissed and black boys rarely found themselves in the position of quarterback. Many white athletes fled the public schools for private academies to ensure they would have playing time, and the celebration of black male athletes on the field seldom translated to a warm welcome off the field.

Chapter 7

"We Never Had a Prom"
Social Integration in the Extracurricular

We first had to change appearances, for appearances mattered. The alteration of the
football uniform, the forced "equality" of black and white student body presidents, all
the window-dressing somebody (not students) came up with to try to symbolize racial
equality and change, were for the sake of appearances and harmless overall. The old
traditions we all knew, black and white, had to evolve, give way to new influences, include other traditions never before considered, or die. Most of all we had to find a way
to get past the prejudice and preconceptions that all of us, black and white, brought to
new relationships we'd never had before and hadn't a clue how to develop.[1]

Unique school identities and cultures manifest themselves not so much in the
formal classroom and curriculum (those tend to be fairly universal and uniform
regardless of where the school is located) but in a school's extracurricular
activities—Homecoming traditions; the annual beauty pageant; senior-class
portraits; pep rallies; choir concerts; the senior play; the battle of the classes;
campaign speeches; Tacky Day; powder puff football; senior skip day; class
favorites, and the junior-senior prom—just to name a few. School colors,
mascots, alma maters, sports traditions, and even the name of the yearbook
or annual are often passed down from generation to generation. For many
students, their personal identities, their social relationships, and their leisure
time are defined by the extracurricular activities at their school. It is no wonder
then that when school desegregation occurred many students rightly asked:
What about football, cheerleading, band, the Beta Club, and prom?

For years, segregationists had warned about the dire consequences of
"race mixing." The Citizens' Council built its campaign to preserve segregated public schools around predictions that integration of schools would
bring about interracial friendships, dating, and marriage, thus the end of
"racial integrity" and the dominance of the white race. And the murders of

Emmett Till in 1955 and Mack Charles Parker in 1959 were all-too-recent reminders to blacks of the deadly consequences of any allegations, whether factual or not, of trying to "mix socially" with whites. Thus, as schools began to desegregate in the late 1960s, at the forefront of everyone's minds was the issue of social integration among black and white students. Should interracial friendships be encouraged? What would be acceptable socializing outside the classroom? Should black and white students be forced to sit together in the cafeteria or play with each other at recess? When was physical contact across race appropriate? When was intermingling definitely off limits? These questions would be worked out, in part, in the extracurricular spaces of schools where race, adolescent identity, and youth culture collided and coalesced in ways that both transformed and reproduced race relations in the South.

"What to Do with the Band?": Deciding the Fate of the Extracurricular

Extracurricular activities were first introduced into urban secondary schools in the early twentieth century for the purpose of assimilating thousands of poor and immigrant students into white, middle-class, Protestant values and norms. Educational reformers of the day believed that participation in sports, student organizations, and school-sponsored social activities would inculcate youth into the virtues of cooperation, teamwork, persistence, and loyalty, which would, in turn, translate into skills needed to be patriotic, hard-working, productive adult citizens of the nation state.[2] By the 1950s, sports, band, cheerleading, honor societies, junior-senior banquets, dances, awards ceremonies and other extracurricular activities were solid fixtures of American high schools and helped define the unique culture of the American teenager. Whether one was black or white or attended Brinkley High School in Jackson or Hancock High on the Gulf Coast, being in the band, singing in the choir, serving as student body president, or playing football defined for many young people who they were and how others perceived them.

Harold Bishop was a football player in the late 1950s in Corinth at Easman High, a segregated all-black school with a rich history of sports and extracurricular activities. Every Friday during football season, the cheerleaders led the high-energy pep rallies with cheers inspired by the music heard out of Memphis and Nashville on WDIA and WCLA and the call-response worship in their Baptist churches. It was a community-bonding event where students, staff, and community members rallied around their Easman High Yellow Jackets. Harold recalls one of his favorite cheers:

Leader: Is Tupelo going to win?

Fans: Yeah man.

Leader: Is Tupelo going to win?

Fans: Yeah man.

Leader: Oh you stop that lie.

    You know it's a sin.

    You know dog-gone well

    Corinth is going to win.[3]

Chryl Covington Grubbs, a cheerleader at the all-white Murrah High in Jackson in 1967, has similar recollections of the electrifying atmosphere of their pep rallies and the crowd support for the mighty Mustangs: "I will NEVER EVER forget my first time to run into the gym for my first Mustang pep rally. I didn't realize that even the teachers and janitorial staff came to watch and participate. My hair stood up on my arms, and I remembered looking up into the bleachers at my classmates and seeing all of them chanting . . . When the football captain of the week got the microphone, the crowd would go WILD!"[4]

The importance of the extra-curricular was not lost on those involved in enforcing desegregation in the South. Title VI of the Civil Rights Act specifically mentioned that racial discrimination in any aspect of schooling was prohibited, including "school sponsored projects outside the classrooms." In a June 1966 brochure, the United States Commission on Civil Rights wrote: "The law says that there can be no discrimination in school facilities, services, and activities. This includes sports participation, social and educational activities, drinking fountains, washrooms, lunchrooms, classroom seating, auditoriums, locker rooms, use of materials, buses, etc. Also, Negro parents may attend PTA meetings, commencement exercises, and all other school events."[5] However, the federal government did not offer any specific guidance on how to deal with the election of school officers, membership in the school band, the selection of class favorites, or any other facet of school life outside the formal curriculum. Perhaps they thought these details too trite for legislative or administrative oversight. Instead superintendents, school boards and principals decided the fate of extracurricular activities in their newly desegregated schools. Whether it was concern over safety, the possibility of students interacting in ways deemed inappropriate by adults, or they were just too busy with curricular issues, many school administrators initially chose to eliminate or greatly curtail all or most extracurricular activities in their schools during the early days of school desegregation.

Thomas and Carolyn Evans were two of seven black students to attend Madison-Ridgeland High School in 1968 under FOC. Both accomplished musicians, they had been actively involved in the band at their segregated school, Rosa Scott. However, when they tried to join the band at their new school, they were repeatedly refused. Their mother, determined that her children would have access to the same opportunities as the white children at Madison-Ridgeland, filed a grievance with the school district. Thomas describes their reception once the band program was ordered to include them:

> By the end of the first semester, Mama decided to take action. We took the matter to court, and the school was forced to allow us in the band during the second semester. The school was charged with violating the Civil Rights Act. But by that time, it was concert season. We were allowed to practice with the band only. As well as I knew that I could play that horn, I had to play last trumpet and Carolyn, last clarinet. When it came time for the band to perform, they either failed to inform us or gave some excuse why we couldn't go. One excuse was that the concert band performed at private functions that didn't allow blacks.[6]

When Thomas and Carolyn returned to Madison-Ridgeland after the summer break, they discovered that their new high school no longer offered a band program. Thomas was stunned: "Now I have heard of many things and had come to expect certain ducks and dodges when it came to equal opportunities, but this took the cake. What kind of administration or school system would go to the extremes of abolishing the entire band program just to keep two black students out?"[7]

When the Jackson School District went through desegregation, some of the formerly black high schools were converted to tenth-grade attendance centers. Brinkley High was one of those. Brinkley had a rich tradition of sports and extracurricular activities. In 1968–69 it won the state basketball championship.[8] But when the school reopened in 1970 under court-ordered desegregation, all extracurricular activities were suspended per order from the school board. Such draconian measures also extended into rural school districts. When the schools in Kemper County were desegregated in January 1970, the school board suspended the rest of the basketball season. Coach Billy Brown, the only white coach who remained in the public schools after desegregation, continued to hold spring football practice, not knowing the future of his football program. When school began in August 1970, virtually every white student had left the public schools, and the school board canceled the first eight football games of the season.[9] Other schools took a more modified approach in curtailing their extracurricular offerings. For example, Yazoo City and Natchez retained the sports programs and the band but canceled pep rallies, Homecoming activities, school assemblies, and all social activities.[10]

Students were typically not consulted about any decisions regarding school desegregation, curricular or extra-curricular. But students often led the charge to reinstate extracurricular activities. At Greenwood High School, the principal threatened to eliminate Homecoming the first semester of desegregation. This infuriated many of the students, including the editor of the paper and a GHS cheerleader, who charged into the principal's office, swooped past the secretary (the principal's wife) and, according to classmate Mary Carol Miller, told the principal in no-uncertain terms: "By God, you're not canceling homecoming. You've taken everything away from us. You're not taking that away from us. You can say we're not going to have it, but we're going to have it. So it can be sanctioned or not." Greenwood High had Homecoming that year but eliminated the annual school-sponsored Homecoming dance.[11]

When schools began reconfiguring their extracurricular offerings, black parents became ever vigilant, carefully monitoring the activities of their children to make sure that they were included in all facets of school life. When instances of discrimination in the classroom or in extracurricular activities were discovered, many black parents lodged complaints with their local school boards. If not remedied, they filed lawsuits. During the first year of desegregation in Rankin County, the school eliminated several extracurricular activities and social events. It also set 1:30 p.m. as the new dismissal time; their justification was the needs of many students who worked after school or had chores at home to complete. For black parents, like Alean and John Adams, this signaled a significant deviation from normal school activities that could only be attributed to the school district's desire to limit the amount of contact white students had with their black peers both in and out of the classroom. On behalf of their son who attended Rankin High, the Adams filed a lawsuit against the Rankin Board of Education for persistent discrimination. Their grievances included discrimination in staffing and curriculum and in extra-curricular activities. The Fifth Circuit Court of Appeals ruled in favor of the Adams and the other plaintiffs and specifically addressed the issue of extracurricular activities:

> There have been several allegations that the closing time of the school has been changed to an earlier hour in the day and that certain social events have been discontinued in order to avoid some of the sociological implications of a unitary school system. Of course we all know that these actions were inescapably products of the Rankin County recalcitrants in the hopes to diminish local sociological reactions. None seem justified now. On the remand, the Court shall make a thorough factual reassessment of the current state of affairs in Rankin County and take all steps necessary to eliminate all vestiges of a dual system including both curricular and extracurricular activities, social, athletic, musical and other groups.[12]

The wholesale elimination of extracurricular activities did not last long, due, in part, to the vocal protest of students. But extracurricular activities were also important to many adults in the community whose social lives were built around their children's activities. They volunteered in the concession stand, collected tickets at football games, held bake sales to raise money for new cheerleading uniforms, and participated in the Booster Club. In many small towns, Friday night football with all its pageantry was the most highly anticipated and attended social event of the week. Even community members who no longer had children in the schools often identified greatly with the accomplishments of their high school football team, their band, or their show choir. Thus, when school desegregation was finally enforced, many adults were at the forefront fighting for the preservation of extracurricular activities in their schools.

Mr. and Miss Greenville High: Representation in Extracurricular Activities

The transition to school desegregation brought intense scrutiny of school policies and practices from both the HEW and concerned parents. As more than one principal commented, "I always felt like someone was looking over my shoulder." To assuage concerns from multiple parties about inclusion and access to extracurricular activities, school administrators often adopted new policies aimed at securing fair and equal representation of black and white students on Homecoming Court, in student leadership positions, and membership in school organizations. According to George Dale, a principal at Moss Point High, "the problem of school integration was not an issue of academics, it was an issue of extracurricular."[13] His most challenging task as a new principal in Moss Point was to ensure that black students, who were numerically a minority after schools were desegregated, were represented in extracurricular activities. He explains: "A kid at the black school might have been president of the student body, head cheerleader, whatever. But when they merged the schools together, because there was approximately 70% white population in the merged situation, the white kids pretty well assumed that it was their school. And 'you're coming in; you're like an outsider coming in. You're not the president of the student body anymore." Charles George, a black assistant principal at West Tallahatchie High in the first year of desegregation, noted that even in desegregated schools in which the black/white ratio was more balanced or black students were the majority, if left to student or teacher selection, white students continued to retain positions of leadership. "When integration came, the same lady [a white student] remained president, and she worked as hard as she could to get them integrated, but the whites kinda dominated the extracurricular. The fact is they had been accustomed to being organized. They had the Lion's Club, the Rotary Club, the Boy Scouts buildings and dens, Cub Scout mothers and that sort of thing."[14]

George Dale implemented a fairly common policy adopted during that time: "We had co-student body president. We had co-class president. We had co-everything." Charles Boone, principal at Quitman High, implemented a similar policy—"co" officers for all clubs and organizations. Dale, Boone, and other principals adopting such measures felt that no one could question the fairness of electing both a black and a white student for positions of leadership (e.g., senior class president). However, such policies were not necessarily popular with either parents or students. Discussions about merit and qualifications sometimes led to accusations of reverse discrimination or favoritism. "Why should someone be elected to a position solely on her race when other more qualified students were denied?" many asked. Principal Charles Boone's response was a pragmatic one: equal representation meant the *same number* of blacks and whites in every facet of extracurricular activities. He explained: "I had to do something, and I did not want anyone to be left completely out, regardless whether they were qualified. In other words, you may have some instances where blacks had four people better than any of the whites, but I'm still going to get a white in and vice versa. I made sure both races were there."

Such policies were often extended to the selection of class favorites and the Homecoming Court. For example, students would elect both a black and white student for "Friendliest" or "Most Likely to Succeed," or a black Mr. and Miss Greenville High and a white Mr. and Miss Greenville High. Alan Huffman described the selection process for class beauties at Murrah High during his senior year: "[W]e had been required to vote for both black and white class beauties and favorites, in equal number, which had been an eye-opener if only because it revealed to us that black and white students often had different ideas about who was beautiful and favored."[15] At Jim Hill High School in Jackson, equal representation in class favorites was handled in a slightly different way. Ricky Nations, a student at Jim Hill High School in Jackson, explained: "If a black male got Mr. Jim Hill—he had the most votes—then the white female with the most votes would be Miss Jim Hill."[16] At Quitman High, Charles Boone made an alteration in how the Homecoming queen and her court (often called "maids") were chosen after his school was desegregated: "I always had the football team choose it [the Homecoming court] by secret ballot. Well, what I did, I told them, 'We'll have a queen and maid of honor, and whoever gets the most votes will be the queen. And the next lady, of the opposite race, will be the maid of honor. And we will recognize both of them.'"

One could certainly argue that without these interventionist policies, black students would have been excluded from many facets of high school life because it was usually black students who were transferred to the white school where whites assumed they would retain the positions of class president, head cheerleader, and Mr. Gulfport High. However, in some school districts, these policies were adopted for a quite different reason—to keep white students in the public schools by assuring them that, even if they were numerically a minority in the new school, they would continue to be selected for prestigious awards and highly sought-after positions. If left to their personal sense of fairness, sometimes students surprised themselves and their teachers. In the first year of desegregation at Murrah High, the top award (Blue Knight and Silver Lady) was not determined by the equal representation dictum. Instead it was decided by popular vote. The student body (comprised of 70 percent black students and 30 percent white students) elected a black boy and a white girl for this highest award.

For hundreds of years blacks and whites in the South were prohibited from any social interaction through laws, social mores, and well-understood and strictly enforced codes of racial etiquette. Prior to school desegregation, it would be rare indeed to have seen black and white young people standing, chatting, or laughing together in any kind of social activity. Yet, with the integration of class favorites and class officers, black boys and white girls standing side by side or posing playfully together were captured in photographs that appeared in newspapers and yearbooks throughout the state. Ricky Nations recalls the reactions of some of his white friends to a picture in his yearbook of the biracial couple selected as Mr. and Miss Jim Hill High: "You didn't see a whole lot of formal pictures with a black guy and a white girl. And we had it in our annual. A lot of my friends from other more white schools couldn't believe that here was a white guy and a black girl or vice versa and that it had been done that way purposefully." Similarly, Alan Huffman recalls how the photograph of Murrah High's Blue Night and Silver Lady was disconcerting to many, for it captured an attractive young black man and white woman who looked like a couple ready for an elegant dinner followed by a night of dancing: "Seeing them posed together in the *Resume,* like some interracial couple in formal attire at a 1973 prom in Jackson, Mississippi, was mildly provocative to some of our parents."[17] Alan and Ricky's comments about the visual image of black and white boys and girls together allude to the symbolic significance of the extracurricular. The smiling faces of a black boy and a white girl dressed in formal suits and evening gowns posed on a spiraling staircase in a local church or home, shoulders almost touching, was an image heretofore unseen in the South. It was tangible evidence, to the dismay of some and hope for many, that social integration was a byproduct of school desegregation and that times were, indeed, changing.

Leave Us Alone, and We'll Get Along:
Students as Leaders in Transforming Race Relations

In chronicling school desegregation in his hometown of Yazoo City, Willie Morris, then the editor of *Harper's Magazine*, expressed great faith that the younger generation would be the catalyst for social change through their discovery, by going to school together, of the commonalities they shared based on their sense of place. Morris wrote:

> They are the first white and black children in America brought together under the courts' specific doctrine of mass integration, and they are intensely curious about each other. They fumble for words to express their new feelings . . . They are as American as they are Southern, but it is this common bond in the South—the rhythms and tempos, the ways of speaking and of remembering, the place and the land their people knew and out of which they suffered together—that makes them, young blacks and whites, more alike than dissimilar; and it is this, before it is all over, that will be their salvation.[18]

Principal William Dodson expressed a similar observation about his black and white students at Greenville High: "There is some mystique about a young kid that they will get together despite what their parents are telling them."[19] Implicit in both comments is the belief that somehow students during desegregation, if left to their own impulses and intuitions, would navigate race relations much better than their parents, even if doing so required them to defy the teachings of their parents, their church, and other adult institutions in their lives. Some students certainly rose to the challenge.

Archie Johnson was a junior when his hometown of Columbia was ordered to desegregate in January 1970. He was apprehensive about leaving Jefferson High for a number of reasons, the prime one being the uncertainty of how the student life he so loved at Jefferson High would continue at the integrated Columbia High. Archie explains:

> We had excellent teachers and a decent facility. The beauty of our system was that we could be in everything. Play football, continue in band, especially in concert band. We were in choir; we were in theater. I was in every yearly play that we had and for the most part, it was great. I enjoyed it. You know, as part of Mississippi's

delaying tactics, they had done a lot of renovation. We had a state-of-the art gymnasium and auditorium that was built maybe a couple, three years before integration. So we had a topnotch facility there. We were just getting settled into that and getting comfortable . . . Jefferson was all that we knew, so there was some resentment, some pain in terms of having to leave the history and all. You know, everything changed.[20]

A student assembly had been planned for the first day where the students at Jefferson High would be joining the students at Columbia High. The junior class presidents of both schools were to meet on the podium and each deliver an address. Archie was the president at Jefferson High and had been working for weeks with his social studies teacher preparing his speech. When it was time for him to speak, he walked up to the podium and gave the student body the peace sign. They erupted in roaring applause. The story was reported in *Time* magazine a few days later: "[S]tudents ignored eight pickets outside and sat down together in an assembly hall to cheer a black student leader who urged them to make their town a lighthouse in Marion County."[21]

When white students expressed views that at the time were considered "moderate" if not downright "liberal," they often made the national news as a juxtaposition to the ways in which southern politicians, parents, and business leaders were responding to court-enforced desegregation. A week before the *Alexander v. Holmes* court ruling, the students at Murrah High in Jackson wrote an article entitled "Time for Tolerance." The tone of the article was not one of ardent desegregationists, but it was clear that the white student writers were determined to give this new experiment of desegregation a try. This student editorial was reproduced in the *Washington Post*:

> We will not attempt to argue the merits or demerits of forced desegregation. The change is inevitable. Integration is not a communist plot; it is merely another of many means to eliminate racial discrimination. We do, however, deplore the attempts of some misguided citizens to circumvent direct Supreme Court orders . . . [T]he only rational alternative is to comply with the law and help maintain the best possible education system. All of us—students, teachers, parents and administrators—must cooperate to achieve quality education.[22]

Willie Morris recounted a meeting he had with Alice DeCell, daughter of state senator Herman DeCell, and a group of white students at Yazoo City High. The schools were in the midst of desegregating, and these students' comments were testimony to Morris that change was coming to Mississippi. Alice told him: "[F]ive years ago the people here were against integration—the rednecks—were in power both in the school and town. Now it's a little unfashionable to say you're against it. There's a generation gap here, just like everywhere else. People say it's the adult leaders who're makin' this work here. I don't think the older generation here realizes how much the white people need the colored people."[23]

In the fall of 1972, Ricky Nations began Jim Hill High School, a formerly all-black school in Jackson. A white student, Ricky was curious about the name of his new school and researched its origins. He discovered that Jim Hill was the first black secretary of state in Mississippi, elected during Reconstruction. Ricky's English teacher was June Meredith, wife of James Meredith. Ricky recalled trying to persuade Mrs. Meredith to talk about the 1962 riots at the University of Mississippi. Her response was always, "We're here to talk about English. We're not here to talk about riots, and we're not here to talk about marches." FOC had been in place in Jackson for several years, so Ricky had attended schools with a few black students prior to total desegregation. When he decided to run for student body president at Jim Hill High School, he wanted solidarity to be the central platform of his campaign. Ricky described how he enlisted the help of a black classmate, Marvis Dennis, whom he met when he was in seventh grade, to stage a dramatic campaign speech:

> The speech was about a page and a half. It talked about how we had gone to school together, and this was our first year that we had done well. And Wingfield was kind of our rival. And we had shown that we were as good or better than they were. [In my speech] I said, "We put white power with black power, and we've gotten Tiger Power. When I said that, the place exploded, and Marvis [up in the catwalks] dropped a sign that said, "Vote United. Vote Nations." And "United Nations" was real big.

Certainly, white and black students often bungled terribly when they tried to interact with each other. After all, most of them had little experience in developing relationships with members of the opposite race, and the adults in their lives were rarely good role models on how to traverse the difficult terrain of race relations. Frank conversations among adults and students or black and white students about power, privilege, accommodation, and assimilation were not part of the routine preparations for desegregation. White students, even the most "liberal" ones, were often clueless about the sense of loss many black students felt in having to come to a white school and conform to their way of doing things. As such, dissent and dissatisfaction between black and white students frequently arose; unfortunately, the adults were not much better attuned to the nuances of loss and accommodation. Such was the case at the first pep rally at newly desegregated Pass Christian High School in 1969.

Pep rallies have long been a contested student space, for they represent, for many students, a site to glorify the students at the top of the hierarchical clique ladder—the students (i.e., jocks and preps) that most conform to adult ideals and expectations.[24] Many students who do not see themselves as part of those groups openly demonstrate their contempt for the "in crowd" by refusing to participate in the cheers, chants, school songs, and skits. During school desegregation, pep rallies could be particularly tense times as the entire student body gathered in close quarters (typically in the gym) far from the direct supervision of teachers and staff. At the first pep rally of the year at Pass Christian High, many of the black students refused to participate in the cheerleaders' mandate to "get on their feet and show their school spirit." The white head cheerleader was distressed by her black peers' refusal to participate in her well-planned pep rally, so in her best "cheerleading" voice, she grabbed the microphone and yelled: "I want you Randolph kids [black students] to get up and yell." Lamar Beaty, the principal, disagreed with her singling out the black students, so he quietly made his way to the podium and pulled the cheerleader to the side. "Look," he told her, "I don't want to be critical, and I don't want to hurt your feelings, but I need to say something." He then took the microphone and addressed the student body: "I want to make one thing very plain. There are no Randolph kids in this building. We are all Pass Christian High School. I know some of you are in a different school, but from this day forward, there's no such thing as Randolph and Pass Christian High School. This is Pass Christian High, and that's it."[25]

Beaty's intent was to emphasize solidarity and unity. While good-intentioned, the problem was that, in reality, the white students *were* Pass Christian High. They did not have to give up anything to assume that identity. The black students from Randolph did not feel any affinity for Pass Christian High with its pep rally rituals and a culture already established and largely defined by the head cheerleader imploring them to "get up and yell." This expectation of accommodation and assimilation was at the heart of why interracial relationships beyond the surface were hard to establish and sustain during early school desegregation despite the best intentions of both black and white students who personally wanted to reach across racial divides.

Becoming White: Extracurricular Activities and Racial Identity

As school districts devised plans to desegregate their schools, they often paid little regard to the rich history and traditions of black schools. They closed black high schools or converted them to junior high or elementary schools, and their names, often in honor of a black educators or other prominent local leaders, were changed. Little care was taken to preserve the artifacts of the school's curricular and extracurricular history. Quite literally in many places, the black schools' trophies and plaques were tossed in the trash as school systems rushed to tear down, renovate, and refurbish school facilities in preparation for massive relocation of students. This was one of the most incredible losses of school desegregation. Typical of many school districts, the Greenville City school system converted the black high school, Coleman High, to a junior high. Not only did it demote a football coach who had an impressive fourteen-year winning history at the school, but in that conversion their trophies, plaques, composite class pictures, and citations were destroyed. "All symbols of blackness . . . were removed," recounts Sarah Johnson, a member of the city council in Greenville and a member of the Mississippi Advisory Committee to the US Commission on Civil Rights.[26]

Certainly, many schools during the desegregation process tried to create new traditions. They allowed the students to choose new school colors, new school mottos, or perhaps a new mascot. But what constitutes a "culture," even high school culture, is not simply in the visible objects (class mottos, colors, mascots). Culture is manifested in the subtleties of "how we do things around here." When black students were relocated to the newly desegregated schools, they were expected to adapt, adopt, and assimilate to the already established white ways of doing things. Robert Gibbs, who was transferred from Brinkley High to Murrah High as part of Jackson's desegregation efforts, commented that it was not the academic challenges that most distressed black students in their new school; rather "it was the changes in culture."[27] For Robert, this cultural difference was most obvious in the high school band.

Black and white high school and college bands have long been known for their distinctive differences in their styles of marching, music, drum majors, and color guard and majorettes. When Robert and his black classmates joined the Murrah High band, they were expected to adapt to the more traditional precision style of marching and playing at Murrah High School, which they reluctantly did. However, Robert noted that had the roles been reversed, whites would not have so easily adapted to the band culture of Brinkley High:

> When you think about integrating schools and the decision made to send blacks to integrate into a white culture how we were probably able to do that easier than doing it the other way if you had made whites try to integrate into our culture. I just don't see them being able to dance a halftime show or play the songs that we played. I think it would have been very, very difficult. You know, we learned how to be a more disciplined regimented band. I don't think they could have done it the other way.[28]

According to Robert, the two different band cultures finally clashed, leading to a confrontation between the former Brinkley High band members and their white band director, Mr. Dollarhide:

> Mr. Dollarhide was deep in tradition and he was used to marching very traditional styles and we were used to the more upbeat style and trying to become disciplined enough to do that was a challenge, and he would have to constantly get on us about our lack of discipline. There was one thing that kind of brought it to a head. Mr. Dollarhide had designed this halftime show with a ship and the song that was going to play was the "Good Ship Lollipop." And we kind of rebelled on that. We just decided that we can't do that. We just can't do it.[29]

Robert and his fellow band members conceded to play the song one time. In return, Robert noted, Mr. Dollarhide agreed to add a few "more upbeat songs to the band's repertoire."

Cheerleading styles were also very different in black and white schools prior to desegregation, as Harold Bishop discovered when he and his father, who was principal of Easman High, visited the all-white Corinth High to watch one of its football games. While the playing on the field was remarkably similar to Harold's experiences as a football player, the cheerleaders, according to Bishop, were vastly different: "The cheerleaders at Corinth High were sequential and militarized in the manner they cheered. They cheered by the numbers. When one arm went up, everybody's arm went up—'Go, go, go, team, go!' And everybody's head dropped the same time. It was practiced and rehearsed carefully. They were motivated but they were militaristic."[30] In contrast, the Easom High cheerleaders were far less rehearsed and much more impromptu. Bishop continues:

> A girl might yell all of a sudden "I've got it." And everyone else in tuning in would say, "got a what?" And then she'd yell a little louder, "I got it" and the other girls would say, "got a what?" And then they'd join the stands. She'd grab her ankles. "It's in my ankles." And they would say, "Where is it? Got a what?" "It's in my knee!" and she'd go all the way up to her brain and finally she'd come down and say, "The Easom Spirit!" and everybody would give a yell and everybody would have the Easom spirit.[31]

Robert Gibbs was similarly surprised: "The cheers from the cheerleaders [at Murrah High] were just totally different than the cheers we were used to. We [at Brinkley High] had a much more lively, more upbeat way of doing things and we had to learn to be a lot more subtle and uptight."[32] Thomas Evans and his black friends referred to the style of cheering at newly desegregated Madison Ridgeland High as "bland" and a far cry from the cheers of his segregated Rosa Scott. Cheers like "Hey, hey Thomas Evans! Hey, hey Thomas Evans! I got my eyes on you! I got my eyes on you! I got my eyes on you and everything that you do! I got my eyes on your, shubedobedo!"[33]

As discussed earlier, some schools adopted policies of equal representation of black and white students in extracurricular activities. However, cheerleading squads were often not included in such policies. While some schools used teacher recommendations, grades, or popular vote to determine the cheerleading squads, during school desegregation, many schools increasingly turned to judges to select the squads. Sometimes the judges were teachers, but often people outside the school setting were used to select the cheerleaders. This resulted in many squads being comprised primarily of white girls, even if white students were a numerical minority, and the athletes for whom they cheered were primarily black. Such was the case at Starkville High, where, according to Fenton Peters, black football players easily integrated into the existing football culture, but black girls struggled in making the cheerleading squad: "The cheerleading thing did not go very well because that is a very sought-after position that parents seek for their children. Black cheerleaders were not able to break into that society very well. If they had eight cheerleaders, probably no more than two were black. The criteria was fixed in such a way that only a few blacks would qualify."[34]

His reference to "criteria" is important because it refers to a particular "look" and "type" of cheerleading valued in the white high schools to which black students were typically transferred. Black girls vying for one of the few coveted positions on their high school squads were expected to adopt the more "white" style of cheerleading. This included tumbling moves, pyramid building, tight arm formations, and highly synchronized cheers and chants. It was the mechanistic style of cheerleading that Harold Bishop saw at Corinth High and the National Cheerleading Association (NCA) taught to white girls throughout the country at their summer camps.[35] For black girls to have any chance of being selected as cheerleaders for their newly desegregated schools, they had to adopt this new style of cheerleading, which was clearly different from the improvisational style of cheerleading in segregated black schools. When black girls failed to make the squads and filed complaints about the overrepresentation of white girls, school officials pointed to the objective criteria being used in the selection process. They argued that black girls simply did not have the requisite technical/athletic skills.

But there was another reason why black girls did not fare so well in the cheerleading selection process. It had to do with the symbolic meaning of the "cheerleader" in American culture and high school life. Grundy notes that "cheerleaders were expected not simply to master routines but to project a 'look,' a combination of clothing, hairstyle, figure, and enthusiastic charm considered to embody the ideals of youthful womanhood."[36] With the feminization of cheerleading in the 1940s and 50s, cheerleaders came to represent a particular type of girl—the kind Olivia Newton-John (as Sandy) portrayed in the movie *Grease*. The kind of girl that other girls envied and boys wanted to date.[37] It was a high-status position with significant social capital, sometimes extending beyond the campus as described by Teena Freeman Horn: "Being one of eight Murrah cheerleaders in a school of over a thousand people was probably the biggest thing that could happen to a north Jackson girl . . . Being a white cheerleader in the 1970s meant entering the closed inner circle of northeast Jackson women and society. Perhaps there was an invitation to the Sub-Debs and the Sub-Deb Ball, which was the high-school version of the pre-debutante."[38] Being a high school cheerleader was the social equivalent of being the quarterback. Just as the quarterback represented the most desirable form of masculinity, the cheerleader signified the wholesome, cute, all-American, girl. And that symbol was most certainly reserved for white girls. As evident in the sharp contrast between the composition of football teams and cheerleading squads in newly integrated schools, whites were far more receptive to black athletes on their football and basketball teams where their masculinity was valued in the highly competitive world of sports than they were to black cheerleaders representing their schools as the prettiest, most popular girls on campus.[39]

Cheerleading survived school desegregation, and black cheers and chants sometimes found their way into a squad's repertoire, although the girls yelling them remained primarily white. Likewise, sports, student government, Homecoming, band, choir, class favorites, and other local school rituals and traditions returned to desegregated schools with as much vigor as before. However, one extracurricular activity did not weather desegregation so well, and in some places, it vanished never to return: the school prom.

Schools Can't Be in the Dance Business: Eliminating the Prom

The school prom is ubiquitous in American youth and high school culture. It is hard to think of a movie about American high school culture that does not feature the prom or a school dance somewhere in its plot, character development, setting, or theme. Amy Best, author of *Prom Night*, traces its roots to debutante balls, where young women of wealthy families were presented into society to signal their availability for courtship and marriage. Borrowing from the glamor and elegance of the debutante ball or the cotillion ball, proms in high schools represented a "democratized version" of the debutante ball that "afforded anyone attending high school the opportunity to feel as they too were 'coming out,' that they could transcend boundaries of class. The message was that you did not have to be rich to wear a fancy frock, to be adorned with a corsage, or to waltz the night away."[40] By the 1950s, the prom (or its close sister—the junior-senior dance and banquet) had become institutionalized in most American high schools. It was the culminating grand gala to which many students looked forward all year. For high school students from Tampa to Des Moines to Portland to Biloxi, the prom signaled a rite of passage marking the end to high school and adolescence and the beginning of adulthood.[41]

The prom was imbued with rituals and traditions. Teens were expected to don evening gowns and tuxedos and to look and act like an adult in ways never allowed anywhere else on their high school campus. It was a time of fun, frivolity, and freedom. The prom was also highly charged with sexuality and romance. Students talked about it in terms of a first date, a first kiss, or a first sexual encounter. The intimate dinner before the prom, the music, the dim lights, the adult clothing, the dancing and intimate touching of bodies made the prom different from all other extracurricular events. This was the reason why almost all schools in the South immediately eliminated school-sponsored proms and other school dances after desegregation.

Principals, superintendents, and school boards sometimes rationalized their decision to eliminate the prom as "schools ought not be in the dance business," although historically, schools had been in the dance business for years. School officials did not publicly cite fears of "amalgamation, mongrelization, and miscegenation" as the reason why the prom was eliminated. However, concerns about improper and inappropriate "race mixing" undergirded the decision to eliminate the prom, codifying a racial trope extensively used by the Citizens' Council in the 1950s and early 1960s to garner support for their anti-integration stance: school integration would compromise the innocence and purity of their white daughters.

In the aftermath of the *Brown* decision, Judge Tom Brady, whose book *Black Monday* became the unofficial handbook of the Citizens' Council, constantly stirred up fears about black men as sexual predators when he addressed white audiences about the dangers of school integration. Here is an excerpt from a speech he delivered in 1957 to the Commonwealth Club of California in San Francisco: "Make no mistake about this, the Southern fathers and mothers are not going to permit their daughters to be humiliated or insulted by Negroes, or by anyone else! They are not going to permit their daughters to have to resist the lewd advances of Negro boys."[42] Socializing their children into a fear of black male sexuality was imperative to maintaining white supremacy, and the Citizens' Council carried this message to white children in a regular feature in the *Citizen* (its official newspaper) called "A Manual for Southerner." Here fifth and sixth graders were warned of the dire consequences of "race mixing" brought about by school desegregation: "Who wants to dance with a boy or girl of another race? Could you enjoy a party where black and white children are mixed? The Race-Mixers even want Negroes and whites to date each other. They know that if boys and girls share the school room, the lunch room, dances, sports, rest rooms, and play grounds, then the boys and girls will want to date each other."[43] For older students, the Citizens' Council sponsored essay contests with the winners receiving $500. In 1960, high school students responded to the following prompt: "Why I Believe in the Social Separation of the Races of Mankind." In one of the winning essays, Mary Rosalind Healy wrote: "I know that the social exposure of one race to another brings about a laxity of principles and a complacency toward differences which can only develop into an incurable epidemic of intermarriage. This malady has but one inevitable result—racial death. This I must believe in the social separation of the races of mankind because I am a Christian and must abide by the laws of God."[44]

Fears about black boys and men as sexual predators of white girls became the basis for a law the Mississippi legislature passed in 1964 allowing school districts to submit desegregation plans based on segregating schools and classrooms by sex. The school districts of Amite County, Carroll County, Coffeeville, and Senatobia submitted such plans to the HEW.[45] The Carroll County superintendent told a federal judge that the primary reason why they wanted sex-segregated schools in his school district was "to keep the black teenage boys away from the white girls."[46] The Natchez-Adams County School Board tried unsuccessfully to pass such a policy. Jack Davis described the rhetoric used to gain support for their proposal: "Segregationist organizations blanketed the state with inflammatory literature, some with alarming images and all carrying the imprimatur of Thomas Dixon's ghost, warning against the dire consequences of school integration: racial mongrelization. No loving white parent, the literature either implied or expressed, would want to open the front door to a black boy—a schoolmate—calling on his/her daughter."[47]

However, while battles were being waged about sex-segregated schools, representation on cheerleading squads, and other issues of access and equality, black and white parents in most Mississippi communities quietly reached an unspoken agreement about the prom. It would be replaced with separate, segregated dances held off campus and privately sponsored. Almost overnight, and with little protest, the prom disappeared as a school-sponsored extracurricular activity. Why did the elimination of the prom precipitate little protest? For teachers and principals tasked with chaperoning dances, the decision seems apparent. It was much easier to eliminate the prom than to try to police student behavior based on unwritten, but clearly understood, rules about the appropriate physical interaction between black and white male and female students. For students, particularly white students, the prom in most places continued in much the same fashion as it had before, other than it was held off campus and funded by parents. But why was there not an outpouring of protest from black parents and students who understood all too well the racist narrative undergirding the decision to eliminate the prom? After all, black parents filed lawsuits about other extracurricular activities and boycotted schools that attempted to institute sex-segregated classrooms during school desegregation.

Unlike other extracurricular activities, the prom's goal was solely and explicitly social; it was an extension of the private sphere designed to promote a form of intimacy and social integration that few black parents desired for their children. As Lillie V. Davis, a longtime black educator in Marks, remarked: "I wasn't interested in socializing with whites, going into their homes and what not."[48] The fight black parents waged on behalf of their children to attend desegregated schools was about equal access to funding, resources, facilities, and educational opportunities so that black children could realize their potential and their dreams without artificial constraints placed on them because of the color of their skin. As Jack Davis notes, "Blacks were no more or no less interested in socially or physically intermingling with the other race than were whites, and blacks had no designs on private white institutions such as family and church."[49] But the elimination of the school-sponsored prom after desegregation without much black protest also points to the presence of an all-too-recent past. Haunted by the ghosts of Emmett Till and Mack Parker, black parents had much more to fear than white parents about the repercussions of even the hint of sexual impropriety across racial lines. They knew all too well the ramifications for their sons of a white girl's accusation of an inappropriate touch or a sexual innuendo while dancing. They also knew very well that their daughters had little recourse if a white boy took sexual liberties in a dark high school parking lot in a state with a long history of looking the other way when white men sexually violated black women. For black parents and community activists, the prom was simply not worth fighting for.

In 1997, actor Morgan Freeman approached the school board in his hometown of Charleston (MS) with an offer to pay for the first school-sponsored prom at Charleston High School since desegregation. The school board declined his offer. In 2008, he made the offer again. This time they accepted, and Freeman challenged the students to plan an integrated prom. On April 19, 2008, Charleston High held its first interracial prom. However, the tradition of having a separate whites-only prom continued. Concerns about interracial dating, dancing, marriage, and sexual contact were the primary reasons given for the continuance of the whites-only prom. Comments such as "I'm not going to have mixed babies in our family" and "ain't no nigger going to rub up on my daughter" were publicly expressed at the first planning meeting for the whites-only prom. Some of the white students at Charleston High refused to attend the segregated prom; others attended both the "white prom" and the school prom, and a few white students snubbed the school prom. Clearly disappointed that the whites-only prom continued, Freeman blamed the white parents for perpetuating in their children a fear of social interaction across racial lines. He described the persistence of such racism as "the shackles around our soul."[50]

The Limitations of the Extracurricular

In the extracurricular activities of schooling, the impenetrability of pervasive racial tropes would be tested with students themselves often being at the forefront of such challenges. John Griffin Jones, the author of the opening quote of this chapter, finishes his explanation of the bridging role of extracurricular activities, particularly sports, during school desegregation with the following: "The key was, again, getting to know something about each other as individuals. And in that critical context, sports performed its historical function as the great leveler, talent on the field providing the common ground. From there we could commit to something we held in common, and, with enough time and constant contact, become friends."[51] Jones personifies the hopes of those who believed in the transformative possibilities of school desegregation to dismantle racism. As students learned together in the same classroom, competed together on the football field and basketball court, and played the trombone side by side, racial stereotypes would be challenged, and progress in race relations would be made. Students, like John Griffin Jones, would be the generation at the vanguard of change. Indeed, it was often at the student level that desegregation worked best as students reached across racial lines to form relationships based on individual commonalities and shared adolescent interests and concerns, often in the context of extracurricular activities.

However, Jones also notes the limitations of a liberal discourse of social change based on individual attitudinal changes: "The sad but honest truth about the early period of desegregation is that, outside those mandates that required black and white students to work together, and of course outside the galvanizing force of Murrah sports, there was little interest in 'mixing'—to use a hateful term trumpeted by the likes of Mississippi governor/senator Theodore G. Bilbo."[52] It was often in the extracurricular that the racial divide was the most visible, serving as a powerful reminder that deeply entrenched beliefs about race relations in the South would not suddenly or simply disappear with a court order, a desegregation plan, and the merging of two student bodies. White and black football players could comfortably banter as they showered together after a victorious game. Black and white Homecoming maids could sit on the sidelines wearing similar crowns and cheer for the same team. White Beta Club members could rally around their black candidate running for a state office. However, such togetherness seldom translated into socializing outside of school. As Jones's confession above illuminates, outside a few school-sanctioned extracurricular spaces, black and white students retreated to fairly segregated social lives. They did not spend the night at each other's homes, attend each other's birthday parties, or hang out in each other's bedrooms on a Saturday night. These were intimate spaces deemed unsuitable for racial mixing. This social separation outside of school was not the result of any formal school policy; but social integration outside a narrowly drawn line was regulated, constrained, and sometimes prohibited through school policies and practices meant to maintain the social separation between the races. The Citizens' Council may have lost its battle to preserve state-run segregated schools, but the ideological underpinnings of its resistance persisted long after schools were finally desegregated.

Chapter 8

"Hell No, We Won't Go"

Protest and Resistance to School Desegregation

Ten years ago, the general feeling was that blood would run in the streets before Mississippi public schools were integrated. Within a month, public school integration will be an accomplished fact and hardly anyone expects violent resistance. "The days of standing in the schoolhouse door to bar black students are over," said Melvin Leventhal, the young white lawyer who heads the NAACP Legal Defense Fund here. "The problem is now what happens inside the school-house—whether black students and faculty are treated the same as whites."[1]

In January 1970, the state that had resisted *Brown* the longest opened its doors to massive court-enforced desegregation. Twelve of the school districts named in the *Alexander v. Holmes* case began classes on January 5, 1970, with thirteen other school districts opening the following week. The state, national, and international press was swarming in towns like Columbia, Yazoo City, Woodville, and Petal waiting to see what would happen. By all accounts, that first day occurred with little incident and no violence. The one exception was in Petal (MS) where a group of primarily white mothers protested with signs saying, "Hell no, we won't go," and white students refused to board busses to transfer to their new school housed in a black neighborhood. The story of white resistance in this small town in Mississippi was picked up by the national press and featured prominently on the front page of the *New York Times* on January 8, 1970. Under the headlines "4,000 Mississippian Whites Go to School, but 300 Balk" is a picture of three white mothers sitting in children's desks and a young white boy clutching his hands in front of a blackboard with the words "We Want Go" boldly emblazoned in chalk.[2]

The newspaper was correct. Blood did not run in the streets in Mississippi when schools opened their doors on the first day of massive desegregation. No superintendent or principal stood at his schoolhouse door refusing black students entrance. The National Guard was not brought in to accompany the mass of black students entering formerly all-white schools. No massive riots erupted as they did in 1962 when James Meredith tried to enroll at the University of Mississippi. No police were captured on TV senselessly beating black students or parents. No white students from Harvard University or Western College hopped on the bus to Mississippi to help in local school desegregation efforts. By the time the Supreme Court ruled in the *Alexander* case, the SNCC and the Congress of Racial Equality (CORE) had moved out of the state to focus their attention elsewhere or had disbanded all together. However, such characterizations of the first days of school desegregation minimize the role of protest and resistance in accomplishing school desegregation. Black parents, students, and local NAACP activists organized marches and boycotts to protest desegregation plans that continued to discriminate against black children. Black students staged walkouts, defied disciplinary policies particularly targeted at black students, and issued demands to their school administrators to be treated equally in their newly integrated schools. Occasionally, racial tension erupted into physical altercations between black and white students. Whites, too, borrowed from the tactics of the civil rights movement and staged their own protests and boycotts.

Burglund, Burnside, and Blackwell: Black Student Activism in Segregated Schools

On February 1, 1960, four black students from North Carolina Agricultural and Technical State College sat down at the whites-only lunch counter at their local Woolworth's in Greensboro, North Carolina. Their actions ignited the student sit-in movement, which was quickly replicated in seventy-eight cities in the South.[3] The state NAACP leaders in Mississippi cautioned students in their youth councils against staging any such sit-ins in Mississippi. They felt the possible repercussions from the Citizens' Council and other ardent segregationists were too great. However, several members of the Tougaloo College NAACP youth council ignored the state leadership, and on March 27, 1961, they staged a sit-in at the Jackson Public Library. The "Tougaloo Nine" were all arrested and jailed. Their act of defiance galvanized not only black youth in Mississippi but also many reluctant black adults. The day after the sit-in, fifteen hundred blacks demonstrated in support of the Tougaloo students.[4] "Here for the first time student activism had created a dynamic that recurred during the 1960s in black communities across the state. Young people on their own initiative confronted the forces of white supremacy publicly and dramatically. Whites responded violently, and this in turn angered and mobilized older blacks who had hitherto steered clear of civil rights activity."[5]

In August 1961, Brenda Travis, a fifteen-year-old high school student at Burglund High in McComb, was working at her part-time job at Sadie's Cleaners. When a white woman berated her for failing to remove a wrinkle from her shirt, Brenda made a split-second decision that would change her life. She set the iron down, grabbed her sandwich, and walked out of the store. She went to the office of C. C. Bryant, president of the McComb branch of the NAACP, which had recently joined forces with the SNCC on a voter registration campaign. At the helm was Robert "Bob" Moses. Moses, recently arrived from New York and a graduate of Hamilton College and Harvard University, inspired Brenda to become active in the local civil rights movement. She volunteered with two other local youth, Ike Lewis and Bobbie Talbert, to integrate the McComb Greyhound bus station by attempting to purchase tickets to New Orleans. All three were arrested and jailed.[6]

Unlike many black high school activists whose parents were involved in local civil rights activities or were members of the local NAACP, Brenda was the daughter of poor parents with no connection with the local movement. Brenda explained why she did not discuss her SNCC/NAACP involvement with her mother:

> I recall not telling my mother anything, not telling her that I had volunteered to go to jail because if I did it wasn't going to happen. So, I guess, at that time, you could've considered it an act of defiance. Many times, that's what we had to do. We had to be defiant, even of our parents because for generations our parents were helpless to do anything to protect us. So then it was up to us to protect ourselves and try to protect generations to follow.[7]

When Brenda and Ike, also a high school student, were released from jail, they tried to return to Burglund High. The principal, Commodore Dewey Higgins, refused them re-entrance and expelled them. Angered by the treatment of their peers, on October 4, 1961, more than one hundred Burglund High students walked out of their school in protest as described by Brenda, who joined the student marchers: "We were just all over the street. We weren't marching orderly, so they [the SNCC workers] came out, and they organized us and told us to march two-by-two. We came to the SNCC office and began to make signs. Not with sticks, because they would have considered that a weapon. We marched to city hall where we proceeded to pray."[8] The SNCC workers were aware of the students' plans, and while Marion Barry and Cordell Reagon were much more supportive than were Bob Moses and Chuck McDew, all four agreed to accompany the students on the march. The SNCC organizers and 116 students were arrested, including Brenda, who found herself, for the second time in less than a month, back in jail. The police eventually released students under the age of eighteen to their parents, but Moses, McDew, Bob Zellner, the lone white SNCC worker in McComb, and 19 black students over the age of eighteen were charged with disturbing the peace and jailed for thirty days. Although Brenda was under the age of eighteen, she was not released to her mother. Brenda was sent to the Oakley Training School, a black reformatory school, where she stayed for more than six months.

The other high school students participating in the march faced further retributions from the school; all 116 were expelled from Burglund High. The criterion for readmission into school was a written pledge from the students stating they would not participate in any further protests or marches. Fifty-four students refused to sign the pledge and were not allowed back into school. To accommodate the students who had nowhere else to attend school, the SNCC volunteers created a makeshift school called "Nonviolent High" which the expelled students attended for the last three weeks of October.[9] Moses, a former teacher at a private preparatory school in New York, was their math teacher. When the 19 older students were released on bail on December 5, those who were seniors finished school at Campbell College, an African Methodist Episcopal school in Jackson.[10]

Many black parents were furious with their children for participating in the walkout and meted out physical punishment at the jail when they picked them up. But many were also angry with the leadership of the SNCC, blaming them for encouraging their children to disobey their parents by participating in the protest. Local activists Nathaniel Lewis and C. C. Bryant were also upset with the SNCC, for they "did not believe McComb was ready for demonstrations, and like many black adults . . . [were] appalled that SNCC would permit a fifteen-year-old girl to participate in a sit-in."[11] However, as Dittmer notes, the SNCC was successful in tapping into a different type of civil rights worker, which, in turn, helped spur others to join:

> Here, SNCC intuitively grasped a vital part of the future mission in Mississippi: developing a sense of worth and leadership among people who had never been held in high regard in their communities. Brenda Travis, for example, had come from a broken home. She was not a "well-known person at school," yet through SNCC she came alive and emerged as a symbol of the student movement in McComb. She had mobilized the Burglund High students, inspiring them to stand up for their principles.[12]

Other confrontations between black students and their parents, teachers, and principals occurred elsewhere in the state as the civil rights movement gained momentum. In May 1963, 500 students walked out of Brinkley High, Jim Hill High and Lanier High to participate in a protest in downtown Jackson.[13] In September 1964, black students at Booker T. Washington, a segregated black high school in Philadelphia (MS), clashed with their black principal when they wore SNCC buttons that read "One Man, One Vote" to school. The principal ordered them to remove the buttons. When they refused, he suspended them.[14] A similar conflict occurred in January 1965 at Henry Weathers High School, a segregated black school in Issaquena County. Thirty students showed up at school wearing freedom buttons displaying a black and a white hand joined together with SNCC inscribed in the margin. Concerned that the buttons were creating a disturbance in her classroom, one teacher sent the students to the principal's office. He demanded they remove the pins. When three students refused, he suspended them. The next school day 1,150 students showed up wearing the freedom buttons. According to court records, several students tried to force the pins on students who had refused to wear them. At the end of the day, the principal suspended 300 students.[15] Eventually, both cases were adjudicated in the Fifth Circuit Court of Appeals.[16]

Today Brenda Travis is one of the sung heroes of the Mississippi movement, her story well known in the annals of student activism in Mississippi. In 2011, she received an honorary diploma from the McComb School District at the fiftieth anniversary of the Burglund High School student walkout.[17] Unrecognized, however, are the hundreds of students involved in the incidents at Booker T. Washington High and Henry Weathers High and the countless others unwilling to accept the gradualist and conservative stance toward desegregation pushed by many black leaders. These unnamed students, along with many other young activists, played a pivotal role throughout the 1960s in the fight for desegregation.[18]

Pickets, Protests, and Walkouts: Black Students Fight Back

When the Meredith March arrived in Grenada in June 1966, local officials decided to leave the marchers alone, believing "the less trouble there was, the sooner the marchers would leave."[19] Dr. King arrived in Grenada that night to address a crowd of four hundred marchers and supporters. For one day and night, these black marchers took to the street with little white interference. Bob Green, a Southern Christian Leadership Conference (SCLC) organizer, climbed on top of a statue of Jefferson Davis and unfurled an American flag to a cheering black crowd. The Meredith March moved on to Greenwood, where Stokely Carmichael fired up a crowd of six hundred with his call for "Black Power." Marchers continued on to Philadelphia where they were met with an angry, violent white mob. In Canton, the police unleashed tear gas into a crowd of nearly twenty-five-hundred marchers who refused to heed police orders of "no tents overnight."[20] When President Lyndon Johnson refused to condemn the actions of the police, Dr. King was disheartened, saying, "I don't know what I'm going to do. The Government has got to give me some victories if I'm gonna keep people nonviolent."[21]

After the marchers moved out of Grenada, SCLC volunteers stayed to help local activists launch a massive voter registration effort. In just two days, thirteen hundred black residents registered to vote. The Grenada movement, as it came to be known, mobilized on many fronts. Local youth tried to buy tickets to the white section of the theater. When they were refused, they staged a sit-in on the sidewalk in front of the theater. Blacks, including many students, attempted to desegregate white churches, restaurants, swimming pools, and other public facilities. Throughout the summer and into the fall, they held mass meetings every night followed by marches downtown. Far different from the earlier responses of whites to do nothing, this time around they pushed back, often with violence. Protesters were arrested, beaten, and jailed. Racial tensions intensified during the summer, culminating in a violent clash in late July in which the peaceful protesters were attacked by a mob of more than seven hundred whites, many of them armed with knives and clubs.[22]

On August 29, 1966, 300 black students and parents filed FOC forms for attendance at John Rundle High and Lizzie Horn Elementary, two all-white schools in Grenada. Within days, 150 more petitioners signed the forms. Many of the petitioners were harassed and threatened with loss of jobs and credit. Eventually, 200 of the 450 black students registered for the white school withdrew their FOC forms.[23] The school board postponed the opening day of school as reported by the local paper: "The opening of Grenada Co. schools was changed to Monday, September 12, necessitated by about 300 of our poor mistreated (?) Negroes 'registering' in our heretofore all-white schools."[24] Despite the delayed opening of school, John Rundle High held its opening football game as planned on September 2, 1966. Two carloads of black students attempted to walk into the game. Bruce Hartford, one of the SCLC workers, described in his weekly Watts report the violence that ensued: "They were assaulted by gangs of white teenagers who were waiting outside the stadium in case any Negroes tried to get in. Pat Lock, Constable of Beat 5 drew his pistol and smashed in the windows of one of the cars. Local youth leader Robert Johnson was beaten by the mob."[25]

Schools finally opened on September 12, 1966. A horde of angry whites tried to prevent the 150 black students from walking into the schools. Some resorted to violence and mercilessly beat several students using clubs, pipes, and whips. The crowd also turned on members of the white press, mauling two cameramen and one reporter. Local law enforcement officers and state troopers sat passively by as the violence unfolded.[26] Fewer than half of the students were able to enter the school buildings that day. The rest returned to Bellflower Baptist Church, the SCLC headquarters. When school was dismissed at the end of the day, school officials gathered all the white girls in the principal's office to protect them from the spate of violence they knew was awaiting the black students once they exited the doors.[27] Once again, a ferocious throng of white protesters attacked the students, injuring three so badly they had to be rushed to the hospital.[28]

Not to be deterred, on the following day, one hundred black students once again tried to desegregate the Grenada public schools. This time they were escorted in cars, which the whites lining the streets attacked. Ten students suffered injuries, but the majority of them entered the school that day.[29] With the national press reporting the violence in Grenada, Governor Paul Johnson finally issued an order to the state troopers to protect the black children when they were dismissed at the end of the school day.[30] When black parents and SCLC organizers tried to meet the students to escort them home, they were stopped by state troopers who informed them that no pedestrians were allowed within two blocks of the school. The children finally returned safely home, but more than five hundred whites showed up at the march that night and once again attacked the black marchers.[31]

Two days later, federal judge Claude F. Clayton finally stepped in and issued a court injunction ordering the children be protected and allowed to go to school.[32] On Monday, September 19, 1966, 169 black students, escorted to and from school by their parents and SCLC workers, walked peacefully into John Rundle High and Lizzie Horn Elementary. Folk singer Joan Baez, who had traveled to Grenada with Dr. King to demonstrate her support for the black students and parents seeking a peaceful school desegregation, was one of those escorting the children.[33] While the students were no longer physically attacked in route to and from school, inside the school they were harassed, spit on, cursed at, excluded, and ostracized. Forty of the black students were expelled in the first few weeks on charges they were "troublemakers."[34]

Students and parents tried to meet with the principals at John Rundle High and Lizzie Horn Elementary, but they refused to meet with them. So, on

October 21, 1966, black students staged a massive walkout to protest the continued harassment of black students.[35] The principal immediately suspended 278 of them for ten days. Several days later, more than 200 black students and adults marched to John Rundle High School and Lizzie Horn Elementary School to protest these mass suspensions. The *Grenada County Weekly* reported what happened next:

> The marchers, singing and chanting, were stopped at the intersection of Margin and College streets by Grenada Police and Highway Patrolmen. After a half-hour of singing, chanting, and demonstrating at the barricade, where they refused to disperse, officers ordered the group into the large "paddy wagon." Monday afternoon officials moved approximately 91 youths, 15-years or older to the state penitentiary at Parchman in cattle trucks to relieve the congestion at the Grenada jail. The adults who were arrested were handcuffed and taken to Parchman in cars by officials. Children under the age of 15 years were released to their parents.[36]

Dr. King was horrified by the actions of the local police and immediately sent a telegram to Acting Attorney General Ramsey Clark, describing the atrocious treatment of the students and SCLC volunteers in Parchman Penitentiary: "Women prisoners were stripped of all but their undergarments and each male prisoner was issued a pair of pants. They were then subjected to deliberate use of the prison air conditioning system. The prisoners have also been threatened and verbally abused." King reminded Clark that the state of Mississippi had already received $80,000 in federal aid as part of the Civil Rights Act to prepare for school desegregation with an additional $33 million authorized for the current year. King concluded: "I recall the pledge of the present Administration to enforce with vigor the Civil Rights Acts and related statutes. It is your sacred obligation to enforce these laws. We strongly urge you to do so in the terror-stricken Negro community of Grenada."[37]

After the arrests, blacks organized a massive boycott of the schools with twenty-two hundred black students participating. Judge Clayton once again intervened, and on November 7, 1966, he ordered black parents not to demonstrate at the school or organize boycotts and ordered the school district to treat the black students equally and fairly and to meet with black parents and students to discuss peaceful resolutions to problems. He also called for clear procedures for filing school complaints.[38]

The Grenada student protest was the most violent protest related to school desegregation in Mississippi, but it was not the last. Black youth continued throughout the decade to be actively involved in the desegregation of their schools. In April 1968, after the assassination of Dr. Martin Luther King Jr., between 600 and 700 black students walked out of their schools in Green-wood. A local minister gathered the protesters together in his church and asked them to channel their rage into the on-going boycott of white mer-chants.[39] Black students in Yazoo City staged a similar walkout after Dr. King's death.[40] In April 1970, black students in Leland High gathered outside the principal's office and later in the auditorium, where they created a list of griev-ances they wanted the superintendent and principal to address immediately.[41] A month later, classes were canceled at Leland High—the reason, according to the local paper: "increased belligerence of the black students."[42] In spring 1970, 108 black students at DeKalb High in Kemper County walked out of their school to protest their treatment as "second class citizens" within the school. At DeKalb High, the black students and teachers were kept completely separate from the white students and white teachers. "We've had enough of being in the same building but being kept apart like animals," the black stu-dents told their former assistant principal.[43] At Greenville High in March 1971, most of the black students walked out of their school to protest what they called the "iron hand rule" of the principal and his remarks about black students needing to "adjust to a white attitude."[44]

In the fall of 1970, Rankin County was the site of a well-organized student walkout involving multiple high schools, including Pearl High where Lamar Beaty was the new principal. One Friday morning in early fall, a teacher at Pearl High School intercepted a note in her classroom that said a walkout was planned for noon that day. She immediately informed Beaty. He confirmed with some of his black students that, indeed, a walkout was planned. New to the area and the racial politics of this small community, Beaty called his direct supervisor, the Attendance Center principal, who told him, "Just handle it the best you can." Beaty next turned to the local law enforcement officials. He called them with the following instructions: "I don't want you on campus. I don't want you to come around. I don't want you to be seen. I just want you to have somebody close by in case I need help." The sheriff agreed and said he would keep a low profile but would be around if he needed him.

As planned, the students walked out at the designated time and gathered in front of the school. Beaty met them. One of the leaders handed him a list of concerns. Beaty looked over the list and commented to the students that only one demand directly concerned Pearl High. The other demands appeared to be aimed at Florence High and Brandon High. Beaty asked them to return to class and told them he would meet with them in the auditorium on Monday for as long as they needed or wanted. The students refused. His assistant prin-cipal whispered to Beaty that he had just stopped someone with a pistol on his seat who was ready to "come on campus to control the kids." His assistant pleaded with him, "You got to do something." At that point Beaty told the students, "You've left me no choice. I'm calling the law." One of the students responded, "Call the law you white motherfucker. We don't care." Then Beaty did something that to this day he says was the worst mistake he ever made as a school administrator. He called the sheriff who stormed onto campus like "gangbusters." With him were members of the Mississippi Highway patrol. When the sheriff pulled up, Beaty told him, "I think if you tell them to go back to class, they will listen to you." The sheriff responded, "to hell with them. I'm taking them to jail." Beaty said, "I don't want you to take them to jail." The sheriff rejoined, "It doesn't make a damn what you want. I'm in control now." The students were arrested and carted off to jail.[45]

In nearby Brandon High, the students staged a similar walkout. Linda and Kenneth Adams were two of the participants. Similar to their counterparts at Pearl High, Linda, Kenneth, and the other Brandon High participants in the walkout were dragged by the police to jail. Their children in jail, Alean and John Adams found themselves in a precarious position. As parents, they were concerned for their children's safety, but as leaders of the local NAACP (John was the president), they felt their first responsibility was to inform the other parents of their children's whereabouts and help secure the release of these children first. Alean remembers well the derision of some of the parents who blamed the Adams for their children's arrest. One woman told Alean, "It's you all's kids that did this. You taught them how to organize, how to protest. You made them think they should."[46] According to Alean, her children were the last to be released from jail, and they were furious:

> Finally our own kids came out, the Adams kids. They were angry at many things, but now they were angry with us. "how long were you gonna keep us in there?" Linda demanded. "You didn't need to be afraid," I protested. "You knew we wouldn't let you stay there! And you are brave!" Linda snorted, "Brave?" she said, wiping angry tears from her eyes. "We're growing up in fear! You two are always doing things that make people furious! People shot at our house! Dad's on the watch list! We are always afraid!" But I could see the strength in her and I was proud.[47]

Black student activists, like Kenneth and Linda Adams, were literally taken from their schools to their local jail; others were punished with school suspensions and expulsions. Some were expelled indefinitely. Long before scholars began writing about the "school-to-prison pipeline," Leon Hall, field director for the Southern Regional Council School Desegregation Project, warned of the serious ramifications of these types of school punishment on black students. He wrote in 1972: "[T]housands of our youth are in jail or roaming the streets because they are prohibited from attending class and not able to find jobs because they cannot obtain their high school credentials. Many of the demonstrations are a result of black students and parents protesting the closing of black schools, and reassignment of black students to formerly all-white schools and the firing and demotion of black teachers, coaches, and administrators."[48]

Hitting Schools in Their Pocketbook: The School Boycott

When the black community of Grenada launched a massive boycott of its school district, it was adapting a commonly used strategy in the civil rights movement, the economic boycott. Natchez and Port Gibson were the sites of two successful boycotts, both led by Charles Evers, brother of slain civil rights leader Medgar Evers.[49] In August 1965, George Metcalfe, president of the Natchez NAACP chapter, was badly injured in a car bomb set by the Ku Klux Klan. Metcalfe had recently filed a petition with the local school board to desegregate the schools. Charles Evers arrived in town the day after the bombing and immediately took over as the local NAACP leader. He and Reverend Shead Baldwin demanded a meeting with city officials to present their formal grievances. Their first demand was that at the meeting the mayor and alderman address Evers and Baldwin with "Mr.," rather than "boy." The list also included hiring more black employees, desegregating public facilities, and denouncing the Ku Klux Klan. The city rejected all demands and asked the governor to send in the National Guard to help keep peace and order. The next day, Evers called for a massive boycott of white merchants.[50] By Thanksgiving, local merchants were financially feeling the effects of the boycott. This empowered local black residents, who realized their "purchasing power and . . . that the white merchant's dependence on their collective patronage was as effective means of persuasion."[51] On November 29, Evers met again with the mayor and city officials. This time they were more willing to make concessions, and Evers called for a mass meeting to vote on ceasing the boycott. The wholesale boycott ended before the busy Christmas shopping season, although blacks continued to boycott the white businesses that did not agree to their demands. One year later, Evers helped lead another effective boycott—this time in Port Gibson in Claiborne County.

Similar to the tactics used in Natchez, in March 1966, Evers and the Claiborne County NAACP presented a list of demands and grievances to city officials: more black employees, addressing black patrons with courtesy titles, and desegregating public accommodations. When city officials refused to concede to any of their demands, the NAACP leaders called for a boycott of white businesses. The boycott lasted almost a year, with the majority of black residents honoring it.[52] City officials, succumbing to the success of the boycott, eventually agreed to many of their demands, including hiring a black policeman, desegregating most public accommodations, and hiring fifteen black clerks. In January 1967, Evers announced that the boycott was over.

Boycotts in other parts of the state (e.g., Indianola) were not always as successful as those in Port Gibson and Natchez; nevertheless, economic boycotts played a significant role in forcing white officials and business leaders to agree to many of the demands and concerns of their black residents.[53] Different from protests and marches, which often drew limited crowds, economic boycotts attracted many blacks who had been reluctant to participate in civil rights activities. Dittmer notes, "Unlike signing school petitions, attempting to register to vote, or marching in picket lines, the boycott guaranteed a large degree of anonymity to the participants; the whole idea of the boycott *was* not to do anything."[54]

As obdurate school districts continued to drag their feet in complying with school desegregation orders, blacks increasingly turned to boycotting schools. Similar to how economic boycotts affected the revenue and profit margins of white merchants, school boycotts could potentially cripple school districts since the amount of money received from the state was derived from the average daily attendance (ADA) of students. An example from Clay County is illustrative. In 1969, the Clay County School system received roughly $1.30 per student based on average daily attendance. When it desegregated its schools, both black and white students boycotted. The school board decided to cancel school until after the district court ruled on their desegregation plan since absentees were not counted when a school was officially closed. These actions were taken, according to Clay County superintendent W. G. McCutston, to prevent the financial collapse of the schools. With only 292 of the 900 students attending schools in Clay County, the school district risked losing approximately $900 a day in funding.[55]

Frequently, boycotts were short term and used as leverage in negotiating with local school boards. When demands were met or a federal court intervened, the boycott was suspended. As discussed earlier, in Grenada, blacks boycotted the schools for more than a week. They returned to school only after a district judge forced the school board to abide by a "fair treatment" policy and to meet with black parents to discuss grievances. In March 1967, in Hazlehurst, black students boycotted their school to bring attention to several issues they had with their school leadership. Charles Evers helped negotiate the demands of the black community with the local school board, which included the removal of the principal from his office and his house. The school board complied with their demands.[56] In Tunica, in February 1969, black students staged a one-day boycott. In addition to calling for the removal of their principal, they also demanded "an improved free-lunch program, black studies in the school curriculum, more social activities including the use of the gymnasium during evening hours, two black members on the County School Board and the elimination of the separate Negro school board, and tighter controls on methods of punishment."[57]

In a few towns, school boycotts lasted much longer as school boards refused to make any concessions toward the demands of their black patrons. When the Coffeeville School District approved a desegregation plan to segregate students by sex, black students responded with a full-fledged boycott that lasted more than a year. As a result of the boycott, attendance numbers declined precipitously from 1,562 in 1969–70 to 918 in 1970–71.[58] In Noxubee County, black students boycotted schools in January 1970 because of the school board's last-minute change to its desegregation plan. The new amended plan called for limiting the enrollment of black students in white schools to 40 percent of the white enrollment. In Noxubee County, the number of black students (thirty-four hundred) far exceeded the number of white students (five hundred); thus, the proposed plan would result in only 200 black students attending desegregated schools. The other thirty-four hundred would continue in segregated schools. So successful was the boycott that only twenty-three black students showed up for class on January 15, 1970. The boycott lasted the entire semester, with almost every black student honoring the boycott.[59] In October 1970, 300 black students in the East Tallahatchie School District boycotted their schools in protest to their district's desegregation plan. One hundred white students withdrew from the school district after the boycott and protests began. By March 1971, the attendance was so low in East Tallahatchie that the school district faced the possibility of losing sixteen or seventeen teachers. Black students finally returned to school in September 1971 after a new desegregation plan was approved.[60]

One of the most effective uses of boycotts around schools was in Clarksdale, the first occurring in November 1961 when the new mayor announced that the bands at Higgins High School and Coahoma Junior College (both all-black schools) would not be invited to participate in the annual Christmas parade. This was an abrupt departure from past tradition. The students responded to the affront by planning a protest march. State NAACP president Aaron Henry dissuaded the students from the march. Instead, the NAACP organized a boycott of the white businesses, and Henry enlisted the help of students to make the boycott effective. Their slogan was apt: "If we can't PARADE downtown should we TRADE downtown?"[61]

Racial tensions in this Delta city remained high throughout the decade, partly around the school district's failure to comply with school desegregation. As late as 1968–69, the Coahoma County School District still operated a dual system of largely segregated schools, resulting in the loss of its federal funding in December 1968. Two months later in February 1969, the school board dismissed thirty-five black teachers and twenty-seven black teacher aides, claiming they had no money to pay them. No white teachers were dismissed. On behalf of the dismissed black teachers, Melvyn Leventhal, attorney for the NAACP Legal Defense Fund, filed a lawsuit charging the school system of failure to comply with desegregation orders and asking for all fired teachers to be reinstated with full salaries and back pay. The suit also asked that the school system institute a desegregation plan using pairing or geographical zoning since its current plan of employing FOC had resulted in only seventeen black students attending white schools.[62]

Federal judge Orma Smith approved the school district's 1969–70 desegregation plan to assign students in grades 1–4 to schools based on achievement test scores. Students scoring in the top 25 percent would attend a formerly all-white school, while those scoring in the lower 75 percent would be assigned to one of the formerly all-black schools. Blacks responded by refusing to have their children tested.[63] In September 1969, 250 blacks, many of whom were students, staged a demonstration near Clarksdale High School. When black students marched onto the campus itself, police arrested 146 of them, charging them with trespassing and disturbing the peace. NAACP president Aaron Henry stated his support for the students but emphasized this was "solely a student movement."[64] A week later, more than 1,000 blacks marched through downtown Clarksdale in continued protest of the desegregation plan and the use of achievement tests to assign students to schools.[65] In November 1969, the NAACP launched another boycott of white merchants in Clarksdale and Coahoma County, this time to force the school district to listen to the concerns of its black constituents. Aaron Henry told the local paper: "[The boycott] will last for an eternity or until members of the black community have an opportunity to participate in every facet of the county and community process. We insist that both the county and city school boards withdraw their school plans and sit down with us at the conference table to reach an agreement."[66] As discussed later in the chapter, when the school system was forced to change its desegregation plan, whites in Clarksdale staged their own marches and protests. When the new desegregation order was implemented in February 1970, virtually all the whites left the public schools.

Riots, Brawls, and Defiance

Popular accounts of the civil rights movement propagate a narrative of social change based primarily on nonviolent direct action, the tactic most closely associated with Dr. Martin Luther King Jr. Yet, as historians have argued, nonviolent direct action was but one of many tactics used to challenge Jim Crow, white supremacy, and state and local resistance to desegregation. Long before "Black Power" became a popular slogan, black southerners turned to more aggressive methods of pushing their fight for equal rights.[67] They not only engaged in outright defiance but also in armed self-defense and violent retaliation. Charles Evers and Rudy Shields were notorious for using violence or threats of violence to protect themselves and others engaged in civil rights activities.[68] Evers is reported to have told a crowd in Nashville in 1964: "I have the greatest respect for Mr. Martin Luther King, but nonviolence won't work in Mississippi . . . We made up our minds . . . that if a white man shoots at a Negro in Mississippi, we will shoot back . . . If they bomb a Negro church and kill our children, we are going to bomb a white church and kill some of their children . . . We are going to use the same thing against them that they use against us."[69] Aaron Henry surrounded his house with armed bodyguards and was ready, when needed, to use the language of violence to scare whites into complying with his demands. Threats of violence were also used to coerce other blacks to cooperate with local NAACP leaders and to participate in local protests. The Deacons for Defense and Justice, a paramilitary organization comprised of black men, openly carried guns while protecting participants in the Meredith March and in marches in Natchez, Port Gibson, and Hattiesburg.[70] They were also known to use coercion and, if necessary, force to ensure full participation of black residents in boycotts of white merchants.[71] Local activists throughout the state armed themselves with guns. Leola Blackmon recalls a voter registration meeting held in 1965 at a secluded house in the Carroll County countryside. When whites rode by and peppered the house with gunfire, "the men who guarded us [were] standing out with high-power guns. They began to shoot back at this car, and they hit it. They say that car left there on a flat 'cause they shot the tires out."[72] According to Akinyele Umoja, this combination of "economic boycotts with paramilitary defense and the potential for retaliation, proved more effective in winning concessions and social and cultural change on the local level than nonviolent direct action or voter registration campaigns depending on federal protections."[73]

In October 1969, on the Friday night following the *Alexander* ruling, fifteen black students brazenly walked into a football game at Liberty High, an all-white school in Amite County. It was a dangerous act—to sit in the stands at a school in a county with a horrific history of violence against blacks. These students knew their defiance of the social norms and expectations of the community both frightened and enraged the white fans sitting around them. Eventually, they left, but the next night they returned and stole the school's Rebel flag, leaving a note in the cafeteria: "Go to Hell, Whites." This bold move in small-town Mississippi was indicative of a nationwide shift in black youth activism, captured in a December 1969 *New York Times* article entitled "Black Activists Shift from Integration Fight to More Militancy."[74] Whites frequently used the term "militant" to describe black students, like those at the Liberty High football game. However, as Gael Graham points out, "being militant" had multiple meanings: "[I]t could mean racial activism, separatism, overt expressions of racial pride, or simply animosity toward whites. Whites used the term 'black militant' to convey strong disapproval of such individuals while many blacks embraced the label proudly."[75] The fifteen black students walking into a segregated school event at Liberty High signified a reversal of traditional power dynamics that would play out in many schools in the early years of desegregation. Graham explains, "[A]s blacks became the arbiters of race and racism, white students lost the comparative advantage they had enjoyed in the early days of desegregation. Many black students on and off campus reveled in making whites feel uncomfortable, if not downright scared."[76]

While violence during school desegregation in Mississippi was minimal, racial tensions sometimes erupted into fights between black and white students. In January 1970 on a bus ride home from the Senior Bowl in Mobile, a fight broke out between two boys from Richton High School. During the altercation, the black student stabbed the white student. He was arrested and jailed. On the following Monday, the white students staged their own sit-in to protest the stabbing, and schools were closed for the day.[77] When schools desegregated in Sharkey-Issaquena in January 1970, most of the white students remained in the public schools, which was unusual in a Delta town where whites were the minority. However, after a fight broke out between some black and white students during the summer of 1970, most of the white parents withdrew their children from the public schools.[78]

In April 1971, the racial tension between black and white students at Central High in Moss Point finally escalated into a schoolwide brawl involving two hundred students. The fight supposedly resulted from the cancelation of the school prom, but there had been an undercurrent of racial unrest simmering throughout the community for months. When the racial tension turned violent, seventy policemen were called to campus to break up the fights.[79]

George Dale, principal at the junior high at the time of the riots, describes what happened that day:

> I'm sure it had probably been brewing for quite some time, and a black kid and a white kid during what they called morning break got to mouthing off at each other, and the next thing you know, they are swinging, and of course, a lot of other folks jumping in. It was kind of a chain reaction, and you look up, and what had been kind of seething underneath immediately came to the top. And they were fighting, and the teachers on duty were trying to break it up. And there were fights breaking out everywhere. And so they called the police, and the police came up and were trying to break it up. By that time, everybody was out on the campus. So the police called the highway patrol. First thing they did was bring their bus up there, and when they finally got it quieted down, people scooted out and went on home. But they had loaded up a bunch of those kids—all they could get. They were fighting them. They put them on the bus to take them down to the jail to send them through the youth court.[80]

When the injured students arrived at the local hospital, they began swinging at each other in the emergency room. Nine students were arrested, and city officials imposed a curfew to help calm the escalating racial situation. The next day the black students boycotted their six-weeks exams and refused to leave campus when ordered to do so. Police were once again called to campus. Twenty-five black students were arrested; several accused the police of using undue force in forcing them to evacuate the campus.[81] The principal and several teachers resigned after the riot.

In 1969, as part of Harrison County's school desegregation plan, North Gulfport High School, an all-black school, was closed, and its students transferred to Harrison Central High, one of the largest high schools in the state. The black students were angry not only about their school closing but also about being sent to a school whose mascot was the Red Rebels and where Confederate flags were omnipresent at every sporting event. Because of Hurricane Camille, the school term did not begin until September 29, 1969. When students finally returned to school, the racial tension was palpable. Shortly thereafter, teachers and administrators began hearing of plans for an organized protest. They were told to be prepared for "Black Friday" and a possible riot. On the day of the rumored riot, the principal assigned all faculty and staff to duty stations throughout campus. The superintendent, hoping his presence would prevent any violent outbursts, arrived early that day. As the busses transporting the black students arrived on campus, the Harrison Central faculty watched as black students exited the busses, many garbed in all black attire. Ominously, because of an earlier storm that had left the school temporarily without electricity, the morning bell did not ring on schedule. William Lewis, a young, new teacher and coach at the school, was stationed on a knoll leading up to the school entrance. He described what happened as students milled about waiting for the bell to ring:

> All of a sudden, a scuffle broke out. And then you started hearing that there was a fight going on over by the cafeteria. And down by the science building. And there were melees all over the campus. And it really was a very challenging situation there for several hours, and it took time to get things under control to get the students in their classrooms. Of course, law enforcement had been placed on alert, because it was not too long until all of the law enforcement showed up. With the size of the campus and the number of students, it was kind of like the water running out of the hole in the dike. You stick your finger in here and it breaks someplace else. And that was exactly what was happening. So it took a good part of the morning to get that under control.[82]

Several students were injured and rushed to the hospital.[83] One student lost several of his teeth when he was hit with a bicycle chain. Superintendent Smith was reportedly injured when trying to separate a group of fighting students.[84] After calm was finally restored, the sheriff reported that they had found several make-shift weapons, including "rake tailed combs, knives, hairbrushes with long stems, and at least 3 chains, one bicycle chain, two other new metal hog chains with rope to lap around the wrist."[85] Several days after the fight, seventeen students were expelled from school, including four white girls whose parents filed a lawsuit against the school district. In an attempt to downplay the seriousness of the fight and alleviate concerns that this was a "race war," district attorney, Boyce Holliman, said, "I saw more fights when I started school."[86] But, according to Lewis, the fights that day were "definitely about race." The school officials tried to reassure parents with statements such as, "[A]ll of the students involved were said to have previous records of misconduct in school." The sheriff offered his own reassurance: he deputized all male teachers, "empowering them to arrest any troublemakers."[87]

One year later, Sheriff Luther Patton was still trying to suppress rumors about the seriousness of the "Black Friday" fights. "The wild rumors after [the] incident at Harrison Central High School last October have caused more trouble than the incident itself."[88] However, he warned students of the strict ban on bringing any item to school that could be perceived as a weapon. Any student discovered with a concealed weapon would be fined one hundred dollars. Patton also said that his officers and local police were prepared to move in quickly if any trouble was suspected.

The Mother Brigade: White Protest and School Desegregation

January 7, 1970, was not a typical return-from-Christmas-break day in the small town of Petal, just on the outskirts of Hattiesburg. It was an unusually cold, blustery day with temperatures dipping into the teens. Also atypical was the group of mothers carrying signs with slogans, such as, "Hell no, we won't go."[89] They were protesting their school district's desegregation plan ordering the transfer of 280 white students to the formerly all-black Earl Travillion School, located in a black section of town. Feeling rather powerless to do much of anything, Superintendent Milton Evens met with the 300 disgruntled parents at Petal Junior High. "We had no other choice," he told the incited crowd. He urged the parents to allow their children to board the buses waiting to transport them to Earl Travillion. They refused, and the busses drove away empty.[90] The *New York Times*, reporting the story on their front page, compared this protest in a small town in Mississippi to other protest movements: "The demonstration resembled those by Negroes all across the South in the civil rights movement and included slogans borrowed from draft resisters." [91] Indeed, after the *Alexander* ruling, white parents and students throughout the state began mobilizing to organize their own countermovement. They staged protests and boycotts; they marched and filed grievances in a last-ditch effort to turn back the school desegregation tide.

White parents in Mississippi staged the first and largest boycott on December 11, 1969, in Forrest County under the direction of a local activist organization called the Committee for Local Control of Education (CLCE). More than 3,000 students participated in the boycott by staying home that day.[92] According to CLCE, the boycott was "90 percent effective."[93] In conjunction with the boycott, several women picketed in Petal and at the Forrest County Courthouse. These women were referred to in the press as the "mother brigade, clad in heavy coats, scarfs, and slacks [and carrying] placards stating: 'No one wants HEW's plan but HEW' and 'We don't need federal interference to run our schools.'"[94] Ray Davis, a member of the CLCE steering committee, reportedly told students to take their textbooks, their uniforms, and other school supplies home with them on December 16, the last day of class before the Christmas holidays. Governor John Bell Williams responded to the boycott by declaring, "Parents who feel it is in the best interest of their child not to attend school have a perfect right to keep the child out of school."[95]

Inciting the white community to support a singular form of protest was not an easy endeavor. Whites had choices: they could send their children to private schools, hop district lines and use false or fictitious addresses to register their children in predominantly white schools, or move to neighborhoods or districts with fewer black pupils. Even less affluent whites were able to attend private schools in many areas with the help of wealthier neighbors who paid their tuition bills. Jim Meadows, a Baptist minister, discovered just how difficult it was to organize a boycott in his hometown in Lauderdale County. On January 5, 1970, he helped convene a group of two hundred white parents at the East Mississippi Electric Power Association auditorium to discuss the proposed boycott of the public schools. Before the meeting, Meadows announced that he personally would not support a boycott unless he had at least 50 percent of white parents supporting it. During the meeting, reaction from the white audience was mixed. Many had already decided to send their children to the private school; others were content to take a "wait and see" attitude and keep their children at home for a few days. After the meeting, Meadows told the local paper that he had not received the support he needed: "It would have been effective if we had gotten 70 or 80 per cent of the parents' support and it would have served its purpose as a voice of opposition." He decided to send his three children to the public schools, at least for the first day, stating, "There may be a time that I may have to send my children to a private school but I believe public schools are the answer and we will send them there until we feel that if we send them they may not be safe."[96]

As discussed earlier, throughout the 1960s, Clarksdale was the site of multiple black protests, boycotts, and marches, including a boycott of local white merchants in November 1969 to protest their school district's desegregation plan of using achievement test scores to assign students to schools. In January 1970, the federal judge struck down the school district's proposed plan and ordered it to eliminate immediately its dual system of desegregated schools. The court ordered grades 7–12 to open under the new plan on February 1, 1970.[97] The mayor and city officials, all white, issued the following statement asking citizens to cooperate with school officials and to support the public schools.

> The implementation of this plan involved many difficulties for both the black and white communities, as well as our school administration. As never before, the people of this city must unite in a determination that these difficulties be resolved. There is no alternative if the city of Clarksdale is to survive and grow into a prosperous community . . . We urge all school parents and students associated with the Clarksdale public school system to maintain and demonstrate a high degree of intelligence and loyalty to the concept of public education.[98]

The vast majority of whites responded differently. A group called "The Silent Majority of Coahoma County" organized a march, and in January 1970, fifteen hundred white residents marched through downtown Clarksdale to protest the court order. Ironically, a central theme of their protest was the right to use FOC to achieve desegregation.[99] After resisting for years any form of school desegregation, even through FOC, the white protestors were now touting "choice" as a basic principle and fundamental right to ensure that the "silent majority [i.e., whites] had a voice in local decisions."[100]

Youth Activism in the Rural South: A Conflicting Narrative

In March 1969, the National Association for Secondary Principals reported that 59 percent of high schools and 56 percent of junior high schools had experienced some form of student protest.[101] Responding to this "state of crisis," practitioner journals (e.g., *The Clearing House, Phi Delta Kappan, School Management,* and *The High School Journal*) from 1968 to 1972 published a plethora of articles about how to handle student unrest on high school campuses. With titles such as "Organizational Response to Student Militancy in the Secondary School" and "Revolutionaries Who Have to Be Home by 7:30," these articles offered school administrators practical strategies for dealing with disruptive student activists. The overarching message of these articles was that principals in urban schools, such as those in New York, Chicago, and Los Angeles, should expect student unrest and be prepared to deal with it appropriately. Missing from these journal articles was any mention of the student unrest occurring in the South during this tumultuous time of school desegregation. Indeed, one article published in 1970 in *The High School Journal* claimed that "the small rural schools have yet to evidence the protest movements in urban America" (364). However, a 1971 NEA report of southern schools embroiled in desegregation paints a very different picture of student activism. It notes that 23,881 students in southern schools were involved in boycotts, walkouts, and demonstrations; 2570 were arrested as a result of "racial clashing" at recently desegregated schools, and 24,866 (primarily black) had been expelled or suspended from July 1970 to May 1971.[102]

Chapter 9

Resistance through Exodus
Private Schools as a Countermovement

Mary Carol Miller was a sophomore at Greenwood High School in January 1970. Her mother was a journalist for the *Memphis Commercial Appeal*, so Mary Carol and her sister were probably better versed than their peers about the desegregation cases making their way through the courts and the possible ramifications of the ruling for them and their school. What Mary Carol was not prepared for was the sudden departure of most of her white friends to Pillow Academy, a private school begun in 1966. She explained: "When the court-ordered integration came full force, kids started bailing out. About half of our tenth-grade class left within a couple of weeks of that. And my memory of that is lockers clanging in the hallway as kids cleaned their lockers out. They were coming to school, handing in whatever they had to hand in to get their records and get out."[1] Eight hundred white students left the Greenwood Municipal Separate School District in the first months of 1970. School board attorney Hardy Lott, in a July 30, 1970, letter to Jerris Leonard, assistant attorney general, blamed the federal lawsuit against the school board as "taking the School District a great deal farther down the road to becoming an all-black school district." On the same day, Lott wrote Senator James Eastland asking his help in ensuring Leonard read his letter: "Dear Jim . . . The time is short, as we must prepare and file in Greenville not later than August 13 any suggestion the School Board has. This is about the last hope for this school district and the School Board and I think it urgent that Mr. Leonard examine the matter, even though we do not have much hope of any results from him."[2] The exodus of white students from public schools in Greenwood was not unique. As court-enforced desegregation occurred, private school enrollment soared. In some towns, like Canton, Woodville, DeKalb, Macon, Holly Springs, Tunica, and Liberty, almost every white student left the public schools within the first year of court-enforced school desegregation.[3]

"What to do with the private schools?" plagued white superintendents and school board members whose immediate concern was the retention of white students in their schools. In many communities, whites organized Friends of the Public Schools (or some variation thereof) to demonstrate their strong opposition to private schools. In other towns, the school board and superintendent openly supported the newly formed private academies with donated (or greatly reduced) gifts of land, facilities, and other resources. The public-private school debate divided the white community in some towns, leaving severed friendships and church divisions in its wake. In a few towns, like Tupelo and Oxford, the private school movement never gained much momentum due largely to the efforts of a well-organized and very vocal business community. And in at least one town, Yazoo City, the white power structure waged a vigorous campaign to support public schools, while many of those same business leaders sent their own children to the local private school. They believed the two systems of schooling could co-exist.

The private school movement also weighed heavily on local black residents, who saw the obvious ploys used by the governor down to the local school boards to support private schools. Tuition grants, retaining private school teachers on the local school system payroll, and selling busses for pennies were simply a continuation of fifteen years of trying to impede school desegregation. Civil rights attorneys and black activists had to devote time and resources to filing lawsuits, not for their children to have the right to go to desegregated schools but to challenge the local, state, and even federal appropriation of public monies to support private schools. In 1970, Charles Evers called for black Mississippians to boycott white merchants who openly supported private schools. "We don't want any violence," he declared. "We just don't want to support private schools in any form. If the white merchants are going to go on record supporting private schools, we're not going to buy from them." Evers predicted that the private school movement would pass and that whites would return to the public schools.[4] Evers was not alone in his optimism that the private school movement would be short-lived. Hodding Carter Jr., editor of the *Delta Democrat* in Greenville, espoused similar sentiments in 1972: "Some of the new academies will undoubtedly continue to operate for a few years more, with ever-fewer students and higher costs. A small handful may become permanent fixtures in their communities, enclaves for the affluent and the irredeemably bigoted."[5]

By the fall 1970, 158 accredited private academies were operating in Mississippi, and by 1971, 20 percent of white students (63,242) in Mississippi attended private schools.[6] Some whites did return to the public schools after the desegregation dust settled; however, in many parts of the state private schools did, indeed, become permanent fixtures. Today, approximately 10 percent of Mississippi's school-age population attends private academies, the bulk of them formed in response to court-enforced desegregation.[7]

The Citizens' Council and the Birth of the Private School Movement in the South

Following the heels of the passage of the Civil Rights Act in July 1964, the Citizens' Council devoted its entire September issue of *the Citizen*, their monthly newspaper, to private schools.[8] This issue signaled a major shift in the council's mission as reflected in the opening editorial entitled "Government Schools": "Until the misuse of Federal power can be reversed, until the conservative white majority can recapture national political power, the obvious alternative for concerned parents who do not wish to surrender their children to government schools is to provide private schools, which will be responsive to the wishes of the patrons."[9] Their rhetorical use of the term "government schools" to refer to public schools was meant to convey that the "public" part of public schools no longer existed; instead, they argued, public schools were the pawns of the federal government. This rhetorical tactic also allowed the council to situate public schools as part of a federal government agenda to override states' rights and the power of the people, that is, white people.[10] The council cited the Civil Rights Act of 1964 as the ultimate imposition of the federal government into the affairs of states by forcing citizens to pay taxes for schools that "instead of being responsive to the wishes of the *public* in a local community, the schools are now forced to obey the wishes of *government* in far-off Washington."[11]

The pages that followed offered a manual for how to start a private school, covering a wide array of topics, from how to select a principal and teachers to finances to curricular and extracurricular issues, to transportation and textbooks to accreditation. The newspaper ends with a sample "Charter of Incorporation" for readers to use in the establishment of their own private school. In 1966 the Citizens' Council of America held its Eleventh Annual Leadership Conference in Chattanooga (TN). Its executive director, Louis W. Hollis, announced there that the "promotion of segregated private schools is [now] the major project of the Citizens' Councils."[12] For ten years, the Citizens' Council had fought to preserve segregated public schools. Now they were calling for a mass exodus from them.

The Citizens' Council opened its first private school, Council School 1, in Jackson in 1964 for grades 1–6 with one principal, 3 teachers, and 22 students. Because their building was not ready, they held classes for several weeks in the home of one of its board members, Dr. Charles Neill. Governor Ross Barnett held a fund-raiser in his home to help raise money for the new school's library. In fall 1965, the school expanded to include grades 1–12, and its student enrollment increased to 110. Council School 2 and Council School 3 opened in fall 1966 with a total attendance at all three schools of 200. In 1968, the Council School Foundation helped form the Mississippi Private School Association. In the 1968–69 school year, enrollment at all three council schools increased to approximately 500 students. By the spring of 1970, it had climbed to 3,000 students. At Council School 3 alone, the enrollment grew from 120 students in fall 1969 to 1,521 students in spring 1970. The influx of new students resulted in the hiring of an additional 51 teachers, 32 new buildings, and 52 new classrooms. By August 1970, the Citizens' Council was operating five private schools in the Jackson area, with an enrollment of 5,000 students.[13]

The Citizens' Council focused on the state's most populous area to launch its private school movement, but private academies also opened in rural areas of the state. Bayou Academy in Bolivar County and Cruger-Tchula Academy in Holmes County both opened in 1964.[14] By 1966, fifty-five private schools were operating in the state.[15] However, private school enrollment did not grow at the rate the council predicted, and the majority of whites chose to remain in the public schools. A number of factors account for the initial slow growth of the private school movement. Many white Mississippians simply could not afford the tuition for a private school, plus community identities in many small towns were attached to their local public schools.[16] Further, most white Mississippians were not ready to concede that desegregation was inevitable, and the adoption of "freedom of choice" plans in many school districts throughout the state allowed most school districts to continue operating a dual and still segregated system of public schooling for most of the 1960s.

As table 9.1 illustrates, the growth of private schools was minimal from 1966 through 1968. However, from 1968 through 1970, the number of students attending private schools in Mississippi almost tripled as the *Alexander v. Holmes Board of Education* case wound its way through the courts, culminating in the 1969 Supreme Court ruling ordering immediate desegregation.[17]

By the mid-1970s, the Citizens' Council's influence and power on state and local politics had greatly waned, and it was plagued by internal struggles.[18] But it laid the foundation for a strong private school network and its Jackson headquarters continued to operate as a clearing house and resource center for the hundreds of private schools operating in the state.

Table 9.1

Private School Growth in Mississippi, 1966–1973

Year	Total Private School Enrollment	Sample Listing of Private Schools Formed
1966	21,333	Delta Academy (primary school) Pillow Academy Tunica Academy
1967	21, 817	Rebul Academy
1968	23,181	Delta Academy High School Humphries Academy Marshall Academy (1–8)
1969	44,497	Benton Academy Greenville Christian Manchester Academy Marshall Academy (high school) Newton Academy Starkville Academy Winston Academy
1970	63,242	East Rankin Academy Jackson Preparatory Academy Kemper Academy Lamar Academy (middle and high) Magnolia Heights Academy Washington School West Tallahatchie Academy
1971	64,196	Heidelberg Academy Hillcrest Christian Strider Academy
1972	62,366	Sylvia Bay Academy
1973	62,021	

Source: Charles Clotfelder, 1976: 30.

Regional Proliferation of White Academies

Most private schools established in the late 1960s were not directly affiliated with the Citizen's Council. Rather, they formed through grass-roots efforts with local parents at the helm. The creation of Kemper Academy in DeKalb is illustrative. In a drenching rainstorm in November 1969, white parents crowded into the Kemper County courthouse in downtown DeKalb to vent their anger with the recent *Alexander* v. *Holmes* case. Their overriding sentiment had been captured a week earlier in the *Kemper County Messenger* with the headline: "Federal Courts Action to Ruin Kemper Schools." The main topic of the meeting was the formation of a new private school. In attendance was the headmaster of the nearby private school in Noxubee County who fielded questions about the problems and possible solutions the community might encounter in opening a private academy. At the end of the meeting, parents completed a form stating their interest in the private school and the names and grades of their children. By the end of November, Kemper Academy had been birthed and was accepting applications for headmaster.[19] When the public schools reopened in January 1970 under court-enforced desegregation, few white students remained in the public schools. Most were enrolled at Kemper Academy.

This type of almost "over-night" creation of private schools was common throughout the state. In Jackson in 1970, a group of mothers conceived of opening a private "neighborhood school," and twenty-four hours later, they were operating a school in a bus directly across the street from Lake Elementary School (a public school) with a full-time (unpaid) certified teacher.[20] In Canton, a local tent factory was converted to a private school. When Canton Academy opened, almost no white students remained in the public school.[21] Lacking a physical facility was not a deterrent in most communities, as local white churches offered to house the academies until more permanent facilities were secured. In 1965, Country Day Academy in Marks opened in Marks Presbyterian Church. That same year, Central Holmes Academy opened with classrooms in First Methodist Church and First Baptist Church in Lexington. In Natchez in January 1970, sixteen Baptist churches partnered to support and establish an all-white private school. That same year in Tunica, their new private school, the Tunica Church School, held classes for an entire semester in the Baptist, Methodist, and Presbyterian churches.[22] By 1972, 19,662 students in Mississippi were attending private schools affiliated with their local Protestant churches.[23]

In 1970, private schools were operating in fifty-six of the eighty-two counties in the state; however, the majority of private schools were located in three main regions: the Delta, the southwest, and in Jackson. From 1963 through 1970, nineteen private schools for whites were opened in the Delta counties of Bolivar, Washington, and Coahoma alone. In contrast, in the northeastern pocket of the state (comprising the counties of Benton, Tippah, Union, Pontotoc, Alcorn, Prentiss, Lee, Tishomingo, and Itawamba), Alcorn was the only county with a private school.[24] The proliferation of private academies in certain regions of the state can be traced to several historical, economic, and demographic factors. Michael Fuquay notes that the Delta was a fertile ground for the birth of the private school movement because of its long-standing antipublic education sentiment. Fearing that an educated slave and, after the Civil War, an educated newly freed slave would be detrimental to the plantation economy, affluent Delta planters fought the establishment of any form of public schooling. Once established, they fought vigorously against any financial support of schools through tax revenues. When desegregation was court enforced in the 1960s, many Delta farmers were wealthy enough to financially back the private schools through donations of cash, land, and buildings. They also often paid the tuition of poor whites in their employ.[25] However, the most significant variable for explaining the concentration of private academies in these regions is the population demographics. In his 1971 senior thesis at Princeton University, Luther Munford studied the correlation between white flight to private schools and the racial demographics of school districts named in the *Alexander* case. Munford reached the following conclusions: "White children abandoned public schools of the *Alexander* districts roughly in proportion to the percentage of black population in each district, no more and no less. Every district with a population 20 per cent or more black lost white students; districts with populations almost 70 per cent Negro lost almost all their white enrollment."[26] As illustrated in table 9.2, the regions of the state with the highest percentage of black students experienced the largest exodus of whites from their public schools.

However, within each of these regions, certain school districts were able to retain white students during the first years of desegregation. For example, in Greenville, 30 to 40 percent of white students remained in the public schools for several years.[27] In the Western Line School District, whites comprised the majority of students at Riverside Elementary and High School, and in Yazoo City the majority of whites stayed in the public school the first semester, although the number significantly decreased by the following semester. Hence, other variables affected the degree of "white flight" in these communities, including the implementation of segregated classrooms within desegregated schools; concerted community support for public schools; income

Table 9.2

Percentage of Black School-Age Population and White Students
in Nonparochial Private Schools by Region, 1971–72

Region	Percentage of School-Age Population – Black Students	Percentage of White Students in Private Academies
Delta	66.7	37.2
Southwest	57.2	33.6
Jackson Metro	47.3	34.1
East Central	46.1	14.6
North	38.1	7.2
Southeast	28.8	4.5

Source: Crespino, 2007: 247.

level of the white population; and strong, cooperative leadership within and
between the black and white communities.

Public Aid to Private Schools

After the *Alexander v. Holmes* ruling, Governor John Bell Williams declared
that Mississippi could easily accommodate both a private and a public school
system as long as the local two systems agreed to "cooperate:"

> For instance, it might be well for our school administrators, in communities
> where needs are great and the facilities limited, to make arrangements with legiti-
> mate private school administrators for the use of their physical facilities at times
> and hours when they are not required for public school purposes. The same spirit
> of cooperation . . . should exist between our churches and private schools, even
> as it exists now between our churches and the public schools. I am strongly of the
> opinion that we must preserve our public school system as an absolute necessity
> for the good of all . . . On the other hand, a strong private school system may very
> well supplement and add strength to our public schools.[28]

By the summer of 1970, the explosion of the private school movement
throughout the South concerned many in the federal government, and they

directed their attention to this "spirit of cooperation" developing between many private and public school systems in the South.

In July 1970, Attorney General Ramsey Clark delivered a passionate address to the Senate Committee on Equal Education Opportunity urging Congress to stop the rapid proliferation of segregationist academies in the South. He implored: "We prohibit segregation in public facilities and public accommodations. Do private schools have less impact on the general welfare than hotels, restaurants, or bowling alleys?"[29] On August 6, 1970, Walter Mondale, chair of the Committee of Equal Education Opportunity, questioned HEW secretary Elliot Richardson as to what his agency was doing to deter the growth of private segregationist schools in the South. Mondale pointed out that it was common knowledge that many of these private schools were being greatly aided by the public schools who were donating land and facilities and transferring teachers and equipment. Mondale pressed Elliot about the HEW conducting a thorough investigation of such practices. Elliot replied that at that time it simply was not feasible to "deploy a large number of investigators to the South to check on the operations of the academies."[30] Five days later, Stephen Pollack, former assistant attorney general for civil rights under President Lyndon Johnson, delivered an eighteen-page report to the Committee on Equal Education Opportunity in which he discussed, among many other problems, private schools in the wake of desegregation enforcement. He argued that "these academies and the racial isolation they perpetuate should be a matter of direct federal concern." Like Mondale and Ramsey, he urged the federal government to intervene when it is clear that "state or local government agencies become involved in their operations."[31]

Back home, ample evidence pointed to a history of the state offering significant help to private schools. In 1964, Governor Paul Johnson called for a special session of the Mississippi legislature to approve a $185 tuition grant for private schools.[32] It passed. Almost immediately six hundred students in sixteen private schools used grant money to attend private schools. By the next year, the tuition of more than seventeen hundred students in twenty-six private schools was being paid or partially paid through these state grants.[33] By 1968, forty-nine academies were being partially funded through these grants, and in 1968, the legislature raised the tuition grant to $240. In 1969, the federal district court in *Coffey v. State Educational Finance Commission* ruled the tuition grants unconstitutional.[34] After the court's ruling, the Mississippi legislature approved a bill allowing students sixteen years and older to borrow money on their own to be used to pay tuition at colleges, universities, junior colleges, vocational schools, and private schools. This "student loan program" allowed money to go directly to students rather than to the private schools, although the bill was clearly intended as aid to private schools. Senator Theo Smith of Corinth, who cast the only dissenting vote in the Senate, noted the irony that minors who did not have the right to vote could, under this law, borrow money and put themselves in debt "thousands of dollars" for a high school education.[35] A provision of the law allowed this debt to be forgiven if students remained in the state to live or study.[36]

Private schools in some areas were greatly boosted by the direct and indirect aid they received from their local school boards and city councils. For example, the Canton City School Board sold Canton Academy a 1967 bus for $250. The Yazoo City School District sold a bus to its local academy for $126. Amite, Canton, and Yazoo County auctioned off school equipment at ridiculously low prices (e.g., 50 cents for a desk). Tunica and Clay Counties continued to keep private school teachers on their payrolls. The Forrest County school system used its busses to transport children to the private school. Leake County Academy opened in 1970 in the old Madden School, a previous public school facility. A new private school in Carroll County opened on the Jennie McBride school ground, a former school in the Carroll County public school system. The teacher apartments adjacent to the land were also leased to the new private school. The two public school teachers living in these apartments were ordered to vacate the building by July 1, 1969. The Madison County superintendent told the white students upon leaving for Christmas break in 1969 to take their textbooks with them to be used at the private schools.[37]

The state also furnished free textbooks to many private schools. In their 1964 instructions on how to start a private school, the editors of the *Citizen* urged whites to take the free textbooks the state offered, but they added the following caveat: "[F]ree textbooks as a state 'handout' are an instrument of cultural retardation and socialistic regimentation." However, they continued: "[W]e do not advise ideological puritanism in this regard. As a practical matter, it will generally be better—for the time being, at least—to take the free textbooks from the state."[38] Richard Brooks, who taught at Macon High School during the first years of desegregation, recalled that when almost all the white students left the Noxubee school system, suddenly textbooks seemed to disappear as well.

When we came back in August, we saw all the books stacked up in the hall. We got new books, but all of a sudden, the books disappeared, and we only got 20 books out of the original 160. All the new books went to the private school. So I didn't know how it happened or who called in but anyway, the State Department came in, and they wanted to know about the new books and why they were at the private school. And so the principal had to get two fellows to drive a truck to go down there and get the books because the State Department guy wouldn't leave. He said, "You're going to have your books back before I leave," and we did. They got all the books on the truck, and some of them already had names in them. So after that, we didn't have any more trouble with the books. [39]

During the 1971–72 school year, 34,000 students in 107 private schools in Mississippi received free textbooks, for which the state paid $490,239. Parents of students in Tunica County filed a class-action lawsuit on behalf of all students in Mississippi, challenging the long-standing practice of the state providing free textbooks to students in private schools. The District Court sustained the validity of the program, stating that the textbooks were going to students, not schools. On appeal, the Supreme Court ruled in *Norwood v. Harrison* (1973) that private schools have the right to operate, but "free textbooks, like tuition grants directed to private school students, are a form of financial assistance inuring to the benefit of the private school themselves." Thus, if a private school in its admission policies discriminated based on race, "the State by tangible aid in the form of textbooks thereby gives support to such discrimination. Racial discrimination in state-operated school is barred by the Constitution." [40] Reluctant to make a blanket rule prohibiting any private school student from receiving free textbooks, the Court ruled that to be eligible for state-provided, free textbooks, the school must submit to the Mississippi Textbook Purchasing Board certification of its nondiscriminatory admission policies and an enrollment report listing the number of minority students in attendance.

With so much public aid going to private schools, civil rights activists and attorneys in the early 1970s had to divert some of their energy from ensuring that schools complied with desegregation orders to challenging the actions of state and local governments in aiding the newly created private schools. In September 1969, civil rights attorneys joined by the Justice Department filed a suit in federal court to block the two-hundred-dollar state loans to students sixteen years and older. In their suit, they referred to the earlier court decision ruling that tuition grants to private schools were unconstitutional. They argued that a loan to students, who could then turn around and use it to pay private school tuition, "would have the effect of encouraging, facilitating, and supporting a system of private schools operated on a racially segregated basis." [41]

In June 1970, a group of black residents in Tate County filed a lawsuit against their superintendent and school board for the 1969 sale of a former school building to Hillcrest Academy. The school board had sold the building to an individual acting on behalf of the Tate County Foundation (the private school organizational group). Board members contended they did not know the individual was purchasing it for the purpose of housing the private school, although they allowed workmen to begin refurbishing the building before the sale was final. In their lawsuit, the black appellants asked that the building be returned to the school board. The Fifth Circuit Court of Appeals ruled in favor of the plaintiffs. The court stated it was common knowledge to everyone in the town that a private school was being formed. The school board's contention it did not know the purchaser planned to use the building was irrelevant since school boards are legally charged with the "affirmative duty to work towards a unitary school system that is free of racial discrimination." The Court reversed the lower district court ruling and ordered that the property be returned to the Tate County Board of Education. It added, "It appears to be appropriate to express a caveat to courts who in the future may have to consider the sale of public school property for use as a private school. Such a sale should be scrutinized with utmost care and caution to the end that public school property shall not be converted to use by private schools which engage in forbidden discriminatory practices." Rather than forcing Tate Academy off its present site, federal district judge Orma Smith ruled in June 1972 that Hillcrest Academy could remain in the former public school building as long as the school did not deny black students admission. Civil rights attorneys disagreed with Smith's ruling, stating that "the net effect of a public school to a private institution—with or without an open-door policy— is the furtherance of school segregation."[42]

Initial aid to private schools also came from the federal government through the Internal Revenue Service (IRS). A private school could qualify for tax-exempt status, thus allowing individuals to claim their contributions to private schools as charitable giving on their tax returns. On July 10, 1970, the IRS announced that private schools that discriminate based on race would no longer be eligible for tax exemptions. Forty-one private schools in Mississippi were affected by the decision. Glenn Swetman, former Biloxi School Board member and president of the Harrison County Private School Foundation, reacted to the ruling with little concern: "We don't see that it will make any difference in our operation whatsoever. Right at first, we relied on donations, but now we are operating solely on our income. The only cause for alarm is that individual donations will not be tax exempt for the donors. I don't think it will cut down on our donations however."[43] Deflating the potential power of the ruling to curtail the growth of private schools, the IRS announced they would accept a private school's "written declaration of nondiscrimination" as proof of compliance. Accepting the "word" of private school administrators that they do not discriminate is "palpably ridiculous," responded Senator Walter Mondale, chairman of the Senate Select Committee on Equal Educational Opportunity.[44]

In March 1971, the IRS revoked the tax-exemptions of 23 private schools in Mississippi. Southwest Academy in Jackson was one of those schools. Its principal, Ralph Martin, appeared unfazed by this revocation when he told a reporter, "If we received public aid we would be obligated to the Government and the less obligation you have to the government the better position you are to provide the kind of education you want." William J. Simmons, director of the Citizens' Councils of America, which operated five private council schools in Jackson, concurred with Martin: "We don't want public aid. All we want is to be left alone. No Negroes have applied for admission, and we wouldn't admit them if they did."[45] On June 30, 1971, in *Green v. Connally,* the United States District Court for the District of Columbia upheld the revoking of tax exempt status for "racially discriminatory private schools."[46] However, for years the IRS and private school supporters wrangled over the role of the IRS and its rules concerning tax exemptions for private religious schools. These schools claimed their policies and practices were protected on grounds of religious freedom. Finally, in 1983, the Supreme Court provided some clear guidance in a ruling involving Bob Jones University (South Carolina): "the Government has a fundamental, overriding interest in eradicating discrimination in education—discrimination that prevailed, with official approval, for the first 165 years of this Nation's constitutional history. That governmental interest substantially outweighs whatever burden denial of tax benefits places on petitioners' exercise of their religious beliefs."[47] Soon thereafter many private schools re-wrote their admission policies to include a "nondiscrimination" clause.

Pragmatic Economics: Organized White Resistance to Private Schools

In some school districts, the white flight to private schools was almost total, and many affluent whites paid the private school tuition of those who could not afford it. However, in some towns, white citizens waged a vigorous campaign to "save our public schools." One of the first organized groups to publicly vocalize its support for public schools was Mississippians for Public Education (MPE) formed in Jackson in 1963 by five middle-class white women: Pat Derian, Elaine Crystal, Mary Ann Henderson, Joan Geiger, and Winifred Green. MPE did not consider itself a political group and members prided themselves on being bipartisan. They had one clear-cut goal: "[W]e are not a forum for debating the pros and cons of desegregation or state's rights or any political question. Our goal is solely to protect, preserve and promote our public school system." MPE chapters were soon formed in Biloxi, Oxford, Greenville, Tupelo and Meridian.[48] They urged women to talk to their husbands and convince them to support public schools and to abstain from any forms of violence. They purchased pro–public school billboards in Jackson that proclaimed: "Their tomorrow depends on you today; send your children to public school." In response to the legislature approving a state tuition grant of $185 to send children to private schools, MPE published a pamphlet entitled *A Time to Speak* that warned: "To responsible Mississippians, the slow erosion of our schools through impractical schemes like tuition grants would be a tragic waste. Closing our schools is unthinkable. Violence, or occupation by federal troops, would be catastrophic."[49] Seven years later, in 1970, a similar organization formed, Jacksonians for Public Education. More than two hundred people attended its first official meeting on August 27, 1970, in Fondren Presbyterian Church. Its chief priority was to encourage whites to keep their children in public school and to support public school personnel.[50]

As discussed in chapter 3, one of the ways in which Dr. Tom Dulin, super-intendent in Winona, sought to ensure that whites stayed in the public schools was to implement a policy barring public school teachers and principals from sending their own children to the private school. He was unsure of its legal-ity, but no one ever challenged it. In 1972, the Calhoun County School Board, upon recommendation of the superintendent and board attorney, adopted a similar policy. Eight white teachers in the district were not rehired because they enrolled their children at Calhoun Academy. Three of them challenged the policy and sued the school district. They lost their case. The US District Court for the Northern District of Mississippi ruled in *Cook v. Hudson* (1973) that the policy was reasonable and necessary for the preservation of public schools in Calhoun County:

> Public school desegregation in Calhoun County was a controversial policy which caused a division in the community; many citizens immediately threw their sup-port to continuing racial segregation in a private school to operate in a competi-tion with the public schools. Since white flight may present a serious obstacle to effective desegregation, a school board is empowered to adopt appropriate mea-sures in aid of the schools under its charge.[51]

Educational psychologists testified to the potentially detrimental emotional and academic effects on the students, leading the Court to conclude that "school teachers who send their own children to a segregated school manifest a belief that segregation is desirable in education and a distrust in desegregated schools. Actions speak louder than words."

In some communities, local businessmen were the moderate voices call-ing for whites to stay with or support the public schools. They argued that if their town wanted to attract business and industry, then a strong public school was imperative. Failure to support public schools, from a business perspective, would precipitate the economic ruin of a community. This was the argument consistently made by John Stone Jenkins, dean of St. Andrews Episcopal Church. He called for the Jackson business community to unify around their public schools, telling them, "If they make their mind up to make school desegregation work, then it will work." He illustrated his point by contrasting the towns of Canton and McComb: "In McComb the local leadership made up its mind to preserve the public schools and to make massive integration work . . . [T]hey brought in a young school superintendent [Julian Prince] to see that it was done. He integrated the schools before the court decision last winter and he brought about more integration than the courts would have required. There is no private school system there today."[52] In contrast, he noted that business leaders in Canton "made the opposite decision. The whites boycotted the public schools and started their own private academy."

In Oxford, local business leaders and members of the University of Mississippi academic community led a successful pro–public school campaign that began with a group called the Oxford Civic Council. Comprised of black and white members of sixteen civic, service, and professional organizations, its initial goal was to unite the black and white community around the preservation of public schools. Ed Meek was one of the original founders of the group. He explained how he and his wife were some of the first in their social group to make the decision to keep their children in the public schools:

> When it came time that Oxford had to integrate, I didn't have a single friend that said I'm going to send my kids to public schools. And my wife and I both said frankly, "We've got to stay in the public schools." This community's got to have a good public school system, and rightfully, wrongfully, I remember I said we recognized that probably the African American students were not at the same level as Caucasian students, but that's the price we're going to have to pay because that will all settle out.[53]

Ed began to hear talk about the forming of a private school in Oxford, and he knew that if the private school movement gained momentum in his hometown, the public schools and the town would suffer. As the president of the Junior Chamber of Commerce, he aggressively began contacting other leaders in town, including Willie B. Tankersley, the chancellor's butler, and Ken Wooten, director of admissions at the University of Mississippi.[54] The Oxford Civic Council met on January 12, 1970, at the Oxford city hall and adopted a resolution expressing their unwavering commitment of public schools: "[W]e do hereby affirm our belief in free public education and pledge our support to the retention of public schools in general and, specifically, to improving the quality of education in the Oxford Municipal Separate School District."[55] In addition to the sixteen members of the council unanimously supporting the resolution, other individuals added their names in support, including the mayor, the aldermen, members of the local clergy, several PTA presidents, the president of the Oxford Municipal School Board and four board members. The Oxford-Lafayette County Chamber of Commerce endorsed the resolution as well with the request that the "Lafayette County School system" be added to the wording of the resolution.

Despite the school board's written support of the resolution, it was slow to develop any definitive plans on how the school system intended to comply with desegregation. This inertia drove the Oxford Civic Council to develop its own plan. Ed explained: "When it was obvious that the leadership for the school board was just not going to do anything, we said let's organize a town meeting and get black and white to come together and let's talk about this because we all have fears; we're all concerned and we all know that we need to solve this issue ourselves and not somebody else." Ed contacted the chairman of the school board to inform him that the Civic Council was planning to host a communitywide meeting at Oxford High to discuss what needed to be done to desegregate their schools. The chairman said, "No—we're not going to do it." Ed would not take "no" for an answer. He told him they planned to host the meeting whether the school board attended or not.

The meeting was planned for Friday, January 16, 1970. To publicize the meeting, the Civic Council placed a one-page ad in the local paper with the headline: "Public Schools Are Vital to the Oxford-University Community!" It also added, "Members of the Oxford Municipal Separate School Board will discuss plans for the second semester of school in the Oxford system."[56] Between twelve and thirteen hundred people (both black and white) crowded into the Oxford High auditorium. The local paper reported that "it was the largest crowd ever assembled" at the school.[57] Ed Meek presided over the meeting. The chancellor of the University of Mississippi, Dr. Porter L. Fortune Jr., talked about the importance of having a strong public school to attract the best faculty to the University of Mississippi. Another guest speaker, Doug McClary, manager of US Plywood, stressed the importance of strong public schools for recruiting employees to the already existing industries in Oxford and Lafayette County. Ken Wooten, chairman of the education committee of the Oxford Civic Council, served as master of ceremonies. He described the meeting:

We got the school board on the stage. Fortune, who was Chancellor of the university, made an address and plea for calm and for the continuation of public education. The fact that it's a must—we've got to have it. So then we turned to the school board. The auditorium was completely filled. We had to put speakers outside. There were people all out on the lawn and everywhere listening to see what the school board was going to do, how it was going to be handled. And so I turned to them and asked them a couple of questions: How many schools are there? How many school buildings do we have? And they said, "Four." But that was not the end of what the Civic Council wanted to do. We wanted to make the transfer reasonable and without violence.

Vocal public support continued for public schools as they prepared for the opening of the second semester on February 2, 1970. At the same time, several townspeople formed a new private school called College Hill Academy. In the January 22, 1970, issue of the *Oxford Eagle,* the Civic Council ran an ad "We Support Public Schools" with the names of 250 people who "have already committed their support," and College Hill Academy had an ad listing the names of the 15 members of their newly formed Board of Trustees with the statement "Inquiries Invited."[58] The potential clash between the private and public schools played out quite visibly when on the same page of the February 3, 1970, issue of *Oxford Eagle,* there were two ads: the predominant one was the propublic school ad with the headline "Hats off to Our Public Schools" followed by a listing of more than 400 people congratulating "administrators, teachers, staff, city officials, school board for a job well done." To its left was a much smaller ad from College Hill Academy listing a membership of 191 students and 12 faculty with the announcement "classes will begin on Tuesday, February 17." The January 29, 1970, editorial summarized what the Oxford Civic Council hoped to accomplish: "There prevails in Oxford a 'positive attitude'—both on the parts of the white and black community—regarding the public school system . . . We feel that in this time of crisis that many forces in Oxford have mobilized and determined in one accord to 'make this work.'"[59] College Hill Academy opened but never attained the enrollment of many other private schools begun during the era of school desegregation. It eventually closed, and today another private school, Regents School of Oxford, occupies its buildings.

In Yazoo City, the business community also rallied around its public schools, but much different from the Oxford Civic Council, the business leaders in Yazoo City sought to support both a public and a private school system. The place is significant because a decade earlier, the local Citizens' Council had so intimidated the fifty-three black residents who signed a petition demanding the schools integrate that no other petitions were filed in the state in the 1950s. In 1969, Yazoo City was home to the Mississippi Chemical Corporation and a significant number of college educated white residents, including John Satterfield, past president of the American Bar Association and the lead attorney for the school districts in the *Alexander* case. Yazoo City was also home to a large black population and a new private school, Manchester Academy. Yazoo City was one of the school districts named in the *Alexander* case, but instead of fleeing the public schools immediately upon the Court's ruling, white business leaders decided to wage a massive campaign to support public schools.[60] They called themselves Friends of Public Schools. Harold Kelly, superintendent during this time period, described the powerful influence of this public-school advocacy group: "We had what we called the tidal wash of the Friends of the Public Schools. And it wasn't necessarily all the people that had the children in the public schools. Some actually had their children in the private school that joined the group and said, 'Yes, we've got to have good public schools from a business standpoint.' They were very vocal about giving us support."[61] Leading the efforts were two powerful men, Owen Cooper, president of the Mississippi Chemical Corporation, and Senator Herman DeCell, elected in 1967. On November 24, 1969, days after the *Alexander* ruling, more than twelve hundred people met in the high school auditorium. Although dominated by white citizens, two hundred blacks attended as well. Twenty-five preachers, politicians, school leaders, parents, and businessmen spoke in support of the public schools.[62] Harriet Kuykendall, wife of Senator DeCell and a teacher at the time, noted the importance of the propublic school business community: "Now we had developed a community in Yazoo City, a group of people called the Friends of the Public School, and they had a meeting one time in the high school auditorium. It's an eight-hundred-seat auditorium, and there wasn't a vacant seat in it. And these are adults, and they are not parents. This was not parents of the public schools; this was friends of the public schools."[63] For Harriet (who kept her children in the public schools) and many others in the established white power structure, the fact that members of the local business community rallied in public support of the public schools was far more important than the personal and individual choice they made about whether or not to send their children to the public school or to Manchester Academy.

The local newspaper, similar to the one in Oxford, also publicly supported the public schools and ran editorials such as the following:

> Yazoo City has been fortunate in many crises because we seem to have a reservoir of enlightened readers (both black and white) willing to persevere through

adversity and do what's right. We urge you all, our readers, to rise to the challenge of the transition being required of us. Certainly there will be perplexities and problems of human misunderstanding, but also opportunities and inspirations to all children of this community and their future.[64]

When schools opened on January 7, 1970, under court-ordered desegregation, the majority of whites remained in the public schools for the first semester. Having the public and vocal support of the larger business community was responsible, according to Superintendent Kelly, for the passing of a bond issue the next year with 84 percent of the voters supporting it. As Kelly stated, "[T]hat was very unusual at that time."

Despite the support of many whites for public schools in Yazoo City, the public-versus-private-school debate created divisions between whites in the community. Willie Morris recounts a conversation with the wife of a southern politician who said, "[Y]ou can't underestimate how all this has divided people—husband and wives, children and parents, brothers and sisters, old friends."[65] Harriet Kuykendall quipped, "We agreed in my bridge club not to discuss it." Indeed, the debate among whites about public versus private schools often turned quite personal.

Will You Send Your Child to the Public Schools?
The Political Becomes Personal

Among the white educators interviewed for this study, no other topic generated as much emotion as that of private schools. Blame for the failure of public school desegregation and its effects on public schools today was often squarely placed on friends, co-workers, and family members who refused to "stick it out" and stay with public schools. Fred Perkins was a first-year principal in 1969 at Sunnyside Elementary in LeFlore County, right outside of Greenwood when the *Alexander* ruling was decided. From stories he had been told, that area was a hotbed for Klan activity. He recalls men sitting in pickup trucks watching what he was doing in the school. He was rightly nervous, keeping his lights on in his house during the night: "We were there, just right in the middle of the Delta, on the edge of a cotton patch, and you didn't know what would happen. It was all a new ballgame. And everybody was kind of nervous about what was happening."[66] He tried to lead his school through the desegregation process, but the lure of the private school was powerful and, in the end, only a few poor whites remained in his school. He explains: "And Pillow Academy left us stripped. Our school was stripped. We had 113 white kids that stayed. I've never thought private schools were a good idea. I thought they were just a way to get around integration. And like I say, my kids never set foot in a private school, and I wouldn't have let them."

Paula Mabry is also critical of the establishment of a private school in her hometown because Starkville could ill afford to financially support both a private and a public school system. Paula began teaching in 1970 at Starkville High, an academically strong high school with a national reputation for its arts program. It had four levels of theater classes, a highly touted band program, and it won the first Kennedy Center for the Arts award, one of only two recipients nationwide. With such a strong public school, Paula questioned why so many whites decided to send their children to Starkville Academy. With two school systems operating, local businesses either had to split their financial support between the two schools or choose to support only one. She explained the economic ramifications for a small and resource-poor town like Starkville:

> I think because of the private school forming there was a definite alignment of loyalty—you know we are going to support this school and this football program or we are going to support this school and this football program. And yes, I think some people were able to successfully support both, but primarily people made a choice. If you are the Coca Cola Company you can give this much to this school and that much to this school, but if you are a small business man, and they want you to advertise in their football program or their annual, you might choose this school over that school.[67]

Jere Nash, who was a school board member in Greenville during school desegregation, understood well the argument for why public schools are essential for economic development. When he discovered that a local realtor was informing newcomers to Greenville that the private schools were the only viable school option, he put a stop to it immediately. But more importantly, Nash viewed the support of public schools to be a moral issue, about which he was passionate. Nash was born in Greenville in 1928—"the year after the Great Flood" that wreaked havoc on the city of Greenville. Nash unabashedly blames private schools for the demise of public education in his city: "I made the statement several years ago that we could overcome the flood, but it was going to be years before we overcame what the private schools were doing to the city of Greenville."[68] He firmly believed that school desegregation could have worked if whites would not have abandoned them for the private schools. "I was fool enough to think that 60/40—55/45 was a good mix. If every white child in the school system of Greenville went to the public

schools, the ratio would be 55/45. And I was fool enough to think, 'Well, anybody can live with that.'" According to Jere, his wife urged him to refrain from
discussing private schools at dinner parties, but it was a topic about which he
was passionate: "I felt very strongly about public education, and integration
became a moral thing for me." Hodding Carter Jr., a fellow resident and editor of the local paper, expounded on how emotional the private versus public
school debate became in the white, middle-class circles of Greenville:

> For many whites who could afford [private schools] it [was a] most agonizing
> kind of moral choice. And one of the reasons why decisions among old friends
> on this subject has been so great, right here, is simply because it was perceived
> finally not as a, just a simple decision about where your children goes to school
> but a moral question. Which those who made on either side felt pretty damn
> strongly about. And an awful lot of people lost their battle with their consciences
> . . . And a lot of other people surprised themselves by standing and then discover-
> ing, much to their fury, that people who they had always respected as being mod-
> erates, or people who cared about the community first, had suddenly deserted
> them. Here they decided to stay in the public schools and they look around and
> this person who they had always understood to be brighter, or more of a moder-
> ate, or whatever, is off to the state academy.[69]

These "agonizing" moral decisions often created divisiveness within the
white community. The most obvious manifestation was the violence and
intimidation (e.g., slashed tires, threatening phone calls, burned crosses,
blown-up mail boxes) many whites experienced because of their decision to
stay in the public schools as teachers or principals or to keep their children
in public schools. In the early years of FOC in the Mississippi Delta town
of Rosedale, Mike Johnson allowed a black boy to try out for the basketball
team.[70] The next night, a cross was burned in his yard. Mike's superintendent glibly told him to buy a gun. His principal called the FBI. The following Sunday, the minister of his Methodist church preached an entire sermon
condemning the actions of those that lashed out against Mike and his family.

When Mike moved to Leland in 1967 to take a coaching position, he was
targeted once again. This time because he continued to teach in the public
school rather than transfer to the private academy. He described how he
and his fellow white teachers were treated: "Because we stayed in the public schools there as teachers, we had more things happen to me physically
then than happened in Rosedale. I don't know how many sets of tires I had
to put on my car because the tires were cut. We had garbage thrown in our
yard consistently over weekends. I had windows broken out of my vehicles.

Very bad phone calls. Calls in the middle of the night and hang up." It is easy to cast these acts of violence as evidence of the divisions between the more radical racist whites and whites who appeared "moderate" because of their refusal to leave the public schools. However, the animosity between those who stayed and those who left often spilled over into the personal relationships of friends, family, and colleagues. Severed relationships, an invitation to a social event declined or never sent, a reserved, cold conversation with someone once considered a close friend, or changes in church membership exemplify the subtle ways in which the private-public school debate caused rifts within the white community. Mike Johnson explained: "There were some teachers who were good friends of ours, who had been in bridge clubs there in Leland that were not asked to come back to that bridge club. There were a lot of people whose church—the people who were in their church just did not have anything to do with them anymore because they stuck with the public schools and wouldn't go away."

It was often students who most felt the rift created when friendship groups were split up by their or their parents' decisions to leave the public schools. When he and his wife decided to keep their children in the Greenville public schools, William Dodson, a principal, noticed that his daughters suddenly were not invited to birthday parties or social events.[71] As white students left Greenwood High in droves, a distinct, and often hostile, division arose between those who attended Pillow Academy and those who stayed in the public schools. Mary Carol Miller, who stayed at Greenwood High, acutely felt this separation. Prior to 1970, she and her friends dismissed Pillow Academy as the place where the "radical racists went. And the kids who didn't fit in and the puny guys who couldn't play football at Greenwood." However, after many of their friends left Greenwood High for Pillow Academy, the animosity between the two groups of whites worsened over the years. Mary Carol recalled: "We felt betrayed by those who left. And I felt like they bailed out for social reasons, and their parents' pressure, and who knows what reason. But we dug our heels in and stayed. But you had a real rift in classes from that point on."[72] One particular day at a pep rally, the enmity between the two took a public ugly turn. Mary Carol described what happened:

At that point, the blacks would stay on one side of the gym and the whites would stay on the other. And a big group from Pillow came in to the gym. A big group of my classmates who had left a couple of months before and gone to Pillow came in. And they came in a door where the blacks could see them come in. And they got quiet at first. I remember the blacks just quit yelling. And we couldn't see who was coming around the side of the bleachers. And it was this big group of mainly girls from Pillow Academy. And this was a big deal. When they came around where we could see them, the band stopped. They just stopped. And one of the senior cheerleaders went over and got the microphone and said, "This is not your place. Leave. Go away." And they did. They turned around and walked out, and we continued with that pep rally.

Mary Carol and her white classmates viewed the Pillow students' coming to "their" pep rally as a serious breach of the unstated but understood rules of how members of this deeply divided white community were to act and interact with each other. She explained how the harassment accelerated:

> You had a real rift in classes from that point on. So there was more verbal joust-ing and trouble between the split whites than there were between the whites and blacks. And it got pretty ugly—at least while I was there. With guys in particular. They would on Friday night, Saturday night, ride around, and the kids at Pillow would come paint "Nigger Tech" on Greenwood High School or on the parking lot, and our guys would go out and paint "Redneck Tech" on theirs. There was just a lot of friction.

Mary Carol's parents gave her the choice to either stay in the public school or attend Pillow Academy. Mary Carol was adamant about staying—so much so that when the conditions of Greenwood High deteriorated to the extent that her parents felt she was not getting the education she needed, Mary Carol graduated a year early rather than transfer to Pillow Academy.

The Cost of Choice: Private Schools Deepening Racial Divisions

Private schools afforded an option to white parents and students during school desegregation not available to any black students, despite their academic or athletic achievements and accomplishments. As Fenton Peters, a black principal in Starkville during this time period, declared, "Blacks had no choices. We only had the public schools."[73] Despite euphemistic references to "quality education and safe schools," the original purpose of these academies was to promulgate segregation based on the pervasive beliefs of many that blacks were inherently socially, culturally, and educationally inferior to whites, as Charles George, a black educator who began his teaching career in the segregated schools of East Tallahatchie, pointedly noted: "As far as helping the county or the town working together, private schools didn't help. In other words, we are better than you are. We are going to do our own thing. In other words, they just thought they were more superior."[74] Lucy Boyd concurred. She was the president of the local NAACP chapter in West Tallahatchie for twenty-two years and was one of the black parents who filed the desegregation lawsuit against her district. She conceded that the creation of the private school in her community may have kept "total eruption" from happening, but the reasons why whites left the public school was very clear to her: "I saw the influx of white students being pulled out. And the pouring in of resources to build that school [Delta Academy]. And I just couldn't see it being done for the right reason—just to avoid being with students of another race, with black students."[75]

As Lucy's comment highlights, choice for white students in the form of private academies had significant consequences for black students. whites, who opted out of the public school, soon divested themselves from any emotional or financial investment in public schools. Without such support, bond issues and tax increases to help fund public schools typically failed, all of which had devastating effects on black students.[76] Herbert Foster, a black educator who began his teaching career in 1971 in Cleveland, explains the detrimental effects of private schools:

> Private schools were not a good thing because if you remove yourself from the public setting, you're not going to do anything to really support the school. I think if they would've accepted the fact that we just had one school and we're going to make it the best school it can possibly be because they wouldn't have had a choice. As long as they had a choice, they didn't put any effort to make the public schools better. They didn't push hard enough for an increase in taxes in support of the public schools.[77]

While many private schools today distance themselves from their segregationist origins, the residual effects of private schools are apparent, particularly in the Delta. Their presence still evokes strong emotions. When the organizers of her thirtieth high school reunion decided to have a joint celebration for graduates of Pillow Academy and Greenwood High, Dr. Mary Carol Miller refused to attend the joint reunion. She blamed the dismal state of public education today in Greenwood, in part, on the whites who left the public schools during school desegregation: "I still like to think that if we could go back forty years, and there was not movement here to start a private school, and you had kept every child in there, and kept the talents and administrative skills and money—for lack of a better word—all those parents who pulled out, if you could have kept all of that in the public schools, then you would not have had that backwards and downwards slide."

The Ultimate Form of Resistance: Leave the Public Schools

On January 2, 1970, the Southern National Party organized a rally in Jackson in hopes of precipitating a statewide response to school desegregation that would "protect your children from being exploited by tyrannical federal government 'bureaucrats.'" They billed the rally as offering a "workable solution to Mississippi's school crisis."[78] The workable solution they proposed was to start a foundation that would help every community organize a private educational system. The Southern National Party never gained much traction; however, the private school movement thrived in the years following the *Alexander* ruling. In the end, the withdrawal of 20 percent of white students from the public schools would be the most consequential form of white resistance to school desegregation

Chapter 10

Unfinished Business
Lessons Learned through School Desegregation

When we began this journey of chronicling the desegregation of public schools, our intent was to build the story around the oral histories of local Mississippians who were directly involved in various ways in the desegregation of public schools. While often dismissed in academic circles, oral histories have long been viewed as a counternarrative to historical accounts that privilege the dominant group. Oral histories have been particularly important in including the marginalized voices of the oppressed, the conquered, the enslaved, and the silenced. Oral histories also highlight the historical importance of context, the everyday world in which people operate, and unique micro forces influencing people's behavior.[1] In organizing the book with separate chapters on black parents, superintendents, principals, and teachers, we hoped to capture the nuances of how school desegregation was accomplished, fought for, resisted, and doomed in differing ways in different parts of the state. Our inclusion of the role of sports, band, the prom, cheerleading, and student government during the school desegregation process is a reminder that educational reformers cannot ignore the importance of the informal curriculum, the hidden curriculum, and the extracurricular of schools. The chapters on protests and private schools illustrate two primary ways in which people responded to this monumental cultural change that threatened the status quo: (1) they resisted in various ways through conventional methods of protest, and (2) they formed a countermovement that sought to retain the tribalism to which they clung and around which their identities were built.

We struggled with where to include the stories of students since, ultimately, they were the ones most affected by the decisions being made for them during this era of school desegregation, yet had the least voice in determining its implementation. Their stories play prominently in the chapters on sports and extracurricular activities because these are the two facets of school life in which students have some power to affect change. The lessons learned from

213

their stories should remind us that the decisions we make today for students have the potential to be life changing in the future. For many students who came of age in the era of school desegregation, that experience fundamentally shaped their beliefs about race, racism, power, and politics. For many, it was a transformational time in their development and set them on a life-long path of being change agents in the state and country. They went on to become politicians, teachers and principals, attorneys, journalists, policy makers, and business leaders, taking with them the lessons they learned about inequalities in schools and in society and the power of ordinary people to bring about change.

As we have shared our research with local civic clubs and attendees at national academic conferences, we inevitably have been asked two questions: (1) Was school desegregation successful in Mississippi? and (2) What's the takeaway from your historical study for schools today? In this closing chapter, we respond to those questions ever mindful of two values we hold dear personally and professionally.

As former public school teachers and now professors in Colleges of Education, we are very sensitive to the easy and frequent scapegoating of public schools for almost every ill in society. Public schools are constantly criticized—from progressives and conservatives alike—for everything from failing to prepare students adequately for the rigors of college and the realities of work in the twenty-first century to reproducing by design social and racial inequalities to educating students into mindless conformity to producing students who can do little more than regurgitate facts and take standardized tests. We have sat through many lectures and conferences in which academicians are quick to point fingers at some "invisible man" or structure (perhaps the superintendent or white school board members) as the primary culprit for the reproduction of social and racial inequalities in the resegregation of public schools while they themselves send their own children to private schools. We are not interested in being part of the "blame public schools for everything" discourse. We are acutely aware of the hard work of "just trying to have school" that goes on every day in classrooms and principal's offices, at PTO meetings and high school gymnasiums, and in the halls, cafeterias, and faculty lounges where educators face complex problems that cannot be fixed as easily as the cacophony of outside voices suggest.

Yet, as we were reminded many, many times writing this book, the story of school desegregation in Mississippi cannot be separated from the omnipresent narrative of race and racism in this country and in our educational institutions. Robert Fortenberry, former superintendent of Jackson Public schools, and Joe Haynes, former superintendent of Greenville city schools, poignantly brought this home during an interview, instructing us, "I trust that your study will not be limited to desegregation of schools because if you do you will have contributed to making the issue much more shallow that it really is. Racism is a deeply embedded part of the fabric of this nation, and it requires action in a lot of places—black and white churches, black and white schools, black and white colleges, who you have lunch with, who you go fishing with—it runs throughout the total gambit of this nation."[2] We hope our contribution here neither scapegoats teachers, principals, and superintendents nor skirts around the issues of racism endemic in our society and our school systems.

Was School Desegregation a Success?

Whether or not school desegregation was successful largely depends on the measures used to determine success, whom you ask, and what region of the state is the unit of analysis. For our purposes here, we employ five criteria to evaluate the "success" of school desegregation. The criteria are derived from an extensive review of the school desegregation literature, our oral history interviews, and discussions with current leaders knowledgeable of and interested in educational policy and practices:

1) White and black students in sizable numbers attended school together and participated in all facets of school life.
2) A significant number of white students with social, cultural, and economic capital stayed in the public schools.
3) Significant segments of the community, both black and white, supported the public schools with their time, talents, and money.
4) The school board and superintendent were committed to providing high quality, academically strong programs in all their schools and in the best interests of *all* their students.
5) The remnants of the above are still evident in the school district today.

Using these five criteria, we offer this answer to "Was school desegregation successful in Mississippi?": yes, no, yes then no, no then yes, and still being decided. What seems like glib responses, in fact, captures the complexity of evaluating the complicated process and outcomes of school desegregation.

Making the Grade: School Desegregation Success Stories

Ever the optimist, Willie Morris, author of numerous books set in his beloved state of Mississippi, proffered in 1986: "[W]ho could have predicted a generation ago, when the Civil Rights Movement was at its crest, that the integration of public schools would someday work best in the small-to middle-size cities in the South? It is the world of proms and cheerleading and classrooms and ballgames."[3] To his death, Morris possessed an interminable belief that Mississippians could work through their differences, including conflicts over school desegregation, because they shared a sense of place marked by community and kinship, a love of sports, music, and religion, and a way of life defined by manners and rituals.[4]

Morris would be pleased to see that his prediction thirty years ago has proven true in many communities, like Columbia, Grenada,[5] Starkville,[6] Kosciusko, Quitman, Oxford, and Tupelo, where school desegregation was worked out rather successfully and continues today. Black and white students learn together in integrated classrooms; they play sports and sing in the choir together; and significant portions of the local power structure, including the school board, are committed to a strong public school system. Probably no town better represents the success of public school desegregation than Clinton.

The Clinton Separate School District was formed in 1970, breaking away from the Hinds County School District and taking with it a significant portion of the white enrollment. After the split, the Hinds County school system had a 68 percent black enrollment. The new Clinton School District was 85 percent white. When Virgil Belue began as Clinton's first superintendent in June 1970, he inherited a brand new elementary school scheduled to open in August, but the school had no sewerage hook-up. Three weeks before opening day he was still trying to locate furniture for it. Despite the shaky start, Belue laid the foundation for what is now a still-thriving public school. He created a grade-based system of schools whereby all children in each grade attended the same school. Students moved as a cohort from one school to the next. Belue had the foresight to know the importance of a community school system in which schools were not identified as "good" or "bad" or "black" or "white." He explained, "I didn't want to fight this thing about drawing lines and counting blacks and whites, and I didn't want to set up a system here where one school could have a lot of support from parents while the other school didn't have support from parents."[7] His proposal was also based on sound educational practices. Principals and teachers would be experts in the curriculum and best practices of their specific grade level.

Over the years the NAACP, the Justice Department and the Office of Civil Rights have challenged the Clinton School District for being a "white flight" school district. In 1977, the federal government filed a lawsuit against the school district demanding it be rejoined with the Hinds County school system. Belue worked with the federal government on a plan that allowed Clinton to absorb a predominantly black neighborhood and convert two of its schools to the sixth- and ninth-grade centers for the entire district. That plan was approved, thus significantly increasing the black population in the district.[8]

Today the Clinton Separate School system is the academic gem of the state. It is a racially diverse, high-performing school system that earned an "A" on the state's 2016–2017 report card. "[In 2015], about 85 percent of its 12th-graders graduated high school, nearly four percentage points higher than the national average, and nearly 10 percentage points higher than the state average. During the 2012–2013 school year . . . nearly 94 percent of black students in Clinton passed the state algebra exam . . . On the state's recent third-grade reading exams, 98 percent of Clinton's third-graders passed on the first try."[9] On other markers imperative for school success, Clinton excels. Parents are highly involved in the schools; teachers and principals set high academic standards for all students; the school system has invested in the latest technology, including iPads or laptops for all students, and the community supports the schools in its academic endeavors and its extracurricular accomplishments. As it was in 1970, all students in the district begin school at Clinton Park East Elementary School, and they graduate as a group from Clinton High School. There are no intradistrict rivalries, either academically or in extracurricular activities. When the Clinton High Arrows won the 2016 6A state football championship, the entire community celebrated the victory.

The Clinton Separate School System is no longer a white-majority school district. Over the last fifteen years, its white school-age population has slowly decreased from 55.41 percent in 2003–4 to 49.43 percent in 2010–11 to 39.15 percent in 2016–17. Today its black population is 52.85 percent with a growing Asian enrollment of 5.79 percent.[10] Socioeconomically the Clinton school system does not reflect the state. The district's median household income of $55,486 is far above the state average of $39,665.[11] Statewide, approximately 70 percent of school-age children are eligible for free or reduced-priced lunches; in Clinton only 43 percent qualify.[12] However, from the perspective of Joy Tyner, principal at Northside Elementary, Clinton's real success with school integration is that it mirrors the racial diversity of the state: "I love the fact that I can walk down the hall and look into any class and it looks like Mississippi."[13]

Flunking Out: Failing at School Desegregation

Eighty-eight percent of school-age children in Mississippi attend public schools. Of them, 48.87 percent are black and 44.35 are white. A cursory look at these figures might suggest that school desegregation was successful.

Mississippi's public schools are comprised almost equally of black and white students. However, such figures are misleading. Overall, the state population is 37.6 percent black and 59.5 percent white, indicating that white students are not proportionately represented in public schools. In some areas of the state, almost no white students enroll in their local public schools. Statewide, approximately 10 percent of white students attend primarily segregated private schools.[14] Almost half (45.2 percent) of black students in Mississippi attend public schools that are 90–100 percent nonwhite schools.[15]

Nationally, much attention has been given to the resegregation of public schools. In 2012, almost 40 percent of US students attended schools that were 90–100% minority.[16] The South, with the largest percentage of black students, remains the least segregated region of the country, but the percent of black students in the South attending majority nonwhite schools slowly increased from 61 percent in 1991 to 71 percent in 2003.[17] As early as 1968, researchers had begun talking about the resegregation of public schools precipitated by school desegregation. In his 1971 analysis of the private school movement in Mississippi, James Palmer identified four types of resegregation:

1. Intra-school resegregation—"results from policies on the part of the administration or, more subtly, by actions of the staff and student body." An example
   would be the use of ability grouping to assign students to primarily segregated classrooms in newly integrated schools.
2. Inter-school resegregation—"occurs when a desegregated school begins to
   return to a segregated status through a shift in racial balance between
   schools." This type of resegregation may occur because of changing residential patterns (e.g., "white flight" to the suburbs" or through intentional zoning policies to ensure certain parts of a city are zoned for a "whiter" school).
3. Inter-system resegregation—"occurs when white families either move or
   attempt to establish fictitious residences." An example would be whites fleeing a city school district with a majority-black population to attend schools
   in the majority-white county system through buying a house in the neigh-
   boring school district or using the address of a family member.
4. Extra-system resegregation—"occurs when parents take their children out of
   the public schools." This kind of resegregation happens when whites remove
   their children from public schools and enroll them in private schools.[18]

One could certainly argue that the term "re-segregation" does not aptly describe what happened in many school districts in Mississippi because *deseg-regation* never occurred despite the abolishing of dual systems of segregated public schools. However, using Palmer's classification above, what occurred in

Table 10.1

Demographic Data of Districts Receiving an "F" on the Annual State Report Card

School District	% Black Students	% White Students	Poverty Rate of District
Amite	81.77	16.43	26.7
Canton	89.37	<5	31.4
Clarksdale Municipal	96.67	<5	37.7
Claiborne	99.13	<5	38.6
Coahoama	89.57	8.16	32.6
Greenville	98.69	<5	35.9
Holmes	99.47	<5	43.2
Humphries	97.31	<5	39.0
Jackson City	96.32	<5	27.0
Jefferson	98.83	<5	32.8
Kemper	95.91	<5	24.6
Leland	90.85	6.86	39.1
Midtown Charter	95.76		Located in Jackson
Montgomery	84.09	12.12	21.2
Natchez-Adams	89.68	8.9	28.1
Noxubee	96.94	<5	32.3
Okalona Separate	94.95	<5	25.5
Quitman County	96.92	<5	33.7
Wilkerson	98.61	<5	30.6
Yazoo City	98.45	<5	45.8

Poverty rates are based on the American Community Survey, 2009 5-year estimates released December 2010 (Proximityone.com/sd_ms.html).

The report card scores are based on Mississippi State Department of Education Figures, 2016-2017 (http://mdereports.mdek12.org/report/report2017.aspx).

Table 10.2

Demographic Data of Districts Receiving
an "A" on the Annual State Report Card

School District	% Black Students	% White Students	Poverty Rate of County
Booneville	22.32	70.25	36.2
Clinton	52.85	39.15	11.4
Desoto	35.55	52.44	9.4
Enterprise	10.5	87.74	11.9
Forrest Agricultural High School	29.76	66.33	Forrest County 21.7
Jackson County	11.37	80.50	11.5
Long Beach	17.08	70.29	8.5
Madison	39.09	51.46	8.9
Ocean Springs	13.63	76.21	8.1
Oxford	35.56	53.80	28.0
Pass Christian	30.68	59.13	9.0
Petal	17.29	74.56	15.9
Rankin	22.53	71.22	8.1
Union Public Schools	21.59	76.25	14.7

Poverty rates are based on the American Community Survey, 2009 5-year estimates released December 2010 (Proximityone.com/sd_ms.html).

The report card scores are based on Mississippi State Department of Education Figures, 2016-2017 (http://mdereports.mdek12.org/report/report2017.aspx).

many school districts in the state was the immediate capitulation of whites to private academies, resulting in extra-system resegregation. The almost totally segregated public school systems left in these communities have suffered for years from under-funding and all the concomitant problems accompanying lack of money and resources, the most important being the academic under-performance of its students.

The State Department of Education's annual report card detailing the academic success of its school districts paints a bleak picture about the correlation between majority-black, high-poverty schools and low academic achievement as demonstrated in Table 10.1 and Table 10.2 listing Mississippi schools receiving an "F" on the annual state report card and those receiving an "A"[19].

The detrimental consequences of the resegregation of American schools on minority and economically disadvantaged students are well-documented. Students that attend desegregated schools score higher on high-stakes standardized tests; they have better access to academically rigorous courses, and have higher rates of graduation, college attendance, and college graduation.[20] On the other hand, "Studies show that high-poverty schools have insufficient curriculum materials; fewer advanced course offerings; unequipped science labs; high student to teacher ratios; inadequate number of professionals to provide counseling, speech, and diagnostic services; less qualified faculty, and fewer athletics, art, or music classes."[21] Segregated, high-poverty schools are prone to more teacher turnover and hire less experienced teachers, and their students have higher dropout rates.[22]

Lillie V. Davis, who began her teaching career in Quitman County and recently retired from the school board, sees every day the residual effects on her students of the total abandonment of public schools by white students forty-five years ago. She explained:

> We still don't have the equal opportunities. We still don't have the type of schools we need. We still don't have the buildings that we need. You take, for example here in Quitman County, we have one gym and we have three schools. Only one gym. And there are some subjects that need to be taught, but they're not taught. We need foreign language taught in the school system, and we don't have that. We want equality for our children. That's all we want. And we want them to have the same chance and the same opportunity that other children have. We should have made more progress than what we have made, but we haven't. It is still a system that we really don't want blacks to achieve.[23]

In the Delta, in the southwest, and in Jackson (the three regions of the state in which 30 percent or more of the whites left the public schools after massive school desegregation), school desegregation has failed miserably. The public school system, largely segregated with black students, poorly funded and woefully underresourced, continues to operate alongside a private school system, largely segregated with white students and, in many places, also poorly funded and underresourced. In the entire Delta region, only three school districts have any semblance of black and white students learning together. In the Greenwood Public School District, one school in the entire district, Bankston Elementary, has a student enrollment of 70 percent black and 30 percent white students. In the Western Line School District, Riverside Elementary and Riverside High have a majority white student population with 73.28 percent and 72.01 percent, respectively. The Cleveland School District has several schools with a racially balanced student population. As discussed below, they were recently ordered by a federal court judge to make significant changes to their school system.[24]

In these regions of segregated schools, not only do black and white students and teachers have very little interaction with one another, thus few opportunities to change racial attitudes or dispel antiquated racial stereotypes, but also both the public and private schools lack the resources to prepare students to be part of an increasingly diverse, global, postindustrial world. This includes a rigorous and robust offering of courses in science and math, foreign languages, arts and humanities, and career and technical education. The limited human, social, and economic capital in these typically resource-poor regions is divided between two systems of schooling, and in the end, both pay dearly for that division.

In 2017, we also see indications that many school districts in the state have recently begun *resegregating* in patterns closely akin to national trends; that is, white students are leaving the public schools either through white flight to public schools with higher white enrollments or to private schools. Philadelphia (MS) is illustrative of a town that successfully achieved school desegregation and maintained it for several decades, but in the last fifteen years has begun experiencing patterns of resegregation. The place, of course, is significant. In 1964, three civil rights workers—James Earl Chaney, Andrew Goodman, and Michael Schwerner—were brutally murdered in Philadelphia. No one was convicted of the murders until 2005.[25] However, the town weathered school desegregation in the early 1970s fairly well, particularly compared to nearby Kemper County, where white students in 1970 left the public schools and never returned. Throughout the 1980s and 1990s, Philadelphia could boast of an integrated school system that seemed to be working.[26] However, recent enrollment figures indicate a steady decline of white students in the Philadelphia school system, from 32 percent in 2003–4 to 19.5 percent in 2016–17.[27] Similar drops in the enrollment of white students have occurred elsewhere in the state. In the East Tallahatchie School District, the white school-age enrollment dropped from 31 percent in 2003–4 to 20.89 percent in 2016–17. In Moss Point, the white population in that school system has decreased from 31 percent in 2003–4 to 20.69 percent in 2016–17.[28] Perhaps it is too early to declare these school districts as "resegregated"; however, if these patterns persist, these communities will almost certainly face the social, economic, and educational problems typically resulting when desegregated schools return to segregated schools.

"The Best Laid Plans": A Good Start, but a Dismal Finish

Making it through the first day, the first week, the first year were all important milestones for the principals, teachers, and superintendents involved in planning the transition from segregated to desegregated schools in the spring and fall of 1970. When 1971 rolled around, many were breathing a sigh of relief, cautiously rejoicing in their endurance and success. This hopefulness can be heard in Willie Morris's 1971 book *Yazoo: Integration in a Deep-Southern Town*, where he chronicles how his hometown fared better than most expected when it desegregated its schools under court order in January 1970: "The lesson in Yazoo City and a number of other communities which largely stayed with their schools was that the majority of white southerners preferred to integrate rather than see the public school destroyed, and that economic considerations played a substantial part."[29] This optimism can also be detected in Frank Reynold's February 1, 1970, commentary on the ABC nightly news about school desegregation efforts in Leland:

> I had a long and instructive talk this afternoon with a school official in Leland, MS, where partial integration has been in effect for several years, and now the schools are completely integrated. The white students have not fled to private, all white schools, nor are they likely to, because to put it bluntly—a lot of people have stuck their necks out. Prominent men in the town, political leaders and others well known to everybody have made it clear they were determined to maintain the quality of the public school system. They have announced that their children were going to stay in the public schools, and the teachers announced that they were going to stay, and were not going to lower their standards. This is what the black people of Leland want, too. A quality education for their children, and a diploma that is not just a certificate of attendance.[30]

One of the groups "sticking their necks out" was a biracial committee of black and white leaders that worked together to promote public schools and school desegregation. At school board meetings, they distributed stickers that read "Think Positive." The local newspaper ran a full-page ad listing the names of more than two hundred white parents who had pledged to keep their children in the public schools. The first year, about 50 percent of the white students remained in the public schools, setting Leland apart from most of the other towns in the Delta.[31]

Today, Yazoo City and Leland are no longer shining examples of how well school desegregation worked. The schools are once again segregated by race. In 2016–17, only fourteen white students attended public schools in the entire Yazoo City school system. The majority of white students either attend Manchester Academy, which opened in 1969, or they have moved into the Yazoo County school system. In 2016–17 only fifty-seven white students attended public schools in Leland. The vast majority of them attend instead one of five private schools within a 30-mile radius. Both the Yazoo City school system and the Leland School District are failing schools according to the Mississippi Department of Education, and over 25 percent of their students fail to graduate from high school (25.2 percent in Yazoo and 35.4 percent in Leland).[32]

The starkest example of a school system that rose and then plummeted in terms of successful school desegregation is Greenville. In many ways, Greenville in the 1960s was an atypical southern town. It was considered moderately progressive in terms of race relations. The editor of the local paper, Hodding Carter Jr., had publicly lashed out against the Citizens' Council in a 1955 article in *Look* magazine, for which the Mississippi legislature attacked him and branded him a "slanderer, a Communist, and an integration-sympathizer."[33] Neither the Ku Klux Klan nor the Citizens' Council had much influence in Greenville. Because of its location as a port city on the Mississippi River, immigrants migrated from New Orleans up the river to Greenville; thus, for a southern town, it was ethnically diverse with a sizable population of Italians, Lebanese, and Chinese living and working there. Greenville had an integrated railroad and bus system long before the rest of the state, and it was the home of several industries that relocated there in the 1950s, including the Alexander Smith Carpets. Stein Mart, a department store chain, was founded in Greenville. In the 1960s Greenville was considered a prospering Delta town.[34]

In 1964, the Greenville School District was the first in the state to voluntarily initiate a school desegregation plan. It did so in defiance of Governor Paul Johnson's declaration for school systems to refrain from responding quickly or affirmatively to the Civil Rights Act.[35] According to school board chair J. Barthelle Joseph Jr., local leaders knew school desegregation was imminent, and they wanted the federal money readily available for school districts that complied with school desegregation. Greenville also prided itself on being a progressive city and wanted to "show the general public that River City will not submit to disorder and chaos but will set the example for the rest of us."[36] "River City" was the pseudonym given to Greenville when it was featured as one of the case studies in the 1965 Coleman Report, the landmark federal "Equality of Educational Opportunity" study.

The desegregation plan first submitted by the Greenville School Board laid out a five-year plan for desegregating its schools using FOC and beginning in 1965–66 with grades 1 and 2. Greenville modified its plan in summer 1965 to include desegregation in grades 1, 2, 7, and 12. Initially, 147 blacks registered to attend formerly all-white schools in fall 1965. Only 135 showed up the first day, and by January 1966 that number had dropped to 120. By 1968 approximately 15 percent of black students attended Greenville High School under the "freedom of choice" plan. No whites had chosen to attend any of the black schools.

Dissatisfied with the slow progress of school desegregation based on FOC, black parents filed a lawsuit against the Greenville School District. In 1969 federal Judge William Keady ordered the school district to abolish completely and immediately its dual system of segregated schooling. In spring 1970, the Greenville Board of Trustees launched a comprehensive communication plan to apprise the community of the new desegregation plan scheduled for fall 1970. Members wrote letters to parents asking for their cooperation in making school desegregation work. They held a forum with all their school personnel to explain the changes, and they made the rounds with a color slide presentation to various civic clubs, PTAs, and other community organizations. They held open houses at all the schools prior to school opening, and they urged the local business community to provide co-op opportunities for high school students and to publicly support the public schools.

Despite two new private schools opening in 1969 (Washington School and Greenville Christian Academy) and the availability of a Catholic education through St. Joseph's Catholic School (a fixture of Greenville for almost a century), fewer than 20 percent of white students left the public schools when they reopened in 1970 as fully desegregated. Many of the middle-class and affluent white Greenville families initially chose to keep their children in the public schools, setting an example for others to follow. By 1975, white students comprised about 30 percent of the overall student population. In a 1976 report, the United States Commission on Civil Rights featured Greenville as one of its twenty-nine case studies of school desegregation efforts in the country. The commission praised the town for its desegregation efforts: "Greenville, Mississippi, might serve as an illustration of the principle that where such a comprehensive approach is combined with good leadership and good will, desegregation works and works well . . . [T]he Greenville public schools and community get "A" marks not only for effort but also for results."[37]

According to many students who attended the Greenville public schools in the 1970s and 1980s, school desegregation was successful. Despite the concerns of many white parents that desegregation would precipitate a decline in academic rigor, test scores in 1971 painted a different picture as reported in the May 7, 1972, issue of the *Delta Democrat-Times*: "Average achievement test scores of eleventh grade students in the public system showed an increase over 1969 scores, despite the implementation of a unitary school system and the simultaneous withdrawal of over one-third of the white students."[38] White students were, by far, the minority, but according to former school superintendent Leeson Taylor II, who graduated from Greenville High in 1989, "we didn't think, was this an African-American school or a Caucasian school, but was it a good school? And most were very good." However, Catherine Carter Sullivan, daughter of Hodding Carter Jr., said she could "already feel the fabric fraying" by the time she graduated from Greenville High in 1976. Her white friends were leaving in droves for the private schools or, for those who could afford it—boarding schools. When Leeson Taylor returned to Greenville in 1993 to teach, he discovered that very few white students remained in the Greenville public schools.[39]

Today, the Greenville school system is 98.69 percent black and received a grade of "F" on the 2016-17 state report card.[40] Plagued by a series of corrupt superintendents (one was jailed for taking bribes from a reading company), Greenville schools are dealing with the all-too-typical problems of underfunded, underresourced, poor, and segregated schools: buildings badly in need of repair, a dearth of qualified teachers, poor academic performance, and a general sense of malaise and frustration. The picture of public schools in Greenville today is, indeed, bleak.

A Slow Start, but Making Strides

As demonstrated above, in many ways, Mississippi reflects nationwide trends in which a growing number of black students and socioeconomically disadvantaged students are being educated once again in segregated, underresourced schools. However, in at least one school district in Mississippi, Carroll County, the pattern is slowly being reversed, although its gains are minimal and its future uncertain. The wind behind this sail has been Superintendent Billy Joe Ferguson. Billy Joe was born and reared in Carroll County and has spent his entire career in his hometown, first as a teacher and coach, then a principal and finally a superintendent. Son of a dairy farmer, he readily admits he has never ventured very far from Carroll County. "You can't leave cows for very long," he quips.[41] Billy Joe, who is white, was first elected superintendent in 1996. In 1998, he closed two schools, Vaiden High and Hawthorn Elementary, as a cost-cutting measure. It was not a popular decision, and Billy Joe was defeated in 2000. However, he was re-elected in 2004, 2008, 2012, and 2016.

Billy Joe made national news in 2015 when he wrote an open letter to Governor Phil Bryant begging the state to help his school district by fully funding the Mississippi Adequate Education Program (MAEP), enacted in 1997 and funded only twice since that time. Governor Bryant did not respond to his letter, but the regional and national press did. MSNBC featured a story on Billy Joe and the Carroll County schools. He also made news by giving up his $86,000 salary to save his school district money. He "retired" and began drawing instead an annual salary of only $18,000 while he continued to work full-time as the superintendent.[42]

Carroll County is a rural, sprawling area covering 635 square miles in the hill country just on the outskirts of the Mississippi Delta. It is poor and predominantly white with a long history of an active KKK and Citizens' Council. When the schools fully desegregated in the fall of 1970, approximately 90 percent of the whites left the public schools for either Holmes Academy or Carroll Academy. Despite the mass exodus of whites from the public schools, the school board continued to be comprised of white members with no investment or interest in strengthening the public schools. It unabashedly diverted public school resources to help Carroll Academy. The private school was opened on the grounds of a former pubic school. Public school busses were used to transport the white children to Carroll Academy, and textbooks intended for public schools were given to the private school.[43] The school board regularly squelched any attempts at raising taxes to aid the public schools. The Council of Conservative Citizens, a descendant of the Citizens' Council, proudly boasted of its affiliation and support of Carroll Academy. In 1999, it helped raise $100,000 for the school, and as late as 2011 sponsored barbeques and other fundraisers for the school.[44]

Today the public school district is still predominantly black, still badly underfunded, and still struggling to help its children achieve academically. But, some slivers of progress have been made. The five-member school board is now comprised of two black and three white members. For the first time ever, one of the white school board members, Daniel Vest, has his three children in the public schools. According to Billy Joe, with the election of Vest in 2013, he now has, for the first time, a school board in which the majority of the members have a *personal* investment in the success of public schools. Whites have trickled back to the public schools in the last fifteen years, an unusual trend in the state. In 2003, 29 percent of the school district was white. By 2010, that number had crept to 32 percent. In 2016–17, whites comprised 39.34

percent of the public school enrollment.[45] Some modicum of success has been achieved in academics as well. In 2015, 81 percent of the students at Marshall Elementary passed the statewide third grade reading test. A 19 percent failure rate is impressive when compared to nearby Holmes County, where 59 percent of its students failed the same test.[46] In fall 2011, Billy Joe applied for a federal grant to fund a four-year-old program in his elementary school. Today, thirty-eight preschool children are enrolled. Many more would like to be, but a shortage of space prevents Billy Joe from expanding the program.

Billy Joe is philosophical about the realities of heading a poor school district with few resources: "In life, when you're poor, you have to do without." But, according to Claiborne Barksdale, former CEO of the Barksdale Reading Institute, Billy Joe is one of the true "heroes" for public education in Mississippi.[47] Billy Joe is vociferous in his support of public schools and has spent his career challenging the white power structure, which, according to Billy Joe, is made up of those who "don't give a lick about children who attend public schools, especially if they're children of color or from low-income families."[48] Whether or not Carroll County will continue this reversal of state and nationwide patterns of resegregation may be determined in 2020 when Billy Joe's tenure as an elected superintendent is finished. According to a new state law, he, like all superintendents in the state, will be appointed by their school board.

The Verdict Is Still Out: School Districts Remain under Court Orders

Many would argue that Cleveland was one town in the Delta that appeared to weather school desegregation much better than the rest of the region. For evidence, they would point to Cleveland High, located on the west side of town. In 2015, Cleveland High was the most racially balanced school in the Delta, with 47.73 percent black students, 45.05 percent white, and 5.02 percent Hispanic.[49] However, across the tracks (literally) on the east side of town, East Side High and D. M. Smith Middle School were almost entirely segregated by race, East Side High with 99.47 percent black students, and D. M. Smith Middle School with 99.29 percent black. In May 2011, the Department of Justice filed a motion asking the district judge to force the Cleveland City School system to comply with school desegregation orders that have been on the books for forty-five years.[50]

Nationwide, approximately 340 school districts are still under school desegregation orders. Mississippi has the most, with sixty-one.[51] School districts still under court orders are required to submit annual reports detailing the progress they have made toward desegregation. Any changes to a school system (e.g., the creation of magnet schools) must first be approved by the court. According to Nikole Hannah-Jones, enforcement of school desegregation orders has increasingly become laxer. She cites a school board attorney in Hollandale (MS), who was not even aware that his school district was still under court orders. In fact, the school district had not submitted an annual report in thirty years. Hannah-Jones emphasizes the importance of these court orders in the desegregation of schools in the South: "For decades, federal desegregation orders were the potent tool that broke the back of Jim Crow education in the South, helping transform the region's educational systems into the most integrated in the country."[52] She points out that once schools are released from desegregation court orders, they tend to resegregate.[53]

Cleveland's school desegregation saga began in July 1965 when the parents of 131 black children filed a lawsuit against the Bolivar School District for failing to comply with school desegregation mandates. On July 22, 1969, federal court judge William Keady ordered the school district to desegregate but allowed it to use geographical attendance zones based on residential housing patterns. Cleveland was geographically a racially divided town. Whites lived west of the railroad tracks; blacks resided on the east side. The school district was divided into two zones and students attended school based on "proximity of residence." Hence, Cleveland High became the high school for white residents on the west side and East Side High the school for blacks.[54]

Over the years, Cleveland has been called back to court a number of times to address its continued patterns of segregated schools. In 1989, a federal judge ordered the school district to implement a majority-to-minority transfer policy, meaning, in practice, black students living anywhere in the district could attend Cleveland High because it was a majority white school. Likewise, any white student could attend East Side High. Many black students began attending the majority-white Cleveland High and Margaret Green Junior High; yet, no whites chose to attend the majority-black East Side High or D. M. Smith Middle School. In 2013, the district courts intervened again. This time federal judge Glen Davidson abolished the attendance zones created in the 1969 decree and allowed students "freedom of choice" to attend any school they wanted. Again, no white students chose to attend East Side or D. M. Smith Middle.

The school district has proposed several measures to make its schools more integrated, including magnet schools in 1990. But the patterns of enrollment and vestiges of segregation remained into the twenty-first century—an integrated Cleveland High and a segregated East Side or as many said, the "white" school and the "black" school." In May 2016, Judge Debra Brown ordered the consolidation of the two high schools and junior high schools with all high school students attending Cleveland High (which would incorporate nearby Margaret Green Junior High) and all middle school students attending East Side. Response to the ruling was mixed. Many black residents viewed it as a victory for ending segregated schools after a forty-five-year battle. Others were concerned about how their children would fare at Cleveland High; the mother of the valedictorian at East Side noted that Cleveland High had never had a black valedictorian. Many whites were perplexed at the ruling, for they saw Cleveland High as a shining example of an integrated school that was working. "It's a big eclectic mix where everyone has a spot," remarked a parent of a child who attended Cleveland High. Former school board member Jim Tims, who is white, expressed concern that whites would not stay with the public schools because the racial composition of the new high school would "tip" toward a ratio with which whites would not be comfortable being the minority since blacks comprise 68 percent of Cleveland's student population.[55] According to Vanita Gupta, head of the Justice Department's Civil Rights Division, the Cleveland ruling is a potent "reminder to districts that delaying desegregation is unacceptable and unconstitutional."[56]

As we write this book, the verdict of whether or not school desegregation was successful in Cleveland is still up for debate. The school district has offered a desegregation plan different from the one Judge Brown ordered. Whatever plan is chosen is scheduled to go into effect in 2017–18. Yet questions linger. Will the white students leave the public schools for Bayou Academy (begun in 1964) or Presbyterian Day School (begun in 1965), thus following the pattern of other Delta towns? Will the Delta State University academic community rally around the school system and help promote public schools, as did the University of Mississippi community in 1970? Will black students feel welcomed and included in all areas of Cleveland High School life? To what extent will black residents feel a loss when East Side High is no longer the centerpiece of the black community?

Lessons Learned

As illustrated throughout this book, ordinary Mississippians, both black and white, were key players in the story of school desegregation. Some came kicking and screaming; many made personal sacrifices to ensure justice for all, and others simply saw themselves as doing their job. Their stories are important in documenting *how* local citizens become involved, willingly or not, in bringing about social change. People fervently disagreed on much during this time period; however, almost everyone featured in this book believed in the late 1960s that their town, their state, and their children were only as strong as their local public school system. As Tom Dulin, the superintendent of Winona public schools during this time period, succinctly explains: "The public school system in the state of Mississippi is the only hope for many, many, many of our children in the state. Their only hope is education. If we do not have good public schools, they are not going to get an education. And that is not right. Everyone is supposed to have a chance."[57] Dr. Dulin's words summarize what we hope is the take away from this book for today's readers, that is, the need in our local communities to build strong public schools for our state and nation's children. This requires both individual actions and collective efforts to strengthen public schools.

Making a Difference: Local Activism and Collective Strategizing

Recently we attended a presentation at the University of Alabama about the resegregation of Tuscaloosa's public schools. After the presentation, a young professor told the audience that this was the fourth lecture she had attended in the last two years about this topic of resegregation in the local schools. She was clearly frustrated by all the talk but little action. She said she was desperately seeking a "movement" that addressed the problem with concrete actions. In the audience were two school board members, the principal of the town's all-black high school, the Dean of the College of Education and numerous university professors. Disappointingly neither the presenter nor anyone in the audience offered her any suggestions. Yet, the history of school desegregation provides an invaluable model for the potential of local activism to affect change around issues of school desegregation. From educators to editors to laundry pressers to nurses to fifteen-year-old students to middle class mothers—people during this time period found ways to support and advocate for the public schools in their community.

For many whites, who were part of their town's established power struc-ture, their activism manifested itself in making the *personal* decision to keep their children in public schools. State Senator Herman DeCell led the petition in Yazoo City to encourage whites to sign their names in support of public schools and kept his own children there while others flocked to the private school. When Jack Reed, a prominent businessman in Tupelo, Ed Meek in Oxford, and Hodding Carter Jr, in Greenville (just to name a few) chose to keep their children in public schools, they influenced others to follow suit. Certainly, one can argue the motivations behind such actions, but the impor-tance of local leaders making public stands in support of public schools by sending their own children to them was instrumental in many locales in making school desegregation a success.

Douglas Blackmon, author of *Slavery by Another Name: The Re-Enslavement of Black Americans from the Civil War to World War II*, began school in Leland during the first year of desegregation and graduated from Leland High in 1982. Writing in 1992 for *Harper's Magazine*, Blackmon questioned the current absence of white activists in his hometown—"preachers and teachers and alderman and grocers and research scientists and high-minded farmers" who banned together during the early days of school desegregation and made a pledge to send their children to public schools. Blackmon contends that their quietness today hearkens to the complicity of many whites in the 1950s and 1960s to perpetuate racism, not by violence or ill-treatment of blacks, but by doing nothing. Blackmon writes, "The moral conviction that integrated my school has given way to an indifference and numbness—the same numbness that allowed me (and most white Deltans) to accept abject black poverty just a stone's throw away from our own homes."[58] Thirty years ago, when a president of one of the state universities decided to enroll his children in the local private school, it is reported that he was met with public outcry and a reprimanding phone call from a state legislator.[59] Recently the president of that same university enrolled his children in the local private school. The public, including his own academic community, hardly batted an eye. No local or state politician gave him a dressing down for his actions; after all, many would argue, where one sends their children to school is nothing more than a personal choice and should not be imbued with any symbolic meaning. The history of whites in positions of power making personal, and often difficult, decisions to invest in their public schools by sending their own children to them should remind us that personal choices do matter. Admittedly, they are not sufficient on their own, but to relegate such decisions to irrelevance negates an entire history of individuals making moral choices to stand as the oppressed or with the oppressed and to fight for social justice within one's local context.

For black parents during school desegregation, their personal decisions to send their children to white schools using FOC, to file lawsuits on their children's behalf, or push their school districts to comply with desegregation in other ways reflect the sacrifices parents were willing to pay for equality not just for their own children but for all black children. They and their children were harassed, intimidated, fired, beaten, and sometimes forced to leave town. Yet, they stood steadfast in their belief that their children had the same rights as white children to get an education, fulfill their dreams, and soar to achieve all they desired. As Alean Adams, one of the mothers at the forefront of the fight for her children to attend integrated schools, said, "When our kids went to school, black children only made up 15 percent of the total population. Sending our kids to school was hell on earth! We had to do it, but it was hard on the children."[60]

Individual choices, while potentially powerful in the local context, were most successful when coupled with collective efforts. During school desegregation, communities organized. In Yazoo City, Sharkey-Issaquena, Rolling Fork, and Tupelo, the Friends of Public School movement, comprised primarily of white business leaders, supported their public schools through appeals to the economic necessity of them. Occasionally white and black residents formed pro–public school coalitions, such as in Leland and Oxford, to ensure a peaceful transition to desegregated schools. Drawing on a long history of collective organizing around civil rights, black Mississippians in Jackson, Biloxi, Columbus, Grenada, Greenville, Harmony, Marks, and countless other small towns joined together to force their school districts to comply with the "law of the land" through protests, boycotts, marches, and lawsuits.

Both black and white Mississippians challenged legislative mandates and local policies designed to weaken public schools. When the 1964 legislature approved a private school tuition voucher, Mississippians for Public Education (MPE) struck back with their own publication, "A Time to Speak," which lambasted the law and its potential repercussions for public schools. They encouraged people to take action by calling their local legislators to express their opposition to the bill. Their activism stimulated a public discussion about why such policies were not aligned with the democratic ideals upon which this country was based. Black citizens challenged their school boards and took them to task when they made policies clearly intended to propagate segregated schools by funding, directly or indirectly, private schools. They held their school boards accountable for enacting discriminatory policies against black teachers, such as inappropriately using GRE and NTE scores to decrease the black teaching staff, or assigning black students to still largely segregated schools or classrooms based on scores on achievement tests. These public challenges to legislative actions and local policies did not always produce the results intended, but, as these local efforts illustrate, strategic organizing requires deploying an array of political, legal, and economic tactics in any fight for social justice.

The lessons learned from ordinary citizens who waged a long and fierce battle for strong desegregated public schools have implications today as we witness what appears to be a waning commitment at the national, state, and local level to educate *all* children in *free, high-quality public schools*. Year after year the Mississippi state legislature fails to fully fund public schools despite the fact that Mississippi ranks last or near the bottom on almost every educational metric.[61] In 2013, legislation was passed allowing the establishment of charter schools without local school board approval in school districts receiving a "D" or "F" ranking. In 2015, the state legislature approved a tuition voucher for students with disabilities to attend private schools. In 2016, in a confusing vote in which initiative 42 was pitted against initiative 42A, state voters failed to approve a measure that would require the state to fund an "adequate and efficient" free public school system.[62]

Supporters of tuition vouchers, charter schools, and privatized education often couch their arguments for these measures in the rhetoric of "choice," "parental rights," and "quality education."[63] These terms all have a troubling historical precedent in the school desegregation era in which prosegregationists used these terms to perpetuate a dual system of segregated public schooling intended to keep blacks undereducated, subjugated, and powerless. When whites abandoned public schools for private schools in the 1960s, they emphasized parents' rights to "choose" a "quality education" for their children, which, in most cases, was thinly disguised language for "I do not choose to have my child sit in classrooms with black students." Another term from the school desegregation era reemerging in the current lexicon of supporters of school choice is "government schools" to refer to public schools. At the Tea Party Unity Rally in 2012, conservative talkshow host Neal Boortz urged the audience to quit using the term "public schools" and instead refer to them as "government schools." In 1964, William Simmons, editor of the Citizens' Council newspaper and director of the Jackson Citizens' Councils, urged his readers to do the same. Simmons followed with a call for whites to leave the "government schools," which, he claimed, were nothing but "pawns" of the federal government. Boorz urged his contemporary audience to defund public schools, support vouchers for private schools, and "preach school choice." Boortz and other "school choice" supporters would adamantly deny that their current usage of "school choice" or references to public schools as "government schools" is intended to exclude black students. Indeed, Empower Mississippi, whose goal is for "50,000 Mississippi students (10% of the public school population) to be enrolled in education choice programs by 2025," makes the opposite claim: "school choice moves students into less racially segregated classrooms than the public schools they were previously attending."[64] Empower Mississippi has been instrumental in helping pass charter school and tuition voucher legislation in the Mississippi legislature. However, if the goal of those touting "choice" is truly to bolster the educational experience and outcomes of all children, regardless of their race or social class, then those making such claims would be well served if they coupled their declarations about the emancipatory possibilities of "choice" with an acknowledgment of the racist legacy of these terms and evidence that "choice" for some will not lead to the separation of white, middle-class students from black and economically disadvantaged students in resegregated schools.

Public Schools as the Bedrock of Democracy

At the height of the school desegregation controversy in her hometown of Lexington (Holmes County), Hazel Brannon Smith, editor of the *Lexington,* wrote in a May 7, 1970 editorial entitled "We Must Save our Public Schools": "Holmes County today is in a state of crisis which must soon be resolved if our county is to survive. What is absolutely essential is that all citizens who care about the future of our county join together in saving our public school system. WITHOUT A GOOD PUBLIC SCHOOL SYSTEM HOLMES COUNTY HAS NO FUTURE, educational, economic, or otherwise."[65] Smith's impassioned plea to her readers about the necessity of a strong public school in their community invokes the spirit of Horace Mann and other public school reformers who believed that foundational to a strong democracy was a strong public school system for the common good. As history demonstrates, the ideological underpinnings of this call for free public schools for all repeatedly failed in practice as blacks, girls, the poor, and immigrants were systematically denied access to free public education, but its ideal was never lost on those who fought valiantly through the years to secure its promise.

The echoes of Horace Mann and Hazel Brannon Smith can be heard in many of the people featured in this book—local people who worked through school desegregation because they believed strong public schools were not only imperative for helping children, regardless of their race, their gender, their birthplace, or their parents' occupations, achieve their individual dreams and goals but also because they knew the civic health and economic viability of their local communities were only as strong as their local public schools.

A book about the history of school desegregation in Mississippi should rightly end with Governor William Winter, revered as the premier educational reformer in Mississippi.[66] Winter's life as a public servant personifies an unwavering belief in the social contract as the heart of democracy. Writing in 2010, Winter warned of the spiritual consequences for our state and our country when we forget our moral obligation to work together for the common good: "In our self-centered preoccupation with our own private interest, we tend to forget that we are bound together by a social contract that requires us to get along with each other and to look out for each other. We ignore the obligations of that contract at the risk of losing our souls."[67] Today public education faces enormous challenges, but our country's dream of providing equal and equitable educational opportunities for all students is as relevant today as it was in the mid-19th century when Horace Mann imagined a common, public education for all and in 1954 when the Supreme Court ruled that "separate [schooling] is inherently unequal [schooling]." If as a community, state, and nation, we forget that strong public schools are a fundamental pillar of democracy, thus worth fighting for, we do, indeed, risk losing our souls.

Notes

Preface

1. Dr. Lamar Weems, interview by author, Jackson, MS.

2. Some of Leon and his family's experiences were reported in Charles Fulton's 1978 PhD dissertation, "Racial Integration in the Public School System in Kemper County, Mississippi, 1954–1974" (104–12), in which Leon reports daily physical fights with older white high school boys. The Johnson children also report being ostracized by other black children.

Introduction

1. Barbara Kingsolver, *Animal Dreams* (New York: Harper Perennial, 1990), 299.

2. The Supreme Court combined five different school desegregation cases: *Brown v. Board of Education of Topeka*, 98 F. Supp. 797 (1951); *Briggs v. Elliott*, 98 F. Supp. 529 (1951); *Davis v. County School Board of Prince Edward County*, 103 F. Supp. 337 (1952); *Gebhart v. Bolton*, 33 Del. Ch. 144, 87A 2d 862 (Del. Ch. 1952); and *Bolling v. Sharpe*, 347 U.S. 497 (1954).

3. *Brown v. Board of Education of Topeka*, 347 U.S. 483 (1954).

4. Ibid.

5. Ibid.

6. Ibid.

7. Richard Kluger, *Simple Justice* (New York: Alfred Knopf, 1976), 722.

8. Ibid., 737.

9. Ibid., 737–38.

10. C. Johnson, "A Southern Negro's View of the South," *The Journal of Negro Education* 26, no. 1 (1957): 8.

11. *Brown v. Board of Education Topeka*, 349 U.S. 294 (1955).

12. "Coleman Claims State Can Force Indefinite Delay on Integration," *State Times* (Jackson, MS), April 26, 1954; W. F. Minor, "Ruling Expected to Bring No Immediate Changes," *Times Picayune* (New Orleans, LA), April 23, 1954.

13. Neil McMillen, *The Citizens' Council: Organized Resistance to the Second Reconstruction, 1954–64* (Urbana: University of Illinois Press, 1971), 15–40; John Martin, *The Deep South Says Never* (New York: Ballantine Books, 1957), 12–21.

14. "Desegregation in Schools Triples," *Clarion-Ledger* (Jackson, MS), December 5, 1966; Harrell Rodgers and Charles Bullock, "School Desegregation: A Policy Analysis," *Journal of Black Studies* 2, no. 4 (June 1972): 412.

15. *Alexander v. Holmes County Board of Education*, 396 U.S. 1218 (1969).

16. "Governor John Bell Williams Address on the Integration of Public Schools in Mississippi." Mississippi Department of Archives and History (AU1062, TR 057), accessed January 21, 2017,

https://www.mdah.ms.gov/arrec/digital_archives/vault/projects/OHtranscripts/AU _1062_117291.pdf.

17. William Street, "The Full Heat of Integration," *Commercial Appeal* (Memphis, TN), January 18, 1970.

Chapter 1

1. "School Men Here Today Give Their Views on Segregation," *Jackson Daily News* (Jackson, MS), May 19, 1954.

2. For a detailed account of the history of the *Brown* decision, see Richard Kluger, *Simple Justice* (New York: Alfred Knopf, 1976); Waldo E. Martin Jr., *Brown v. Board of Education: A Brief History with Documents* (Boston: St. Martin's, 1998); Charles J. Ogletree Jr., *All Deliberate Speed* (New York: W. W. Norton, 2004). See also "Segregation and the Supreme Court," *The Atlantic*, July 1954, http://www.theatlantic.com/magazine/archive/1954/07 /segregation-and-the-supreme-court/.

3. *Brown v. Board of Education, Topeka, Kansas*, 347 U.S. 483 (1954).

4. Arthur Sutherland, "Segregation by Race in Public Schools Retrospect and Prospect," *Law and Contemporary Problems* 20, no. 1 (Winter 1955): 169.

5. Mississippi Constitution, section 6220.5 of the Mississippi Code.

6. Erle Johnston, *Mississippi's Defiant Years, 1953–1973* (Forest, MS: Lake Harbor, 1990), 17.

7. John Bartlow Martin, *The Deep South Says Never* (New York: Ballantine Books, 1957); James Nabrit, "Legal Invention and the Desegregation Process," *The Annals of the American Academy of Political and Social Science* 304 (March 1956): 35–43.

8. Charles Bolton, *The Hardest Deal of All: The Battle over School Integration in Mississippi, 1870–1980* (Jackson: University Press of Mississippi, 2005), 61.

9. "Transcript of Meeting of Legal Educational Advisory Committee and Negro Leaders, July 30, 1954," Segregation Integration-Schools, vertical file, Mississippi Department, Mississippi State Universities Libraries, Starkville, MS; see also W. A. Bender, "Desegregation in the Public Schools of Mississippi," *Journal of Negro Education* 24, no. 3 (Summer 1956): 288.

10. Bender, 291–92.

11. Nabrit, 38–39; Johnston, 1990, 4–6; Erle Johnston, interview by Yasuhiro Katagiri, August 13, 1993, University of Southern Mississippi Center for Oral History and Cultural Heritage, http://anna.lib.usm.edu/~spcol/crda/oh/ohjohnstone2b.html.

12. Michael Butler, "The Mississippi State Sovereignty Commission and Beach Integration, 1959–1963: A Cotton-Patch Gestapo?" *Journal of Southern History* 68, no. 1 (February

2002): 109; Preston Valien, "The Status of Educational Desegregation, 1956: A Critical Summary," *Journal of Negro Education* 25, no. 3 (Summer 1956): 359.

13. Butler, 110.

14. Erle Johnston, *I Rolled with Ross: A Political Portrait* (Baton Rouge: Moran Industries, 1980), 26.

15. Charles Bolton, "Mississippi's School Equalization Program, 1945–54: 'A Last Gasp to Try to Maintain a Segregated Educational System,'" *The Journal of Southern History* 66, no. 4 (November 2000): 806.

16. Glenn L. Swetman, President of Biloxi Board of Trustees, to Senator James Eastland, July 25, 1952. James O. Eastland Collection, File Series 3, Subseries 4, Box 3, Folder 11, the University of Mississippi Libraries, Oxford, MS.

17. "Message of the Honorable Hugh White, Governor of Mississippi," November 3, 1953. Speech delivered before the joint session of the Mississippi legislature extra-ordinary session, Segregation Integration-Schools, vertical file, Mississippi Department, Mississippi State Universities Libraries, Starkville, MS; Bolton, 2000: 807–8; Johnston, 1990, 3.

18. Eunice Newton and Earle West, "The Progress of the Negro in Elementary and Secondary Education," *The Journal of Negro Education* 32, no. 4 (Autumn 1963): 466–84.

19. Johnston, 1990, 4; Charles Fulton, "Racial Integration in the Public School System in Kemper County, Mississippi, 1954–1974" (PhD dissertation, University of Mississippi, 1978), 80; Bolton, 2005, 59; Jack Davis, *Race against Time: Culture and Separation in Natchez since 1930* (Baton Rouge: Louisiana State University Press, 2001), 212.

20. Bolton, 2005, 54.

21. James Haney, "The Effects of the *Brown* Decision on Black Educators," *Journal of Negro Education* 47, no. 1 (Winter 1978): 88–95.

22. Charles Payne, *I've Got the Light of Freedom: The Organizing Tradition and the Mississippi Freedom Struggle* (Berkeley: University of California Press, 1995), 53.

23. John Dittmer, *Local People: The Struggle for Civil Rights in Mississippi* (Urbana: University of Illinois Press, 1994), 43; Roy Wilkins, "The Role of the National Association for the Advancement of Colored People in the Desegregation Process," *Social Problems* 2, no. 4 (April 1955): 201–4.

24. Dittmer, 46.

25. Medgar Evers telegram to Roy Wilkins, July 19, 1955, Folder 5, II: A227, NAACP Records, General Office File: Desegregation of Schools: Branch Action: Mississippi, Library of Congress, Washington, DC; "Those Who Signed," *Vicksburg Evening Post* (Vicksburg, MS), July 19, 1955; "Vicksburg School Board Says Negroes' Petition Not Legal," *Clarion-Ledger* (Jackson, MS), July 20, 1955; "Jackson Petition Is Filed," *Natchez Times* (Natchez, MS), July 26, 1955.

26. Martin, 1957, 30.

27. Dr. Maurice Mackel to Roy Wilkins, July 18, 1955, Folder 5, II: A227, NAACP Records, General Office File: Desegregation of Schools: Branch Action: Mississippi, Library of Congress, Washington, DC.

28. Dr. Maurice Mackel to Roy Wilkins. July 25, 1955, Folder 5, II: A227, NAACP Records, General Office File: Desegregation of Schools: Branch Action: Mississippi, Library of Congress, Washington, DC.

29. David Bacon and A. M. Mackel to Brent Forman. July 25, 1955, Folder 5, II: A227, NAACP Records, General Office File: Desegregation of Schools: Branch Action: Mississippi, Library of Congress, Washington, DC; see also "Petition Filed NAACP Calls for Integration in Schools," *Natchez Times* (Natchez, MS), July 26, 1955.

30. "Jackson Petition Is Filed," *Natchez Times* (Natchez, MS), July 26, 1955.

31. Neil McMillen, *The Citizens' Council: Organized Resistance to the Second Reconstruction, 1954–64* (Urbana: University of Illinois Press, 1971), 211; Martin, 30.

32. Roy Wilkins to Dr. Robert Fullilove. September 23, 1955, Folder 5, II: A227, NAACP Records, General Office File: Desegregation of Schools: Branch Action: Mississippi, Library of Congress, Washington, DC.

33. James Wright to NAACP, November 8, 1955, Folder 5, II: A227, NAACP Records, General Office File: Desegregation of Schools: Branch Action: Mississippi, Library of Congress, Washington, DC.

34. Roy Wilkins to James Wright. November 10, 1955, Folder 5, II: A227, NAACP Records, General Office File: Desegregation of Schools: Branch Action: Mississippi, Library of Congress, Washington, DC.

35. Martin, 30.

36. Dittmer, 51–52.

37. Bender, 285.

38. Ibid., 288.

39. Dittmer, 53–58, 83–84; Payne, 36–42, 53–54.

40. Dittmer, 57.

41. Ibid.

42. William Robinson, "Integration's Delay and Frustration Tolerance," *Journal of Negro Education* 28, no. 4 (Autumn 1959): 472.

43. Martin, 2.

44. Ibid., 34; McMillen, 15–40.

45. Editorial, *Citizens' Council* 1, no. 1 (October 1955), http://www.citizenscouncils.com/index.php?option=com_content&view=newspaper&file=1-Oct55-Dec55.swf.

46. Letter from Ellett Lawrence, Finance Chairman of the Association to Citizens' Councils of Mississippi, to all district and county chairmen, and the executive committee Mississippi-Citizens' Council, FBI files (105–34237–225) accessed May 10, 2013, https://archive.org/stream/CItizensCouncilMovement/CitCouncils-LA-MS-2#page/n15/mode/2up.

47. McMillen, 161–88, 235–66.

48. Ibid., 162.

49. "Winning Essays in the 1960 Contest," http://lib.usm.edu/legacy/spcol/exhibitions/anti-somm/civil_rights-3.html (accessed July 16, 2014).

50. "How to Save Our Public Schools," 1959, Citizens' Council/Civil Rights Collection, Series 1, Box 1, Folder 29 (Brochures, 1955–1957, 1960–1966), McCain Library and Archives, University of Southern Mississippi Library, Hattiesburg, MS.

51. "Community Plan to Counteract Racial Agitators," July 21, 1965. Citizens' Council/Civil Rights Collection, Series 1, Box 1, Folder 29 (Brochures, 1955–1957, 1960–1966), McCain Library and Archives, University of Southern Mississippi Library, Hattiesburg, MS.

52. Gilbert Mason, *Beaches, Blood, and Ballots: A Black Doctor's Civil Rights Struggle* (Jackson: University Press of Mississippi, 2000), 143–45.

53. Robinson, 474–75.

54. For a detailed discussion of the April 24, 1960, wade-in, see Mason, chapter 6 (65–87), and Butler, 107–48.

55. Mason, 114–15, 141–57; "Group of Negroes Ask Integration Biloxi Schools," *Daily Herald* (Mississippi Coast), March 19, 1963; Bolton, 2005, 98–99.

56. Mason, 152.

57. Ibid., 153–55; "'Stay Calm' Mayor, School Board Say," *Jackson Times* (Jackson, MS), March 14, 1963; Winson Hudson and Constance Curry, *Mississippi Harmony: Memoirs of a Freedom Fighter* (New York: Palgrave, 2002), 47–73; Bolton, 2005, 99–102.

58. *Evers v. Jackson Municipal Separate School District* 328 F. 2d 408 (5th Cir. 1964).

59. "Appeal in School Case Won't Stop Integration," *Clarion-Ledger* (Jackson, MS), July 8, 1964.

60. "School Officials Grudgingly Yield," *Commercial Appeal* (Memphis, TN), July 8, 1964: Bolton, 102–3.

61. "Public Education: 1964 Staff Report," Submitted to the United States Commission on Civil Rights, October 1964: 130–37, https://www.law.umaryland.edu/marshall/usccr/documents/cr12ed82964.pdf.

62. Hudson and Curry, 66.

63. "Lone Negro Girl Enters Previous White School," *Carthaginian* (Carthage, MS), September 3, 1964.

64. *Henry v. Clarksdale-Coahoma School Board*, 352 F. 2d 648 (5th Cir. 1966); "Public Education: 1964 Staff Report," 138; Bolton, 103–4.

65. Hudson and Curry, 68; Mason, 156; Dittmer, 165–66; Payne, 288–90; Myrlie Evers, *For Us, the Living* (Jackson: University Press of Mississippi, 1967).

66. Harrell Rodgers, "The Supreme Court and School Desegregation: Twenty Years Later," *Political Science Quarterly* 89, no. 4 (1974–75): 752–53; Myron Lieberman, "Desegregation since 1964: The Civil Rights Fiasco in Public Education," *Phi Delta Kappan* 47, no. 9 (May 1966): 482–85.

67. For a detailed explanation of how the ESEA affected Mississippi schools after its passage, see Crystal Sanders, "'Money Talks': The Elementary and Secondary Education Act of 1965 and the African-American Freedom Struggle in Mississippi," *History of Education Quarterly* 56, no. 2 (May 2016): 361–67. For a discussion of the unusual alliance of all three branches of government, see Ginny Lane and Amy White, "The Roots of Resegregation: Analysis and Implications," *Race, Gender & Class* 17, nos. 3–4 (2010): 81–102.

68. William Peart, "Desegregation of Schools Lacked Leadership in State," *Clarion Ledger* (Jackson, MS), September 19, 1965.

69. Bolton, 2005, 121.

70. Superintendent Robert Taylor to Senator James Eastland, December 21, 1967, James O. Eastland Collection, File Series 3, Subseries 4, Box 53, Folder 24, the University of Mississippi Libraries, Oxford, MS.

71. Bolton, 2005, 118.

72. Ibid., 121.

73. Sanders, 2016a, 365–66.

74. Peart.

75. For a critique written by the Student Nonviolent Coordinating Committee (SNCC) of the Office of Education's handling of the implementation of Title VI, see Marion S. Berry and Betty Garmin, *SNCC: A Special Report on Southern School Desegregation*, Fall 1965, http://www.crmvet.org/docs/65_sncc_school-rpt.pdf.

76. United States Commission on Civil Rights, "Federal Rights under School Desegregation Law," CCR Clearinghouse Publication 6, June 1966, http://www.law.umaryland.edu /marshall/usccr/documents/cr1106.pdf.

77. *Federal Rights under School Desegregation Law,* 19.

78. James McPhail, *A History of Desegregation Developments in Certain Mississippi School Districts* (Hattiesburg: Mississippi School Study Council, Spring 1971), 78–79.

79. "US Charges 13 in Noxubee Intimidate Negro Parents," *Commercial Appeal* (Memphis, TN), September 12, 1967.

80. *United States v. Jefferson County Board of Education* 372 F. 29 836 (5th Cir. 1966). For commentary, see also, James Bolner "The Supreme Court and Racially Imbalanced Public Schools in 1967," *Journal of Negro Education* 38, no. 4 (Autumn 1969): 125–34.

81. *Green v. County School Board of New Kent County* 391 U.S. 430 (1968). For commentary, see William Gordon, "The Implementation of Desegregation Plans Since *Brown,*" *Journal of Negro Education* 63, no. 3 (Summer 1994): 311–12.

82. *Alexander v. Holmes County Board of Education,* 396 U.S. 1218 (1969). For in-depth examination of *Alexander v. Holmes*, see Patrick Doherty, "Integration Now: A Study of *Alexander v. Holmes* County Board of Education," *Notre Dame Law Review* 45, no. 3 (March 1970): 489–514.

83. Doherty, 497.

84. "Local Freedom of Choice Plans Upheld by Court," *Neshoba Democrat* (Philadelphia, MS), May 15, 1969.

85. Doherty, 501.

86. For a discussion of Nixon's "Southern Strategy" and a softening on the federal enforcement of school desegregation in the South, see Lawrence McAndrews, "The Politics of Principle: Richard Nixon and School Desegregation," *The Journal of Negro History* 83, no. 3 (Summer 1998): 187–200; Joseph Crespino, *In Search of Another Country: Mississippi and the Conservative Counterrevolution* (Princeton, NJ: Princeton University Press, 2007; "Requiem for a Liberal Dream?" *Newsweek* (March 2, 1970): 18–21. For a detailed discussion of the role of Mississippi Senator John Stennis in influencing Nixon towards an attack on northern school segregation, see Joseph Crespino, "The Best Defense Is a Good Offense: The Stennis Amendment and the Fracturing of Liberal School Desegregation Policy, 1964–1972," *Journal of Policy History* 18, no. 3 (2006): 304–25. For newspaper accounts of the "Stennis Amendment," see Peter Milius, "Most Classrooms Still Segregated, U.S. Study Finds," *Washington Post,* January 4, 1970; Tom Wicker, "In the Nation: One Evil, Two Problems." *New York Times,* February 12, 1970; Roy Reed, "Southern Blacks Fear a Growing Northern Apathy," *New York Times,* March 21, 1970; Garnett Horner, "Nixon to Discuss Federal Policy on Integration," *Washington Star,* March 21, 1970.

87. Horace Barker, "The Federal Retreat in School Desegregation," Southern Regional Council, December 1969, 30–46; David Norman, "The Strange Career of the Civil Rights Division's Commitment to Brown," *The Yale Law Journal* 93, no. 6 (May 1984): 983–89; "Civil Rights Chief Canned for Meddling in White House Ruling," *Daily Herald* (Biloxi-Gulfport, MS), February 22, 1970.

88. Doherty, 502.

89. Fred Graham, "More Delay Seen in Desegregation," *New York Times*, September 22, 1969; Warren Weaver, "High Court Takes Key School Case," *New York Times*. October 10, 1969; Barry Schweid, "Fed Gov't Stands with State at Hearing Delay School Mix," *Natchez Democrat* (Natchez, MS), October 24, 1969.

90. *Alexander v. Holmes County Board of Education* 396 U.S. 1218 (1969).

91. For a sampling of newspaper reports of this momentous day, see James Wooten, "2 Whites and 1,391 Blacks in a Mississippi School," *New York Times*, January 6, 1970; "Mississippi Integration Due Today," *Washington Post*, January 5, 1970; William Street, "The Full Heat of Integration," *Commercial Appeal* (Memphis, TN), January 18, 1970; "Public School System in Wilkinson County Abandoned to Negroes," *Meridian Star* (Meridian, MS), January 4, 1970; "Public School Desegregation Goes into Effect Across State," *Delta Democrat-Times* (Greenville, MS), January 5, 1970; "Governor Urges Restraint in Mix Crisis," *Meridian Star* (Meridian, MS), January 4, 1970; Floyd Johnson, "Calmness Arrives for Yazoo Citizens," *Jackson Daily News* (Jackson, MS), January 8, 1970.

92. Tom Herman, "'Integrated' Schools in South Sometimes Keep Races Separated," *Wall Street Journal*, May 15, 1970; Bruce Galphin, "Mississippi Takes Step to Integrate," *Washington Post*, January 6, 1970; Charles Fulton, "Racial Integration in the Public School System in Kemper County, Mississippi, 1954–1974" (PhD dissertation, University of Mississippi, 1978).

93. William Keady, *All Rise: Memoirs of a Mississippi Federal Judge* (Boston: Recollections Bound, 1988), 106; *United States v. Hinds County School Board v. Amite County School Board* 560 F. 2d 619 (5th Cir., 1977); "Public School System in Wilkinson County Abandoned to Negroes" (Meridian, MS), January 6, 1970; Ken Tolliver, "Court Approves County Plan for All-Boy, All-Girl Schools," *Commercial Appeal* (Memphis, TN), May 20, 1969.

94. Keady, 105; "IQ to Be Segregation Basis in County's First 3 Grades," *Clarion Ledger* (Jackson, MS), June 4, 1969. Luther Munford, "Sunflower, Boliver Tests Over," *Delta Democrat-Times* (Greenville, MS), August 3, 1969; "Unique Desegregation Plan Offered," *The Delta Democrat-Times*, May 16, 1969.

95. National Education Association, *Report of NEW Task Force III. School Desegregation: Louisiana and Mississippi*, November 1970, 25–26.

96. Ted Simmons, "Wholesale Desegregation of Southern Schools Set," *Clarion-Ledger* (Jackson, MS), August 23, 1970.

Chapter 2

1. Alean and John Adams, interview by author, Brandon, MS. All quotes from an interviewee are from author interviews unless otherwise noted. A list of the oral history interviews appears in the bibliography.

2. For an account of Alean's involvement in bringing a Head Start program to her community as part of the Child Development Group of Mississippi, see Crystal Sanders, *A Chance for Change: Head Start and Mississippi's Black Freedom Struggle* (Chapel Hill: University of North Carolina Press, 2016), 134–35, 138, 188–89.

3. Alean M. Adams, *Way beyond Pisgah: Surviving Integration in Smalltown Mississippi* (self-published, 2009), 5.

4. For an analysis of how one of the leading civil rights workers in the state and one of the staunchest segregationist southern politicians hailed from the same rural county, see Chris Asch, *The Senator and the Sharecropper: The Freedom Struggles of James O. Eastland and Fannie Lou Hamer* (New York: New Press, 2008).

5. Constance Curry, *Silver Rights* (Chapel Hill, NC: Algonquin Books of Chapel Hill, 1995).

6. Ibid., 29.

7. Ibid., 36–37.

8. Gloria Carter Dickerson, interview by author, Drew, MS.

9. Curry, 112–13.

10. Alean Adams, 141–75; Alean Adams, interview by author, Brandon, MS. Unless otherwise cited, information about the Adamses was taken from our interview with Alean and John Adams.

11. Alean Adams, 132.

12. Ola Crockett, interview by author, Laurel, MS.

13. Mason, 158–59.

14. Gloria Carter Dickerson, interview by author, Drew, MS. Gloria's story is also told in Constance Curry's book *Silver Rights*. Unless otherwise cited, information about Gloria's experiences was taken from our interview.

15. For more information about the organization, see http://we2gether.org/.

16. Clarence Hall, interview by author, Avon, MS. Clarence's involvement in his local civil rights movement is briefly discussed in Unita Blackwell and JoAnne Prichard Morris, *Barefootin': Life Lessons from the Road to Freedom* (New York: Crown, 2006).

17. Ann Hall Evans and Clarence Hall, interview by author, Avon, MS.

18. Robert Jackson, interview by author, Marks, MS.

19. Curry, 11.

20. Ibid., 108.

Chapter 3

1. Julian Prince, "Balancing the Scales: School Desegregation in McComb, Mississippi," unpublished manuscript, 53. Manuscript shared with authors by Dr. Prince.

2. Mrs. Lilla D. Ware, speech delivered at a retirement dinner hosted by black teachers and employees of the Scott County public schools, December 20, 1955, personal manuscript shared with authors by Dr. Lamar Weems.

3. Lamar Weems letter to author, July 25, 2014.

4. Prince, 54.

5. Dan Dodson, "School Administration, Control and Public Policy Concerning Integration," *Journal of Negro Education* 34, no. 3 (1965): 249.

6. United States Commission on Civil Rights, "Federal Rights under School Desegregation Law," CCR Clearinghouse Publication, 6, June 1966, http://www.law.umaryland.edu/marshall/usccr/documents/cr1106.pdf.

7. Luther Munford, "Black Gravity: Desegregation in 30 Mississippi School Districts" (senior thesis, Princeton University, 1971); James Palmer, *Mississippi School Districts: Factors in the Disestablishment of Dual Systems* (MS: Social Science Research Center, 1971).

8. Ruby Martin to Superintendent Henry Hull, January 3, 1969, James O. Eastland Collection, File Series 3, Subseries 4, Box 46, Folder 3, University of Mississippi Libraries, Oxford, MS.

9. Henry Hull to Senator James Eastland. January 14, 1969, James O. Eastland Collection, File Series 3, Subseries 4, Box 46, Folder 3, University of Mississippi Libraries, Oxford, MS.

10. Senator James Eastland to Superintendent H.C. Hull, January 22, 1969, James O. Eastland Collection, File Series 3, Subseries 4, Box 46, Folder 3, University of Mississippi Libraries, Oxford, MS.

11. Harrell Rodgers and Charles Bullock, "School Desegregation: A Policy Analysis," *Journal of Black Studies* 2, no. 4 (June 1972): 429.

12. "Voluntary Plan of Desegregation by the Okolona Municipal Separate School District to the Department of Health, Education and Welfare," James O. Eastland Collection, File Series 3, Subseries 4, Box 46, Folder 3, University of Mississippi Libraries, Oxford, MS.

13. H. C. Hull to Senator James Eastland, February 28, 1969, James O. Eastland Collection, File Series 3, Subseries 4, Box 46, Folder 3, University of Mississippi Libraries, Oxford, MS.

14. Prince, 49–50; Julian Prince, interview by author, Tupelo, MS. There is significant overlap between the information shared in the interview and Dr. Prince's unpublished manuscript. When appropriate, the manuscript pages are cited. All quotes from an interviewee are from author interviews unless otherwise noted. A list of the oral history interviews appears in the bibliography.

15. See also Prince, 51–52.

16. Ibid., 54.

17. See also Prince, 46–50, 54–55.

18. For a detailed account of McComb in the early 1960s, see Charles Payne, *I've Got the Light of Freedom: The Organizing Tradition and the Mississippi Freedom Struggle* (Berkeley: University of California Press, 1995), 111–31, and John Dittmer, *Local People: The Struggle for Civil Rights in Mississippi* (Urbana: University of Illinois Press, 1994), 99–115.

19. Payne, 113.

20. J. Oliver Emmerich, *Two Faces of Janus: The Saga of Deep South Change* (Jackson: University College Press of Mississippi, 1973), 137.

21. Dittmer, 109–15; Payne, 233.

22. Emmerich, 132.

23. Prince, 60.

24. Dr. Charles Nash, interview by author, Tuscaloosa, AL.

25. Emmerich, 149.

26. Ibid., 150.

27. Another component of Prince's plan, unpopular with many, was the renaming of the black and white high schools. McComb High was renamed Gibson High, in honor of the president of Southeastern Louisiana College (Joseph E. Gibson). Burglund High was renamed Higgins High, in honor of Commodore Dewey Higgins (the longtime black principal of the school).

28. See also Prince, 88–89.

29. Fielding Wright, "Prince Explains McComb Change," *Mississippi Press* (Pascagoula, Moss Point), October 17, 1969.

30. J. D. Prince to Senator James Eastland, April 23, 1971, James O. Eastland Collection, File Series 3, Subseries 4, Box 27, Folder 95, University of Mississippi Libraries, Oxford, MS.

31. Prince, 106.

32. Dr. Tom Dulin, interview by author, Winona, MS.

33. Brandon Hembree, "Winona Mix Plan Holds," *Jackson Daily News* (Jackson, MS), August 29, 1969.

34. Dr. Clyde Muse, interview by author, Jackson, MS.

35. *Ayers v. Allain,* 674 F. Supp. 1523 (ND Mississippi, 1987).

36. Utica's president, Louis Stokes, was appointed vice president of the Utica campus.

37. Harold Kelly, interview by author, Yazoo City, MS.

38. Willie Morris was only twenty-nine years old at the time.

39. Thomas Bevier, "All's Well in Yazoo City, but What about Tomorrow?" *Commercial Appeal* (Memphis, TN), January 18, 1970; Leon Lindsay, "Making Integration Work: Yazoo City, Miss. Copes with School Challenge," *Christian Science Monitor,* November 12, 1970. For a more critical perspective of Yazoo City's desegregation attempts, see Luther Munford, "Black Gravity: Desegregation in 30 Mississippi School Districts" (senior thesis, Princeton University, 1971), 120–22.

40. Munford, 121–22.

41. "Toughest Job in U.S.," *Clarion-Ledger* (Jackson, MS), August 18, 1970; see also Maybelle Gorringe, "Dr. Martin Resigns Post as City Schools Head," *Jackson Daily News* (Jackson, MS), August 28, 1970; "Martin Quits City's Troubled Schools," *Clarion Ledger* (Jackson, MS), August 28, 1970.

42. "Chaos for Mississippi Schools?" *Meridian Star* (Meridian, MS), December 1, 1969.

Chapter 4

1. Ernest Zebrowski and Judith Howard, *Category 5: The Story of Camille* (Ann Arbor: University of Michigan Press. 2005), 226; R. H. Simpson, Arnold Sugg, and Staff, "The Atlantic Hurricane Season of 1969," *Monthly Weather Review* (National Hurricane Center, Weather Bureau, ESSA, Miami, FL, April 1970): 300.

2. Lamar Beaty, interview by author, Houston, MS. All quotes from an interviewee are from author interviews unless otherwise noted. A list of the oral history interviews appears in the bibliography.

3. Dr. William Lewis, interview by author, Poplarville, MS.

4. Mark Chesler, James Crowfoot, and Bunyan Bryant, "Institutional Changes to Support School Desegregation: Alternative Models Underlying Research and Implementation," *Law and Contemporary Problems* 42, no. 4 (Autumn 1978): 174–213; Gary Orfield, "How to Make Desegregation Work: The Adaptation of Schools to Their Newly-Integrated Bodies," *Law and Contemporary Problems* 39, no. 2 (Spring 1975): 314–40; Pat Cordisco, "The Phantom Challenge of the Principalship," *American Secondary Education* 1, no. 1 (December 1970): 16–19.

5. Charles Boone, interview by author, Quitman, MS.

6. John Allen Flynt, interview by author, New Hebron, MS.

7. Dr. James Brewer, interview with author, Hazlehurst, MS. Dr. Brewer wrote about his experiences preparing for desegregation in James Brewer, "We Made the Transition from Dual to Unitary," *Mississippi Educational Advance* 61, no. 8, (May 1970): 14, 31.

8. *Report of NEA Task Force III, School Desegregation: Louisiana and Mississippi*, (Washington, DC: National Education Association, November 1970), 28.

9. Dr. Fenton Peters, interview by author, Starkville, MS.

10. This pairing of schools to achieve desegregation was referred to as the Princeton Plan.

11. Ken Clawson, "MS County Integrates Reluctantly," *Washington Post*, August 25, 1970.

12. Sid Salter, interview by author, Starkville, MS.

13. Larry Van Dyke, interview by author, Meridian, MS.

14. Lewis Lord, "Like Watching Something Wonderful Die, Students Say of Total Integration Move," *Meridian Star* (Meridian, MS), January 11, 1970.

15. Galen Drewry, "The Principal Faces Desegregation," *Educational Leadership* (October 1955): 17.

16. "Public School Notice: Starkville Municipal Separate School District," *Starkville Daily News*, September 9, 1970.

17. "Statement of Policy: Vicksburg Public Schools," *Vicksburg Post* (Vicksburg, MS), September 3, 1970.

18. Dale Findley and Henry O'Reilly, "Secondary School Discipline," *American Secondary Education* 2, no. 1 (December 1971): 26–31.

19. George Dale, interview by author, Jackson, MS.

20. Charles George, interview by author, Webb, MS.

21. Dr. Larry Box, interview by author, Starkville, MS.

22. "Judge Orders Students Readmitted in Hair Case," *Delta Democrat Times* (Greenville, MS), February 16, 1970; "Riverside Students Sue for Hair Right," *Delta Democrat-Times* (Greenville, MS), February 13, 1970; "Judge Keady OKs Hair at Riverside," *Delta Democrat-Times* (Greenville, MS), February 17, 1970; Bob Boyd, "Coleman Youth Suspended," *Delta Democrat Times* (Greenville, MS), March 16, 1970.

23. Gael Graham, *Young Activists: American High School Students in the Age of Protest* (DeKalb: Northern Illinois University Press, 2006), 82–95.

24. Frederick Rodgers, *The Black High School and Its Community* (Lexington, MA: Lexington Books, 1967), 16. See also Linda Tillman, "African American Principalship and the Legacy of *Brown*," *Review of Research in Education*, 28 (2004): 101–46; Vanessa Siddle Walker, "The Architects of Black Schooling in the Segregated South: The Case of One

Principal Leader," *Journal of Curriculum and Supervision* 19, no. 1 (2003): 54–72; Vanessa Siddle Walker, "Valued Segregated Schools for African American Children in the South, 1935–1969: A Review of Common Themes and Characteristics," *Review of Educational Research* 70, no. 3 (Autumn 2001): 253–85.

25. Chesler, Crowfoot, and Bryant. 193–94; Adam Fairclough, "The Costs of *Brown*: Black Teachers and School Integration," *Journal of American History* 91, no. 1 (June 2004): 43–55; Michael Fultz, "The Displacement of Black Educators Post-*Brown*: An Overview and Analysis," *History of Education Quarterly* 44, no. 1 (Spring 2004): 11–45; Willard Gandy, "Implications of Integration for the Southern Teacher," *Journal of Negro Education* 31, no. 2 (Spring 1962): 191–97: James Haney, "The Effects of the *Brown* Decision on Black Educators," *Journal of Negro Education* 47, no. 1 (Winter 1978): 88–95; Robert Hooker, "Displacement of Black Teachers in the Eleven Southern States," *Afro-American Studies* 2 (December 1971): 165–80.

26. NEA Task Force, 8.

27. Ibid., 8–14.

28. Ted Simmons, "Wholesale Desegregation of Southern Schools Set," *Clarion-Ledger* (Jackson, MS), August 23, 1970.

29. Haney, 94.

30. Fairclough, 54.

31. NEA Task Force, 9–10.

32. *Cousin v. Board of Trustees of Houston Municipal Separate School District*, 726 F. 2d 262 (5th Cir. 1984).

33. Luther Munford. "Black Gravity: Desegregation in 30 Mississippi School Districts." (senior thesis, Princeton University, 1971), 160–63.

34. Casey Banas, "Seek to Avoid School Order in Mississippi," *Chicago Tribune,* November 4, 1969.

35. Dr. Charles Nash, interview by author, Tuscaloosa, AL.

36. See chapter, 3, for a discussion of McComb in the early 1960s.

37. NEA Task Force, 11.

Chapter 5

1. Harriet Kuykendall, interview by author, Jackson, MS. All quotes from an interviewee are from author interviews unless otherwise noted. A list of the oral history interviews appears in the bibliography.

2. JoAnne Prichard Morris, interview by author, Jackson, MS.

3. Casey Banas, "Mississippi Schools: Effect of Court Order," *Chicago Tribune,* April 19, 1970.

4. Philip Hearn, "Indianola School Superintendent Says Schools Losing Strength," *Daily Journal* (Tupelo, MS), February 3, 1970; "Third of Clarksdale's Teachers Quit in Change," *Daily Journal* (Tupelo, MS), February 9, 1970; Ken Tolliver, "Coahoma, Other Schools Get Deadline," *Commercial Appeal* (Memphis, TN), January 21, 1970.

5. *United States v. Tunica County School District,* 323 F. Supp. 1019 (ND, Mississippi, 1970); William Keady, *All Rise: Memoirs of a Mississippi Federal Judge* (Boston: Recollections Bound, 1988), 108.

6. Jerry Bustin, interview by author, Forest, MS.

7. Dalton McAlpin, interview by author, Starkville, MS.

8. Lillie V. Davis, interview by author, Marks, MS.

9. Cyndie Harrison, interview by author, Jackson, MS. For another personal account of a young, white teacher assigned to a black school in the Delta (Leland) during the same time period, see David Beckwith, *A New Day in the Delta: Inventing School Desegregation as You Go* (Tuscaloosa: University of Alabama Press, 2009).

10. NEA Task Force, 21–22.

11. Jerry DeLaughter, "Jackson to Shift Teachers by Lottery," *Commercial Appeal* (Memphis: TN), December 10, 1969.

12. "Fewer Whites Expected When Jackson Classes Open," *Hattiesburg American* (Hattiesburg, MS), February 5, 1970.

13. Carol Kelley, "Detailed Plans for City Faculty Integration Set," *Starkville Daily News* (Starkville, MS), February 4, 1970.

14. Dr. Larry Box, interview by author, Starkville, MS.

15. Willard Gandy, "Implications of Integration for the Southern Teacher," *Journal of Negro Education* 31, no. 2 (Spring 1962): 191.

16. American Friends Service Committee, "Status of School Desegregation in the South: 1970," 85.

17. Morris, 128.

18. Bobby Cooper, "The Effects of Desegregation on Black Elementary and Secondary Teachers in Mississippi 1970–1973" (EdS thesis, University of Colorado, 1977).

19. *Report of NEA Task Force III, School Desegregation: Louisiana and Mississippi* (Washington, DC: National Education Association, November 1970), 17–22.

20. NEA Task Force, 4.

21. Gandy, 197.

22. Emma Bragg, "Changes and Challenges in the '60s," *Journal of Negro Education* 32, no. 1 (Winter 1963): 25–34.

23. Paul Pittman, "School Dilemma Weighs Heavy on Delta in Summer of 1969," *Leland Press,* July 31, 1969.

24. Dr. Charles Nash, interview by author, Tuscaloosa, AL.

25. Dr. Fenton Peters, interview by author, Starkville, MS.

26. Bragg, 28.

27. "170 Marchers Arrested in Mississippi," *Atlanta Constitution,* June 12, 1970; "100 Mississippi Blacks Held," *New York Times,* June 5, 1970.

28. *Armstead v. Starkville,* 325 F. Supp. 560 (ND, Mississippi, 1971); Charles Bolton, *The Hardest Deal of All: The Battle over School Integration in Mississippi, 1870–1980* (Jackson: University Press of Mississippi, 2005), 213.

29. "Superintendent Discusses Teacher Mixing," *Enterprise-Tocsin* (Indianola, MS), April 22, 1971.

30. *Baker v. Columbus Municipal Separate School District,* 329 F. Supp. 706 (ND, Mississippi, 1971); David Brown, "Ruling Is Due Today in Suit by Black Columbus Teachers," *Commercial Appeal* (Memphis, TN), September 3, 1970.

31. *Armstead v. Starkville,* 325 F. Supp. 560 (ND, Mississippi, 1971). See also *Baker v. Columbus Municipal Separate School District,* 329 F. Supp. 706 (ND, Mississippi, 1971).

32. *Earlean McCormick v. Attala County Board of Education,* 407 F. Supp. 586 (ND, Mississippi, 1976).

33. *Keglar v. East Tallahatchie School District,* 378 F. Supp. 1269 (ND, Mississippi, 1974).

34. William Chaze, "Core Leader Sees School Mix Failing," *Daily Herald* (Biloxi-Gulfport), December 17, 1969.

35. "New Discrimination Forms Charged in Integration," *Daily Herald* (Mississippi Gulf Coast), January 12, 1970.

36. James George, interview by author, Carrollton, MS.

37. NEA Task Force, 31.

38. For a detailed discussion of the shootings at Jackson State, see Tim Spofford, *Lynch Street: The May 1970 Slayings at Jackson State College* (Kent, OH: Kent State University Press, 1988).

39. Jason Sokol, *There Goes My Everything: White Southerners in the Age of Civil Rights, 1945–1975* (New York: Vintage Books, 2006), 4.

40. David Haplin, "The Nature of Hope and Its Significance for Education," *British Journal of Educational Studies* 49, no. 4 (December 2001): 396.

41. Ibid., 397.

42. Ibid.

Chapter 6

1. Eddie Payton played for Jackson State University and then for the NFL from 1977 to 1982. Walter Payton went on to play for Jackson State University and then had a stellar career as a running back in the NFL for the Chicago Bears, helping them win the Super Bowl in 1985. In 1993, he was inducted into the Pro Football Hall of Fame. Walter died in 1999 at the age of forty-five.

2. Dr. Tommy Davis, interview by author, Meridian, MS. All quotes from an interviewee are from author interviews unless otherwise noted. A list of the oral history interviews appears in the bibliography.

3. Charles Boston, interview by author, Columbia, MS.

4. Hamilton "Ham" Stevens, interview by author, Forest, MS.

5. Hugh McCarthy, interview by author, Forest, MS.

6. Charles Martin, "Jim Crow in the Gymnasium: The Integration of College Basketball in the American South," *International Journal of the History of Sports* 10, no. 1 (April 1993): 68–86.

7. Erle Johnston, *Mississippi's Defiant Years, 1953–1973* (Forest, MS: Lake Harbor), 40–43; Kirby Lee, "Members of 1955 Compton Team that Broke Color Barrier Honored," *Los Angeles Times,* October 27, 1994; Manque Winters, "To Hell with Race and Segregation—We Just

Wanted to Play: The Historic 1955 Junior Rose Bowl Compton College (CA) vs Jones County Junior College (MS)," *North American Society for Sports History Proceedings*, 1996: 97–98.

8. Russell Henderson, "The 1963 Mississippi State University Basketball Controversy and the Repeal of the Unwritten Law: 'Something More than the Game Will Be Lost,'" *Journal of Southern History* 63, no. 4 (November 1997): 827–54; Johnston, 1990, 191–99.

9. Henderson, 839.

10. Ibid.

11. Ibid., 853.

12. Clarence Johnson, *Integration versus Segregation in Mississippi Schools* (New York: Vantage, 1992), 76.

13. Dr. Fenton Peters, interview by author, Starkville, MS.

14. George Dale, interview by author, Jackson, MS.

15. Mike Johnson, interview by author, Oakdale, MS.

16. Dr. William Lewis, interview by author, Poplarville, MS.

17. Dalton McAlpin, interview by author, Starkville, MS.

18. Thomas J. Evans, *The First Day: The Integration Pioneers of the Mississippi School System* (Bloomington, IN: iUniverse, 2010), 82.

19. Richard Dent, interview by author, Waynesboro, MS.

20. Archie Johnson, interview by author, Biloxi, MS.

21. Sid Salter, interview by author, Starkville, MS.

22. Allen Barra, "The Integration of College Football that Didn't Happen in One Game," *The Atlantic*, November 15, 2013, http://www.theatlantic.com/entertainment/archive/2013/11/the-integration-of-college-football-didnt-happen-in-one-game/281557/.

23. Willie Morris, *The Courting of Marcus Dupree* (Jackson: University Press of Mississippi. 1983), 133.

24. Barra.

25. Pamela Grundy, *Learning to Win: Sports, Education, and Social Change in Twentieth-Century North Carolina* (Chapel Hill: University of North Carolina Press. 2001).

26. Grey and Alice Spencer, interview by author, Avon, MS.

27. Owen Makamson, interview by author, Avon, MS.

28. Billy Brown, interview by author, DeKalb, MS.

29. Harry Breeland, interview by author, Oak Grove, MS.

30. John Allen Flynt, interview by author, New Hebron, MS.

31. Jack Davis, *Race against Time: Culture and Separation in Natchez since 1930* (Baton Rouge: Louisiana State University Press, 2001), 222.

32. Charles George, interview by author, Webb, MS.

33. Charles Boston, interview by author, Columbia, MS.

34. Bob Boyd, "School Board Backs New Coach Assignments," *Delta Democrat-Times* (Greenville, MS), May 5, 1980; Bob Boyd, "Coaching Choice Defended," *Delta Democrat Times* (Greenville, MS), May 1, 1970.

35. LynNell Hancock, "The Anonymous Town that Was the Model of Desegregation in the Civil-Rights Era," *The Nation*, October 4, 2016, https://www.thenation.com/article/the-anonymous-town-that-was-the-model-of-desegregation-in-the-civil-rights-era/.

36. "Black Coaches Meet to Solve Problems," *Daily Herald* (Biloxi-Gulfport, MS), January 17, 1970.

37. Dr. Beverly Moon, interview by author, Cleveland, MS.

38. "Friends Reunited 60 Years after Memorable Handshake," January 30, 2015. Retrieved from Today.com.

39. Joe Kincheloe and William Pinar, eds. *Curriculum as Social Psychoanalysis: The Significance of Place* (Albany: State University of New York Press, 1991), 127.

Chapter 7

1. Teena Horn, Alan Huffman, and John Griffin Jones, eds. *Lines Were Drawn: Remembering Court-Ordered Integration at a Mississippi High School* (Jackson: University Press of Mississippi, 2016), 177.

2. For a more detailed discussion of the role of extracurricular activities in early American high schools, see Joel Spring, *The American* School (1642–1990) (New York: Longman, 2004); Charles Foster, *Extra-curricular Activities in the High School* (Richmond, VA: Johnson, 1925).

3. Dr. Harold Bishop, interview by author, Tuscaloosa, AL, September 27, 2002. Dr. Bishop's story is also related in Natalie Adams and Pamela Bettis, *Cheerleader! An American Icon* (New York: Palgrave, 2003a), 97–99. All quotes from an interviewee are from author interviews unless otherwise noted. A list of the oral history interviews appears in the bibliography.

4. Horn, Huffman, and Jones, 181–82.

5. United States Commission on Civil Rights, "Federal Rights under School Desegregation Law" CCR Clearinghouse Publication 6, June 1966, 8, http://www.law.umaryland.edu/marshall/usccr/documents/cr1106.pdf.

6. Thomas J. Evans, *The First Day: The Integration Pioneers of the Mississippi School System* (Bloomington, IN: iUniverse, 2010), 49.

7. Ibid., 50.

8. Horn, Huffman, and Jones, 162.

9. "DeKalb Cancels Eupora Game," *Webster Progress-Times* (Eupora, MS), October 15, 1970.

10. Willie Morris, *Yazoo: Integration in a Deep-Southern Town* (Fayetteville: University of Arkansas Press, 1971), 94; Jack Davis, *Race against Time: Culture and Separation in Natchez since 1930* (Baton Rouge: Louisiana State University Press, 2001), 228.

11. Dr. Mary Carol Miller, interview by author, Greenwood, MS.

12. *Adams. V. Rankin County Board of Education,* 485 F. 2d 324 (5th Cir. 1973).

13. George Dale, interview by author, Jackson, MS.

14. Charles George, interview by author, Webb, MS.

15. Horn, Huffman, and Jones, 199.

16. Ricky Nations, interview by author, Clinton, MS.

17. Horn, Huffman, and Jones, 199.

18. Morris, 86.

19. Dr. William Dodson, interview by author, Brandon, MS.

20. Archie Johnson, interview by author, Biloxi, MS.

21. Cited in James Brewer, "We Made the Transition from Dual to Unitary," *Mississippi Educational Advance* 61, no. 8 (May 1970): 31. *Newsweek,* the *Wall Street Journal,* and the *Times-Picayune* also featured stories about the smooth transition in Columbia.

22. Richard Harwood, "Integration Comes to Mississippi," *Washington Post,* February 15, 1970.

23. Morris, 93.

24. For an excellent analysis of the "jock-and-prep" culture at many high schools, see Penelope Eckert, *Jocks and Burnouts: Social Categories and Identity in the High School* (New York: Teachers College Press, 1989), and Pamela Bettis and Natalie Adams, "The Power of the Preps and a Cheerleading Equity Policy," *Sociology of Education* 76, no. 2 (April 2003): 128–42.

25. Lamar Beaty, interview by author, Houston, MS.

26. United States Commission on Civil Rights, "School Desegregation in Greenville, Mississippi: A Staff Report of the U.S. Commission on Civil Rights," August 1977, 11.

27. Horn, Huffman, and Jones, 193.

28. Ibid.

29. Ibid.

30. Adams and Bettis, 2003a, 98.

31. Ibid.

32. Horn, Huffman, and Jones, 193.

33. Evans, 74.

34. Dr. Fenton Peters, interview with author, Starkville, MS.

35. Adams and Bettis, 2003a, 91–110.

36. Grundy, 287.

37. Mary Ellen Hanson, *Go! Fight! Win! Cheerleading in American Culture* (Bowling Green, OH: Bowling Green State University Press, 1995), 1–7.

38. Horn, Huffman, and Jones, 184.

39. Natalie Adams and Pamela Bettis, "Commanding the Room in Short Skirts: Cheering as the Embodiment of Ideal Girlhood," *Gender and Society* 17, no. 1 (2003b): 73–91; Grundy, 285–90.

40. Amy Best, *Prom Night: Youth, Schools, and Popular Culture* (New York: Routledge, 2000), 6.

41. Louise Edna Goeden, "Prom Magic: Event of the Term at Washington High," *Clearing House* 25, no. 3 (November 1950): 167–69; Sidney G. Gould. "Senior Prom: Costly, Exclusive, Deserted," *Clearing House* 22, no. 6 (February 1948): 339–40; Frank Sisk, "Greater Holding Power for the Big Prom: Something Better than Dancing," *Clearing House* 28, no. 9 (May 1954): 545–46.

42. Tom Brady, "Segregation and the South," Address, Commonwealth Club of California, San Francisco, October 4, 1957, http://dc.lib.odu.edu/cdm/ref/collection/npsdp/id/1151.

43. "A Manual for Southerner," *Citizen* 2, no. 10, July 1957.

44. "Winning Essays in the 1960 Contest: Sponsored by the Association of Citizens' Councils of Mississippi," accessed July 16, 2014 http://lib.usm.edu/legacy/spcol/exhibitions/anti-somm/civil_rights-3.html.

45. "Public Education: 1964 Staff Report" (Submitted to United States Commission on Civil Rights, October 1964), 136, accessed January 20, 2017, https://www.law.umaryland.edu/marshall/usccr/documents/cr12ed82964.pdf; William Keady, *All Rise: Memoirs of a Mississippi Federal Judge* (Boston: Recollections Bound Inc. 1988), 106.

46. Bolton, 2005, 180.

47. Jack Davis, 233.

48. Lillie V. Davis, interview by author, Marks, MS.

49. Jack Davis, 232.

50. "Prom Night in Mississippi," DVD (Return to Mississippi Productions, 2008).

51. Horn, Huffman, and Jones, 177.

52. Ibid., 176.

Chapter 8

1. State Shuns Violence in School Change-Over," *Delta Democrat-Times* (Greenville, MS), August 30, 1970.

2. James Wooten, "4,000 Mississippi Whites Go to School, but 300 Balk," *New York Times,* January 8, 1970.

3. Jeffrey Turner, *Sitting in and Speaking Out: Student Movements in the American South 1960–1970* (Athens: University of Georgia Press, 2010), 45–50; Ellen Levine, *Freedom's Children: Young Civil Rights Activists Tell Their Own Stories* (New York: Puffin Books, 1993), 58–76.

4. John Dittmer, *Local People: The Struggle for Civil Rights in Mississippi* (Urbana: University of Illinois Press, 1994), 87–89.

5. Ibid., 89.

6. Brenda Travis, interview by Wazir Peacock, Jean Wiley, and Bruce Hartford, accessed January 21, 2017 http://www.crmvet.org/nars/travisb.htm. See also Dittmer, 107–15, and Charles Payne, *I've Got the Light of Freedom: The Organizing Tradition and the Mississippi Freedom Struggle* (Berkeley: University of California Press, 1995), 120–24.

7. Brenda Travis, interview by Wazir Peacock, Jean Wiley, and Bruce Hartford.

8. Ibid.

9. For an insightful analysis of how "Nonviolent High" laid the foundation for the Freedom Schools established in 1964, see Jon Hale, *The Freedom Schools: Student Activists in the Mississippi Civil Rights Movement* (New York: Columbia University Press, 2016).

10. Dittmer, 111; Travis interview.

11. Dittmer, 111.

12. Ibid., 113.

13. Hale, 44–45.

14. *Burnside v. Byars,* 363 F.2d 744 (5th Cir. 1966).

15. *Blackwell v. Issaquena Board of Education,* 363 F.2d (5th Cir. 1966); Unita Blackwell and JoAnne Prichard Morris, *Barefootin': Life Lessons from the Road to Freedom* (New York: Crown, 2006), 133–37.

16. Hale attributes the youth activism during the 1964–65 school year to the participation of over 2000 black students in Freedom Schools during the summer of 1964. For additional examples of walkouts staged by black students in segregated schools in 1964–65, see Hale, 160–66

17. "Burglund High School Walkout 50th Anniversary," *McComb Legacies,* October 8, 2011, http://mccomblegacies.org/2011/10/Burglund-walkout-50th-anniversary/.

18. For accounts of other high school students involved in such movements, see Gael Graham, *Young Activists: American High School Students in the Age of Protest* (DeKalb: Northern Illinois University Press, 2006); Rebecca de Schweinit. *If We Could Change the World: Young People and America's Long Struggle for Racial Equality* (Chapel Hill: University of North Carolina Press, 2009); Ellen Levine, *Freedom's Children: Young Civil Rights Activists Tell Their Own Stories* (New York: Puffin Books, 1993); Jon Hale, "'The Fight Was Instilled in Us': High School Activism and the Civil Rights Movement in Charleston," *South Carolina Historical Magazine* 114, no. 1 (January 2013): 4–28; John A. Stokes, *Students on Strike: Jim Crow, Civil Rights, Brown, and Me* (Washington, DC: National Geographic, 2008); Vincent Willis, "'Let Me In, I Have the Right to Be Here': Black Youth Struggle for Equal Education and Full Citizenship after the *Brown* Decision, 1954–1969," *Citizenship Teaching & Learning* 9, no. 2 (2014): 53–70. For an examination of how black school-age students were involved in the Freedom School movement in 1964, see Jon Hale, *The Freedom Schools: Student Activists in the Mississippi Civil Rights Movement* (New York: Columbia University Press, 2016).

19. Dittmer, 395.

20. For detailed description of the Meredith March from Grenada to Canton, see Dittmer, 395–402.

21. Dittmer, 401.

22. Bruce Hartford, "Grenada Mississippi—Chronology of a Movement," 1967, accessed January 15, 2017 www.crmvet.org/docs/66_sclc_grenada_log.pdf. Hartford.

23. Ibid.

24. Andrew Whitaker, "Seen, Heard, and Told," *Grenada County Weekly* (Grenada, MS), September 1, 1966.

25. Bruce Hartford, "Weekly Watts Report-Grenada Miss.," September 16, 1966, http://www.crmvet.org/info/grenada.htm.

26. James Bonney, "White Crowd Beats Negroes, Newsmen," *Clarion-Ledger* (Jackson, MS), September 13, 1966; Jack Cantrell, "Jack Cantrell's Story: 'They Beat Me with Broomsticks,'" *Memphis Press-Scimitar,* September 13, 1966.

27. Hartford, 1967.

28. Gail Falk, "Court Orders Protection for Negro Pupil," *Southern Courier* (Montgomery, AL), September 24–25, 1966.

29. Hartford, 1967.

30. "Governor Promises to Use More Force if Necessary," *Commercial Appeal* (Memphis, TN), September 14, 1966.

31. "Show of Force Keeps Tempers under Control," *Commercial Appeal* (Memphis, TN), September 14, 1966.

32. "Grenada Officials Told to Stop Mix Violence," *Memphis Press-Scimitar* (Memphis, TN), September 14, 1966.

33. John Pearce, "Sunday Was Peaceful in Race-Tense Areas," *Times-Picayune* (New Orleans, LA), September 19, 1966; John Pearce, "Martin Luther King Arrives in Grenada," *Times-Picayune* (New Orleans, LA), September 20, 1966.

34. "Negro Students Stand Tall in Midst of Grenada Strife," *Commercial Appeal* (Memphis, TN), September 15, 1966.

35. "Walkout Is Staged by Negro Students," *Clarion-Ledger* (Jackson, MS), October 22, 1966.

36. "Happenings in Grenada during Past Week Recorded," *Grenada Weekly* (Grenada, MS), October 27, 1966; "Grenada Police Arrest 200 in School March," *Clarion-Ledger* (Jackson, MS), October 25, 1966.

37. "News: Southern Christian Leadership Conference," October 28, 1966, http://www.crmvet.org/docs/pr/66_sclcnews_661028.pdf.

38. Hartford, "Chronology Events."

39. Graham, 53.

40. Harriet Kuykendall, interview by author, Jackson, MS; JoAnne Prichard Morris, interview by author, Jackson, MS. All quotes from an interviewee are from author interviews unless otherwise noted. A list of the oral history interviews appears in the bibliography.

41. "School Board Works on Plans to Prevent Another Day like Friday," *Leland Progress* (Leland, MS), April 9, 1970.

42. "Final Few Days of High School Changed," *Leland Progress* (Leland, MS), May 21, 1970.

43. Tom Herman, "Integrated Schools in South Sometimes Keep Races Separated," *Wall Street Journal*, May 15, 1970.

44. "GHS Hit by Black Walkout," *Delta Democrat-Times* (Greenville, MS), March 19, 1971.

45. Lamar Beaty, interview by author, Houston, MS.

46. Alean and John Adams, interview by author, Brandon, MS.

47. Alean M. Adams, *Way beyond Pisgah: Surviving Integration in Smalltown Mississippi* (self-published, 2009), 134.

48. "Southern Schools Expelling Students," *News-Herald* (Panama City, FL), June 3, 1972.

49. For a detailed description of these boycotts, see Jack Davis, *Race against Time: Culture and Separation in Natchez since 1930* (Baton Rouge: Louisiana State University Press, 2001), 180–206, and Emily Crosby, *A Little Taste of Freedom: The Black Struggle in Claiborne County, Mississippi* (Chapel Hill: University of North Carolina Press, 2005).

50. Davis, 184–85.

51. Ibid., 190.

52. Crosby, 128–47.

53. See, for example, J. Todd Moye, *Let the People Decide: Black Freedom and White Resistance Movement in Sunflower County, Mississippi, 1945–1986* (Chapel Hill: University of North Carolina Press. 2004).

54. Dittmer, 121.

55. "Clay High, Beasley Schools Closed until after Court Hearing," *Starkville Daily News* (Starkville, MS), September 12, 1969.

56. "Negroes End Boycott of Hazlehurst Schools," *Copiah County News* (Hazlehurst, MS), March 29, 1967.

57. Earl Harvish, "School Boycott Called 'Success,'" *Commercial Appeal* (Memphis, TN), February 27, 1969.

58. "Negroes in Mississippi Boycotting Classes," *Dispatch* (Lexington, NC), September 2, 1970; *United States v. Coffeeville Consolidated School District*, 365 F. Supp. 990 (ND, Mississippi, 1973); "Under Age Pickets Released," *The Daily Herald* (Biloxi-Gulfport, MS), September 30, 1970.

59. Richard Brooks, interview by author, Macon, MS; *U.S. v. Hinds County School Board v. Noxubee County School District*, 433 F. 2d 619 (5th Cir. 1970); "Attendance Off in Public Schools," *Macon Beacon* (Macon, MS), January 15, 1970; "Some Mississippi Schools Are All Black," *Boca Raton News*, January 13, 1970; "School Mixing Hits Snag in Mississippi," *Columbus Dispatch* (Columbus, MS), January 13, 1970.

60. *Keglar v. East Tallahatchie School District*, 378 F. Supp. 1269 (ND, Mississippi, 1974).

61. Dittmer, 120–23.

62. Billy Skelton, "Dismissed Coahoma Teachers to Work, Seek Aid for Pay," *Jackson Daily News* (Jackson, MS), February 16, 1969; Curtis Wilkie, "'Fired' Teachers Continue Classes," *Clarksdale Press Register* (Clarksdale, MS), February 17, 1969; "Rights Suit Filed Against Coahoma," *The Commercial Appeal* (Memphis, TN), February 23, 1969.

63. Emily Braddock, "Coahoma Integration Snarl Will Go to Court Tuesday," *The Commercial Appeal* (Memphis, TN), August 30, 1969.

64. "Police Arrest 146 Negroes in Delta City," *Starkville Daily News* (Starkville, MS), September 23, 1969; Emily Braddock, "Rejected Negro Students Picket High School Campus in Clarksdale," *The Commercial Appeal* (Memphis, TN), September 23, 1969.

65. "Marching Blacks Oppose Tests in Clarksdale," *Delta Democrat-Times* (Greenville, MS), October 19, 1969; "1,200 March in Clarksdale," *Commercial Appeal* (Memphis, TN), October 19, 1969; "Mississippi Blacks Appeal 'IQ' Test Desegregation," *Chicago Daily Defender*, October 21, 1969.

66. "Negroes Plan Boycott of Clarkdale Stores," *Commercial Appeal* (Memphis, TN), October 11, 1969.

67. Lance Hill, *The Deacons for Defense: Armed Resistance and the Civil Rights Movement* (Chapel Hill: University of North Carolina Press, 2004); Annelieke Dirks, "Between Threat and Reality: The National Association for the Advancement of Colored People and the Emergence of Armed Self-Defense in Clarksdale and Natchez, Mississippi, 1960–1965," *Journal for the Study of Radicalism* 1, no. 1 (2006): 71–98; Akinyele Omowale Umoja, "'We Will Shoot Back': The Natchez Model of Paramilitary Organization in the Mississippi Freedom Movement," *Journal of Black Studies* 32, no. 3 (January 2002): 271–94.

68. Willie Morris in *Yazoo: Integration in a Deep-Southern Town* writes of Rudy Shields: "He was carrying a .38 up West Powell Street to the NAACP house when I cruised by in a car to meet him, and inside he put the pistol on his desk and complained about the segregation of classes and the demotion of all the black principals and assistants" (99).

69. Robert Penn Warren, *Who Speaks for the Negro?* (New Haven, CT: Yale University Press, 1965), 109.

70. Dittmer, 393–95.

71. Dirks, 88–92; Umoja, 277–86.

72. Youth of the Rural Organizing and Culture Center, *Minds Stayed on Freedom: The Civil Rights Struggle in the Rural South, an Oral History* (Boulder, CO: Westview, 1991), 166.

73. Umoja, 291.

74. "Black Activists Shift from Integration Fight to More Militancy," *New York Times,* December 30, 1969.

75. Graham, 60.

76. Ibid., 63.

77. "13 Districts Mix Quietly; Whites Few," *Clarion-Ledger* (Jackson, MS), January 13, 1970; "Negro Student Held in Stabbing; School Closed," *Daily Journal* (Tupelo, MS), January 14, 1970.

78. Morris, 131.

79. "Coastal City Quiet after Racial Flareup," *Jackson Daily News* (Jackson, MS), April 16, 1971.

80. George Dale, interview by author, Jackson, MS.

81. "Moss Point Again Scene of Violence," *Jackson Daily News* (Jackson, MS), April 17, 1971.

82. Dr. William Lewis, interview by author, Poplarville, MS.

83. Tom Cook. "Harrison Central Trouble," *Daily Herald* (Gulfport-Biloxi, MS), October 9, 1969.

84. Richard Glaczier, "Attendance at School Reduced," *Daily Herald* (Mississippi Coast), October 10, 1969.

85. Jimmie Bell, "Officials Assure Student Safety," *Daily Herald* (Gulfport-Biloxi, MS), October 11, 1969.

86. Tom Cook, "Harrison Central Trouble," *Daily Herald* (Gulfport-Biloxi, MS), October 9, 1969.

87. Tom Cook, "17 Pupils Expelled at School," *Daily Herald* (Mississippi Coast), October 12, 1969.

88. Dorothy Leggett, "Sheriff Calls for Quiet Integration," *Daily Herald* (Mississippi Coast), August 24, 1970.

89. "Angry Parents Defy Court Order," *Meridian Star* (Meridian, MS), January 7, 1970.

90. Jerry DeLaughter, "Whites in Forrest County Refuse to Integrate," *Commercial Appeal* (Memphis, TN), January 8, 1970; "Whites Defy a Federal School Busing Order in Mississippi," *Chicago Tribune,* January 8, 1970; "White Parents Stage Sit-in in Mississippi," *Los Angeles Times,* January 8, 1970; "Sit-in at Petal," *Jackson Daily News* (Jackson, MS), January 8, 1970.

91. James Wooten, "4,000 Mississippi Whites Go to School, but 300 Balk," *New York Times,* January 8, 1970.

92. "White Pupils Boycott Schools in Mississippi," *Chicago Tribune,* December 12, 1969.

93. "White Mothers Launch Boycott in Mississippi," *New Journal and Guide* (Norfolk, VA), December 20, 1969; "3,000 Skip School in Mississippi," *Atlanta Constitution,* December 12, 1969.

94. "Whites Boycott Schools in Forrest Mix Protest," *Meridian Star* (Meridian, MS), December 11, 1969.

95. "School's Operations Are Normal during Boycott," *Daily Herald* (Biloxi-Gulfport), December 11, 1969.

96. "Baptist Minister Giving Up Boycott," *Meridian Star* (Meridian, MS), January 7, 1970.

97. Fred Grimm, "Clarksdale Gets Push on Schools," *Commercial Appeal* (Memphis, TN), January 11, 1970.

98. Miriam Dabbs, "Clarksdale Backs Public Education," *Jackson Daily News* (Jackson, MS), January 14, 1970.

99. "Whites Walk against School Integration in Clarksdale," *Delta Democrat-Times* (Greenville, MS), January 19, 1970; "FOCUS March through City Draws 1,500," *Clarksdale Press Register* (Clarksdale, MS), January 17, 1970; "FOCUS Unit Formed for School Freedom," *Daily Herald* (Mississippi Coast), January 31, 1970.

100. FOCUS handout, nd.

101. Ronald Abrell and Charles Hanna, "High School Student Unrest Reconsidered," *The High School Journal* 54, no. 6 (March 1971): 396-404

102. "Southern Schools Expelling Students," *News-Herald* (Panama City, FL), June 3, 1972.

Chapter 9

1. Dr. Mary Carol Miller, interview by author, Greenwood, MS. All quotes from an interviewee are from author interviews unless otherwise noted. A list of the oral history interviews appears in the bibliography.

2. Letter from Hardy Lott to Jerris Leonard, July 30, 1970, James O. Eastland Collection, File Series 3, Subseries 4, Box 15, Folder 10, University of Mississippi Libraries, Oxford, MS; Letter from Hardy Lott to Senator James Eastland, July 30, 1970, James O. Eastland Collection, File Series 3, Subseries 4, Box 15, Folder 10, University of Mississippi Libraries, Oxford, MS.

3. This chapter deals with the proliferation of segregation academies. According to a 1973 Yale Law Journal Company report, different types of private schools exist: parochial schools, elite prep schools, and segregation academies. Segregation academies can be further divided into "rebel yell" academies, and "segregation academies second generation." For an explanation of the differences, see the Yale Law Journal Company, "Segregation Academies and State Action," *The Yale Law Journal* 82, no. 7 (June 1973): 1436-61.

4. William Vaughn, "Evers Opposes Private Schools in Mississippi," *Meridian Star* (Meridian, MS), January 11, 1970.

5. Hodding Carter, "Editorial," *Delta Democrat-Times* (Greenville, MS), January 27, 1972.

6. Charles Clotfelter, "School Desegregation, 'Tipping,' and Private School Enrollment," *The Journal of Human Resources* 11, no. 1 (Winter 1976): 29-30; Michael Fuquay. "Civil Rights and the Private School Movement in Mississippi, 1964–1971," *History of Education Quarterly* 42, no. 2 (Summer 2002): 167. Another report lists the number of private schools in 1970 as 208: Mark Lowry, "Schools in Transition," *Annals of the Association of American Geographers* 63, no. 2, (June 1973): 176.

7. National Center for Education Statistics, Private School Enrollment, 2012–13, accessed January 22, 2017 https://nces.ed.gov/programs/digest/d15/tables/dt15_205.80.asp.

8. For an in-depth discussion of the Citizens' Council, see Neil McMillen, *The Citizens' Council: Organized Resistance to the Second Reconstruction, 1954–64* (Urbana: University of Illinois Press, 1971).

9. William Simmons, "Government Schools," *The Citizen* 8 (September 1964): 2. The Citizens' Council released another pamphlet in January 1970 about how to organize a private school. Among articles included were "How to Disorganize the Public Schools." "Special Educational Issue Foundation Executive Tells How to Organize a Private School," January 1970, MS. F25A, Allen Eugene Cox Papers, Box 12, Manuscript Department, Mississippi State University Libraries, Starkville, MS.

10. For analysis of the Citizens' Council role in shaping modern conservatism, see Joseph Crespino, *In Search of Another Country: Mississippi and the Conservative Counterrevolution* (Princeton, NJ: Princeton University Press, 2007), and Michael Fuquay, "Civil Rights and the Private School Movement in Mississippi, 1964–1971," *History of Education Quarterly* 42, no. 2 (Summer 2002): 159–80.

11. William Simmons, 2.

12. McMillen, 303.

13. Billy Skelton, "Council School 3 Enrollment Soars," *Clarion-Ledger* (Jackson, MS), April 3, 1970; Fuquay, 164–66; "Welcome to Council Schools: A Handbook of Information and School Policy" (Jackson: Council School Foundation, 1970); "Registration Hits 5,000," *Jackson Daily News* (Jackson, MS), August 23, 1970.

14. Fuquay, 169.

15. Clotfelter, 30.

16. See Luther Munford, "Black Gravity: Desegregation in 30 Mississippi School Districts" (senior thesis, Princeton University, 1971); Kenneth Andrews, "Movement-counter-movement Dynamics and the Emergence of New Institutions: The Case of 'White Flight' Schools in Mississippi," *Social Forces* 80, no. 3 (2002): 911–36; Jeremy Porter, Frank Howell, and Lynn Hempel, "Old Times Are Not Forgotten: The Institutionalization of Segregationist Academies in the American South," *Social Problems* 61, no. 4 (November 2014): 576–601.

17. Yale Law Journal Company, 1442.

18. Charles Overby, "Citizen Council Political Activities Results in Internal Power Fight," *Daily Herald* (Biloxi-Gulfport), August 24, 1970.

19. "Federal Courts Action to Ruin Kemper Schools," *Kemper County Messenger* (DeKalb, MS), November 13, 1969; Billy Brown, interview with author, DeKalb, MS.

20. "School Opens in an Old Bus," *Commercial Appeal* (Memphis, TN), September 18, 1970.

21. James Jones. "Whites Leave Schools en Masse in Canton," *Delta Democrat-Times* (Greenville, MS), January 13, 1970; Fuquay, 177.

22. *Norwood v. Harrison,* 382 F. Supp. 921 (ND, Mississippi, 1974); *United States v. Tunica County School District,* 323 F. Supp. 1019 (ND, Mississippi, 1970); Sara Criss, "Whites in Holmes County Leave Integrated Schools," *Commercial Appeal,* September 9, 1965.

23. The Baptist-church affiliation was the highest with 3525 students followed by Presbyterians with 1198. See Yale Law Journal Company, 1436.

24. Lowry, 177.

25. Fuquay, 163.

26. Munford, xi.

27. Yale Law Journal Company, 1443.

28. "Governor John Bell Williams on the Integration of Public Schools in Mississippi," Mississippi Department of Archives and History (AU1062, TR 057), accessed January 21, 2017

"https://www.mdah.ms.gov/arrec/digital_archives/vault/projects/OHtranscripts/AU _1062_117291.pdf.

29. "Statement by Ramsey Clark before the Select Committee on Equal Educational Opportunity United States Senate," July 7, 1970, Stennis Collection, Box 12, Series 29, Folder 19. Mississippi State University Libraries, Starkville, MS.

30. "Lawyer Group to Monitor Desegregation," *Washington Evening Star,* August 7, 1970.

31. "Statement by Stephen J. Pollack before the Select Committee on Equal Educational Opportunity, United States Senate," August 11, 1970, Stennis Collection, Box 12, Series 29, Folder 19, Mississippi State University Libraries, Starkville, MS.

32. In 1959, Virginia was the first state to pass tuition grant legislation. Alabama, Georgia, Louisiana, Mississippi, North Carolina, and South Carolina soon passed their own form of private school tuition vouchers.

33. Jim Leeson, "Private School Continue to Increase in the South," Southern Education Report, November 1966; Yale Law Journal Company, 1436–61.

34. *Coffey v. State Educational Finance Commission,* 296 F. Supp. 1389 (SD, Mississippi, 1969).

35. Leroy Morganti, "Teenagers Can Borrow for Education Under Law," *Daily Herald* (Mississippi Coast), January 20, 1970.

36. This program is still part of the Mississippi Code 1972 37–51–1 (Financial Assistance to Children Attending Non-Sectarian Private Schools). Our thanks to Jim Keith, an expert in school law issues, for this information.

37. Willie Morris, *Yazoo: Integration in a Deep-Southern Town* (Fayetteville, AR: University of Arkansas Press, 1971), 110; Fuquay, 178; *United States v. Tunica County School District,* 323 F. Supp. 1019 (ND, Mississippi, 1970); "Private School Announced at Madden," *Neshoba Democrat* (Philadelphia, MS), November 27, 1969; "Private School Principal Named," *Conservative* (Carrollton, MS), May 22, 1969.

38. "Q & A," *Citizen* 8 (September 1964): 16.

39. Richard Brooks, interview by author, Macon, MS.

40. *Norwood v. Harrison,* 413 U.S. 455.

41. "Fed Court Asked to Overturn State Law," *Starkville Daily News* (Starkville, MS), September 23, 1969; "Civil Rights Lawyers Ask Private Aid Block," *Starkville Daily News* (Starkville, MS), September 20, 1969.

42. *McNeal v. Tate County School District,* 460 F.2d.568 (5th Cir. 1971); "Tate Academy Gets Federal Court Order," *Jackson Daily News* (Jackson, MS), June 21, 1972; Mike McCall, "Judge Ok's Private School with Warning Policies," *Commercial Appeal* (Memphis, TN), June 22, 1972.

43. Ron Harrist, "Officials Threaten Look at Schools in the North," *Hattiesburg American* (Hattiesburg, MS), August 20, 1970.

44. "End of Tax Exemption Ordered for 23 Mississippi Academies," *New York Times,* March 27, 1971; Reese Cleghorn, "Segregation by Tax Exemption," *The Nation* (June 29, 1970): 785–86; "IRS Says It Will Take Southern Schools' Word about Racial Polices," *Wall Street Journal,* August 13, 1970; Kitty Terjen, "The Segregation Academy Movement," in Robert E. Anderson Jr., *The South and Her Children: School Desegregation 1970–1971,* Southern Regional Council, Atlanta, 1971, 72.

45. "White Academies in the South-Booming Despite Obstacles," *U.S. News & World Report,* April 19, 1971.

46. *Green v. Connally,* 330 F. Supp. 1150 (D.C. 1971).

47. *Bob Jones University v. United States,* 461 U.S. 574 (1983); "Race and Ethnicity in a New Era of Public Funding of Private Schools: Private School Enrollment in the South and the Nation," Southern Education Foundation, March 2016: 12.

48. "Mississippi Women Fight Valiantly to Keep Schools," *Commercial Appeal* (Memphis, TN), November 1, 1964; Winifred A. Green, interview by Charles Bolton, 1997, vol. 704, University of Southern Mississippi, Center for Oral History & Cultural Heritage, Hattiesburg, MS.

49. *A Time to Speak,* Mississippians for Public Education, n.d. Constance W. Curry papers. Manuscript, Archives, and Rare Book Library, Robert W. Woodruff Library, Emory University, 0818–002.tif.

50. "New Jackson Organization Supports Public Schools," *Clarion-Ledger* (August 23, 1970); "Public Education Friends Organize," *Clarion-Ledger* (Jackson, MS), August 29, 1970; Billy Skelton, "Public Schools Allies Rally: It's a Personal, Real Thing," *Clarion-Ledger* (Jackson, MS), August 23, 1970.

51. *Cook v. Hudson,* 365 F. Supp. 855 (ND, Mississippi, 1973).

52. "We Have Great Opportunities . . . Blacks and Whites Can Communicate Here," *Delta Democrat-Times* (Greenville, MS), February 15, 1970.

53. Dr. Ed Meek, interview by author, Oxford, MS.

54. Dr. Ken Wooten, interview by author, Oxford, MS.

55. "Resolution Adopted," *Oxford Eagle* (Oxford, MS): "Council to Back Schools," *Oxford Eagle* (Oxford, MS), January 15, 1970.

56. "Public Schools Are Vital to the Oxford-University Community," *Oxford Eagle* (Oxford, MS), January 15, 1970.

57. "Capacity Crowd of 1,200 to 1,300 Attended," *Oxford Eagle* (Oxford, MS), January 22, 1970.

58. "College Hill Academy" (ad), *Oxford Eagle* (Oxford, MS), January 22, 1970; "We Support Public Schools," *Oxford Eagle* (Oxford, MS), January 22, 1970.

59. "Now's the Time," *Oxford Eagle* (Oxford, MS), January 29, 1970.

60. A group of white parents and business leaders in Sharkey-Issaquena launched a similar campaign with a published ad in the November 20, 1969, issue of the *Deer Creek Pilot.* The ad read, "We, the undersigned parents and patrons of the Sharkey-Issaquena Line Consolidated School District . . . hereby signify our intent and that of our children to remain in the public schools. We hold no malice toward those who may disagree, and respect their opinion, as being as sincerely held as our own. However, we are taking this informal and unorganized action in an effort to lend our support to our public schools, and invite others

of like mind to join us." A number of white students in the Sharkey-Issaquena School District remained in the public schools in January 1970, but by fall 1970, most had left for the private school.

61. Harold Kelly, interview by author, Yazoo City, MS.

62. "An Important Message from Concerned Citizens," *Yazoo City Herald* (Yazoo City, MS), November 20, 1969.

63. Harriet Kuykendall, interview by author, Jackson, MS.

64. Morris, 35.

65. Ibid., 124.

66. Dr. Fred Perkins, interview by author, Starkville, MS.

67. Paula Mabry, interview by author, Starkville, MS.

68. Jere Nash, interview by author, Greenville, MS.

69. Hodding Carter, interview conducted by Jack Bass and Walter Devries, April 1, 1974, Interview A-0100, Southern Oral History Program Collection (#4007), accessed June 16, 2011 http://docsouth.unc.edu/sohp/A-0100/A-0100.html.

70. Mike Johnson, interview by author, Oakdale, MS.

71. Dr. William Dodson, interview by author, Brandon, MS.

72. Dr. Mary Carol Miller, interview by author, Greenwood, MS.

73. Dr. Fenton Peters, interview by author, Starkville, MS.

74. Charles George, interview by author, Webb, MS.

75. Lucy Boyd, interview by author, Charleston, MS.

76. The Yale Law Journal 1973 report argues that once it is determined that segregated private schools benefit from state action (e.g., free textbooks), they should be subjected to reasonable state regulation. See Yale Law Journal Company, 1459–61 for an analysis of why private should be held to the same desegregation orders as public schools.

77. Herbert Foster, interview by author, Marks, MS.

78. Billy G. James, "New Southern Party Calls for School Rally," *Atlanta Constitution*, January 2, 1970.

Chapter 10

1. Sally French and John Swain, "Telling Stories for a Politics of Hope," *Disability & Society* 21, no. 5 (2006): 383–96; Valerie Janesick, "Oral History as a Social Justice Project: Issues for the Qualitative Researcher," *Qualitative Report* 12, no. 1 (2007): 111–21; Richard Quantz, "The Complex Visions of Female Teachers and the Failure of Unionization in the 1930s: An Oral History," *History of Education Quarterly* 25, no. 4 (1985): 439–58; Joan Sangster, "Telling Our Stories: Feminist Debates and the Use of Oral History," *Women's History Review* 3, no. 1: 5–28. For a history of school desegregation in the South based on oral histories, see George Noblit, ed., *School Desegregation: Oral Histories toward Understanding the Effects of White Domination* (Rotterdam, Amsterdam: Sense, 2015).

2. Dr. Robert Fortenberry and Dr. Joe Haynes, interview by author, Jackson, MS.

3. Willie Morris, "Is There a South Anymore?" *Southern Magazine*, October 1986, http://www.southerner.net/v1n3_99/southern.html.

4. For a critique of this notion of shared southern values, see Jane Adams and D. Gorton, "Confederate Lane: Class, Race, and Ethnicity in the Mississippi Delta," *American Ethnologist* 33, no. 2 (2006): 293–97.

5. As discussed in chapter 8, Grenada was the site of the worst violence associated with school desegregation in 1966. However, today the Grenada School District is comprised of more than four thousand students with a school population of 50.02 percent black and 47.5 percent white.

6. In 2013, the Mississippi legislature (Senate Bill 2818) ordered the consolidation of the Starkville city school system and the Oktibbeha County school system, effective July 1, 2015. Since 2012, the legislature has consolidated thirteen school districts in the state. The Starkville-Oktibbeha consolidation was the first that merged a failing system (Oktibbeha) with a successful school system (Starkville city schools).

7. Dr. Virgil Belue, interview by author, Clinton, MS.

8. See also Jackie Mader, "How One Mississippi District Made Integration Work," *Huffington Post,* April 18, 2016, http://www.huffingtonpost.com/entry/mississippi-integration_us_57151ff2e4b0060ccda3df.

9. Mader.

10. Mississippi State Department of Education Figures, 2016–2017, http://ors.mde.k12.ms.us/data/.

11. http://www.census.gov/quickfacts/table/INC110215/2814420,28.

12. See http://datacenter.kidscount.org for 2010–2011 free and reduced-lunch figures; NCES 2010–2011 free and reduced lunch figures by state, https://nces.ed.gov/programs/digest/d12/tables/dt12_046.asp.

13. Mader.

14. National Center for Education Statistics, Private School Enrollment, 2012–13, accessed January 22, 2017 https://nces.ed.gov/programs/digest/d15/tables/dt15_205.80.asp.

15. Gary Orfield, Jongyeon Ee, Erica Frankenberg, and Genevieve Siegel-Hawley, "Brown at 62: "School Segregation by Race, Poverty and State," *The Civil Rights Project* (May 16, 2016): 5.

16. Dana Thompson Dorsey, "Segregation 2.0: The New Generation of School Segregation in the 21st Century," *Education and Urban Society* 45, no. 5 (2013): 533; Nikole Hannah-Jones, "Segregation Now. . . ." *The Atlantic* (May 2014): 68–81; Jerry Rosiek and Kathy Kinslow, *Resegregation as Curriculum: The Meaning of the New Racial Segregation in U.S. Public Schools* (New York: Routledge, 2016).

17. Gary Orfield and Erica Frankenberg, "Increasingly Segregated and Unequal Schools as Courts Reverse Policy," *Educational Administration Quarterly* 50, no. 5 (2014), 728; Gary Orfield and Chugnmei Lee, "Racial Transformation and the Changing Nature of Segregation," the Civil Rights Project, January 2006.

18. James Palmer, "Unitary School Systems: One Race or Two," (paper presented at the annual meeting of the Association of Southern Agricultural Workers, Jacksonville, FL, February 2, 1971).

19. A notable exception is that of Davis Magnet Elementary School, a high-poverty, high-performing school located in Jackson. While the Jackson School District overall received an "F" rating, Davis Magnet Elementary (comprised of 97.8 percent black students)

was ranked the top elementary school in the state in 2015–16. It received an "A" ranking for several consecutive years.

20. Gary Orfield, Erica Frankenberg, and Genevieve Siegel-Hawley, "Integrated Schools: Finding a New Path," *Educational Leadership* 68, no. 3 (November 2010): 22–27.

21. Ginny Lane and Amy White, "The Roots of Resegregation: Analysis and Implications," *Race, Gender & Class* 17, nos. 3–4 (2010): 83.

22. Roslyn Mickelson, "Twenty-first Century Social Science on Racial Diversity and Educational Outcomes," *Ohio State Law Journal* 60, no. 6 (2008): 1173–228.

23. Lillie V. Davis, interview by author, Marks, MS.

24. Mississippi State Department of Education Figures, 2016–2017, http://ors.mde.k12 .ms.us/data/.

25. In 2005, Edgar Ray Killen was convicted of manslaughter and sentenced to sixty years in prison.

26. Willie Morris, in *The Courting of Marcus Dupree,* provides a beautifully written account of how both black and white residents of Philadelphia rallied around Marcus Dupree, a black running back for Philadelphia High School and one of the most highly recruited high school players in the country. The story also chronicles the rise and fall of Marcus Dupree as he transitioned to college football at the University of Oklahoma and then quit the team. Today, Marcus Dupree is a part-time truck driver.

27. Mississippi State Department of Education Figures, 2016–2017, http://ors.mde.k12 .ms.us/data/.

28. Ibid.

29. Willie Morris, *Yazoo: Integration in a Deep-Southern Town* (Fayetteville, AR: University of Arkansas Press, 1971), 107.

30. "Frank Reynolds Commentary," February 2, 1970. Personal memento of Mike Johnson shared with authors.

31. Douglas A. Blackmon, "The Resegregation of a Southern School," *Harper's Magazine,* September 1992, http://www.slaverybyanothername.com/other-writings/ harpers-magazine-the-resegregation/.

32. Mississippi State Department of Education Figures, 2016–2017, http://ors.mde.k12 .ms.us/data/; Mississippi State Department of Education, 4-year Graduation Rates, http:// reports.mde.k12.ms.us/pdf/a/2016/Grad%20Dropout%20Rates%20-%202016%20Report%20 (002).pdf.

33. Carter's rebuttal to the legislature appeared on the front page of the *Delta Democrat-Times* on April 3, 1955, in which he wrote: "I herewith resolve by a vote of 1 to 0 that there are 89 liars in the State legislature beginning with Speaker Sillers and working way on down to Rep. Eck Windham of Prentiss, a political loon whose name is fittingly made up of the words 'wind' and 'ham.'" See "Liar by Legislation," *Delta Democrat-Times* (Greenville, MS), April 3, 1955.

34. United States Commission on Civil Rights, "School Desegregation in Greenville, Mississippi: A Staff Report of the U.S. Commission on Civil Rights," August 1977; LynNell Hancock, The Anonymous Town that was the Model of Desegregation in the Civil-Rights Era." *The Nation,* October 4, 2016, accessed November 1, 2016, https://www.thenation.com /article/the-anonymous-town-that-was-the-model-of-desegregation-in-the-civil-rights-era/.

35. The Tupelo city school system was the second school district and Vicksburg the third to sign a pledge to desegregate their schools by September 1, 1965, under the terms of the Civil Rights Act (see "Civil Rights Pledge Signed in Tupelo" and "Vicksburg Agrees to Comply"), MSS. 45, Allen Eugene Cox Papers, Box 1, Manuscript Department, Mississippi State University Libraries, Starkville, MS.

36. United States Commission on Civil Rights, 3.

37. Ibid., 17.

38. The Yale Law Journal Company, "Segregation Academies and State Action," *The Yale Law Journal* 82, no. 7 (June 1973): 1436.

39. Hancock.

40. Mississippi State Department of Education Figures, 2016–2017, http://ors.mde.k12 .ms.us/data/.

41. Billy Joe Ferguson, interview by author, Carrollton, MS.

42. See also Monique Harrison-Henderson, "Under Pressure: Some Mississippi Educators Silenced on School-Funding Battle," *The Hechlinger Report.* October 16, 2015, http:// www.jacksonpress.com/news/2015/oct/16/under-pressure-some-mississippi-edu; "Retired Superintendent is Still on the Job," *Education Reporter,* March 2015, http://eagleforum.org /publications/educate/mar15/retired-superintendent-is-still-on-the-jo/; "A 'Chicken Coop' in a Mississippi School," accessed December 13, 2016, http://www.civilrights.org/publications/ reports/education-resource-equity-report/chapter-i/; Kayleigh Skinner, "Q & A: Mississippi Superintendent Explains Why He Gave Up His Salary to Help Relieve 'Wretched Conditions' at His Schools," *The Hechlinger Report,* February 2, 2015, http://hechingerreport.org/q-a -mississippi-superintendent-explains-why-he-gave-up-his-salary-to-help-relieve-wretched -conditions-at-his-schools/.

43. James George, interview by author, Carrollton, MS.

44. Heidi Beirich, "Council of Conservative Citizens Funds Miss. Private Schools," Southern Poverty Law Center, accessed June 4, 2014, https://www.splcenter.org/fighting -hate/intelligence-report/2011/council-conservative-citizens-funds-miss-private-schools

45. Mississippi State Department of Education Figures, 2016–2017, http://ors.mde.k12 .ms.us/data/.

46. Nick Chiles, "Tests on Trial," *The Hechinger Report,* May 27, 2015, http://www.jack sonfreepress.com/news/2015/may/27/tests-trial/.

47. Claiborne Barksdale, interview by author, Oxford, MS.

48. "A 'Chicken Coop' in a Mississippi School," accessed December 13, 2016, http://www .civilrights.org/publications/reports/education-resource-equity-report/chapter-i/.

49. Mississippi State Department of Education Figures, 2016–2017, http://ors.mde.k12 .ms.us/data/.

50. Jimmie Gates, "Schools Must Desegregate," *The Clarion-Ledger* (Jackson, MS), May 17, 2016.

51. "A National Survey of School Desegregation Orders," accessed April 14, 2016, https:// projects.propublica.org/graphics/desegregation-orders.

52. Nikole Hannah-Jones, "Lack of Order: The Erosion of a Once-Great Force for Integration," ProPublica, May 1, 2014, https://www.propublica.org/article/lack-of-order -the-erosion-of-a-once-great-force-for-integration.

53. Nikole Hannah-Jones, "Segregate Now," ProPublica, accessed April 12, 2016, https://www.propublica.org/article/segregation-now-full-text. In this article, Hannah-Jones chronicles the resegregation of public schools in Tuscaloosa, AL.

54. *Cowan v. Bolivar County Board of Education*, 914 F. Supp. 2d 801 (ND, Mississippi, 2012).

55. Sharon Lerner, "A School District that Was Never Desegregated," *The Atlantic*, February 5, 2015, https://www.theatlantic.com/education/archive/2015/02/a-school-district-that-was-never-desegregated/385184/.

56. Gates.

57. Dr. Tom Dulin, interview by author, Winona, MS.

58. Blackmon.

59. Personal conversation (interviewee did not want to be cited).

60. Alean M. Adams, *Way beyond Pisgah: Surviving Integration in Smalltown Mississippi* (self-published, 2009), 111.

61. According to Parents' Campaign, Mississippi ranks fiftieth in national student achievement rankings. It ranks forty-nine of fifty-one in percent of adults with at least a bachelor's degree. It ranks forty-eight of fifty-one in per student funding and last in the Southeast ($7,926). It ranks forty-nine out of fifty in average teacher salary. On the 2013 National Assessment of Education Progress, only 21 percent of fourth graders in the state scored proficient or above in reading, and only 26 percent scored proficient or above in math. In 2014, two-thirds of kindergarten students in Mississippi scored below the benchmark associated with 70 percent mastery of literacy skills. Accessed January 29, 2017, http://www.tpcref.org/facts-about-education-in-mississippi/. See also "Miles to Go Mississippi: Rebuilding Education: The Next Big Challenge." Southern Education Foundation, 2006.

62. Supporters of Initiative 42, a grass-roots effort, collected approximately 200,000 signatures, so the measure could be brought to a public vote. The state legislature created a counterinitiative, called Initiative 42A, the wording of which was very similar to that of Initiative 42. The primary difference was that Initiative 42 used the language contained in the 1997 Mississippi Adequate Education Program (MAEP) and called for the state to fund an "*adequate and efficient* free public school system." Initiative 42A required the state to fund an "*effective* free public school system without judicial enforcement." According to Luther Munford, the sponsor of Initiative 42, the legislature's choice of wording in Initiative 42A was a "deceptive strategy" meant to confuse the voters.

63. For a general overview of school choice, see James E. Ryan and Michael Heise, "The Political Economy of School Choice," *The Yale Law Journal* 111, no. 8 (June 2002): 2043–136. For a historical analysis of the origins of school choice with roots in liberal educational reform movements, see James Forman Jr., "The Secret History of School Choice: How Progressives Got There First," *The Georgetown Law Journal* 93 (2005): 1287–319 and Richard D. Kahlenberg and Halley Potter, "Restoring Shanker's Vision for Charter Schools," *American Educator* 38, no. 4 (Winter 2014–15): 4–13. For a critique of "choice" as part of market-driven initiatives in education, see Janelle Scott and Rand Quinn, "The Politics of Education in the Post-*Brown* Era: Race, Markets, and the Struggle for Equitable Schooling," *Educational Administration Quarterly* 50, no. 5 (2014): 749–63; Anna Wolfe, "Then and Now: When 'School Choice' Creates a Divide," *Jackson Free Press*. December 17, 2014, http://www.jacksonfreepress.com/news/2014/dec/17/when-choice-creates-divide/.

64. See http://empowerms.org/about/; Brett Kittredge, "How Does School Choice Effect Racial Segregation?" May 19, 2016, http://empowerms.org/how-does-school-choice-effect -racial-segregation/.

65. Hazel Brannon Smith, "We Must Save our Public Schools," *Lexington* (Lexington, MS), May 7, 1970.

66. For an in-depth discussion of Winter's contributions to public education in Mississippi, particularly his role in the passage of the 1982 Mississippi Education Reform Act, see Charles Bolton, *William F. Winter and the New Mississippi: A Biography* (Jackson: University Press of Mississippi, 2013); *The Measure of Our Days: Writings of William F. Winter* (Jackson: University Press of Mississippi, 2006); Andrew P. Mullins Jr., *Building Consensus: A History of the Passage of the Mississippi Education Reform Act* (Jackson: Mississippi Humanities Council and the Phil Hardin Foundation, 1992).

67. William Winter, "Opening Doors in a Closed Society," Kalamazoo, MI: Fetzer Institute, Essay no. 16 (Winter 2010), 13.

Bibliography

Books

Adams, Alean McIntyre. "Way beyond Pisgah: Surviving Integration in Smalltown Mississippi." Self-published, 2009.

Adams, Natalie, and Pamela Bettis. *Cheerleader! An American Icon*. New York: Palgrave, 2003a.

Andrews, Kenneth. *Freedom Is a Constant Struggle: The Mississippi Civil Rights Movement and Its Legacy*. Chicago: University of Chicago Press, 2004.

Asch, Chris. *The Senator and the Sharecropper: The Freedom Struggles of James O. Eastland and Fannie Lou Hamer*. New York: New Press, 2008.

Beckwith, David. *A New Day in the Delta: Inventing School Desegregation as You Go*. Tuscaloosa: University of Alabama Press, 2009.

Best, Amy. *Prom Night: Youth, Schools, and Popular Culture*. New York: Routledge, 2000.

Blackwell, Unita, and JoAnne Prichard Morris. *Barefootin': Life Lessons from the Road to Freedom*. New York: Crown, 2006.

Bolton, Charles. *The Hardest Deal of All: The Battle over School Integration in Mississippi, 1870–1980*. Jackson: University Press of Mississippi, 2005.

———. *William F. Winter and the New Mississippi: A Biography*. Jackson: University Press of Mississippi, 2013.

Childers, Sara. *Urban Educational Identity: Seeing Students on Their Own Terms*. New York: Routledge, 2016.

Cooper, Bobby. "The Effects of Desegregation on Black Elementary and Secondary Teachers in Mississippi 1970–1973." EdS thesis, University of Colorado, 1977.

Crespino, Joseph. *In Search of Another Country: Mississippi and the Conservative Counterrevolution*. Princeton, NJ: Princeton University Press, 2007.

Crosby, Emilye. *A Little Taste of Freedom: The Black Struggle in Claiborne County, Mississippi*. Chapel Hill: University of North Carolina Press, 2005.

Curry, Constance. *Silver Rights*. Chapel Hill, NC: Algonquin Books of Chapel Hill, 1995.

Davis, Jack. *Race against Time: Culture and Separation in Natchez since 1930*. Baton Rouge: Louisiana State University Press, 2001.

De Schweinitz, Rebecca. *If We Could Change the World: Young People and America's Long Struggle for Racial Equality*. Chapel Hill: University of North Carolina Press, 2009.

Dittmer, John. *Local People: The Struggle for Civil Rights in Mississippi.* Urbana: University of Illinois Press, 1994.

Eckert, Penelope. *Jocks and Burnouts: Social Categories and Identity in the High School.* New York: Teachers College Press, 1989.

Emmerich, J. Oliver. *Two Faces of Janus: The Saga of Deep South Change.* Jackson: University and College Press of Mississippi, 1973.

Evans, Thomas J. *The First Day: The Integration Pioneers of the Mississippi School System.* Bloomington, IN: iUniverse, 2010.

Evers, Myrlie. *For Us, the Living.* Jackson: University Press of Mississippi, 1967.

Foster, Charles. *Extra-curricular Activities in the High School.* Richmond, VA: Johnson, 1925.

Fulton, Charles. "Racial Integration in the Public School System in Kemper County, Mississippi, 1954–1974." (PhD dissertation, University of Mississippi, 1978).

Graham, Gael. *Young Activists: American High School Students in the Age of Protest.* DeKalb: Northern Illinois University Press, 2006.

Grundy, Pamela. *Learning to Win: Sports, Education and Social Change in Twentieth-Century North Carolina.* Chapel Hill: University of North Carolina Press, 2001.

Hale, Jon. *The Freedom Schools: Student Activists in the Mississippi Civil Rights Movement.* New York: Columbia University Press, 2016.

Hanson, Mary Ellen. *Go! Fight! Win! Cheerleading in American Culture.* Bowling Green, OH: Bowling Green State University Press, 1995.

Hill, Lance. *The Deacons for Defense: Armed Resistance and the Civil Rights Movement.* Chapel Hill: University of North Carolina Press, 2004.

Horn, Teena, Alan Huffman, and John Griffin Jones, eds. *Lines Were Drawn: Remembering Court-Ordered Integration at a Mississippi High School.* Jackson: University Press of Mississippi, 2016.

Hudson, Winson, and Constance Curry. *Mississippi Harmony: Memoirs of a Freedom Fighter.* New York: Palgrave, 2002.

Johnson, Clarence. *Integration versus Segregation in Mississippi Schools.* New York: Vantage, 1992.

Johnston, Erle. *I Rolled with Ross: A Political Portrait.* Baton Rouge, LA: Moran Industries, 1980.

———. *Mississippi's Defiant Years 1953–1973.* Forest, MS: Lake Harbor, 1990.

Keady, William. *All Rise: Memoirs of a Mississippi Federal Judge.* Boston: Recollections Bound, 1988.

Kincheloe, Joe, and William Pinar, eds. *Curriculum as Social Psychoanalysis: The Significance of Place.* Albany: State University of New York Press, 1991.

Kingsolver, Barbara. *Animal Dreams.* New York: Harper Perennial, 1990.

Kluger, Richard. *Simple Justice: The History of* Brown v. Board of Education *and Black America's Struggle for Equality.* New York: Alfred A. Knopf, 1975.

Levine, Ellen. *Freedom's Children: Young Civil Rights Activists Tell Their Own Stories.* New York: Puffin Books, 1993.

Linn, R. L., and Welner, K. G., eds. *Race-conscious Policies for Assigning Students to Schools.* Washington, DC: National Academy of Education, 2007.

McMillen, Neil. *The Citizens' Council: Organized Resistance to the Second Reconstruction, 1954–64*. Urbana: University of Illinois Press, 1971.

Martin, John Bartlow. *The Deep South Says Never*. New York: Ballantine Books, 1957.

Martin, Waldo E., Jr. *Brown v. Board of Education: A Brief History with Documents*. Boston: St. Martin's, 1998.

Mason, Gilbert. *Beaches, Blood, and Ballots: A Black Doctor's Civil Rights Struggle*. Jackson: University Press of Mississippi, 2000.

The Measure of Our Days: Writings of William F. Winter. Jackson: University Press of Mississippi, 2006.

Morris, Willie. *The Courting of Marcus Dupree*. Jackson: University Press of Mississippi, 1983.

Morris, Willie.. *Yazoo: Integration in a Deep-Southern Town*. Fayetteville: University of Arkansas Press, 1971.

Moye, J. Todd. *Let the People Decide: Black Freedom and White Resistance Movement in Sunflower County, Mississippi, 1945–1986*. Chapel Hill: University of North Carolina Press, 2004.

Mullins, Andrew P., Jr. *Building Consensus: A History of the Passage of the Mississippi Education Reform Act*. Jackson: Mississippi Humanities Council and the Phil Hardin Foundation, 1992.

Noblit, George, ed. *School Desegregation: Oral Histories toward Understanding the Effects of White Domination*. Rotterdam, Amsterdam: Sense, 2015.

Ogletree, Charles J., Jr. *All Deliberate Speed*. New York: W. W. Norton, 2004.

Payne, Charles. *I've Got the Light of Freedom: The Organizing Tradition and the Mississippi Freedom Struggle*. Berkeley: University of California Press, 1995.

Prince, Julian. "Balancing the Scales: School Desegregation in McComb, Mississippi." Unpublished manuscript.

Reyes, Pedro, Jay D. Scribner, and Alicia Paredes Scribner, eds. *Lessons from High-performing Hispanic Schools: Creating Learning Communities*. Teachers College, 1999.

Rodgers, Frederick. *The Black High School and Its Community*. Lexington, MA: Lexington Books, 1967.

Rosiek, Jerry, and Kathy Kinslow. *Resegregation as Curriculum: The Meaning of the New Racial Segregation in U.S. Public Schools*. New York: Routledge, 2016.

Sanders, Crystal. *A Chance for Change: Head Start and Mississippi's Black Freedom Struggle*. Chapel Hill: University of North Carolina Press, 2016b.

Sokol, Jason. *There Goes My Everything: White Southerners in the Age of Civil Rights, 1945–1975*. New York: Vintage Books, 2006.

Spofford, Tim. *Lynch Street: The May 1970 Slayings at Jackson State College*. Kent, OH: Kent State University Press, 1988.

Spring, Joel. *The American School (1642–1990)*. New York: Longman, 2004.

Stokes, John A. *Students on Strike: Jim Crow, Civil Rights, Brown, and Me*. Washington, DC: National Geographic, 2008.

Terjen, Kitty. "The Segregation Academy Movement." In Robert E. Anderson Jr., *The South and Her Children: School Desegregation 1970–1971*, edited by Robert Anderson (69–79). Atlanta, GA: Southern Regional Council, March 1971.

Turner, Jeffrey. *Sitting in and Speaking Out: Student Movements in the American South 1960–1970*. Athens: University of Georgia Press, 2010.

Warren, Robert Penn. *Who Speaks for the Negro?* New Haven, CT: Yale University Press, 1965.

"Welcome to Council Schools: A Handbook of Information and School Policy." Jackson: Council School Foundation, 1970.

Winter, William. *Opening Doors in a Closed Society*. Kalamazoo, MI: Fetzer Institute, 2010.

Youth of the Rural Organizing and Culture Center. *Minds Stayed on Freedom: The Civil Rights Struggle in the Rural South, an Oral History*. Boulder, CO: Westview, 1991.

Zebrowski, Ernest, and Judith Howard. *Category 5: The Story of Camille*. Ann Arbor: University of Michigan Press. 2005.

Articles

Abrell, Ronald, and Charles Hanna. "High School Student Unrest Reconsidered." *The High School Journal* 54, no. 6 (March 1971): 396-404.

Adams, Jane, and D. Gorton. "Confederate Lane: Class, Race, and Ethnicity in the Mississippi Delta." *American Ethnologist* 33, no. 2 (2006): 288–309.

Adams, Natalie, and Pamela Bettis. "Commanding the Room in Short Skirts: Cheering as the Embodiment of Ideal Girlhood." *Gender and Society* 17, no. 1 (2003b): 73–91.

Andrews, Kenneth. "Movement-Countermovement Dynamics and the Emergence of New Institutions: The Case of 'White Flight' Schools in Mississippi." *Social Forces* 80, no. 3 (2002): 911–36.

Barra, Allen. "The Integration of College Football That Didn't Happen in One Game." *The Atlantic*, November 15, 2013, http://www.theatlantic.com/entertainment/archive/2013/11/the-integration-of-college-football-didnt-happen-in-one-game/281557/.

Beirich, Heidi. "Council of Conservative Citizens Funds Miss. Private Schools." Southern Poverty Law Center, https://www.splcenter.org/fighting-hate/intelligence-report/2011/council-conservative-citizens-funds-miss-private-schools.

Bender, Wm. A. "The Status of Educational Desegregation in Mississippi." *Journal of Negro Education* 25, no. 3 (Summer 1956): 285–88.

Bettis, Pamela, and Natalie Adams. "The Power of the Preps and a Cheerleading Equity Policy." *Sociology of Education* 76, no. 2 (April 2003): 128–42.

Blackmon, Douglas A. "The Resegregation of a Southern School." *Harper's Magazine*. September 1992, http://www.slaverybyanothername.com/other-writings/harpers-magazine-the-resegregation/.

Bolner, James. "The Supreme Court and Racially Imbalanced Public Schools in 1967." *Journal of Negro Education* 38, no. 4 (Autumn 1969): 125–34.

Bolton, Charles. "Mississippi's School Equalization Program, 1945–54: 'A Last Gasp to Try to Maintain a Segregated Educational System.'" *The Journal of Southern History* 66, no. 4 (November 2000): 781–814.

Brady, Tom Brady. "Segregation and the South." Address, Commonwealth Club of California, San Francisco, October 4, 1957, http://dc.lib.odu.edu/cdm/ref/collection/npsdp/id/1151.

Bragg, Emma. "Changes and Challenges in the '60s." *Journal of Negro Education* 32, no. 1 (Winter 1963): 25–34.

Brewer, James. "We Made the Transition from Dual to Unitary." *Mississippi Educational Advance* 14 (May 1970): 14, 31.

Butler, J. Michael. "The Mississippi State Sovereignty Commission and Beach Integration, 1959–1963: A Cotton-Patch Gestapo?" *Journal of Southern History* 68, no. 1 (February 2002): 107–48.

Chesler, Mark, James Crowfoot, and Bunyan Bryant. "Institutional Changes to Support School Desegregation: Alternative Models Underlying Research and Implementation." *Law and Contemporary Problems* 42, no. 4 (Autumn 1978): 174–213.

Clotfelter, C. "School Desegregation, 'Tipping,' and Private School Enrollment." *The Journal of Human Resources* 11, no. 1 (1976): 28–50.

Cordisco, Pat. "The Phantom Challenge of the Principalship." *American Secondary Education* 1, no. 1 (December 1970): 16–19.

Crespino, Joseph. "The Best Defense Is a Good Offense: The Stennis Amendment and the Fracturing of Liberal School Desegregation Policy, 1964–1972." *Journal of Policy History* 18, no. 3 (2006): 304–25.

Dirks, Annelieke. "Between Threat and Reality: The National Association for the Advancement of Colored People and the Emergence of Armed Self-Defense in Clarksdale and Natchez, Mississippi, 1960–1965." *Journal for the Study of Radicalism* 1, no. 1 (2006): 71–98.

Dodson, Dan. "School Administration, Control and Public Policy concerning Integration." *Journal of Negro Education* 34, no. 3(1965): 249–57.

Doherty, Patrick. "Integration Now: A Study of *Alexander v. Holmes County Board of Education*." *Notre Dame Law Review* 45, no. 3 (March 1970): 489–514.

Dorsey, Dana Thompson. "Segregation 2.0: The New Generation of School Segregation in the 21st Century." *Education and Urban Society* 45, no. 5 (2013): 533–47.

Drewry, Galen. "The Principal Faces Desegregation." *Educational Leadership* (October 1955): 14–17.

Fairclough, Adam. "The Costs of *Brown*: Black Teachers and School Integration." *Journal of American History* 91, no. 1 (June 2004): 43–55.

Findley, Dale, and Henry O'Reilly. "Secondary School Discipline." *American Secondary Education* 2, no. 1 (December 1971): 26–31.

Forman, James, Jr. "The Secret History of School Choice: How Progressives Got There First." *The Georgetown Law Journal* 93 (2005): 1287–1319.

French, Sally, and John Swain, "Telling Stories for a Politics of Hope." *Disability & Society* 21, no. 5 (2006): 383–96.

Fultz, Michael. "The Displacement of Black Educators Post-Brown: An Overview and Analysis." *History of Education Quarterly* 44, no. 1 (Spring 2004): 11–45.

Fuquay, Michael. "Civil Rights and the Private School Movement in Mississippi, 1964–1971." *History of Education Quarterly* 42, no. 2 (Summer 2002): 159–80.

Gandy, Willard. "Implications of Integration for the Southern Teacher." *Journal of Negro Education* 31, no. 2 (Spring 1962): 191–97.

Goeden, Louise Edna. "Prom Magic: Event of the Term at Washington High." *Clearing House* 25, no. 3 (November 1950): 167–69.

Gordon, William. "The Implementation of Desegregation Plans Since Brown." *Journal of Negro Education* 63, no. 3 (Summer 1994): 310–22.

Gould, Sidney G. "Senior Prom: Costly, Exclusive, Deserted." *Clearing House* 22, no. 6 (February 1948): 339–40.

Hale, Jon. "'The Fight Was Instilled in Us': High School Activism and the Civil Rights Movement in Charleston." *South Carolina Historical Magazine* 114, no. 1 (January 2013): 4–28.

Hancock, LynNell. "The Anonymous Town That was the Model of Desegregation in the Civil-Rights Era." *The Nation.* October 4, 2016, https://www.thenation.com/article/the-anonymous-town-that-was-the-model-of-desegregation-in-the-civil-rights-era/.

Haney, James. "The Effects of the Brown Decision on Black Educators." *Journal of Negro Education* 47, no. 1 (Winter 1978): 88–95.

Hannah-Jones, Nikole. "Lack of Order: The Erosion of a Once-Great Force of Integration." *ProPublica* (May 1, 2014), https://www.propublica.org/article/lack-of-order-the-erosion-of-a-once-great-force-for-integration.

———. "Segregation Now...." *The Atlantic* (May 2014), 68–81.

Haplin, David. "The Nature of Hope and Its Significance for Education." *British Journal of Educational Studies* 49, no. 4 (December 2001): 392–410.

Henderson, Russell. "The 1963 Mississippi State University Basketball Controversy and the Repeal of the Unwritten Law: 'Something More than the Game Will Be Lost.'" *Journal of Southern History* 63, no. 4 (November 1997): 827–54.

Hooker, Robert. "Displacement of Black Teachers in the Eleven Southern States." *Afro-American Studies* 2 (December 1971): 165–80.

Janesick, Valerie. "Oral History as a Social Justice Project: Issues for the Qualitative Researcher." *Qualitative Report* 12, no. 1 (2007): 111–21.

Kahlenberg, Richard, and Halley Potter. "Restoring Shanker's Vision for Charter Schools." *American Educator* 38, no. 4 (Winter 2014–2015): 4–13.

Kannapel, Patricia, and Stephen Clements. "Inside the Black Box of High-performing High-poverty Schools." Lexington, KY: Prichard Committee for Academic Excellence, 2005, http://www.prichardcommittee.org/Ford%20Study/FordReportJE.pdf.

Kittredge, Brett. "How Does School Choice Effect Racial Segregation?" May 19, 2016, http://empowerms.org/how-does-school-choice-effect-racial-segregation/.

Lane, Ginny, and Amy White. "The Roots of Resegregation: Analysis and Implications." *Race, Gender & Class* 17, nos. 3–4 (2010): 81–102.

Leeson, Jim. "Private Schools Continue to Increase in the South." *Southern Education Report,* November 1966.

Lerner, Sharon. "A School District That Was Never Desegregated." *The Atlantic* (February 5, 2015), https://www.theatlantic.com/education/archive/2015/02/a-school-district-that-was-never-desegregated/385184/.

Lieberman, Myron. "Desegregation since 1964: The Civil Rights Fiasco in Public Education." *Phi Delta Kappan* 47, no. 9 (May 1966): 482–86.

Lowry, Mark. "Schools in Transition." *Annals of the Association of American Geographers* 63, no. 2 (June 1973): 167–80.

McAndrews, Lawrence. "The Politics of Principle: Richard Nixon and School Desegregation." *The Journal of Negro History* 83, no. 3 (Summer 1998): 187–200.

Martin, Charles. "Jim Crow in the Gymnasium: The Integration of College Basketball in the American South." *International Journal of the History of Sports* 10, no. 1 (April 1993): 68–86.

Mickelson, Roslyn. "Twenty-first Century Social Science on School Racial Diversity and Educational Outcomes." *Ohio State Law Journal* 69, no. 6 (2008): 1173–1228.

Morris, Willie. "Is There a South Anymore?" *Southern Magazine,* October 1986, http://www.southerner.net/v1n3_99/southern.html.

Munford, Luther. "Black Gravity: Desegregation in 30 Mississippi School Districts." Senior thesis, Princeton University, 1971.

Nabrit, James. "Legal Invention and the Desegregation Process." *The Annals of the American Academy of Political and Social Science* 304 (March 1956): 35–43.

Newton, Eunice, and Earle West. "The Progress of the Negro in Elementary and Secondary Education." *The Journal of Negro Education* 32, no. 4 (1963): 466–84.

Norman, David. "The Strange Career of the Civil Rights Division's Commitment to Brown." *The Yale Law Journal* 93, no. 6 (May 1984): 983–89.

Orfield, Gary. "How to Make Desegregation Work: The Adaptation of Schools to Their Newly-Integrated Bodies." *Law and Contemporary Problems* 39, no. 2 (Spring 1975): 314–40.

Orfield, Gary, and Erica Frankenberg. "Increasingly Segregated and Unequal Schools as Courts Reverse Policy." *Educational Administration Quarterly* 50, no. 5 (2014): 718–34.

Orfield, Gary, Erica Frankenberg, and Genevieve Siegel-Hawley. "Integrated Schools: Finding a New Path." *Educational Leadership* (November 2010): 22–27.

Palmer, James. "Unitary School Systems: One Race or Two." Paper presented at the annual meeting of the Association of Southern Agricultural Workers, Jacksonville, FL, February 2, 1971.

Porter, Jeremy, Frank Howell, and Lynn Hempel. "Old Times Are Not Forgotten: The Institutionalization of Segregationist Academies in the American South." *Social Problems* 61, no. 4 (November 2014): 576–601.

Quantz, Richard. "The Complex Visions of Female Teachers and the Failure of Unionization in the 1930s: An Oral History." *History of Education Quarterly* 25, no. 4 (1985): 439–58.

Reeves, Douglas B. "High Performance in High Poverty Schools: 90/90/90 and Beyond." *Center for Performance Assessment* (2003): 1–20.

"Requiem for a Liberal Dream?" *Newsweek* (March 2, 1970): 18–21.

Robinson, William. "Integration's Delay and Frustration Tolerance." *Journal of Negro Education* 28, no. 4 (Autumn 1959): 472–75.

Rodgers, Harrell. "The Supreme Court and School Desegregation: Twenty Years Later." *Political Science Quarterly* 89, no. 4 (1974–75): 751–76.

Rodgers, Harrell, and Charles Bullock. "School Desegregation: A Policy Analysis." *Journal of Black Studies* 2, no. 4 (June 1972): 409–37.

Ryan, James, and Michael Hese. "The Political Economy of School Choice." *The Yale Law Journal* 111, no. 8 (June 2002): 2043–136.

Sanders, Crystal. "'Money Talks': The Elementary and Secondary Education Act of 1965 and the African-American Freedom Struggle in Mississippi." *History of Education Quarterly* 56, no. 2 (May 2016a): 361–67.

Sangster, Joan. "Telling Our Stories: Feminist Debates and the Use of Oral History." *Women's History Review* 3, no. 1 (1994): 5–28.

Scott, Janelle, and Rand Quinn. "The Politics of Education in the Post-*Brown* Era: Race, Markets, and the Struggle for Equitable Schooling." *Educational Administration Quarterly* 50, no. 5 (2014): 749–63.

"Segregation and the Supreme Court." *The Atlantic,* July 1954, http://www.theatlantic.com /magazine/archive/1954/07/segregation-and-the-supreme-court/.

Simpson, R. H., Arnold Sugg, and Staff. "The Atlantic Hurricane Season of 1969." *Monthly Weather Review* (National Hurricane Center, Weather Bureau, ESSA, Miami, FL, April 1970): 300.

Sisk, Frank. "Greater Holding Power for the Big Prom: Something Better Than Dancing." *Clearing House* 28, no. 9 (May 1954): 545–46.

Sutherland, Arthur. "Segregation by Race in Public Schools Retrospect and Prospect." *Law and Contemporary Problems* 20, no. 1 (Winter 1955): 169–83.

Tillman, Linda. "African American Principalship and the Legacy of *Brown.*" *Review of Research in Education* 28 (2004): 101–46.

Valien, Preston. "The Status of Educational Desegregation, 1956: A Critical Summary." *Journal of Negro Education* 25, no. 3 (Summer 1956): 359–68.

Umoja, Akinyele Omowale. "'We Will Shoot Back': The Natchez Model of Paramilitary Organization in the Mississippi Freedom Movement." *Journal of Black Studies* 32, no. 3 (January 2002): 271–94.

Walker, Vanessa Siddle. "The Architects of Black Schooling in the Segregated South: The Case of One Principal Leader." *Journal of Curriculum and Supervision* 19, no. 1 (2003): 54–72.

———. "Valued Segregated Schools for African American Children in the South, 1935–1969: A Review of Common Themes and Characteristics." *Review of Educational Research* 70, no. 3 (Autumn 2001): 253–85.

Wilkins, Roy. "The Role of the National Association for the Advancement of Colored People in the Desegregation Process." *Social Problems* 2, no. 4 (April 1955): 201–4.

Willis, Vincent. "'Let Me In, I have the Right to Be Here': Black Youth Struggle for Equal Education and Full Citizenship after the *Brown* Decision, 1954–1969." *Citizenship Teaching & Learning* 9, no. 2 (2014): 53–70.

Yale Law Journal Company. "Segregation Academies and State Action." *The Yale Law Journal* 82, no. 7 (June 1973): 1436–61.

Oral History Interviews

Adams, Alean, interview by author, Brandon, MS.

Adams, John, interview by author, Brandon, MS.

Barksdale, Claiborne, interview by author, Oxford, MS.

Beaty, Lamar, interview by author, Houston, MS.

Belue, Virgil, interview by author, Clinton, MS.

Bishop, Harold, interview by author, Tuscaloosa, AL.

Boone, Charles, interview by author, Quitman, MS.

Boston, Charles, interview by author, Columbia, MS.

Boyd, Lucy, interview by author, Charleston, MS.

Box, Larry, interview by author, Starkville, MS.

Breeland, Harry, interview by author, Oak Grove, MS.

Brewer, James, interview with author, Hazlehurst, MS.

Brooks, Richard, interview by author, Macon, MS.

Brown, Billy, interview by author, DeKalb, MS.

Bustin, Jerry, interview by author, Forest, MS.

Carter, Hodding, interview by Jack Bass and Walter Devries, April 1, 1974, Interview A-0100, Southern Oral History Program Collection (#4007), http://docsouth.unc.edu/sohp/A -0100/A-0100.html.

Crockett, Ola, interview by author, Laurel, MS.

Dale, George, interview by author, Jackson, MS.

Davis, Lillie V., interview by author, Marks, MS.

Davis, Tommy, interview by author, Meridian, MS.

Dent, Richard, interview by author, Waynesboro, MS.

Dickerson, Gloria Carter, interview by author, Drew, MS.

Dodson, William, interview by author, Brandon, MS.

Dulin, Tom, interview by author, Winona, MS.

Evans, Ann Hall, interview by author, Avon, MS.

Ferguson, Billy Joe, interview by author, Carrollton, MS.

Flynt, John Allen, interview by author, New Hebron, MS.

Fortenberry, Robert, interview by author, Jackson, MS.

Foster, Herbert, interview by author, Marks, MS.

George, Charles, interview by author, Webb, MS.

George, James, interview by author, Carrollton, MS.

Green, Winifred A., interview by Charles Bolton, 1997, vol. 704, University of Southern Mississippi, Center for Oral History & Cultural Heritage, Hattiesburg, MS.

Hall, Clarence, interview by author, Avon, MS.

Harrison, Cyndie, interview by author, Jackson, MS.

Haynes, Joe, interview by author, Jackson, MS.

Jackson, Robert, interview by author, Marks, MS.

Johnson, Archie, interview by author, Biloxi, MS.

Johnson, Mike, interview by author, Oakdale, MS.

Johnston, Erle, Interview by Yasuhiro Katagiri, August 13, 1993, University of Southern Mississippi Center for Oral History and Cultural Heritage, http://anna.lib.usm .edu/~spcol/crda/oh/ohjohnstone2b.html.

Kelly, Harold, interview by author, Yazoo City, MS.

Kuykendall, Harriet, interview by author, Jackson, MS.

Lewis, Williams, interview by author, Poplarville, MS.

Mabry, Paula, interview by author, Starkville, MS.

McAlpin, Dalton, interview by author, Starkville, MS.

McCarthy, Hugh, interview by author, Forest, MS.

Makamson, Owen, interview by author, Avon, MS.

Meek, Ed, interview by author, Oxford, MS.

Miller, Mary Carol, interview by author, Greenwood, MS.

Moon, Beverly, interview by author, Cleveland, MS.

Morris, JoAnne Prichard, interview by author, Jackson, MS.

Muse, Clyde, interview by author, Jackson, MS.

Nash, Charles, interview by author, Tuscaloosa, AL.

Nash, Jere, interview by author, Greenville, MS.

Nations, Ricky, interview by author, Clinton, MS.

Perkins, Fred, interview by author, Starkville, MS.

Peters, Fenton, interview by author, Starkville, MS.

Prince, Julian, interview by author, Tupelo, MS.

Salter, Sid, interview by author, Starkville, MS.

Spencer, Alice, interview by author, Avon, MS.

Spencer, Grey, interview by author, Avon, MS.

Stevens, Hamilton, interview by author, Forest, MS.

Travis, Brenda, interview by Wazir Peacock, Jean Wiley, and Bruce Hartford, accessed
    January 21, 2017, http://www.crmvet.org/nars/travisb.htm.

Van Dyke, Larry, interview by author, Meridian, MS.

Weems, Lamar, interview by author, Jackson, MS.

Wooten, Ken, interview by author, Oxford, MS.

Court Cases

Adams. v. Rankin County Board of Education, 485 F. 2d 324 (5th Cir 1973).

Alexander v. Holmes County Board of Education, 396 U.S. 1218 (1969).

Armstead v. Starkville, 325 F. Supp. 560 (ND, Mississippi, 1971).

Baker v. Columbus Municipal Separate School District, 329 F. Supp. 706 (ND, Mississippi 1971).

Blackwell v. Issaquena Board of Education, 363 F.2d (5th Cir. 1966).

Bob Jones University v. United States, 461 U.S. 574 (1983).

Bolling v. Sharpe, 347 U.S. 497 (1954).

Briggs v. Elliott, 98 F. Supp. 529 (1951).

Brown v. Board of Education of Topeka, 98 F. Supp. 797 (1951).

Brown v. Board of Education of Topeka, 347 U.S. 483 (1954).

Brown v. Board of Education Topeka, 349 U.S. 294 (1955).

Burnside v. Byars, 363 F.2d 744 (5th Cir. 1966).

Coffey v. State Educational Finance Commission, 296 F. Supp. 1389 (SD, Mississippi, 1969).

Cook v. Hudson, 365 F. Supp. 855 (ND, Mississippi, 1973).

Cousin v. Board of Trustees of Houston Municipal Separate School District, 726 F.2d 262
    (5th Cir. 1984).

Cowan v. Bolivar County Board of Education, 914 F. Supp. 2d 801 (ND Mississippi, 2012).

Davis v. County School Board of Prince Edward County, 103 F. Supp. 337 (1952).

Earlean McCormick v. Attala County Board of Education, 407 F. Supp. 586 (ND, Mississippi, 1976).

Evers v. Jackson Municipal Separate School District, 328 F.2d 408 (5th Cir. 1964).

Gebhart v. Bolton, 33 Del. Ch. 144, 87A 2d 862 (Del. Ch. 1952).

Green v. Connally, 330 F. Supp. 1150 (DC 1971).

Green v. County School Board of New Kent County, 391 U.S. 430 (1968).

Henry v. Clarksdale-Coahoma School Board, 352 F.2d 648 (5th Cir. 1966).

Keglar v. East Tallahatchie School District, 378 F. Supp. 1269 (ND, Mississippi, 1974).

McNeal v. Tate County School District, 460 F. 2d568 (5th Cir. 1971).

Norwood v. Harrison, 382 F. Supp. 921 (ND Mississippi 1974).

Singleton v. Jackson Municipal Separate School System (1969)

United States v. Jefferson County Board of Education, 372 F.29 836 (5th Cir. 1966).

United States v. Hinds County School Board v. Amite County School Board, 560 F.2d 619 (5th Cir. 1977).

United States v. Tunica County School District, 323 F. Supp. 1019 (ND, Mississippi, 1970).

United States v. Coffeeville Consolidated School District, 365 F. Supp. 990 (ND, Mississippi 1973).

US v. Hinds County School Board v. Noxubee County School District, 433 F.2d 619 (5th Cir. 1970).

Newspapers

"An Important Message from Concerned Citizens," *Yazoo City Herald* (Yazoo City, MS), November 20, 1969.

"Angry Parents Defy Court Order," *Meridian Star* (Meridian, MS), January 7, 1970.

"Appeal in School Case Won't Stop Integration," *Clarion-Ledger* (Jackson, MS), July 8, 1964.

"Attendance Off in Public Schools," *Macon Beacon* (Macon, MS), January 15, 1970.

Banas, Casey. "Mississippi Schools: Effect of Court Order," *Chicago Tribune*, April 19, 1970.

———. "Seek to Avoid School Order in Mississippi," *Chicago Tribune*, November 4, 1969.

"Baptist Minister Giving up Boycott," *Meridian Star* (Meridian, MS), January 7, 1970.

Bell, Jimmie. "Officials Assure Student Safety," *Daily Herald* (Gulfport-Biloxi, MS), October 11, 1969.

Bevier, Thomas. "All's Well in Yazoo City, but What about Tomorrow?" *Commercial Appeal* (Memphis, TN), January 18, 1970.

"Black Activists Shift from Integration Fight to More Militancy," *New York Times*, December 30, 1969.

"Black Coaches Meet to Solve Problems," *Daily Herald* (Biloxi-Gulfport, MS), January 17, 1970.

Bonney, James. "White Crowd Beats Negroes, Newsmen," *Clarion-Ledger* (Jackson, MS), September 13, 1966.

Boyd, Bob. "Coaching Choice Defended," *Delta Democrat Times* (Greenville, MS), May 1, 1970.

———. "Coleman Youth Suspended," *Delta Democrat Times* (Greenville, MS), March 16, 1970.

———. "School Board Backs New Coach Assignments," *Delta Democrat-Times* (Greenville, MS), May 5, 1980.

Braddock, Emily. "Coahoma Integration Snarl Will Go to Court Tuesday," *Commercial Appeal* (Memphis, TN), August 30, 1969.

———. "Rejected Negro Students Picket High School Campus in Clarksdale," *Commercial Appeal* (Memphis, TN), September 23, 1969.

Brown, David. "Ruling Is Due Today in Suit by Black Columbus Teachers," *Commercial Appeal* (Memphis, TN), September 3, 1970.

"Burglund High School Walkout 50th Anniversary," *McComb Legacies,* October 8, 2011, http://mccomblegacies.org/2011/10/Burglund-walkout-50th-anniversary/.

Cantrell, Jack. "Jack Cantrell's Story: 'They Beat Me with Broomsticks,'" *Memphis Press-Scimitar,* September 13, 1966.

"Capacity Crowd of 1,200 to 1,300 Attended," *Oxford Eagle* (Oxford, MS), January 22, 1970.

Carter, Hodding. "Editorial." *Delta Democrat-Times* (Greenville, MS)., January 27, 1972.

"Chaos for Mississippi Schools?" *Meridian Star* (Meridian, MS), December 1, 1969.

Chaze, William. "Core Leader Sees School Mix Failing," *Daily Herald* (Biloxi-Gulfport), December 17, 1969.

"A 'Chicken Coop' in a Mississippi School," accessed December 13, 2016, http://www.civil rights.org/publications/reports/education-resource-equity-report/chapter-i/.

Chiles, Nick. "Tests on Trial," *Hechinger Report,* May 27, 2015, http://www.jacksonfreepress.com/news/2015/may/27/tests-trial/.

"Civil Rights Chief Canned for Meddling in White House Ruling," *Daily Herald* (Biloxi-Gulfport, MS). February 22, 1970.

"Civil Rights Lawyers Ask Private Aid Block," *Starkville Daily News* (Starkville, MS), September 20, 1969.

Clawson, Ken. "MS County Integrates Reluctantly," *Washington Post,* August 25, 1970.

"Clay High, Beasley Schools Closed Until after Court Hearing," *Starkville Daily News* (Starkville, MS), September 12, 1969.

Cleghorn, Reese. "Segregation by Tax Exemption," *The Nation,* June 29, 1970, 785–86.

"Coastal City Quiet after Racial Flareup," *Jackson Daily News* (Jackson, MS), April 16, 1971.

"Coleman Claims State Can Force Indefinite Delay on Integration," *State Times* (Jackson, MS), April 26, 1954.

"College Hill Academy," (ad), *Oxford Eagle* (Oxford, MS), January 22, 1970.

Cook, Tom. "Harrison Central Trouble," *Daily Herald* (Gulfport-Biloxi, MS), October 9, 1969.

———. "17 Pupils Expelled at School," *Daily Herald* (Mississippi Coast), October 12, 1969.

Criss, Sara. "Whites in Holmes County Leave Integrated Schools," *Commercial Appeal,* September 9, 1965.

Dabbs, Miriam. "Clarksdale Backs Public Education," *Jackson Daily News* (Jackson, MS), January 14, 1970.

"DeKalb Cancels Eupora Game," *Webster Progress-Times* (Eupora, MS), October 15, 1970.

DeLaughter, Jerry. "Jackson to Shift Teachers by Lottery," *Commercial Appeal* (Memphis: TN), December 10, 1969.

———. "Whites in Forrest County Refuse to Integrate," *Commercial Appeal* (Memphis, TN), January 8, 1970.

Desegregation in Schools Triples," *Clarion-Ledger* (Jackson, MS), December 5, 1966.

Editorial. *Citizens' Council* 1, no. 1 (October 1955), http://www.citizenscouncils.com/index .php?option=com_content&view=newspaper&file=1-Oct55-Dec55.swf.

"End of Tax Exemption Ordered for 23 Mississippi Academies," *New York Times,* March 27, 1971.

Falk, Gail. "Court Orders Protection for Negro Pupil," *Southern Courier* (Montgomery, AL), September 24–25, 1966.

"Fed Court Asked to Overturn State Law," *Starkville Daily News* (Starkville, MS), September 23, 1969.

"Federal Courts Action to Ruin Kemper Schools," *Kemper County Messenger* (DeKalb, MS), November 13, 1969.

"Fewer Whites Expected When Jackson Classes Open," *Hattiesburg American* (Hattiesburg, MS), February 5, 1970.

"Final Few Days of High School Changed," *Leland Progress* (Leland, MS), May 21, 1970.

"FOCUS March through City Draws 1,500," *Clarksdale Press Register* (Clarksdale, MS), January 17, 1970.

"FOCUS Unit Formed for School Freedom," *Daily Herald* (Mississippi Coast), January 31, 1970.

Galphin, Bruce. "Mississippi Takes Step to Integrate," *Washington Post,* January 6, 1970.

Gates, Jimmie. "Schools Must Desegregate," *Clarion-Ledger* (Jackson, MS), May 17, 2016.

"GHS Hit by Black Walkout," *Delta Democrat-Times* (Greenville, MS), March 19, 1971.

Glaczier, Richard. "Attendance at School Reduced," *Daily Herald* (Mississippi Coast), October 10, 1969.

Gorringe, Maybelle. "Dr. Martin Resigns Post as City Schools Head," *Jackson Daily News* (Jackson, MS), August 28, 1970.

"Governor Promises to Use More Force if Necessary," *Commercial Appeal* (Memphis, TN), September 14, 1966.

"Governor Urges Restraint in Mix Crisis," *Meridian Star* (Meridian, MS), January 4, 1970.

Graham, Fred. "More Delay Seen in Desegregation," *New York Times,* September 22, 1969.

"Grenada Officials Told to Stop Mix Violence," *Memphis Press-Scimitar* (Memphis, TN), September 14, 1966.

"Grenada Police Arrest 200 in School March," *Clarion-Ledger* (Jackson, MS), October 25, 1966.

Grimm, Fred. "Clarksdale Gets Push on Schools," *The Commercial Appeal* (Memphis, TN), January 11, 1970.

"Group of Negroes Ask Integration Biloxi Schools," *Daily Herald* (Mississippi Coast), March 19, 1963.

"Happenings in Grenada during Past Week Recorded," *Grenada Weekly* (Grenada, MS), October 27, 1966.

Harrison-Henderson, Monique. "Under Pressure: Some Mississippi Educators Silenced on School-Funding Battle," *Hechlinger Report,* October 16, 2015, http://www.jacksonfreepress .com/news/2015/oct/16/under-pressure-some-mississippi-edu.

Harrist, Ron. "Officials Threaten Look at Schools in the North," *Hattiesburg American* (Hattiesburg, MS), August 20, 1970.

Harvish, Earl. "School Boycott Called 'Success,'" *Commercial Appeal* (Memphis, TN), February 27, 1969.

Harwood, Richard. "Integration Comes to Mississippi," *Washington Post,* February 15, 1970.

Hearn, Philip. "Indianola School Superintendent Says Schools Losing Strength," *Daily Journal* (Tupelo, MS), February 3, 1970.

Hembree, Brandon. "Winona Mix Plan Holds," *Jackson Daily News* (Jackson, MS), August 29, 1969.

Herman, Tom. "'Integrated' Schools in South Sometimes Keep Races Separated," *Wall Street Journal,* May 15, 1970.

Horner, Garnett. "Nixon to Discuss Federal Policy on Integration," *Washington Star,* March 21, 1970.

"IQ to Be Segregation Basis in County's First 3 Grades," *Clarion Ledger* (Jackson, MS), June 4, 1969.

"IRS Says It Will Take Southern Schools' Word about Racial Polices," *Wall Street Journal,* August 13, 1970.

"Jackson Petition Is Filed," *Natchez Times* (Natchez, MS), July 26, 1955.

James, Billy G. "New Southern Party Calls for School Rally," *Atlanta Constitution,* January 2, 1970.

Johnson, Floyd. "Calmness Arrives for Yazoo Citians," *Jackson Daily News* (Jackson, MS), January 8, 1970.

Jones, James. "Whites Leave Schools en Masse in Canton," *Delta Democrat-Times* (Greenville, MS), January 13, 1970.

"Judge Keady OKs Hair at Riverside," *Delta Democrat-Times* (Greenville, MS), February 17, 1970.

"Judge Orders Students Readmitted in Hair Case," *Delta Democrat Times* (Greenville, MS), February 16, 1970.

Kelley, Carol. "Detailed Plans for City Faculty Integration Set," *Starkville Daily News* (Starkville, MS), February 4, 1970.

"Lawyer Group to Monitor Desegregation," *Washington Evening Star,* August 7, 1970.

Lee, Kirby. "Members of 1955 Compton Team That Broke Color Barrier Honored," *Los Angeles Times,* October 27, 1994.

Leggett, Dorothy. "Sheriff Calls for Quiet Integration," *Daily Herald* (Mississippi Coast), August 24, 1970.

"Liar by Legislation," *Delta Democrat-Times* (Greenville, MS), April 3, 1955.

Lindsay, Leon. "Making Integration Work: Yazoo City, Miss. Copes with School Challenge," *Christian Science Monitor,* November 12, 1970.

"Local Freedom of Choice Plans Upheld by Court," *Neshoba Democrat* (Philadelphia, MS), May 15, 1969.

"Lone Negro Girl Enters Previous White School," *Carthaginian* (Carthage, MS), September 3, 1964.

Lord, Lewis. "Like Watching Something Wonderful Die, Students Say of Total Integration Move," *Meridian Star* (Meridian, MS), January 11, 1970.

McCall, Mike. "Judge Ok's Private School with Warning Policies," *Commercial Appeal* (Memphis, TN), June 22, 1972.

Mader, Jackie. "How One Mississippi District Made Integration Work," *Huffington Post,* April 18, 2016, http://www.huffingtonpost.com/entry/mississippi-integration_us _57151ff2e4b0060ccda3df.

"A Manual for Southerner," *Citizen* 2, no. 10, July 1957.

"Marching Blacks Oppose Tests in Clarksdale," *Delta Democrat-Times* (Greenville, MS), October 19, 1969.

"Martin Quits City's Troubled Schools," *Clarion Ledger* (Jackson, MS), August 28, 1970.

Milius, Peter. "Most Classrooms Still Segregated, U.S. Study Finds," *Washington Post,* January 4, 1970.

Minor, W. F., "Ruling Expected to Bring No Immediate Changes," *Times Picayune* (New Orleans, LA), April 23, 1954.

"Mississippi Blacks Appeal 'IQ' Test Desegregation," *Chicago Daily Defender,* October 21, 1969.

"Mississippi Integration Due Today," *Washington Post,* January 5, 1970.

"Mississippi Women Fight Valiantly to Keep Schools," *Commercial Appeal* (Memphis, TN), November 1, 1964.

Morganti, Leroy. "Teenagers Can Borrow for Education under Law," *Daily Herald* (Mississippi Coast), January 20, 1970.

"Moss Point Again Scene of Violence," *Jackson Daily News* (Jackson, MS), April 17, 1971.

Munford, Luther. "Sunflower, Boliver Tests Over," *Delta Democrat-Times* (Greenville, MS), August 3, 1969.

"Negro Students Stand Tall in Midst of Grenada Strife," *Commercial Appeal* (Memphis, TN), September 15, 1966.

"Negroes End Boycott of Hazlehurst Schools," *Copiah County News* (Hazlehurst, MS), March 29, 1967.

"Negroes in Mississippi Boycotting Classes," *Dispatch* (Lexington, NC), September 2, 1970.

"Negroes Plan Boycott of Clarkdale Stores," *Commercial Appeal* (Memphis, TN), October 11, 1969.

"Negro Student Held in Stabbing; School Closed," *Daily Journal* (Tupelo, MS), January 14, 1970.

"New Discrimination Forms Charged in Integration," *Daily Herald* (Mississippi Gulf Coast), January 12, 1970.

"New Jackson Organization Supports Public Schools," *Clarion-Ledger,* August 23, 1970.

"Now's the Time," *Oxford Eagle* (Oxford, MS), January 29, 1970.

"100 Mississippi Blacks Held," *New York Times,* June 5, 1970.

"170 Marchers Arrested in Mississippi," *Atlanta Constitution,* June 12, 1970.

"1,200 March in Clarksdale," The *Commercial Appeal* (Memphis, TN), October 19, 1969.

Overby, Charles. "Citizen Council Political Activities Results in Internal Power Fight," *Daily Herald* (Biloxi-Gulfport), August 24, 1970.

Pearce, John. "Martin Luther King Arrives in Grenada," *Times-Picayune* (New Orleans, LA), September 20, 1966.

———. "Sunday Was Peaceful in Race-Tense Areas," *Times-Picayune* (New Orleans, LA), September 19, 1966.

Peart, William. "Desegregation of Schools Lacked Leadership in State," *Clarion Ledger* (Jackson, MS), September 19, 1965.

"Petition Filed: NAACP Calls for Integration in Schools," *Natchez Times* (Natchez, MS), July 26, 1955.

Pittman, Paul. "School Dilemma Weighs Heavy on Delta in Summer of 1969," *Leland Press*, July 31, 1969.

Police Arrest 146 Negroes in Delta City," *Starkville Daily News* (Starkville, MS), September 23, 1969.

Private School Announced at Madden," *Neshoba Democrat* (Philadelphia, MS), November 27, 1969.

"Private School Principal Named," *Conservative* (Carrollton, MS), May 22, 1969.

"Public Education Friends Organize," *Clarion-Ledger* (Jackson, MS), August 29, 1970.

"Public School Desegregation Goes into Effect Across State," *Delta Democrat-Times* (Greenville, MS), January 5, 1970.

"Public School Notice: Starkville Municipal Separate School District," *Starkville Daily News*, September 9, 1970.

"Public Schools Are Vital to the Oxford-University Community," *Oxford Eagle* (Oxford, MS), January 15, 1970.

"Public School System in Wilkinson County Abandoned to Negroes," *Meridian Star* (Meridian, MS), January 4, 1970.

"Q & A," *Citizen* 8, September 1964, 16.

Reed, Roy. "Southern Blacks Fear a Growing Northern Apathy," *New York Times*, March 21, 1970.

"Registration Hits 5,000," *Jackson Daily News* (Jackson, MS), August 23, 1970.

"Resolution Adopted," *Oxford Eagle* (Oxford, MS); "Council to Back Schools," *Oxford Eagle* (Oxford, MS), January 15, 1970.

"Retired Superintendent Is Still on the Job," *Education Reporter*, March 2015, 2016, http://eagleforum.org/publications/educate/mar15/retired-superintendent-is-still-on-the-job/.

"Rights Suit Filed against Coahoma," *Commercial Appeal* (Memphis, TN), February 23, 1969.

"Riverside Students Sue for Hair Right," *Delta Democrat-Times* (Greenville, MS), February 13, 1970.

"School Board Works on Plans to Prevent Another Day like Friday," *Leland Progress* (Leland, MS), April 9, 1970.

"School Men Here Today Give Their Views on Segregation," *Jackson Daily News* (Jackson, MS), May 19, 1954.

"School Mixing Hits Snag in Mississippi," *Columbus Dispatch* (Columbus, MS), January 13, 1970.

"School Officials Grudgingly Yield," *Commercial Appeal* (Memphis, TN), July 8, 1964.

"School Opens in an Old Bus," *Commercial Appeal* (Memphis, TN), September 18, 1970.

"School's Operations Are Normal during Boycott," *Daily Herald* (Biloxi-Gulfport), December 11, 1969.

Schweid, Barry. "Fed Gov't Stands with State at Hearing Delay School Mix," *Natchez Democrat* (Natchez, MS), October 24, 1969.

"Show of Force Keeps Tempers under Control," *Commercial Appeal* (Memphis, TN), September 14, 1966.

Simmons, Ted. "Wholesale Desegregation of Southern Schools Set," *Clarion-Ledger* (Jackson, MS), August 23, 1970.

Simmons, William. "Government Schools," *Citizen* 8, September 1964, 2.

"Sit-in at Petal," *Jackson Daily News* (Jackson, MS), January 8, 1970.

Skelton, Billy. "Council School 3 Enrollment Soars," *Clarion-Ledger* (Jackson, MS), April 3, 1970.

———. "Dismissed Coahoma Teachers to Work, Seek Aid for Pay," *Jackson Daily News* (Jackson, MS), February 16, 1969.

———. "Public Schools Allies Rally: It's a Personal, Real Thing," *Clarion-Ledger* (Jackson, MS), August 23, 1970.

Skinner, Kayleigh, "Q & A: Mississippi Superintendent Explains Why He Gave Up His Salary to Help Relieve 'Wretched Conditions' at His Schools," *Hechlinger Report,* February 2, 2015, http://hechingerreport.org/q-a-mississippi-superintendent-explains-why-he-gave-up-his-salary-to-help-relieve-wretched-conditions-at-his-schools/.

Smith, Hazel Brannon, "We Must Save Our Public Schools," *Lexington* (Lexington, MS), May 7, 1970.

"Some Mississippi Schools Are All Black," *Boca Raton News,* January 13, 1970.

Southern Schools Expelling Students," *News-Herald* (Panama City, FL), June 3, 1972.

"Statement of Policy: Vicksburg Public Schools," *Vicksburg Post* (Vicksburg, MS), September 3, 1970.

"State Shuns Violence in School Change-Over," *Delta Democrat-Times* (Greenville, MS), August 30, 1970.

"State to Have the 'Most Integrated' Public Schools," *Mississippi Press* (Pascagoula, MS), August 19, 1970.

"'Stay Calm' Mayor, School Board Say," *Jackson Times* (Jackson, MS), March 14, 1963.

Street, William. "The Full Heat of Integration," *Commercial Appeal* (Memphis, TN), January 18, 1970.

"Superintendent Discusses Teacher Mixing," *Enterprise-Tocsin* (Indianola, MS), April 22, 1971.

"Tate Academy Gets Federal Court Order," *Jackson Daily News* (Jackson, MS), June 21, 1972.

"Third of Clarksdale's Teachers Quit in Change," *Daily Journal* (Tupelo, MS), February 9, 1970.

"13 Districts Mix Quietly; Whites Few," *Clarion-Ledger* (Jackson, MS), January 13, 1970.

"Those Who Signed," *Vicksburg Evening Post* (Vicksburg, MS), July 19, 1955.

"3,000 Skip School in Mississippi," *Atlanta Constitution,* December 12, 1969.

Tolliver, Ken. "Coahoma, Other Schools Get Deadline," *Commercial Appeal* (Memphis, TN), January 21, 1970.

———. "Court Approves County Plan for All-Boy, All-Girl Schools," *Commercial Appeal* (Memphis, TN), May 20, 1969.

"Toughest Job in U.S.," *Clarion-Ledger* (Jackson, MS), August 18, 1970.

"Under Age Pickets Released," *Daily Herald* (Biloxi-Gulfport, MS), September 30, 1970.

"Unique Desegregation Plan Offered," *Delta Democrat-Times,* May 16, 1969.

"US Charges 13 in Noxubee Intimidate Negro Parents," *Commercial Appeal* (Memphis, TN), September 12, 1967.

Vaughn, William. "Evers Opposes Private Schools in Mississippi," *Meridian Star* (Meridian, MS), January 11, 1970.

"Vicksburg School Board Says Negroes' Petition Not Legal," *Clarion-Ledger* (Jackson, MS), July 20, 1955.

"Walkout Is Staged by Negro Students," *Clarion-Ledger* (Jackson, MS), October 22, 1966.

"We Have Great Opportunities . . . Blacks and Whites Can Communicate Here," *Delta Democrat-Times* (Greenville, MS), February 15, 1970.

"We Support Public Schools," *Oxford Eagle* (Oxford, MS), January 22, 1970.

Weaver, Warren. "High Court Takes Key School Case," *New York Times,* October 10, 1969.

Whitaker, Andrew. "Seen, Heard, and Told," *Grenada County Weekly* (Grenada, MS), September 1, 1966.

"White Academies in the South—Booming Despite Obstacles," *U.S. News & World Report,* April 19, 1971.

"White Mothers Launch Boycott in Mississippi," *New Journal and Guide* (Norfolk, VA), December 20, 1969.

"White Parents Stage Sit-in in Mississippi," *Los Angeles Times,* January 8, 1970.

"White Pupils Boycott Schools in Mississippi," *Chicago Tribune,* December 12, 1969.

"Whites Boycott Schools in Forrest Mix Protest," *Meridian Star* (Meridian, MS), December 11, 1969.

"Whites Defy a Federal School Busing Order in Mississippi," *Chicago Tribune,* January 8, 1970.

"Whites Walk against School Integration in Clarksdale," *Delta Democrat-Times* (Greenville, MS), January 19, 1970.

Wicker, Tom. "In the Nation: One Evil, Two Problems," *New York Times,* February 12, 1970.

Wilkie, Curtis. "'Fired' Teachers Continue Classes," *Clarksdale Press Register* (Clarksdale, MS), February 17, 1969.

"Winning Essays in the 1960 Contest." http://lib.usm.edu/legacy/spcol/exhibitions/antisomm/civil_rights-3.html.

Wolfe, Anna. "Then and Now: When 'School Choice' Creates a Divide," *Jackson Free Press,* December 17, 2014, http://www.jacksonfree press.com/news/2014/dec/17/when-choice -creates-divide/.

Wooten, James. "4,000 Mississippi Whites Go to School, but 300 Balk," *New York Times,* January 8, 1970.

———. "2 Whites and 1,391 Blacks in a Mississippi School," *New York Times,* January 6, 1970.

Wright, Fielding. "Prince Explains McComb Change," *Mississippi Press* (Pascagoula, Moss Point), October 17, 1969.

Collections

Civil Rights Pledge Signed in Tupelo" and "Vicksburg Agrees to Comply," MS. 45, Allen
    Eugene Cox Papers, Box 1, Manuscript Department, Mississippi State University Librar-
    ies, Starkville, MS.
"Community Plan to Counteract Racial Agitators," July 21, 1965. Citizens' Council/Civil
    Rights Collection, Series 1, Box 1, Folder 29 (Brochures, 1955–1957, 1960–1966), McCain
    Library and Archives, University of Southern Mississippi Library, Hattiesburg, MS.
David Bacon and A. M. Mackel to Brent Forman, July 25, 1955, Folder 5, II: A227, NAACP
    Records, General Office File: Desegregation of Schools: Branch Action: Mississippi,
    Library of Congress, Washington, DC.
Dr. Maurice Mackel to Roy Wilkins, July 18, 1955, Folder 5, II: A227, NAACP Records, Gen-
    eral Office File: Desegregation of Schools: Branch Action: Mississippi, Library of Con-
    gress, Washington, DC.
———, July 25, 1955, Folder 5, II: A227, NAACP Records, General Office File: Desegregation
    of Schools: Branch Action: Mississippi, Library of Congress, Washington, DC.
Glenn L. Swetman, President of Biloxi Board of Trustees, to Senator James Eastland, July 25,
    1952. James O. Eastland Collection, File Series 3, Subseries 4, Box 3, Folder 11, the Univer-
    sity of Mississippi Libraries, Oxford, MS.
"Governor John Bell Williams on the Integration of Public Schools in Mississippi," Missis-
    sippi Department of Archives and History (AU1062, TR 057), "https://www.mdah
    .ms.gov/arrec/digital_archives/vault/projects/OHtranscripts/AU_1062_117291.pdf.
H. C. Hull to Senator James Eastland, February 28, 1969, James O. Eastland Collection, File
    Series 3, Subseries 4, Box 46, Folder 3, University of Mississippi Libraries, Oxford, MS.
Henry Hull to Senator James Eastland, January 14, 1969, James O. Eastland Collection, File
    Series 3, Subseries 4, Box 46, Folder 3, University of Mississippi Libraries, Oxford, MS.
"How to Save Our Public Schools," 1959, Citizens' Council/Civil Rights Collection, Series 1,
    Box 1, Folder 29 (Brochures, 1955–1957, 1960–1966), McCain Library and Archives, Uni-
    versity of Southern Mississippi Library, Hattiesburg, MS.
James Wright to NAACP, November 8, 1955, Folder 5, II: A227, NAACP Records, General
    Office File: Desegregation of Schools: Branch Action: Mississippi, Library of Congress,
    Washington, DC.
J. D. Prince to Senator James Eastland, April 23, 1971, James O. Eastland Collection, File
    Series 3, Subseries 4, Box 27, Folder 95, University of Mississippi Libraries, Oxford, MS.
Letter from Ellett Lawrence, Finance Chairman of the Association to Citizens' Councils
    of Mississippi, to all district and county chairmen, and the executive committee
    (Mississippi-Citizen's Council, FBI files (105–34237–225), https://archive.org/stream
    /CItizensCouncilMovement/CitCouncils-LA-MS-2#page/n15/mode/2up.
Letter from Hardy Lott to Jerris Leonard, July 30, 1970, James O. Eastland Collection, File
    Series 3, Subseries 4, Box 15, Folder 10, University of Mississippi Libraries, Oxford, MS.
Medgar Evers telegram to Roy Wilkins, July 19, 1955, Folder 5, II: A227, NAACP Records,
    General Office File: Desegregation of Schools: Branch Action: Mississippi, Library of
    Congress, Washington, DC.

"Message of the Honorable Hugh White, Governor of Mississippi." November 3, 1953. Speech delivered before the joint session of the Mississippi legislature extra-ordinary session, Segregation Integration-Schools, vertical file, Mississippi Department, Mississippi State Universities Libraries, Starkville, MS.

Mrs. Lilla D. Ware, speech delivered at a retirement dinner hosted by black teachers and employees of the Scott County public schools, December 20, 1955. Personal manuscript shared with authors by Dr. Lamar Weems.

Roy Wilkins to Dr. Robert Fullilove, September 23, 1955, Folder 5, II: A227, NAACP Records, General Office File: Desegregation of Schools: Branch Action: Mississippi, Library of Congress, Washington, DC.

Roy Wilkins to James Wright. November 10, 1955, Folder 5, II: A227, NAACP Records, General Office File: Desegregation of Schools: Branch Action: Mississippi, Library of Congress, Washington, DC.

Ruby Martin to Superintendent Henry Hull, January 3, 1969, James O. Eastland Collection, File Series 3, Subseries 4, Box 46, Folder 3, University of Mississippi Libraries, Oxford, MS.

Senator James Eastland to Superintendent H.C. Hull, January 22, 1969, James O. Eastland Collection, File Series 3, Subseries 4, Box 46, Folder 3, University of Mississippi Libraries, Oxford, MS.

"Special Educational Issue Foundation Executive Tells How to Organize a Private School," January 1970, MS. F25A, Allen Eugene Cox Papers, Box 12, Manuscript Department, Mississippi State University Libraries, Starkville, MS.

"Statement by Ramsey Clark before the Select Committee on Equal Educational Opportunity United States Senate," July 7, 1970, Stennis Collection, Box 12, Series 29, Folder 19. Mississippi State University Libraries, Starkville, MS.

"Statement by Stephen J. Pollack before the Select Committee on Equal Educational Opportunity, United States Senate," August 11, 1970, Stennis Collection, Box 12, Series 29, Folder 19, Mississippi State University Libraries, Starkville, MS.

Superintendent Robert Taylor to Senator James Eastland, December 21, 1967, James O. Eastland Collection, File Series 3, Subseries 4, Box 53, Folder 24, the University of Mississippi Libraries, Oxford, MS.

"A Time to Speak," Mississippians for Public Education, n.d., Constance W. Curry Papers. Manuscript, Archives, and Rare Book Library, Robert W. Woodruff Library, Emory University, 0818–002.tif.

"Transcript of Meeting of Legal Educational Advisory Committee and Negro Leaders, July 30, 1954, Segregation Integration-Schools, vertical file, Mississippi Department, Mississippi State Universities Libraries, Starkville, MS.

"Voluntary Plan of Desegregation by the Okolona Municipal Separate School District to the Department of Health, Education and Welfare," James O. Eastland Collection, File Series 3, Subseries 4, Box 46, Folder 3, University of Mississippi Libraries, Oxford, MS.

Reports

American Friends Service Committee, "Status of School Desegregation in the South, 1970." Washington, DC.

Barker, Horace, "The Federal Retreat in School Desegregation." Southern Regional Council, December 1969, 30–46.

Berry, Marion S., and Betty Garmin, *SNCC: A Special Report on Southern School Desegregation,* fall 1965, http://www.crmvet.org/docs/65_sncc_school-rpt.pdf.

Hartford, Bruce, "Grenada Mississippi—Chronology of a Movement," 1967, www.crmvet.org /docs/66_sclc_grenada_log.pdf.

———, "Weekly Watts Report-Grenada Miss.," September 16, 1966, http://www.crmvet.org /info/grenada.htm.

Kids Data Center, http://datacenter.kidscount.org.

McPhail, James, "A History of Desegregation Developments in Certain Mississippi School Districts."Hattiesburg: Mississippi School Study Council, Spring 1971.

Mississippi State Department of Education Figures, 2016–2017, http://ors.mde.k12.ms.us/data/.

National Education Association,*Report of NEW Task Force III. School Desegregation: Louisiana and Mississippi,* November 1970.

National Center for Education Statistics, Private School Enrollment, 2012–13, https://nces .ed.gov/programs/digest/d15/tables/dt15_205.80.asp.

A National Survey of School Desegregation Orders," accessed April 14, 2016, https://projects .propublica.org/graphics/desegregation-orders.

NCES 2010–2011 free and reduced lunch figures by state, https://nces.ed.gov/programs /digest/d12/tables/dt12_046.asp.

Orfield, Gary, and Chugnmei Lee, "Racial Transformation and the Changing Nature of Segregation." The Civil Rights Project, January 2006.

Palmer, James, *Mississippi School Districts: Factors in the Disestablishment of Dual Systems.* MS: Social Science Research Center, 1971.

ProximityOne, Proximityone.com/sd_ms.html.

"Public Education: 1964 Staff Report," Submitted to the United States Commission on Civil Rights, October 1964: 130–37, https://www.law.umaryland.edu/marshall/usccr/docu ments/cr12ed82964.pdf.

Southern Education Foundation, "Race and Ethnicity in a New Era of Public Funding of Private Schools: Private School Enrollment in the South and the Nation,"March 2016.

"State Superintendent Applauds JPS Schools for Academic Excellence," http://www.jackson .k12.ms.us/davis.

United States Census, Quick Facts, Clinton, Mississippi, http://www.census.gov/quickfacts /table/INC110215/2814420,28.

United States Commission on Civil Rights, "Federal Rights Under School Desegregation Law," CCR Clearinghouse Publication, no. 6, June 1966. accessed January 20, 2017, http:// www.law.umaryland.edu/marshall/usccr/documents/cr1106.pdf

United States Commission on Civil Rights. "School Desegregation in Greenville, Mississippi: A Staff Report of the U.S. Commission on Civil Rights," August 1977.

Index

Ability grouping, 32, 119, 218
Achievement tests, 32, 180, 186, 233
Activism. *See* Arrest and incarceration of
    youth; Community organizing; Pro-
    tests; Sit-in; Walk-out
Adams, Alean, 34–35, 37–39, 150, 176, 232
Adams, John, 34–35, 37–39, 150, 176
Adams, Kenneth, 39, 150, 176
Adams, Linda, 38, 176
*Adams v. Rankin County Board of Educa-
    tion*, 150
Adcox, Bill, 83
Alcorn County, 194
Alcorn State University, 115, 125, 140
Alexander, Beatrice, 29, 31
*Alexander v. Holmes County Board of Edu-
    cation*, 29–33, 44, 54, 67, 78, 155, 167, 191,
    193, 195
American Football Coaches Association,
    143
Amite County, 32, 58, 163, 182, 197, 219
Anderson, Johnny, 142–43
Arrest and incarceration of youth, 168–70,
    173–74, 176–77, 180, 182–83, 187

Bacon, David, 15
Baez, Joan, 173
Baldwin, Shead, 177
Band, 41, 72, 148–49, 151, 154, 158–59, 179,
    207, 210, 213. *See also* Extracurricular
    activities
Barnett, Ross, 13, 57, 127, 191
Baseball. *See* Sports

Basketball. *See* Sports
Bayou Academy, 191, 230
Beaty, Lamar, 76–77, 88, 90, 96, 157, 175–76
Bellflower Baptist Church, 173
Belue, Virgil, x, 216–17
Bender, W. A., 17
Biesecker, Carl, 144–45
Biloxi, 13, 21–25, 42, 199, 200, 233
Bishop, E. S., 12
Bishop, Harold, 147, 159–60
Black, Hugo, 31
Blackmon, Douglas, 232
Blackmon, Leola, 181
Black teachers, 108–13; academic qualifica-
    tions during segregation, 41, 109–10,
    154; alliance with whites after *Brown*
    decision, 14, 30; demotions and dismiss-
    als, 93, 108–13, 177, 180, 233; experiences
    in white schools, 113–14, 115–17, 135–36;
    response to *Brown* decision, 4–5; salary
    equalization, 14. *See also* Teachers
Bob Jones University v. United States, 200
Bolivar County, 32, 71, 191, 194, 229. *See also*
    Cleveland
Boone, Charles, 78–81, 86, 88, 98, 152
Boortz, Neil, 234
Boston, Charles, xi, 124–25, 135–37, 139–42
Box, Larry, 91, 107–8
Boycotts, 143, 168, 174, 177–80, 185–87
Boyd, J. D., 12
Boyd, Lucy, 211
Boyer, Roscoe, 64
Brady, Tom, 5–6, 162

291

Brandon, 37, 39, 175–76
Breeland, Harry, xi, 135–36
Brewer, James, 81–84
Brinkley High School, 147, 149, 158–59, 171
Brookhaven, 18
Brooks, Richard, 197
Brown, Billy, 133–34, 149
Brown v. Board of Education, 3–5, 11–14, 51
Brown v. Board of Education II, 5
Bryant, C. C., 169, 170
Bryant, Coach Paul, 132–33
Buchannan, B. Hall, 82
Burger, N. R., 12
Burglund High School, 169–70, 171
Burten, Elbert, 112–13
Bus drivers, 38, 43, 85
Business, support of public schools, 102, 189, 202–6, 223–24, 231, 233, 262n60

Calhoun County, 201
Canton, 40, 172, 188, 193, 197, 202, 219
Carroll County, x, 14, 32, 57, 62–63, 115–16, 163, 181, 197, 226–28
Carter, Gloria. *See* Dickerson, Gloria Carter
Carter, Hodding, Jr., 189, 208, 224, 226, 231
Carter, Mae Bertha, 35–37, 43, 49, 50
Carter, Matthew, 35–37, 49
Carter children (Beverly, Deborah, Gloria, Larry, Pearl, Ruth, and Stanley), 36, 42–44
Carthage, 24–25
Chaney, James, 34, 222
Charter schools, 234
Charleston, 164–65
Cheerleading, 143–44, 147–48, 150, 151, 157, 159–61, 210, 213. *See also* Extracurricular activities
Chickasaw County, 55, 93
Christmas party, 116–18, 123
Citizens' Council: Council schools, 143, 190–91; formation of, 6, 19–20; ideology,

20, 146–47, 162–63, 166; influence on private school movement, 21, 190–91, 193, 200, 227, 234; intimidation of whites, 20–21, 126, 224; and violence against blacks, 16, 18, 20, 168, 204–5
Civil Rights Act of 1964, 6–8, 25–27, 36, 49, 52–57, 148–49, 174, 190, 224
Claiborne County, 177, 219. *See also* Port Gibson
Clark, Ramsey, 174, 196
Clark County. *See* Quitman
Clarksdale, 15, 24, 179–80, 186, 219
Clay County, 178, 197
Clayton, Claude E., 173–74
Cleveland, 35, 71, 104, 115, 117, 211, 222, 228–30. *See also* Bolivar County
Clinton, 69, 216–17, 220
Coaches, 132–37, 139–43, 145, 177. *See also* Sports
Coahoma County, 102, 179–80, 186, 194. *See also* Clarksdale
Coffeeville, 32, 163
Coffey v. State Educational Finance Commission, 196
Coleman, J. P., 5, 13, 16
Columbia, ix, 81, 124, 131, 136–37, 139–41, 154–55, 167, 216
Columbus, 111–12, 233
Colvard, D. W., 127
Committee for Local Control of Education, 185
Community organizing, 15–16, 19, 34, 37–38, 169–70, 172–74, 177–80, 185–86, 200–206, 233
Congress of Racial Equality (CORE), 113, 168
Cook v. Hudson, 201
Cooper, Owen, 205
Corinth, 57–58, 147, 159–60, 197
Corporal punishment, 47, 88–89. *See also* Discipline
Council of Conservative Citizens, 227
Council schools. *See* Citizens' Council

Courts, Gus, 18
Cousin, Warren, 93
Covington County, 93
Cox, Harold, 31
Crockett, Isom, 39–42
Crockett, Ola, 39–42
Cruger-Tchula Academy, 191
Cunningham, Sam, 132

Dale, George, 89, 97–98, 128, 151–52, 183
Davis, Lillie V., 103–4, 113, 115–17, 122, 123,
    164, 221
Davis, Tommy, 124–25
Deacons for Defense and Justice, 181
DeCell, Alice, 155
DeCell, Herman, 100, 155, 205, 231
DeKalb, ix, xii, 14, 32, 134, 175, 188, 193. *See
    also* Kemper County
Delta State University, 64, 230
Democracy: invoked in *Brown* decision
    and response to *Brown*, 3–5, 12, 15, 56,
    233; and public schools, 9, 235–36
Dent, Richard, 130
Departmentalization, 117
Department of Health, Education, and
    Welfare (HEW), 26–27, 29–31, 53–58,
    62–63, 67–68, 71–75, 78, 101, 121, 151, 163,
    185, 196
Department of Justice (DOJ), 23, 25, 28,
    57–58, 63, 73, 121, 198, 216, 228, 230
Desegregation, voluntary, 26, 28, 53, 56, 63,
    266n35
Dickerson, Gloria Carter, 36, 42–45
Discipline, 8, 68–69, 77, 85–91
Dodson, William, 209
Dress code, 91–92
Drew, 35–37, 42, 44–45, 49–50
Dulin, Tom, x, 8, 56, 62–66, 70, 201,
    231

Eastland, James, x, 11, 13, 26, 35, 55–56, 62,
    188
East Tallahatchie, 112–13, 179, 210, 222

Elementary and Secondary Education Act,
    25–26
Empower Mississippi, 234
Equalization program, 13–14, 21, 154–55
Evans, Ann Hall, 46–48
Evans, Carolyn, 148
Evans, Thomas James, 148–49, 159–60
Evens, Milton, 185
Evers, Charles, 177–78, 181, 189
Evers, Medgar, 14–15, 22, 24–25, 177
Extracurricular activities, 146–66. *See also*
    Sports

Federal Bureau of Investigation (FBI), ix,
    13, 24, 61, 63, 95, 208
Federal funding, termination of, 25–26, 62,
    178–80
Femininity, 160–61
Ferguson, Billy Joe, 226–28
Fighting, 90, 182–84
Finch, Robert, 30, 67
Flynt, John Allen, 80–81, 89–91, 137–38
Football. *See* Sports
Forman, Brent, 15
Forrest County, 185, 197, 220
Fortenberry, Robert, 214
Foster, Herbert, 211
Franklin County, 93
Freedom of choice, 34–50; appropriation
    by whites, 186–87; as a delaying tactic,
    28–31, 55–56, 180, 191, 225; experiences
    of black children, 24–25, 38–39, 42–49,
    134, 172–74; experiences of black par-
    ents, 35–42; implementation of, 26–27,
    53, 58, 60, 63–65, 172–74; intimidation of
    black parents, 25, 28–29, 36–37, 40, 46,
    172; origins of, 26–29, 53
Freedom of Choice in the United States
    (FOCUS), 187
Freeman, Morgan, 164–65
Friends of Public Schools, 73, 102, 189,
    200–201, 205, 233, 262n60
Funding, school, 13–14, 25–26, 29, 178–80, 227

George, Charles, 89, 97–99, 139, 151–52, 210
George, James, 115–16, 122
Gibbs, Robert, 158–59
Glen Allan, 45, 47, 91
Goodman, Andrew, 34, 222
Goolsby, James E., 111
Government schools, 190, 234
Graduate Record Examination (GRE), 110–11, 233
Green, Inez, 89, 97–98
Green, James Earl, 121
Greene, Percy, 12
Greene v. County School Board of New Kent County (1968), 29
Green v. Connally, 200
Greenville, 53, 91, 142, 154, 158, 175, 188–89, 192, 194, 200, 207–9, 214, 219, 224–26, 231, 233
Greenwood, 5, 71, 150, 172, 175, 188, 206, 209–11, 222
Grenada, 171–74, 177–78, 216, 233, 264n5
Grubbs, Chryl, 148
Gulfport, 142, 183

Hall, Ann. See Evans, Ann Hall
Hall, Clarence, 45–46
Harrison, Cyndie, xi, 105–6, 114, 117–19, 121–22
Harrison Central High, 77, 128, 139, 142, 183–84
Harrison County, 77, 128, 139, 142, 183–84, 199
Hawthorne, Larry, 128
Hayes, Emit, 119–20
Haynes, Joe, 214
Hazlehurst, 178
Henry, Aaron, 179–81
HEW. See Department of Health, Education, and Welfare
Higgins, Dewey, 169, 246n27
Hinds County, 15, 30, 57, 66–70, 93, 108, 216
Holly Springs, 84, 103, 188

Holmes County, 102, 191, 193, 219, 227–28, 235
Homecoming. See Extracurricular activities
Hope, 121–23
Hudson, Dovie, 24
Hudson, Winson, 24
Huffman, Alan, 153
Humes, H. H., 12
Hurricane Camille, 76–77, 183

Indianola, 6, 19, 35, 102, 178
Internal Revenue Service (IRS), 199–200
Interracial relationships, 130–132, 143–46, 153–57, 161–66
Issaquena County, 45–46, 171, 182, 233. See also Sharkey-Issaquena

Jackson, 12, 14–17, 24–25, 37, 45, 52, 66, 68, 74, 103, 106–8, 112, 116, 129, 140, 143, 147–49, 152–53, 155–58, 161, 168, 170, 190–95, 200–202, 212, 214, 219, 221, 223, 234
Jackson, Robert, 48–49
Jacksonians for Public Education, 201
Jackson State University, 120, 126, 140
Jefferson High School, 81, 136–37, 140, 154–55
Jenkins, John Stone, 202
Jim Hill High School, 107, 119–20, 129, 152–53, 156, 171
Johnson, Archie, 124, 131, 136–37, 154
Johnson, Leon, ix, xii, 134
Johnson, Lindy, 134
Johnson, Lyndon, 172, 196
Johnson, Mike, 128, 208–9
Johnson, Paul, 26, 173, 196, 224
Johnston, Erle, 13
Jones, John Griffin, 165–66
Jones County, 39–40
Justice Department. See Department of Justice

Keady, William, 91, 225, 229

Keglar v. East Tallahatchie School District, 112

Kelly, Harold, x, 8, 56, 70–74, 205

Kemper County, ix, 14, 32, 133–34, 149, 175, 192, 193, 219, 222

King, Martin Luther, Jr., 43, 46, 101, 133, 171–75, 181

Ku Klux Klan, 5, 46, 58, 134, 177, 224

Kuykendall, Harriet DeCell, 100–102, 122, 205–6

Lauderdale County, 134, 186

Lawrence County. *See* New Hebron

Leake County, 24, 93, 197. *See also* Carthage

Lee, George W., 18

Lee, Herbert, 58

LeFlore County, 206. *See also* Greenwood

Legal Education Advisory Committee (LEAC), 5, 13, 16

Leland, 109, 128, 175, 208–9, 219, 223–24, 232–33

Leonard, Jerris, 188

Leventhal, Melvin, 72, 167, 180

Lewis, A. J., 24–25

Lewis, Debra, 24–25

Lewis, Ike, 169

Lewis, Minnie, 24–25

Lewis, William, 77, 128–29, 131, 138, 142, 184

Liberty, 32, 181–82, 188

Loans, student, 196–97, 198

Long Beach, 28, 220

Lott, Hardy, 188

Lottery, 68, 106–8, 133

Mabry, Paula, 207

Mackel, Maurice, 15

Madison-Ridgeland, 129, 148–49

Makamson, Owen, 133

Marks, 49, 103–4, 113, 123, 164, 193, 223. *See also* Quitman County

Martin, John S., 74, 106–7

Martin, Maye Dee, 104–6, 115, 117, 122

Masculinity, 92, 161, 163

Mason, George, 21–23, 25, 42

Mason, Natalie, 21–23, 42

Meadows, Jim, 186

Media, coverage of desegregation, 68, 73, 83–85, 167, 173, 185. *See also* Newspapers

McAlpin, Dalton, 103, 107, 119–22, 129

McCarthy, Babe, 127

McCarthy, Hugh, 126

McComb, 51, 57–62, 95, 98, 109, 169–71, 202

McCormick, Earlean, 112

McDonald, Douglas, 64

McNeal v. Tate County School District, 199

Meek, Ed, 202–3, 231

Meredith, James, 23, 57, 126, 156, 168

Meredith, June, 156

Meredith March, 171–72

Meridian, 30, 57, 69–70, 74, 85, 200

Metcalfe, George, 177

Militants, 182

Military, 23, 45

Miller, Mary Carol, 150, 188, 209–11

Millsaps College, 52, 105

Mississippians for Public Education (MPE), 200, 233

Mississippi Citizens Council on Education (MCCE), 13

Mississippi Educational Services Center, 96

Mississippi legislature: amendment to abolish public schools, 13; attack of Hodding Carter, Jr., 224, 265n33; recent policies, 228, 233–34, 264n6, 267n62; response to *Brown* decision, 5, 13–14; support of private schools, 196, 201; support of sex-segregated schools, 163; and tuition grants, 196, 233

Mississippi Negro Teachers Association, 12, 14, 113

Mississippi Private School Association, 191

Mississippi State Department of Education, 26, 79, 197–98, 220–21, 224

Mississippi State Sovereignty Commission, 13
Mississippi State University, 19, 76, 96, 109–10, 126–27, 142
Mississippi Teachers' Association. *See* Mississippi Negro Teachers Association
Mississippi Valley State College, 140, 142
Mize, Sidney, 23
Mondale, Walter, 196, 199
Moon, Beverly, 143–44
Morris, JoAnne Prichard, 100–102, 122
Morris, Willie, 73, 108, 154–55, 206, 215, 233
Moses, Robert, 60, 169–70
Moss Point, 61, 97, 128, 151, 182, 222
Munford, Luther, xi, 93, 194
Murrah High School, 148, 152–53, 155, 158–59, 161, 166
Muse, Clyde, x, 8, 56, 66–71, 74

NAACP Legal Defense Fund, 37, 72, 112, 167, 180
Nash, Charles, 58, 60, 95–96, 98, 109
Nash, Jere, 207–8
Natchez, 14, 15–16, 85, 138, 149, 163, 177–78, 181, 193, 219
National Association for Secondary Principals, 187
National Association for the Advancement of Colored People (NAACP): aid to victims of violence, 17–18; cost of affiliation to black teachers, 39–40; criticism of black teachers, 14; legal challenges related to school desegregation, 22–23, 37, 72, 112, 168, 180, 216; local chapters, 15–16, 35, 37, 58, 168–69, 176, 179, 181, 211; petitions, 15–18, 23; response to *Brown* ruling, 4, 17
National Education Association (NEA), 81, 92–93, 96, 106, 108, 112, 117, 187
National Teachers Examination (NTE), 110, 111, 233
Nations, Ricky, 152–53, 156

Neshoba County, 34, 84, 99. *See also* Philadelphia
New Hebron, 80–81, 89–90, 137–38
Newspapers: coverage of school desegregation, 24, 53, 73, 85–87, 109, 123, 155, 167, 172, 174, 175, 223; support of public education, 204, 219, 223. *See also* Media
Nixon, Richard, 30, 55
"Nonviolent High," 170
Norwood v. Harrison, 198
Noxubee County, 28, 134, 179, 193, 197, 219

Oak Grove, 135–36
Office of Civil Rights (OCR), 62, 216
Okalona, 55, 219
Otis, J. R., 12
Oxford, 105, 114, 117–19, 189, 200, 202–4, 216, 220, 231, 233
Oxford Civic Council, 202–4
Owens, George, 14

Parchman prison, 174
Parker, Mack Charles, 147, 164
Pass Christian, 76, 88, 90, 96, 156–57, 220
Patterson, Joe, 23
Patterson, Robert, 6, 19
Payton, Eddie, 124
Payton, Walter, 124, 141
Pearl, 175–76
Pep rally, 88, 147–48, 156–57, 209–10. *See also* Extracurricular activities
Perkins, Fred, 206
Perry County, 83
Petal, 167, 185, 220
Peters, Fenton, xi, 82–83, 91, 94, 98, 110–11, 128, 160, 210
Petitions, 15–18
Philadelphia, 34–35, 84, 132, 171–72, 222, 265n26
Pillow Academy, 188, 192, 206, 209–10, 211
Pisgah, 37
Police, 23, 40, 59, 84–85, 170, 172, 173, 174, 176, 178, 180, 182–83, 184

Pollack, Stephen, 196

Port Gibson, 177–78, 181

Prince, Julian, x, 51, 52, 57–62, 95, 202

Principals, 76–99; demotions and dismissals of black principals, 92–94; discipline, 85–92; experiences of black principals, 94–98, 119–20; leadership during desegregation, 76–99; relationship to assistant principals, 8, 79–80, 89–90, 93–98, 139–41, 151, 175; retirements and resignations, 77–78

Private schools, 188–212; black challenges to, 189, 198–99; Citizens' Council support of, 191–92, 197, 200; cost to public schools, 210–12; Council schools, 191–93, 200; critique of, 189, 196, 199, 200–201, 206–12, 220, 222–23, 232; enrollment figures, 218; expansion of, 189–90, 192–95; public aid of, 195–200; and tax exemptions, 199–200; textbooks, 197–98; white resistance, 64–65, 200–210, 225, 231, 233

Proms, 9, 161–65, 213, 216

Protests, 9, 23, 61, 69–70, 111, 136, 167, 168–74, 180, 182, 185–87, 213, 233

Public aid to private schools, 189, 195–200

Quitman, 78–81, 86, 152, 216

Quitman County, 48–49, 103–4, 123, 219, 221. See also Marks

Rankin County, 35, 37–38, 93, 102, 150, 175, 192, 220

Reddix, Jacob, 12

Resegregation, 214, 218, 220–22, 228, 231, 235

Richardson, Elliot, 196

Riverside, 46–47, 91, 133, 194, 222

Rolling Fork, 233

Rosedale, 128, 208

Salter, Leo, 84, 99

Salter, Sid, x, 99, 132

Satterfield, John, 13, 71, 205

School choice, 9, 211, 234–35

Schwerner, Michael, 34, 222

Scott County, xii, 52

Seeley, David, 57, 59

Segregationist academies. See Private schools

Senate Committee on Equal Education Opportunity, 196, 199

Sex-segregated schools, 32, 163–64, 179

Sexuality, 161, 162–63, 165

Sharkey-Issaquena, 182, 233, 262n60

Shields, Rudy, 181, 257n68

Simmons, William, 17, 200, 234

"Singleton factors," 112

Singleton v. Jackson Municipal Separate School System, 112

Sit-in, 127, 168, 170, 172, 182

Smith, Hazel Brannon, 235

Smith, Lamar, 18

Smith, Orma, 65, 180, 199

Smith, Theo, 197

Southern Christian Leadership Conference (SCLC), 171, 172

Southern National Party, 212

Spencer, Alice, 133

Spencer, Grey, 133

Sports, 9, 124–45, 147–50, 154, 158–61, 163, 165, 172, 181, 207, 213. See also Extracurricular activities

Starkville, 66, 76, 82–83, 86, 91, 94, 96, 98, 107–8, 110–12, 128, 160, 192, 207, 210, 216, 264n6

Stevens, Hamilton, 125

Student activism, 167–87; arrest and incarceration of students, 168–70, 173–74, 176–77, 180, 182–83, 187; in Grenada, 172–74; in newly desegregated schools, 174–80; in Rankin County, 175–76; representation in practitioner journals, 187; in segregated schools, 169–71; statistics, 187. See also Boycotts; Sit-in; Suspension and expulsion; Violence; Walk-out

Student government. *See* Extracurricular
    activities
Student Non-violent Coordinating Com-
    mittee (SNCC), 58, 168–71
Students: and conflicts over private schools,
    188, 209–10; extracurricular activities,
    146–66; freedom of choice, 36–50; pro-
    tests, 168–87; sports, 124–45
Sunflower County, 19, 32, 35, 44, 102
Superintendents, 51–75; cooperation with
    federal government, 57–60, 63, 65, 68;
    leadership, 8, 56–75, 82–83, 116, 185, 216–
    17, 226–28; prior to *Brown* ruling, 51–52;
    relationship to black constituents, 14,
    28, 40, 49, 52–53, 95–96, 103–5, 142, 175,
    198; resistance to desegregation, 26, 32,
    52–56, 71–73, 163; response to *Brown*
    ruling, 11; retirements and resignations,
    74, 107
Suspension and expulsion, 69, 85, 86, 87, 90,
    91, 92, 169, 170, 171, 173, 174, 176, 184, 187
Swetman, Glenn, 199

Talbert, Bobbie, 169
Taliaferro, George, 144–45
Tate County, 198–99
Tax-exemptions for private schools,
    199–200
Teachers, 100–128; assignment of, 68, 80–81,
    103–8, 133; demotions and dismissals of
    black teachers, 93, 108–13, 136, 177, 180,
    233; experiences during school desegre-
    gation, 100–123. *See also* Black teachers;
    White teachers
Teachers' lounge, 106, 115
Testing. *See* Achievement tests; Graduate
    Record Examination (GRE); National
    Teachers Examination (NTE)
Textbooks, 43, 102, 138, 185, 190, 197–98, 227
Thompson, W. B., 142
Till, Emmett "Bobo," 18, 147, 164
Title VI. *See* Civil Rights Act of 1964
Todd, L. O., 74

Tougaloo College, xi, 17, 52, 97, 168
Tougaloo Nine, 168
Travis, Brenda, 169–71
Tubbs, Jack, 26
Tuition grants, 189, 196, 198, 201, 261n32
Tunica, 102, 179, 188, 192, 193, 197, 198
Tupelo, 53, 62, 189, 200, 216, 231, 233

*United States v. Jefferson County Board of
    Education*, 28
University of Mississippi, 23, 45, 57, 64, 70,
    105, 109, 126, 127, 142, 156, 168, 202, 203,
    230
University of Southern Mississippi, 49, 109,
    125, 135

Van Dyke, Larry, 84–85
Vicksburg, 15–16, 87, 98, 143
Violence: and Citizens' Council, 6, 19–20;
    Charles Evers's stance on, 181; Deacons
    for Defense and Justice, 181; directed at
    blacks and civil rights activists, 18, 23,
    25, 34, 58, 147, 164, 172–74, 222; fights at
    desegregated schools, 182–84; Grenada,
    172–74; McComb, 58–59; retaliation for
    petitions or freedom of choice, 6, 25, 28,
    36, 38, 40, 43–44, 172–74; white experi-
    ences of, 61, 116, 208–9

Walk-out, 136, 168–70, 174–76, 187
Walthall County, 15
Ware, Lilla, 52
Warren, Earl, 3–5
Waynesboro, 130
Weapons, 87, 91–92, 181, 184
Weathersby, Davis, 142
Weems, Lamar, xii
Weems, Mack, 52
West Tallahatchie County, 14, 26, 89, 97–98,
    139, 151, 192, 211
Western Line, 47, 71, 91, 194, 222
White, Hugh, 5, 12
White, J. H., 12

White Citizens' Council. *See* Citizens' Council

White flight, 194, 200, 201, 216, 218, 222

White supremacy, 20, 56, 109, 111, 143–44, 162–64, 168, 181, 234

White teachers: exodus from public schools, 102–3, 197; experiences in segregated black schools, 100–102, 117–21; harassment of, 208–9; refusal to send children to public schools, 201; treatment of black children during freedom of choice, 39, 43, 47. *See also* Teachers

Wilkins, Roy, 15, 17

Williams, John Bell, 6, 185, 195

Winona, 19, 57, 63–66, 201, 231

Winston County, 93

Winter, William, 235

Woodville, 167, 188

Wooten, Ken, 202–3

Wright, J. H., 17

Yazoo City, ix, 16–17, 33, 70–74, 85, 100–102, 149, 154–55, 167, 175, 189, 194, 197, 204–6, 219, 223–24, 231, 233

CPSIA information can be obtained
at www.ICGtesting.com
Printed in the USA
LVHW090905240723
753027LV00079B/42